THE CORRESPONDENCE

OF

JONATHAN SWIFT, D.D.

VOL. II

LONDON : G. BELL AND SONS, LTD.
PORTUGAL STREET, KINGSWAY, W.C.
CAMBRIDGE : DEIGHTON, BELL & CO.
NEW YORK : THE MACMILLAN CO.
BOMBAY : A. H. WHEELER & CO.

THE CORRESPONDENCE

OF

JONATHAN SWIFT, D.D.

EDITED BY

F. ELRINGTON BALL

HONORARY LITT.D., DUBLIN

WITH AN INTRODUCTION BY

THE RIGHT REV. J. H. BERNARD, D.D.

BISHOP OF OSSORY, FERNS AND LEIGHLIN

VOL. II

LONDON

G. BELL AND SONS, LTD.

1911

CHISWICK PRESS : CHARLES WHITTINGHAM AND CO.
TOOKS COURT, CHANCERY LANE, LONDON.

CONTENTS

LETTERS

v

CONTENTS

PAGE

CONTENTS

CONTENTS

PAGE

CONTENTS

CONTENTS

SUPPLEMENTAL LETTERS

APPENDIXES

LIST OF ILLUSTRATIONS

[1] The view is taken from the tower of the church.

[2] The plot of ground shown in the illustration is the original glebe, Swift's "half acre of Irish bog." Under the tree in the centre of the plot there is a well, and to the right of the farm-house a block of masonry, which tradition connects with the site of Swift's vicarage. As is subsequently shown (*infra*, p. 240), apart from other reasons, the distance between the two objects gives room for doubt as to the accuracy of the conjecture, and it is far more probable that the block of masonry is a fragment of "a fair manse house with a castle and other houses of office," which stood upon the glebe in earlier times (Ussher's "Works," i, lxxxii).

ERRATA

Page 278, note 6, line 4, *for* " Wharton " *read* " Walpole."
Page 370, note 2, line 2, *for* " Archbishop King was discarded as
being too favourable to the Irish interest and " *read* " in addition
to Archbishop King."

CORRESPONDENCE OF JONATHAN SWIFT

CLXIII. [*Sheridan.*]

SWIFT TO ARCHBISHOP KING

London, *January* 3, 1712-13.

MY LORD,

SINCE I had the honour of your Grace's letter,[1] we have had a dead time of news and politics; and I make a conscience of writing to you without something that will recompense the trouble of reading. I cannot but grant that your Grace, who are at a distance, and argue from your own wisdom and general observations and reading, is likely to be more impartial than I, who, in spite of my resolutions and opinion to the contrary, am forced to converse only with one side of the world, which fastens prejudices to me, notwithstanding all I can do to avoid them. Your Grace has certainly hit upon the weak side of our peace; but I do not find you have prescribed any remedies, for that of limiting France to a certain number of ships and troops was, I doubt, not to be compassed. While that mighty kingdom remains under one monarch, it will be always in some degree formidable to its neighbours. But we flatter ourselves it is likely to be less so than ever, by the concurrence of many circumstances too long to trouble you with. But, my Lord, what is to be done? I will go so far with your Grace as to tell you, that some of our friends are of opinion with the other party, that if this last campaign had gone on with the conjunction of the British troops, France might have been in danger of being driven to great

[1] *Supra*, vol. i, p. 348.

extremes. Yet I confess to you, at the same time, that if I had been first Minister, I should have advised the Queen to pursue her measures toward a peace.

Some accidents and occasions have put it in my way to know every step of this treaty better, I think, than any man in England;[1] and I do assert to your Grace that if France had been closely pushed this campaign, they would, upon our refusal, have made offers to Holland, which the Republic would certainly have accepted; and in that case the interests of England would have been wholly laid aside, as we saw it three years ago at the Hague and Gertruyden-berg. The Marshal d'Uxelles and Mesnager, two of the French plenipotentiaries, were wholly inclined to have begun by the Dutch; but the third, Abbé de Polignac, who has most credit with Monsieur Torcy, was for beginning by England.[2]

There was a great faction in France by this proceeding: and it was a mere personal resentment, in the French King and Monsieur Torcy, against the States, which hindered them from sending the first overture there. And I believe your Grace will be convinced, by considering that the demands of Holland might be much more easily satisfied than those of Britain. The States were very indifferent about the article of Spain being in the Bourbon family, as Monsieur Buys publicly owned when he was here, and among others to myself.[3] They valued not the demolition

---

[1] Swift is alluding chiefly to his work on the "History of the Four Last Years of the Queen," in connection with which he was given access to official correspondence and State documents. Although its authenticity has been questioned, there seems no longer room for doubt that the treatise known to us by that name was Swift's composition ("Prose Works," x, v-xxv, and cf. Sir Henry Craik's "Life," ii, 290-8). In his preface Swift says ("Prose Works," x, 13) that the History was written while he was at Windsor in the year 1712, but as the Journal to Stella shows it occupied him to the exclusion of everything else for a considerable time also after his return to London. In September he tells Stella that he is engaged on a long work, and is waiting for papers which the Ministers are to send him. A month later he has hundreds of letters to read and squeezes "a line out of each, or at least the seeds of a line." In November he has still "a world of writing to finish" and complains that "these toads of Ministers are so slow in their helps," and in December he thinks that "this business" will still keep him employed for six weeks (*ibid.*, ii, 382, 391, 396, 397). Of the fate of the History which Swift was hastening to have ready before Parliament met we shall learn farther on (*infra*, p. 16, n. 2).

[2] *Cf.* "Prose Works," x, *passim.*   [3] *Supra*, vol. i, p. 315.

of Dunkirk, the frontier of Portugal, nor the security of
Savoy. They abhorred the thoughts of our having Gibraltar
and Minorca, nor cared what became of our dominions in
North America. All they had at heart was the sovereignty
of Flanders, under the name of a barrier, and to stipulate
what they could for the Emperor, to make him easy under
their encroachments.

I can farther assure your Grace, before any proposals
were sent here from France, and ever since, until within
these few months, the Dutch have been endeavouring constantly, by private intrigues with that Court, to undermine
us, and put themselves at the head of a treaty of peace;
which is a truth that perhaps the world may soon be informed in, with several others that are little known.[1] Besides,
my Lord, I doubt whether you have sufficiently reflected
on the condition of this kingdom, and the possibility of
pursuing the war at that ruinous rate. This argument is
not the weaker for being often urged. Besides, France is
likely to have a long minority; or, if not, perhaps to be
engaged in a civil war. And I do not find that in public
affairs, human wisdom is able to make provisions for
futurity, which are not liable to a thousand accidents. We
have done all we can, and for the rest, *curent posteri.*

Sir William Temple's Memoirs, which you mentioned, is
his first part, and was published twenty years ago. It is
chiefly the treaty of Nimeguen, and was so well known,
that I could hardly think your Grace has not seen it.

I am in some doubt whether a fall from a horse be suitable to the dignity of an archbishop. It is one of the chief
advantages in a great station that one is exempt from
common accidents of that kind. The late King indeed got
a fall; but his Majesty was a fox-hunter. I question whether
you can plead any precedent to excuse you; and therefore,
I hope you will commit no more such errors: and in the
mean time, I heartily congratulate with your Grace that I
can rally you upon this accident.

I am in some fear that our peace will hardly be concluded in several weeks, by reason of a certain incident
that could not be foreseen;[2] neither can I tell whether the

---

[1] This is a further reference to the " History of the Four Last Years
of the Queen."

[2] The incident appears to have been the " idle quarrel " between the

Parliament will sit before the conclusion of the peace, because some persons differ in their politics about the matter. If others were no wiser than I, your session should not be deferred upon that account. I am, with the greatest respect,

Your Grace's most dutiful and humble servant.

CLXIV. [*Manuscripts of the Marquis of Bath.*[1]]

SWIFT TO THE EARL OF OXFORD

January 5, 1712-13.

I MOST humbly take leave to inform your Lordship that the Dean of Wells died this morning at one o'clock.[2] I entirely submit my poor fortunes to your Lordship.

CLXV. [*Original.*[3]]

VISCOUNT BOLINGBROKE TO SWIFT

Thursday Morning, Two o'Clock [*January* 8, 1712-13].[4]

THOUGH I have not seen you, I did not fail to write to Lord Treasurer. *Non tua res agitur*, dear Jonathan. It is

French plenipotentiary, Mesnager, and the Dutch plenipotentiary, Rechteren ("Prose Works," x, *passim*).
[1] Hist. MSS. Com. (1904), i, 228.
[2] As has been already noticed (*supra*, vol. i, p. 335, n. 2), the deanery of Wells had become vacant in February 1712. According to "Fasti Ecclesiae Anglicanae," it was not filled until April 1713, but this letter indicates that in the interval some person had been at least designated to the dignity. Two other deaneries, those of Ely and Lichfield, had become also vacant about the same time, and Swift had been kept for many months in a state of suspense. In September he wrote to Stella that if he was not given one of the vacant preferments he would return at once to Ireland, and in December he tells her of his intention to forbear publishing the "Four Last Years of the Queen" until the Court decided something about him ("Prose Works," ii, 383, 406).
[3] In the British Museum. See Preface.
[4] Swift has endorsed this letter January 5, 1712-3, which was Monday. The letter evidently relates, like the preceding one, to the deanery

the Treasurer's cause; it is my cause; it is every man's cause, who is embarked in our bottom. Depend upon it, that I never will neglect any opportunity of showing that true esteem, that sincere affection, and honest friendship for you, which fill the breast of your faithful servant,

BOLINGBROKE.

Dr. Swift.

CLXVI. [*Sheridan.*]

SWIFT TO THE DUKE OF ARGYLL

January 20, 1712-13.

MY LORD,

I WOULD myself have delivered the answer I sent yesterday to your Grace at Court by Dr. Arbuthnot, if I had not thought the right of complaining to be on my side; for, I think it was my due, that you should have immediately told me whatever you had heard amiss of my conduct to your Grace. When I had the honour to be first known to those in the Ministry, I made it an express condition, that whoever did me ill offices, they should inform me of what was said, and hear my vindication, that I might not be mortified with countenances estranged of the sudden, and be at a loss for the cause.[1] And I think, there is no person alive, whose favour or protection I would purchase at that expense. I could not speak to the disadvantage of your Grace without being ungrateful (which is an ill word) since you were pleased voluntarily to make so many professions of favour to me for some years past; and your being a Duke and a General would have swayed me not at all in my respect for your person, if I had not thought you to abound in qualities, which I wish were easier to be found in those

of Wells, and not, as has been suggested, to the bishopric of Hereford, which was also vacant. It appears more probable that it was written on Monday than on Thursday.

[1] The allusion is to Swift's conversation with Bolingbroke two years previously: "I warned him . . . that I expected every great Minister who honoured me with his acquaintance, if he heard or saw anything to my disadvantage, would let me know in plain words, and not put me in pain to guess by the change or coldness of his countenance or behaviour" ("Prose Works," ii, 148).

of your rank. I have, indeed, sometimes heard what your Grace was told I reported; but as I am a stranger to coffee-houses, so it is a great deal below me to spread coffee-house reports. This accusation is a little the harder upon me, because I have always appeared fond of your Grace's character; and have, with great industry, related several of your generous actions, on purpose to remove the imputa-tion of the only real fault (for I say nothing of common frailties) which I ever heard laid to your charge. I confess, I have often thought that Homer's description of Achilles bore some resemblance to your Grace, but I do not re-member that ever I said so.[1] At the same time, I think few men were ever born with nobler qualities to fill and adorn every office of a subject, a friend and a protector, etc.

CLXVII. [Copy.[2]]

ARCHBISHOP KING TO SWIFT

Dublin, January 22, 1712-13.

REVEREND SIR,

I RECEIVED yours of the 8th instant by last packets. I may tell you that I never could prevail with myself to confine myself to the conversation of any one party of men of any one sort, but have acquaintance of all—Papists, Protestants, Dissenters, Whigs, Tories, tradesmen, gentle-men, even loose and wicked men, as well as religious and devout, provided that I am satisfied that their business is not to betray and do me mischief; and even then [I] have not always declined them. And I think my present station, not only justifies me in this, but obliges me to it; for the

---

[1] From the reference to Achilles, Scott thinks ("Works," xvi, 25) that the fault attributed to Argyll was "impetuous ambition." It is probable from this letter and from a passage in the Journal to Stella ("Prose Works," ii, 455) that there had been dissension between Swift and Argyll before the publication of "The Public Spirit of the Whigs," and that Swift's bitter attack upon Argyll had its origin in their per-sonal no less than their public relations (supra, vol. i, p. 248, n. 5). The ill-feeling can only have existed for a few days, as a fortnight before Argyll had been chatting with Swift at Court and had introduced him to the French ambassador ("Prose Works," ii, 410).

[2] In King's Correspondence. See Preface.

whole need not a physician so much as the sick; and I thank God [that] I have this comfort from it, and that many have been benefited by it, and I never knew one was the worse. I know this is a great objection against me by some, but I am resolved never to remove it. I have been acquainted with a man many years and never can tax him with an ill office, but he differs from me in some opinions; must I turn his enemy on that account? This is to leave him in his errors, if they chance to be errors. No, surely to continue my friendship is in my judgement the way to gain on him, and if not to reclaim him, yet to make him easy and moderate in his conversation, which is a great step gained. If a set of men fall under the displeasure of the Government shall I immediately look on them as abandoned wretches, and avoid their conversation as infected, when then I must have no friends at all, for the Government changes perhaps in three or four years and then those that I broke with are favourites, and men of the former sort brow-beaten? If a man therefore will follow this method he must have no friends at all in ten or twelve years. These are measures I never followed, nor ever will with God's help. I will choose conversation for myself, and no man shall ever have it in his power to choose for me. If a man find it his interest to avoid me, I am not concerned, and that will allow him to come again. I receive him as if no such thing had happened, provided he has not been guilty of treachery; [there]fore I dispense with a man to pursue an interest which I cannot serve as [well as the] person he applies to, so he only do[es] good to himself without doing mischief to others. I know all must not follow my rules, but I reckon it an unhappiness when they cannot, and perhaps that is your case.

As to the affair you write of in yours I conceive there are two ways of showing things, that is to say, they have a fair and plausible side generally and another that is not so popular; now in my opinion the great[est] care ought to be taken, especially in public businesses, to put them in the most advantageous light and show that face of them that is most defensible. If a man have a good design to carry on, which must be secret in concealing it, he must advance by fair and specious colours that may both satisfy the world, and if possible the true and real purpose. But I have no rule for those that design ill, but to lay aside their evil intention. Now I have observed of the French that they have the advantage of all Europe in this particular, for be their designs good or bad, they never want colours and glosses to set them off, and though they satisfy nobody yet they silence them, and I find it true, what has often been said, one plausible reason is harder to be answered than ten real ones. I would wish a little more dexterity this way in some of my friends than they have in my [opinion] shown hitherto; and that they would not show the ugly shocking face of things, and make the honourable and fair altogether a secret. Perhaps if it were proper I would give you a great many instances of this sort, that in my view of things might and ought to have been avoided. I and the world at a distance and in reality see only the outside of affairs, and when that is not lovely we are apt to conclude as the poet doth in a contrary case *si quae latent pejore putant*. You say that I have " hit upon " one. I can by no means allow you that word, it looks as if there were something of chance in it. Assure yourself that I believe there is hardly a man between Cape Clear and Rushpoint in the north, Papists or Protestants, but he has hit on this very thing: the former repeat it with triumph, and the latter with dread and amazement. They reckon their all depends on this point, and the fear they are in distracts them in some degree. If there were not something of this nature they would never be guilty of such mad practices as I believe you have account of from hence.[1]

As to the minority of a King of France, I am mistaken if ever you see it, or if it happen, that it will be of long continuance. As to security of one Prince from encroachments of another, I know only two ways to obtain it effectually. One is to disenable him from hurting his neighbours, another to make it his interest not to do it. I wish somebody would as earnestly show the world that Europe on

---

[1] Since the parliamentary session of 1711 political feeling in Ireland had continued to run high. " The rage and folly" of the Whigs, according to Secretary Southwell, knew no bounds (Departmental Correspondence in P.R.O. of Ireland). Their chief offence was that on the anniversary of King William's birthday in the previous year, when according to custom "Tamerlane" was acted in the Dublin theatre, they had insisted on the recitation of the prologue written by Garth, which the Lords Justices had prohibited as offensive to England's new allies.

the peace will have either of those securities: it would be of great service.

I remember formerly it has been a maxim to make peace with sword-hand, which the French King has always pursued with the exactest care and carried his point in every treaty by it. I find several here join with your friends in their opinion that if the French had been pushed last campaign, and we had redoubled our attempts against him, it would have got a better and [general] peace for all the confederates than we are like to have, and the nearer to [Paris] the confederate armies had got, still the better. As to what you say of the Dutch tricking us, they say it is to be considered whether the Dutch or French are most in interest engaged to preserve the balance of power in Europe, and which have broken their faith and treaties oftenest, and in prudence trusted them; but they pretend there neither was nor would be any danger, for it would have been in our power to turn short on them, when we pleased, and if they began to falter. If the French had been soundly beaten, we might at any time [have] turned to them, and they would have embraced us on any terms whatsoever; nor say they, doth it appear that the demands of Holland were so easily satisfied, witness the treaty at the Hague and Gertruydenberg. They pretend from this that England was never asked till Holland twice refused.

These are the pretences I have met with, and perceive that amongst people that see only the outside of things they carry some show, especially since even the best affected seem to be in the dark and can say nothing to them. There were two gentlemen with me not long ago and they fell into a dispute—the occasion I need not tell you—whether it was easier to send a fleet and army from the Downs to Calais on the French coast, or to the Mediterranean. He that maintained the latter to be more difficult called for a map, and began to show the way they must sail, and the winds that are necessary, the other cut him short, and told him none but a Whig would maintain such a paradox, which struck him silent, but whether it satisfied him I did not ask.

I have two notions, when or how I come by them, or whether I was born with them I cannot tell, but they are these: that to prefer the public to private interest is virtue, and what a man loses that way will be made good to him by the author of goodness; the other is, that to prefer the future good of myself and posterity to the present is wisdom. Perhaps I had this from my own practice, and other children's, with their butter-cakes. I remember we would thrust off the butter from one part of the cake, and eat it without any, that we might have the more on the last, and that it might be the more pleasing and relishing. How this will agree with your *curent posteri* I cannot say, but I think all wise States have had the greatest regard to posterity, and though they would not prevent all mischiefs, yet they never left gaps open to chance which was visible, and which with any care would probably be stopped. A good gamester leaves as little to chance as he can. In short I never saw any great thing done without a certain scheme and plan of the whole business adjusted before hand. What is done in such a way is regular and steady, and rewards at last generally. Such as trust to time, place and occasions often want necessaries. I am, etc.

W. D[UBLIN].

Dr. Swift.

CLXVIII. [*Original.*[1]]

ROBERT HUNTER TO SWIFT

New York [received *March* 1, 1712-13].[2]

I THINK I am indebted to you for two letters, and should have continued so, had it not been for the apprehension of your putting a wrong construction upon my neglect. My friends being few in number, I would not willingly, or by my own fault, lose those I have. The true cause is this. My unhappy circumstances have so soured me,[3] that what-

[1] In the British Museum. See Preface.
[2] The letter is dated 1 November.
[3] During the opening years of his government of the province of New York (*supra*, vol. i, p. 169, n. 3) Hunter had to contend with opposition from the Assembly, as well as to suppress a Negro insurrection, and suffered great disappointment from the failure of a Palatine settlement for which he was responsible. But he survived to gain the reputation of being one of the ablest and most judicious administrators ever sent to America by England, and "no future governor could earn higher praise than to be likened to him" (*cf.* "The

ever I write must be vinegar and gall to a man of your mirth; for the better understanding of which, be pleased to read them in the words of one of my most renowned predecessors:—*Cuando pensé venir á este gobierno á comer caliente y á beber frio, y á recrear el cuerpo entre sábanas de holanda sobre colchones de pluma, he venido á hacer penitencia como si fuera ermitanno, y como no la hago de mi voluntad, pienso que al cabo al cabo me ha de llevar el diablo.*[1] This worthy was indeed but a type of me, of which I could fully convince you by an exact parallel between our administrations and circumstances, which I shall reserve to another opportunity. The truth of the matter is this: I am used like a dog after having done all that is in the power of man to deserve a better treatment, so that I am now quite jaded. *Male vehi malo alio gubernante, quam tam ingratis rectoribus bene gubernare.*

The approaching peace will give leisure to the Ministry to think of proper remedies for the distracted state of all the Provinces; but of this more particularly, the importance of it by its situation being greater, and the danger by their conduct more imminent than that of the rest. I have done my duty in representing their proceedings, and warning them of the consequences; and there I leave it. *Neque tam me εὐελπιστία consolatur ut antea quam ἀδιαφορία, qua nulla in re tam utor quam in hac civili et publica.* I have purchased a seat for a bishop, and by orders from the Society have given direction to prepare it for his reception. You once upon a day gave me hopes of seeing you there.[2] It would be to me no small relief to have so good a friend to complain to. What it would be to you to hear me when you

---

English in America" by J. A. Doyle, and "The Story of the Palatines," by Sanford H. Cobb).

[1] This passage occurs in Sancho Pança's letter from his island to Don Quixote. See "Don Quixote," translated by John Ormsby, vol. iv, p. 139.

[2] From this reference it appears certain that Swift himself entertained in his Whig days the idea of obtaining a colonial bishopric as a possibility (*supra*, vol. i, p. 134, n. 1). In relating the various attempts made during the reign of Queen Anne by the Society for the Propagation of the Gospel to establish such a bishopric, Mr. Doyle conjectures ("The Colonies under the House of Hanover," p. 276) that Swift probably continued to cherish the ambition until the accession of the House of Hanover, but for such an opinion there is no ground.

could not help me, I know not. *Cætera desunt*—for the
post cannot stay. Adieu. I am,
Very sincerely yours,
Ro. HUNTER.

CLXIX. [*Copy.*[1]]

SWIFT TO SIR ANDREW FOUNTAINE

Friday morning, *March* 6, 1712-13.

GOOD SIR ANDREW,[2]
I RECEIVED your kind and friendly letter last night,
indeed I think I may truly say I received it this morning,
for it was past twelve o'clock—for the bellman had gone
about—for I had been abroad a playing at cards with some
good friends that you know and love.[3] Now as to what you
say of hoping I will excuse your boldness and the trouble:
I do not take it in good part that you should please to
think that I think that anything that you think to command me in is any boldness or trouble. I hope I am better
bred than so, and that I know how to behave myself to my
betters as well as another. Now as to what you say, that
you desire my good company—as you are pleased to call
it so, much above my deserts, unless you will accept the
will, as we say, for the deed—at Madam Vanhumree's[4] at
the hour of three to-morrow (for so it was when you wrote
it, although it be now to-day) I stand very much bounden
to Madam's good will and friendly invitation, if so be she
desired you to tell me (as I suppose she did) to come. But
so it is, that I did in some sort make a kind of a promise
to eat a bit of beef with a friend of mine in York Buildings;

[1] The copy, which is preserved in the Forster Collection, was made
by Forster from the original at Narford (*supra*, vol. i, p. 153, n. 1).
The latter was sold by Sotheby, Wilkinson, and Hodge, on 15 December, 1906.
[2] Swift's intercourse with Fountaine (*supra*, vol. i, p. 183, n. 1) had
been renewed on Swift's return to London, and notwithstanding the
change in Swift's political views, there had been frequent meetings
between the two friends at Mrs. Vanhomrigh's house and other places
(" Prose Works," ii, *passim*).
[3] The day before Swift had paid a visit to Lord Pembroke in order
to see " some curious books " (*ibid.*, p. 437).
[4] Swift spells here the Vanhomrigh name phonetically.

but if my said friend will by any means have me excused,
I will accept Madam Vanhumree's invitation with many
thanks.[1]

But now as to what you say that I am to decide, whether
Madam Hessy or you be most silliest, I am sure it is but a
jest—for Madam Hessy is a very ripe-witted young gentlewoman; and, Sir Andrew, as for you, all the world knows
that you are a bookish gentleman, and admired far and
near for your forwardliness in deep learning. But now if
you mean that you will both strive to counterfeit yourselves
silly, mayhap to pass away the time and make your friends
merry, if I am to decide, why then I am a judge, and as a
judge, I must be sillier than you both. And so, good Sir
Andrew, you call me fool by craft.

Now as to what you say in your postscript, I cannot
answer all your fine compliments, but I wish you as well as
those that can—and would go as far by night as by day to
serve my honoured friend Sir Andrew—as any he that
wears a head—for I will not be behindhand with the best
in well doing or in well wishing, when it lies in my power.
I desire you will present my service to the good gentlewoman and her two daughters and the same to yourself,
who am, good Sir Andrew,

Yours to command in all faithful service,
                    JONATHAN SWIFT.

Good Sir Andrew, when I say you call me fool by craft
I pray you take it not amiss as though I should take it
unkindly that you should take me for a fool, for fool
enough I am, God he knows, but I know you do but jest,
and pray pardon me that I indite no better, and I pray
pardon these many blots and this sad scrawl.

Addressed—For his honoured friend Sir Andrew Fountaine,
   Knight, at his dwelling house in St. James's Place, near
   St. James's Street, on the right hand at the upper end of
   all before you turn to the right hand up again, there
   present, in London.

[1] As appears from the Journal to Stella ("Prose Works," ii, 438) the
friend in York Buildings, namely Oxford, did not excuse Swift.

CLXX. [*Faulkner.*]

SWIFT TO ARCHBISHOP KING

London, *March* 28, 1713.

MY LORD,

ALTHOUGH your humour of delaying, which is a good deal in fashion, might serve me for authority and example in not sooner acknowledging your Grace's letter,[1] I shall not make that use of it; but naturally tell you, that the public delay has been the cause of mine. We have lived almost these two months past by the week, expecting that the Parliament would meet, and the Queen tell them that the peace was signed. But unforeseen difficulties have arisen, partly by some mistakes in our plenipotentiaries, as well as of those of France, too long to trouble your Grace with, since we now reckon all will be at an end;[2] and the Queen has sent new powers to Utrecht, which her ministers there must obey, I think, or be left without excuse. The peace will be signed with France, Holland, the Emperor, Savoy, Portugal, and England; but Spain has yet no minister at Utrecht, the Dutch making difficulties about the Duke d'Ossuna's passports; but the Marquis de Monteleon will soon begin his journey, at least he tells me so.[3] However, it is of no great moment whether Spain comes in now, or a month hence; and the Parliament will be satisfied with the rest. People here have grumbled at those prorogations until they are weary;[4] but they are not very convenient, considering how many funds are out, and how late it is in the year. They think of taking off two shillings in the

---

[1] *Supra*, p. 6.

[2] The English plenipotentiaries had hesitated to sign the treaty of peace until representatives of all the powers concerned were present, and the French plenipotentiaries had continued to insist upon conditions which had been abandoned by the French government in their conferences with the Duke of Shrewsbury at Paris.

[3] Monteleon, who had been in England for some months as the ambassador of Philip V of Spain, had paid great court to Swift, saying that his master was more obliged to him than to any man in Europe ("Prose Works," ii, *passim*). Spain was ultimately represented at Utrecht by Ossuna (*ibid.*, x, 190).

[4] Parliament had been eleven times prorogued.

pound from the land-tax,[1] which I always argued earnestly against; but the Court has a mind to humour the country gentlemen, and the thing is popular enough; but then we must borrow upon new funds, which it will be of the last difficulty to invent or to raise.

The other party are employed in spreading a report most industriously, that the Lord Treasurer intends, after the peace, to declare for the Whigs. They have spread it in Scotland, to prepare people for the next election; and Mr. Annesley[2] told me the other day at my Lord Steward's,[3] that he had heard I writ the same to my friends in Ireland; which, as it is wholly without ground, so the fact is what I never had the least belief of, although his Lordship is somewhat of your Grace's mind, in not refusing to converse with his greatest enemies; and therefore he is censured, as you say you are, upon the same account.[4] And to those who charge him with it—as some are free enough to do it—he only says, his friends ought to trust him; and I have some reason to believe, that after a peace, the direct contrary will appear. For my own part, I entirely agree with your Grace, that a free man ought not to confine his converse to any one party; neither would I do so, if I were free; but I am not, and perhaps much less is a great minister in such a juncture as this. Among many qualities I have observed in the Treasurer, there is one which is something singular, that he will be under an imputation, how wrong soever, without the pains of clearing himself to his nearest friends, which is owing to great integrity, great courage, or

---

[1] The rate was in time of war four shillings, which produced a revenue of about two millions.

[2] Francis Annesley, to whom Swift alludes, was a grandson of the first Viscount Valentia of that family, and from him the present Earl of Annesley descends. He was an English barrister, and represented the borough of Westbury in the British Parliament. In the reign of William III he had sat for the borough of Downpatrick in the Irish Parliament, but in the first session of Queen Anne's reign he had been expelled on account of the part which he had taken as a commissioner to inquire into the grants of the forfeited estates in Ireland. Between Archbishop King and Annesley a close friendship existed.

[3] Lord Poulett (*supra*, vol. i, p. 193, n. 3) then held that office, to which he had been appointed when Oxford became Lord Treasurer.

[4] As is now known there was good ground for the rumour that Oxford meditated at that time a coalition with Halifax and other Whigs, and Swift himself admits in the Journal to Stella that a conference had taken place ("Prose Works," ii, 444, 445).

great contempt of censure. I know he has abundance of the two last, and I believe he has the first.[1]

Your Grace's observations on the French dexterity in negotiation, as well as their ill faith, are certainly right; but let both be as great [as] possible, we must treat with them one time or other; and if Ministers will not be upon their guard against such notorious managers, they are altogether inexcusable. But I do assure your Grace, that as it has fallen in my way to know more of the steps of this whole treaty, than perhaps any one man besides, I cannot see that anything in the power of human prudence, under many difficult conjunctures, has been omitted. We have been forced to conceal the best side, which I agree has been unfortunate and unpopular; but you will please to consider that this way of every subject interposing their sentiments upon the management of foreign negotiations, is a very new thing among us; and the suffering it has been thought, in the opinion of wise men, too great a strain upon the prerogative; especially giving a detail of particulars, which, in the variety of events, cannot be ascertained during the course of a treaty. I could easily answer the objection of your Grace's friends in relation to the Dutch, and why they made those difficulties at the Hague and Gertruydenberg. And when the whole story of these two last intriguing years comes to be published, the world will have other notions of our proceedings. This perhaps will not be long untold, and might already have been, if other people had been no wiser than I.[2] After all, my Lord, I grant that from

---

[1] A reference in a letter written from London on the previous day by the illustrious Berkeley, then a Fellow of Trinity College, Dublin, suggests the possibility that Swift may have been a party to the negotiations between Oxford and the Whig leaders, notwithstanding what he says to Archbishop King. The passage is a curious one, and is as follows: "I breakfasted with Mr. Addison at Dr. Swift's lodgings. His coming in while I was there, and the good temper he showed was construed by me as a sign of an approaching coalition of parties, Mr. Addison being more earnest in the Whig cause than Mr. Steele (the former having quitted an employment rather than hold it under the Tories, which by a little compliance he might have done), and there having passed a coldness if not a direct breach between those two gentlemen and Dr. Swift on the score of politics. Dr. Swift's wit is admired by both of them and indeed by his greatest enemies. . . . I think him one of the best natured and agreeable men in the world" (Hist. MSS. Com., Report vii, App., p. 238).

[2] "The History of the Four Last Years of the Queen," to which

a distant view of things, abundance of objections may be
raised against many parts of our conduct. But the difficulties which gave room to these objections are not seen,
and perhaps some of them will never appear; neither may
it be convenient they should. If in the end it appears that
we have made a good bargain for you, we hope you will
take it without entering too nicely into the circumstances.

I will not undertake to defend our proceedings against
any man who will not allow this postulatum, that it was
impossible to carry on the war any longer; which, whoever
denies, either has not examined the state of the nation with
respect to its debts, or denies it from the spirit of party.
When a friend of mine objected this to Lord Nottingham,
he freely confessed it was a thing he had never considered.
But, however, he would be against any peace without
Spain; and why? Because he was not Privy Seal. But
then, why does he vote with the Whigs in everything else,
although peace has no concern? Because he was not Privy
Seal. I hope, my Lord, we shall in time unriddle you many
a dark problem, and let you see that faction, rage, rebellion,
revenge, and ambition, were deeply rooted in the hearts of
those who have been the great obstructors of the Queen's
measures, and of the kingdom's happiness; and if I am not
mistaken, such a scene may open, as will leave the present
age and posterity little room to doubt who were the real
friends and real enemies of their country. At the same
time I know nothing is so rash as predicting upon the
events of public councils; and I see many accidents very
possible to happen which may soon defeat all my wise conjectures. I am, my Lord,

Your Grace's most dutiful and most humble obedient
servant.

Swift again alludes, had made no progress since January (*supra*,
p. 2). The delay in its publication was not due to Swift. Although
as a composition the History is not placed high by modern critics,
Swift's own estimate of it was different, and led him to tell Stella that
she might expect "something very notable" ("Prose Works," ii, 392).
Such value did Swift attach to it that he even thought at one time it
might be used as a lever to extort preferment (*ibid.*, p. 406). But the
reason it was not issued was the same as prevented its appearance in
the closing years of Swift's life, namely, the opinion of more sapient
politicians that a great portion of it was too dangerous to publish, and
that only what related to the peace ought to be printed (*ibid.*, 417, 434).

CLXXI. [*Original.*[1]]

MATTHEW PRIOR TO SWIFT

Paris, *April* 8 [O.S. *March* 28], 1713.

PRAY take this word writ after our packets closed, and the messenger staying for it, as an equivalent for yours dispatched at midnight and when the writer was half asleep.[2] Hang me if I know how to go on, though I am in a country where everybody does not only write letters but prints them. Our great affair goes on very successfully. We transmit the Spanish treaty, concluded at Madrid, for your approbation in England, and transmission to Utrecht; after which I think, *pax sit* will become authentic Latin; after which, I suppose, our Society will flourish,[3] and I shall have nothing to do but to partake of that universal protection, which it will receive. In the mean time, pray give my great respects to our brethren, and tell them that, while in hopes of being favoured, they are spending their own money, I am advancing my interests in the French language, and forgetting my own mother tongue. But we shall have time enough to perfect our English when we have done with other matters. I want mightily to hear from Lord Treasurer. Tell him so. I owe brother Arbuthnot a letter; excuse my not writing to him, till I know what to say.[4] I cannot find Vanhomrigh since he brought

---

[1] In the British Museum. See Preface.

[2] Prior had accompanied Bolingbroke to Paris in the previous August, and had remained there in the position of an informal ambassador. It was at this time that the famous correspondence was carried on by Prior and Bolingbroke under the names of Mat and Harry.

[3] The composition and history of " The Society," to which allusion has been so often made, is discussed at length by Sir Leslie Stephen (" Swift," pp. 104-6). Of the " Brothers' Club," as Stephen calls it, Prior and Arbuthnot, who is mentioned by Prior later on, were original members. Although he was absent from London when the Society was started (" Prose Works," ii, 194) Swift appears to have been its life and soul, and to have acted for a time as its secretary. Before this letter was written, however, his interest in the Society had begun to decline.

[4] Swift was then very frequently in Arbuthnot's company (*supra*, vol. i, p. 338, n. 1). Three days later on the eve of All Fools' Day,

me your letter.[1] I have a rarity of a book to send you by
the first fair occasion. I make but little of the English wit,
the Guardian;[2] but, possibly, I do not yet enter into his
design. Let Lord Bolingbroke know I love him mightily;
and pray do you as much for Dick Shelton.[3] Adieu, my
good friend. I am, very truly,

Your obedient and faithful servant,
M. PRIOR.

Addressed—To Dr. Jonathan Swift.

CLXXII. [*Original.*[4]]

THE EARL POULETT TO SWIFT

Sunday Afternoon [*March* 29, 1713].

I WAS called away presently after chapel upon some business which hindered my going up stairs at St. James's, and
occasions Dr. Swift the trouble of this, to make my excuse
for not returning the paper, which I here send you;[5] and
though it is not in my power to serve you in any proportion to my unfeigned respects for you, yet I would not be
wanting, of my part, in any opportunity where I can, to
express myself, Sir,

Your most faithful humble servant,
POULETT.

they contrived with the assistance of Lady Masham "a lie," of which
some particulars will be found in Appendix I.

[1] It appears from a subsequent reference that Vanessa's brother
(*supra*, vol. i, p. 339, n. 1) was then residing in Paris.

[2] On 1 April Swift says to Stella, "Did I tell you that Steele has
begun a new daily paper called the Guardian? They say good for
nothing. I have not seen it" ("Prose Works," ii, 450).

[3] The friend who appears in Prior's "Alma."

[4] In the British Museum. See Preface.

[5] Swift's application to Earl Poulett (*supra*, p. 15, n. 3) was probably
in connection with an unsuccessful effort which Swift made at that time
to obtain a dispensation for a Fellow of Trinity College, Dublin, from
the obligation to take holy orders. The Fellow was one of the Grattans,
who became Swift's great friends. This appears to have been his
first acquaintance with the family.

CLXXIII. [*Copy.*[1]]

ARCHBISHOP KING TO SWIFT

Dublin, *April* 14, 1713.

SIR,

I RETURN you my hearty thanks for yours of the 28th of March last. It was a little shocking to find her Majesty's plenipotentiaries made any demur of signing the peace, but I find all that is over. I have not heard from any hand one word of the articles, but assure yourself if there be sufficient security against the Pretender, the people of Ireland will receive it gratefully, and not trouble their minds about anything else, but the fear of him put them almost out of their wits and hurries them into many inconveniences.

I cannot imagine what grounds any would have to say that you had wrote into Ireland that my Lord Treasurer after the peace intended to declare for the Whigs. I am sure you never hinted any such thing to me, but the contrary, but if you had, it would have remained with me, for you may rest satisfied, that for above this twelve months, no one ever saw any letter you wrote to me, nor did I so much as hint that I had any correspondence with you; partly for fear of importunity and partly of pumping; nay, there want not such as would make no scruple to quote me that were thought to have a good correspondent for a piece of news of their own inventing, of which I have instances. I cannot conceive what great occasion there will be for money considering we have had little campaigning these last two years.

The Ministers as you observe had need to look sharp, considering with whom they have to deal, for if you look back on all the treaties that have been between England and France for the last four hundred years, you will not find one in which they have not notoriously overreached us; and this is I reckon the great ground of the jealousies of the people which is increased by the secrecy with which it is transacted. And if you reflect on the management of former Ministries, particularly of those of the four last reigns, you will be of opinion that these kingdoms have no

[1] In King's Correspondence. See Preface.

great reason to be over confident of their Ministers, or trust much to them.

I find that few here grant your postulatum; they say that the confederates were content to carry on the war if Britain would have for the future contributed but four million yearly towards it, which they say we might have done for twenty years, without running one shilling in debt. This is a matter of which I am no judge and therefore can say nothing to it. I have nothing to add but my hearty prayers that this may prove a firm and lasting peace, that may answer the expectations of good people, and be for the honour of those that have negotiated it.

I have been extremely ill all this winter, and intend God willing for Bath after my visitation is over. I hope to be there the latter end of this month, or the beginning of the next. I am unwilling to go to London, because there are already too many of the Bishops and other clergy of Ireland there. I have a cause in the House of Lords between Christ Church and me.[1] Judgement has been given for me in the Common Pleas and Queen's Bench here, and Queen's Bench in England, unanimously by all the judges in every court, but it is now removed by them into the Lords' House in Great Britain; pray speak to such Lords as you are acquainted with to be there at the hearing.

Dr. Swift.

CLXXIV. [*Original.*[2]]

DEAN ATTERBURY TO SWIFT

Chelsea, Tuesday Morning, *April* 21, 1713.

MR. DEAN,

GIVE me leave to tell you, that there is no man in England more pleased with your being preferred than I am.[3]

---

[1] This litigation was a renewal of that to which reference has been made (*supra*, vol. i, p. 48, n. 2), and arose from the contention of the Dean of Christ Church that his Cathedral was a royal foundation, and was therefore not subject to the Archbishop (Stokes, *op. cit.*, p. 223).

[2] In the British Museum. See Preface.

On the previous day Swift had been promised the deanery of St. Patrick's. At the beginning of the month no less than six ecclesiastical dignities were vacant, the three English deaneries already

I would have told you so myself at your lodgings, but that my waiting[1] confines me. I had heard a flying report of it before; but my Lord Bolingbroke yesterday confirmed the welcome news to me. I could not excuse myself without saying thus much; and I have not time to say more, but that I am,

Your most affectionate and faithful servant,

FR. ATTERBURY.[2]

Addressed—To the Reverend Dr. Swift.

CLXXV. [*Sheridan.*]

SWIFT TO ARCHBISHOP KING

London, *April* 30, 1713.

MY LORD,

I HAD the honour of your Grace's letter of the 14th, which at present I cannot answer particularly. I send this to welcome your Grace to the Bath, where we conclude you

mentioned (*supra*, p. 4, n. 2), a canonry at Windsor, and two Irish bishoprics, those of Raphoe and Dromore. A week before this letter was written, on learning that the deaneries were filled, Swift had for the first time asserted his right to receive from the Ministers open and honourable recognition of his labours for their party. It had been suggested to him in the previous October that he should obtain one of the Irish bishoprics for Dean Stearne, and the deanery of St. Patrick's for himself. At the time he had scouted the idea of helping Stearne, recalling the old grievance of the curacy (*supra*, vol. i, p. 72, n. 1); but after some months he began to think that the influence over Queen Anne of his enemies, the Duchess of Somerset and Archbishop Sharpe, would preclude the possibility of preferment in the gift of the Crown, and that the deanery of St. Patrick's, which was in the gift of the Lord Lieutenant, might prove after all a useful alternative. For some time he had therefore urged the claims of Stearne to one of the vacant bishoprics, and now demanded Stearne's promotion and his own appointment in Stearne's place. For a few days the question was complicated by the efforts of some of his friends to secure for him the Windsor canonry, but finally it was settled in what Swift had come to see was the only possible way (*cf.* " Prose Works," ii, 390, 418, 424, 453, 456-9).

[1] As the Queen's chaplain.
[2] When writing this letter I wonder did Atterbury recall his condemnation of "the profane strokes" in the "Tale of a Tub."

are now arrived; and I hope the design of your journey is
more for prevention than cure.   I suppose your Grace has
heard that the Queen has made Dr. Stearne Bishop of
Dromore, and that I am to succeed him in his deanery.
Dr. Parnell, who is now in town, writ last post to your
Grace, to desire the favour of you that he may have my
small prebend:[1] he thinks it will be some advantage to come
into the Chapter, where it may possibly be in my power to
serve him in a way agreeable to him, although in no degree
equal to his merits; by which he has distinguished himself
so much, that he is in great esteem with the Ministry, and
others of the most valuable persons in this town.[2]   He has
been many years under your Grace's direction, and has a
very good title to your favour, so that I believe it will be
unnecessary to add how much I should be obliged to your
Grace's compliance in this matter;[3] and I flatter myself
that his being agreeable to me, will be no disadvantage to

[1] Parnell's letter to King, asking for the prebend of Dunlavin
(*supra*, vol. i, p. 53, n. 2) is preserved in the Library of Trinity College,
Dublin (MS. No. 1122).
[2] Thomas Parnell, the poet, to whom allusion has already been
made in connection with his appointment to the archdeaconry of
Clogher (*supra*, vol. i, p. 42, n. 2) had been overwhelmed with grief by
the death of his wife, and had been in England for a year trying to
restore his health, which had been seriously affected. While in
London he had been taken under Swift's wing, and had been introduced by him to Oxford, under flattering circumstances which have
been often told (*cf.* " Prose Works," ii, 422; Delany's " Observations,"
p. 20), and to Bolingbroke, with a result that led Swift to observe to
Stella how pleasant it was to see one, " who hardly passed for anything in Ireland," make his way in London " with a little friendly for-
warding." It was at this time Parnell wrote his " Essay on the Different
Styles of Poetry," which had the benefit of revision from Bolingbroke
(" Prose Works," ii, *passim*).
[3] King had been one of the guardians of Thomas Parnell, and his
brother John Parnell, an Irish judge, from whom the Lords Congleton
and Charles Stewart Parnell were descended. From correspondence
between King and their mother, who must have been a relation or
very intimate friend of the Archbishop, some interesting particulars of
Thomas Parnell's early life can be gathered. It appears from these
letters that he was naturally very diffident, and did not feel justified
for some years in making use of deacon's orders which King had
thought fit to confer upon him before he had reached canonical age.
These years he spent in travel which he hoped would be of advantage
to him, " whether it improved his mind or no," by " dazzling the un-
thinking with the name of a travelled man" (MS. cited *supra*, n. 1,
and King's Correspondence, *passim*).

him in your Grace's opinion. I am, with the greatest respect, my Lord,

Your Grace's most dutiful and most humble servant,

JON. SWIFT.

CLXXVI. [*Copy.*[1]]

SWIFT TO THE REV. WILLIAM DIAPER

London, *April* 30, 1713.

SIR,[2]

I AM ashamed to tell you how ill a philosopher I am; that a very ill situation of my own affairs for three weeks past, made me utterly incapable of answering your obliging letter, or thanking you for your most agreeable copy of verses. The prints will tell you that I am condemned to live again in Ireland; and all that the Court or Ministry did for me was to let me choose my station in the country where I am banished. I could not forbear showing both your letter and verses[3] to our great men, as well as to the men of wit of my acquaintance; and they were highly approved by all. I am altogether a stranger to your friend Oppian; and am a little angry when those who have a genius lay it out in translation.[4] I question whether *res angusta domi* be not one of your motives. Perhaps you want such a bridle as a translation, for your genius is too fruitful, as appears by the frequency of your similes; and this employment may teach you to write more like a mortal man, as Shakespeare expresseth it.[5]

I have been minding my Lord Bolingbroke, Mr. Har-

---

[1] In the Forster Collection. See Preface.

[2] Diaper, who was a native of Somersetshire, appears to have been a *protégé* of his countryman, Sir William Wyndham, then Secretary-at-War. He had been educated at Balliol College, Oxford. His death took place only four years later at the early age of twenty-nine.

[3] "Dryades or the Nymph's Prophecy," which Swift describes as "sea eclogues, poems of Mermen, resembling pastorals of shepherds," and praises as very pretty and original (" Prose Works," ii, 353), was published by Diaper in that year. In the following one he published "An Imitation of the Seventeenth Epistle of the First Book of Horace address'd to Dr. S—ft."

[4] A translation of "Oppian's Halieuticks of the Nature of Fishes and Fishing of the Ancients," by Diaper, was published after his death.

[5] "How many years a mortal man may live" (3 Hen. VI, ii, 5).

court, and Sir William Wyndham, to solicit my Lord Chancellor to give you a living, as a business which belongs to our Society, who assume the title of rewarders of merit.[1] They are all very well disposed, and I shall not fail to negotiate for you while I stay in England, which will not be above six weeks; but I hope to return in October, and if you are not then provided for, I will move heaven and earth that something may be done for you. Our Society hath not met of late, else I would have moved to have two of us sent in form to request a living for you from my Lord Chancellor; and, if you have any way to employ my service, I desire you will let me know it, and believe me to be, very sincerely, Sir,

Your most faithful humble servant,

J. SWIFT.

Addressed—To the Reverend Mr. William Diaper, at Dean, near Basingstoke, Hampshire.

CLXXVII. [*Original.*[2]]

PROVOST PRATT AND SWIFT TO EDWARD SOUTHWELL

May 5, 1713.

Memorial about Dr. Raymond

THE rectory of Moymet within two miles of Trim in the county of Meath, value about forty pounds per annum [is]

---

[1] Lord Harcourt, whose title had been advanced from that of Lord Keeper to that of Lord Chancellor, was, like Oxford, not allowed to be a member of the Society, but in the opinion of Swift both of them were sufficiently honoured by the admission of their sons to render it their duty to assist anyone whom the Society patronized. Swift had already been instrumental in securing for Diaper priest's orders, telling Stella, with the usual depreciation of his own kindness, that " it is a poor, little, short wretch, but will do best in a gown " (" Prose Works," ii, 403).

[2] The original of this memorial, in Swift's handwriting, is preserved in the Marquess of Ormonde's evidence room at Kilkenny Castle. So far as is known, it is the only relic of Swift left by his friend the second Duke of Ormond. To the Marquess of Ormonde I am indebted for permission to include the memorial in the Correspondence, as well as to make use in these notes of information which could only have been obtained by access to his manuscript collection.

in the gift of Lady Roscommon,[1] but now on Dr. Stearne's promotion in the gift of the government. It hath been usually given to the minister of Trim, and is no sinecure, but the Bishop will oblige whoever has it to keep a curate. It is only convenient for the minister of Trim, being hardly worth while for anybody else to pass patent for it. Therefore his Grace is desired to bestow it to Dr. Raymond, minister of Trim, unless anybody whom his Grace hath a mind to oblige, think it worth their acceptance. The cure of Trim is very great, and profits small.[2]

CLXXVIII. [*Sheridan.*]

SWIFT TO JOSEPH ADDISON

May 13, 1713.

SIR,

I WAS told yesterday, by several persons, that Mr. Steele had reflected upon me in his Guardian;[3] which I could hardly believe, until, sending for the paper of the day, I found he had, in several parts of it, insinuated with the utmost malice, that I was author of the Examiner; and abused me in the grossest manner he could possibly invent, and sent his name to what he had written.[4] Now, Sir, if I

[1] The widow of the well-known fourth Earl of Roscommon:

"... in all Charles's days
Roscommon only boasts unspotted lays."

She had married, after Lord Roscommon's death, Thomas Carter of Robertstown in the county of Meath, whose son was prominent in the Irish Parliament of George II, and became Master of the Rolls and Secretary of State in Ireland, and it was probably through her second husband that Lady Roscommon had the gift of Moymet.

[2] It is a somewhat interesting example of the Church government of that time to find that Bishop Stearne on his promotion from Trim to the deanery of St. Patrick's (*supra*, vol. i, p. 120, n. 2) was allowed to deprive his successor of part of his legitimate emoluments by retaining Moymet. In approaching the Duke of Ormond as Lord Lieutenant, through his Chief Secretary Edward Southwell, on behalf of Raymond, Provost Pratt was doubtless actuated by regard for one who had been a brother Fellow, and Swift by gratitude for kind attention which Raymond had paid to Stella. As will be seen farther on their application was eventually successful.

[3] *Supra*, p. 19, n. 2.

[4] The cause of the reflections upon Swift was an attack in the "Examiner" on Lord Nottingham, which in part took the form of a libel on that nobleman's daughter.

am not author of the Examiner,[1] how will Mr. Steele be able to defend himself from the imputation of the highest degree of baseness, ingratitude, and injustice? Is he so ignorant of my temper, and of my style? Has he never heard that the author of the Examiner, to whom I am altogether a stranger,[2] did a month or two ago vindicate me from having any concern in it? Should not Mr. Steele have first expostulated with me as a friend? Have I deserved this usage from Mr. Steele, who knows very well that my Lord Treasurer has kept him in his employment upon my entreaty and intercession?[3] My Lord Chancellor and Lord Bolingbroke will be witnesses, how I was reproached by my Lord Treasurer, upon the ill returns Mr. Steele made to his Lordship's indulgence, etc.

CLXXIX. [*Copy.*[4]]

ARCHBISHOP KING TO SWIFT

Chester, *May* 16, 1713.[5]

REVEREND SIR,

THIS is to welcome you to my neighbourhood at St. Sepulcher's. I have a very great loss in the removal of the Bishop of Dromore, who was not only a neighbour, but a bosom friend. I understand that was not much his advantage,[6] but I am sure it was to mine, and the Church's.

[1] The editor of the "Examiner" at that time was William Oldisworth (see "Prose Works," *passim*).

[2] With respect to Oldisworth Swift observes to Stella, "he is an ingenious fellow, but the most confounded vain coxcomb in the world, so that I dare not let him see me, nor am acquainted with him" ("Prose Works," ii, 440).

[3] After the accession of the Tory government Steele had been deprived of the office of Gazetteer (*supra*, vol. i, p. 80, n. 1), but allowed to retain a commissionership of the stamp office, which was also held by him. In granting this favour Harley was actuated, in the opinion of Forster ("Life," p. 287), by more selfish motives than Swift thought, and would have been glad to gain Steele's support on any terms.

[4] In King's Correspondence. See Preface.

[5] Writing on that day to Edward Southwell, Archbishop King says: "I came [here] yesterday about six in the afternoon having left Dublin about noon the day before; I intended to have been here three weeks ago, but a continued easterly wind kept me on the other side."

[6] In this surmise King was not mistaken. Ormond, who only con-

I hope that will not discourage you from reckoning yourself amongst my friends, which I earnestly desire. I had wrote sooner to you, but expected every day a wind to bring me here, it continued cross for many days, and gave me opportunity to consecrate your predecessor before I came away.[1] I go directly from hence to the Bath, my health requiring it, where I shall be glad to hear from you. I know not whether I shall be obliged to go to London before I return. I will not if I can avoid it, for considering the great number of Irish Bishops and clergy that are there, I am ashamed to add to the number. I should be very much pleased to have an hour or two of your conversation before I returned or you went to Ireland, but am afraid I can hardly expect it, though perhaps it might be of use to us both.

I have a cause before the Lords in the Parliament to be heard this session.[2] It is between Christ Church and me. I think I gave you an account of it before, you may do me good service in it if you would speak to Mr. Annesley,[3] who manages for me, and knows when it comes on, and get some number of the states of the case when printed and distribute them to your friends, with a request to be present at the hearing. I would reckon [it] a great obligation. I have had the unanimous judgement of all the judges in the Common Pleas and Queen's Bench in Ireland, and likewise of the Queen's Bench in England, for me; what weight those will have with the Lords I cannot tell, but the cause seems so plain to all that heard it argued that they say there is no colour against me.

Your predecessor in St. Patrick's did a great deal to his church and house, but there is still work for you; he designed a spire for the steeple, which kind of ornament is much wanting in Dublin; he has left your economy clear and two hundred pounds in bank for this purpose. The steeple is one hundred and twenty feet high, twenty-one

sented to Stearne's promotion in order to secure the deanery for Swift, alleged as his chief objection to Stearne that "he was influenced by the Archbishop of Dublin" ("Prose Works," ii, 459).

[1] King lost no time in consecrating his friend. Stearne's patent is dated 1 May, and his consecration took place in St. Patrick's Cathedral on 10 May. As a suffragan of the Armagh province Stearne ought to have been consecrated by Primate Marsh, but owing to the Primate's infirmities the duty fell to King.

[2] *Supra*, p. 21.   [3] *Supra*, p. 15, n. 2

feet in the clear wide, where the spire is to stand; the design was to build it of brick, one hundred and twenty feet high, the scaffolding we reckoned to be the principal cost, which yet is pretty cheap in Dublin, the brick and lime are good and cheap. But we have no workman that understands anything of the matter. I believe you may be acquainted with several that are conversant with such kind of work, and if you would discourse some of them, and push on the work as soon as settled, it might be of use to you, and give the people there an advantageous notion of you, *dimidium facti qui bene capit habet.*[1]

I add no more, but my hearty prayers for you, and that you may enjoy with comfort and reputation the provision her Majesty has made for you,[2] which shall be the study and endeavour of, etc.

W. D[UBLIN].

Dr. Swift.

CLXXX. [*Sheridan.*]

RICHARD STEELE TO SWIFT

May 19, 1713.

SIR,

MR. ADDISON showed me your letter, wherein you mention me.[3] They laugh at you, if they make you believe your

---

[1] The tower, which stands at the north-west corner of St. Patrick's Cathedral, and which is one of the most noble structures of the kind in the United Kingdom, was built in the fourteenth century, but the spire, which now surmounts it, was not erected until some years after Swift's death. As the present Dean of St. Patrick's remarks ("The Cathedral Church of St. Patrick," p. 33), "although quite incongruous to the architect's eye," the spire is not displeasing in effect. This, however, could hardly have been the case if it had been built of brick as suggested in this letter, but fortunately better taste prevailed, and it was constructed of stone.

[2] In the letter to Southwell cited above Archbishop King indicates that he had desired a different successor to Stearne, and compares Swift's appointment to that of a clerical peer of small parts, Thomas, sixth Viscount Ikerrin, who had been thrust into the deanery of Tuam. His words are as follows: "The deanery [of St. Patrick's] has taken a new turn which I could not foresee; you will bear me witness that I had no hand in putting my Ikerrin by it."

[3] As Sir Henry Craik says ("Life," i, 337), in writing to Addison Swift meant that the subject of his letter (*supra*, p. 26) should be dealt

opportunity of giving your Lordship my humblest thanks, for a hundred favours you have done me. I wanted the sight of your Lordship this day in York Buildings.[1] Pray, my Lord, come to town before I leave it, and supply all my wants. My Lord Treasurer uses me barbarously: appoints to carry me to Kensington, and makes me walk four miles at midnight. He laughs when I mention a thousand pounds which he gives me; though a thousand pounds is a very serious thing, etc.[2]

CLXXXIII. [*Sheridan.*]

SWIFT TO ARCHBISHOP KING

London, *May* 23, 1713.

MY LORD,

I HAD the honour of a letter from your Grace, the 18th instant, from Chester. I was confidently told, about three weeks ago, that your Grace was expected every day at the Bath; and you will find a letter there as old as that, with a requisition in favour of Dr. Parnell, who, by his own merit, is in the esteem of the chief ministers here. I am very sensible, that the loss your Grace has suffered in the removal of Dr. Stearne, will never be made up by me, upon a great many accounts: however, I shall not yield to him in respect and veneration for your Grace's character and person; and I return you my most grateful acknowledgments for the offer you make me of your favour and pro-

---

Lord Chancellor of Ireland, Sir Constantine Phipps, who had been Harcourt's junior when defending Sacheverell.

[1] Harcourt had invariably attended the Cabinet dinners given by Oxford at York Buildings on Saturdays. The date which I have appended to this letter fell on Saturday, and from Swift's reference to his approaching departure for Ireland is at least not altogether unlikely to be accurate.

[2] On assuming his dignity Swift was obliged to pay £800 on account of the house built by Bishop Stearne (*supra*, vol. i, p. 82, n. 3), £150 in respect of first fruits, and £50 for his patent; and although in writing to Stella he does not speak so confidently, he had some ground for hoping that a grant of £1,000 might be made to him from the privy purse for the purpose of defraying these expenses ("Prose Works," ii, 460, 463).

tection. I think to set out for Ireland on Monday sevennight, to be there before the term ends; for so they advise me, because the long vacation follows, in which I cannot take the oaths, unless at a Quarter Sessions, and I had better have two chances than one. This will hinder me from paying my respects to your Grace at the Bath; and indeed my own health would be better, I believe, if I could pass a few weeks there; but my remedy shall be riding, and a sea voyage. I have been inquiring, and am told your Grace's cause will hardly come on this session; but indeed I have been so much out of order for these ten days past, that I have been able to do nothing.

As to the spire to be erected on St. Patrick's steeple, I am apt to think it will cost more than is imagined; and I am confident that no bricks made in that part of Ireland, will bear being exposed so much to the air; however, I shall inquire among some architects here. I hope your Grace will find a return of your health in the place where you are. I humbly beg your blessing; and remain, with great respect, my Lord,

Your Grace's most dutiful and most humble servant,
JON. SWIFT.

CLXXXIV. [*Sheridan.*]

SWIFT TO RICHARD STEELE

[*May* 23, 1713.]

SIR,

. . .[1] THE case was thus: I did, with the utmost application, and desiring to lay all my credit upon it, desire Mr. Harley (as he was then called) to show you mercy. He said he would, and wholly upon my account: that he would appoint you a day to see him: that he would not expect you should quit any friend or principle. Some days after, he told me, he had appointed you a day, and you had not kept it; upon which he reproached me, as engaging for more than I could answer, and advised me to more caution another time. I told him, and desired my Lord Chancellor

---

[1] This letter, which is a reply to the one from Steele (*supra*, p. 29), has been injured, and the only words deciphered in the first lines are: " I may probably know better when they are disposed."

and Lord Bolingbroke to be witnesses, that I would never speak for, or against you, as long as I lived; only I would add, that it was still my opinion, you should have mercy till you gave further provocations. This is the history of what you think fit to call, in the spirit of insulting, their laughing at me; and you may do it securely, for, by the most inhuman dealings, you have wholly put it out of my power, as a Christian, to do you the least ill office. Next I desire to know, whether the greatest services ever done by one man to another, may not have the same turn as properly applied to them? And, once more, suppose they did laugh at me, I ask whether my inclinations to serve you merit to be rewarded by the vilest treatment, whether they succeeded or not? If your interpretation were true, I was laughed at only for your sake; which, I think, is going pretty far to serve a friend. As to the letter I complain of, I appeal to your most partial friends, whether you ought not either to have asked, or written to me, or desired to have been informed by a third hand, whether I were any way concerned in writing the Examiner? And if I had shuffled, or answered indirectly, or affirmed it, or said I would not give you satisfaction, you might then have wreaked your revenge with some colour of justice. I have several times assured Mr. Addison, and fifty others, that I had not the least hand in writing any of those papers; and that I had never exchanged one syllable with the supposed author in my life, that I can remember, nor ever seen him above twice, and that in mixed company, in a place where he came to pay his attendance. One thing more I must observe to you, that a year or two ago, when some printers used to bring me their papers in manuscript, I absolutely forbid them to give any hints against Mr. Addison and you, and some others; and have frequently struck out reflections upon you in particular, and should, I believe, have done it still, if I had not wholly left off troubling myself about those kind of things.

I protest I never saw anything more liable to exception, than every part is of the letter you were pleased to write me. You plead that I do not in mine to Mr. Addison, in direct terms, say I am not concerned in the Examiner, and is that an excuse for the most savage injuries in the world a week before? How far you can prevail with the Guardian, I shall not trouble myself to inquire; and am more concerned how you will clear your own honour and conscience, than my reputation. I shall hardly lose one friend by what you [say:] I know not any [person who would] laugh at me for any [inaccurate] absurdity of yours. There are solecisms in morals as well as in languages; and to which of the virtues you will reconcile your conduct to me, is past my imagination. Be pleased to put these questions to yourself:—If Dr. Swift be entirely innocent of what I accuse him, how shall I be able to make him satisfaction? And how do I know but he may be entirely innocent? If he was laughed at only because he solicited for me, is that a sufficient reason for me to say the vilest things of him in print under my hand, without any provocation? And how do I know but he may be in the right, when he says I was kept in my employment at his interposition? If he never once reflected on me the least in any paper, and has hindered many others from doing it, how can I justify myself, for endeavouring in mine to ruin his credit as a Christian and a clergyman?[1] I am, Sir,

Your most obedient humble servant,

J. S.

CLXXXV. [Copy.[2]]

ARCHBISHOP KING TO SWIFT

Bath, *May* 25, 1713.

REVEREND SIR,

I GAVE you the trouble of a letter from Chester[3] and proposed beginning my journey to this place the Monday after, but it pleased God to afflict me with a relapse into the gout, which being both in my knee and foot hindered me venturing on it, however I ventured to set out on

[1] After quoting in the "Guardian" a passage from the "Examiner," in which Lord Nottingham's daughter is described as tatting "in the immediate presence of God and her Majesty," Steele had inserted the comment that it was very evident which of those persons the writer in the "Examiner" was "the more fearful of offending." He had also called the writer a *miscreant*, but had subsequently expressed regret for using a word which he believed signified an unbeliever (Aitken's "Life of Steele," i, 382).

[2] In King's Correspondence. See Preface.   [3] *Supra*, p. 27.

Wednesday and got here on Saturday,[1] through most insufferable ways; my gout still continues, but I thank God, it is more easy. I met here yours of April the 30th in favour of Dr. Parnell; there is no person I would more willingly oblige and am very glad to find it would be grateful to you, but I promised that prebend long ago to Mr. Espin that has the cure, and is very ill provided of a maintenance, and before I left Ireland gave order for his titles as soon as it should be vacant.[2] I have laid a scheme for the supplying the cures of the diocese, the best that the present circumstances will afford, and of which I shall be glad to have your opinion and approbation in due time.

I reckon the first care of a Bishop ought to be the provision for the cures of his diocese, and the next a proper encouragement for some clergyman of a superior form, that may be able to subsist not only in parochial offices, but also in managing the more general and political part of his pastoral charge. I find myself by the improportionable scantiness of the provision for Church ministers, both as to the number and duty required of them, unable in any measure to accomplish either of these; but I must do the best I can, and I think it necessary in many places to grant the prebends that are in my gift to those that serve the cures; by which means I obtain both their attendance at the Cathedral in their turns, and likewise encourage better men to undertake the cures, whereas when they are given to persons that have no other obligation to keep them in the diocese, I entirely lose their service in both places. By this means you may have a chapter of ten or twelve members at any time in a day's warning, and there are generally six or seven resident in the city whose advice and assistance is of great moment both to the Dean and me in the affairs of the Church, and I hope you will find it so.

I find Dr. Parnell cannot be very useful where he is, though I gave him effectual help to obtain what he has,[3] and perhaps it may be in my way (as I have it in my

---

[1] Archbishop King was writing on Monday.

[2] Joseph Espin, who continued a prebendary of St. Patrick's Cathedral until his death, had other claims to the dignity than want of means, as he had been a scholar of Trinity College, Dublin—an academic distinction which Parnell had not obtained.

[3] *Supra*, p. 23, n. 2.

thought) to give him a removal, where he may be more
easy to himself and serviceable to the public. But this
must be a work of time. I add no more but my hearty
prayers for, etc.

W. D[UBLIN].

Since the writing of this I received yours of the 23rd
instant. I have nothing to add but my prayers for your
good journey into Ireland, as I take it if you be not installed before the next term, you must stay till Quarter
Sessions or next term to take the oaths as the law requires.
I should be sorry my cause were delayed till next session,
which must be another year. Our Irish brick will do very
well for the steeple, and five or six thousand will finish it.
Dr. Swift.

CLXXXVI. [*Sheridan.*]

RICHARD STEELE TO SWIFT

Bloomsbury, *May* 26, 1713.

SIR,
I HAVE received yours,[1] and find it impossible for a man
to judge in his own case. For an allusion to you, as one
under the imputation of helping the Examiner, and owning I was restrained out of respect to you, you tell Addison, under your hand, you think me the vilest of mankind,
and bid him tell me so. I am obliged to you for any kind
things said in my behalf to the Treasurer; and assure you,
when you were in Ireland, you were the constant subject
of my talk to men in power at that time. As to the vilest
of mankind, it would be a glorious world if I were: for I
would not conceal my thoughts in favour of an injured
man, though all the powers on earth gainsaid it, to be
made the first man in the nation. This position, I know,
will ever obstruct my way in the world; and I have conquered my desires accordingly. I have resolved to content
myself with what I can get by my own industry, and the
improvement of a small estate, without being anxious

[1] *Supra*, p. 33.

whether I am ever in a Court again or not.[1] I do assure
you, I do not speak this calmly, after the ill usage in your
letter to Addison, out of terror of your wit, or my Lord
Treasurer's power; but pure kindness to the agreeable
qualities I once so passionately delighted in, in you. You
know, I know nobody; but one that talked after you, could
tell, "Addison had bridled me in point of party." This was
ill hinted, both with relation to him, and, Sir,

Your most obedient humble servant,
RICHARD STEELE.

I know no party; but the truth of the question is what
I will support as well as I can, when any man I honour
is attacked.

CLXXXVII. [*Sheridan.*]

SWIFT TO RICHARD STEELE

May 27, 1713.

SIR,
THE reason I give you the trouble of this reply to your
letter, is because I am going in a very few days to Ireland;
and although I intended to return toward winter, yet it
may happen, from the common accidents of life, that I
may never see you again. In your yesterday's letter, you
are pleased to take the complaining side, and think it hard
I should write to Mr. Addison as I did, only for an allusion. This allusion was only calling a clergyman of some
little distinction an infidel: a clergyman who was your
friend, who always loved you, who had endeavoured at
least to serve you, and who, whenever he did write anything, made it sacred to himself never to fling out the least
hint against you.

One thing you are pleased to fix on me, as what you are
sure of; that the Examiner had talked after me, when he
said, "Mr. Addison had bridled you in point of party." I
do not read one in six of those papers, nor ever knew he

---

[1] As Sir Henry Craik says ("Life," i, 338) Steele's reply amounts to
a flimsy and conditional expression of gratitude to Swift and a boast
of his own independence and nobility of spirit.

had such a passage; and I am so ignorant of this, that I cannot tell what it means: whether, that Mr. Addison kept you close to a party, or that he hindered you from writing about party. I never talked or writ to that author in my life,[1] so that he could not have learned it from me; and in short, I solemnly affirm, that with relation to every friend I have, I am as innocent, as it is possible for a human creature to be; and whether you believe me or not, I think, with submission, you ought to act as if you believed me, till you have demonstration to the contrary.[2] I have all the Ministry to be my witnesses, that there is hardly a man of wit of the adverse party, whom I have not been so bold as to recommend often and with earnestness to them; for, I think, principles at present are quite out of the case, and that we dispute wholly about persons. In these last you and I differ; but in the other I think, we agree, for I have in print professed myself in politics, to be what we formerly called a Whig.

As to the great man whose defence you undertake,[3] though I do not think so well of him as you do, yet I have been the cause of preventing five hundred hard things being said against him. I am sensible I have talked too much when myself is the subject: therefore I conclude with sincere wishes for your health and prosperity, and am, Sir,

Yours, etc.

You cannot but remember, that in the only thing I ever published with my name, I took care to celebrate you as much as I could, and in as handsome a manner, though it was in a letter to the present Lord Treasurer.[4]

---

[1] *Supra*, p. 27, n. 2.

[2] "We cannot wonder that Steele found it difficult to believe that Swift had no connection with the Examiner," says Mr. Aitken (*op. cit.*, i, 385); "his name was constantly joined to the paper, and we have his own admission that he assisted the writer with hints."

[3] The Duke of Marlborough.

[4] In his "Proposal for Correcting, Improving, and Ascertaining the English Tongue," Swift speaks of the great success with which Steele had "tried the force and compass of our language" ("Prose Works," xi, 17).

CLXXXVIII. [*Scott.*]

SWIFT TO MISS ESTHER VANHOMRIGH

[*May* 31, 1713.]

I PROMISED to write to you, and I have let you know that it is impossible for anybody to have more acknowledgments at heart for all your kindness and generosity to me. I hope this journey will restore my health.[1] I will ride but little every day, and I will write a common letter to you all from some of my stages, but directed to you. I could not get here till ten this night.[2] Pray be merry, and eat, and walk, and be good, and send me your commands, whatever Mr. L[ewis][3] shall think proper to advise you. I have hardly time to put my pen to paper, but I would make good my promise. Pray God preserve you, and make you happy and easy; and so adieu brat. Service to mother and Molkin.

Mrs. B[arber]'s house, eleven at night, company waiting who come to take leave of me.[4]

CLXXXIX. [*Original.*[5]]

ERASMUS LEWIS TO SWIFT

Whitehall, *June* 2, 1713.

I HOPE this will meet you at Chester, and that your passage at sea will be favoured with as mild weather as your journey by land has been these two first days. The division yester-

---

[1] On the following day, Monday, 1 June, Swift set out for Ireland (Forster Collection, No. 509).

[2] It appears from Swift's account-book that he had spent the day at Kensington.

[3] As has been already mentioned Erasmus Lewis was an intimate of the Vanhomrigh family.

[4] Swift was probably spending the night before his journey in the City with his printer. Writing to Stella, when the deanery was in the balance, he says: " I dined in the City, and ordered a lodging to be ready for me against I come to pack up my things " (" Prose Works," ii, 457).

[5] In the British Museum. See Preface.

day, in the House of Lords, was fifty-four against fifty-four. Proxies were called for, and we had seventeen to thirteen.[1] This is the greatest victory we ever had. The Duke of Argyll[2] and the Scotch were against us to a man. The Lords Weymouth and Carteret[3] were with them. It was very comical to see the Tories, who voted with Lord Treasurer against the dissolution of the Union, under all the perplexities in the world, lest they should be victorious; and the Scotch, who voted for a bill of dissolution, under agonies lest they themselves should carry the point they pretended to desire. In all the time I have been conversant in business, I never before observed both sides, at the same time, acting parts which they thought contrary to their interests. Let us hear from you sometimes, and believe there is nobody with more sincerity yours, than.

CXC. [*Original.*[4]]

REV. JOHN SHARPE TO SWIFT

London, *June* 4, 1713.

REVEREND SIR,

I WAS commanded by his Excellency Brigadier Hunter, Governor of New York,[5] to deliver the enclosed with my own hand. Had I been so happy, for his service and my own satisfaction, as to have seen you at London, I am persuaded your influence here might have contributed to create a better opinion of him, amongst some leading men in the Society for Propagation of the Gospel in Foreign Parts, who have been much imposed on by the clamorous memorials of some indiscreet missionaries abroad. He has the just esteem of two-thirds of the clergy in his govern-

---

[1] The division was on a motion for leave to bring in a bill to dissolve the Union with Scotland. The origin of the motion was chiefly the extension of a tax on malt to that country, and a resolution rendering Scotch peers incapable of being made peers of Great Britain.

[2] Argyll (*supra*, p. 6, n. 1) supported the motion " with soldierlike energy" (Wyon, *op. cit.*, ii, 454).

[3] As already mentioned (*supra*, vol. i, p. 144, n. 3) Lady Carteret was a granddaughter of Lord Weymouth.

[4] In the British Museum. See Preface.   [5] *Supra*, p. 10.

ment, and the greatest part of the laity, who have either sense, probity, or honour; but his adversaries have made the Church's cause a favourable handle for their repeated complaints, which, with the application of their friends here, makes them very hopeful of success.

I have been twelve years abroad, in the service of the Church in America: the last ten were in the station of chaplain to her Majesty's forces at New York, where I had the opportunity of being very near to the several governors, and assure you, that if I had ever observed in him any inclination to weaken the interest of the Church there, I could not in conscience offer to excuse him; but he is better known to you, than that I, who am altogether unknown, should presume to give his character.

What I beg leave to entreat of you is, to recommend me in my endeavours for his service, to the advice and assistance of your friends. The perplexity of all his affairs at this time claims the good offices of all that wish him well. If, in favour to his Excellency, you are pleased to honour me with the pardon of this, and what return the enclosed may require, direct for me to the care of Mr. James Douglas, merchant, in Fen Court, Fenchurch Street, London. I beg leave to subscribe myself, with great respect, Reverend Sir,

Your most obedient and most humble servant,
JOHN SHARPE.

Enclosure—

ROBERT HUNTER TO SWIFT

New York, *March* 14, 1712-13.

Quonoroghquaniou diadadega generoghqua aguegon tchit-chenagaree; or, lest you should not have your Iroquoise dictionary at hand, "Brother, I honour you and all your tribe;" though that is to be taken *cum grano salis*; for one of them has done me much harm; God reward him, etc. For that, and what besides you want to know that relates to me, I refer you to the bearer, Mr. Sharpe, our chaplain; a very worthy, ingenious, and conscientious clergyman. I wrote to you some time ago by a merchant ship, and therein gave you some hints of my sufferings, which are not diminished since that time. In hopes of a better settlement, I wished for your company.

Until that comes, I can contribute to nothing but your spleen. Here is the finest air to live upon in the universe; and if our trees and birds could speak, and our assemblymen be silent, the finest conversation too. *Fert omnia tellus*, but not for me. For you must understand, according to the custom of our country, the Sachems[1] are of the poorest of the people. I have got the wrong side of Sir Polydore's office; a great deal to do, and nothing to receive.[2] In a word, and to be serious at last, I have spent three years of life in such torment and vexation, that nothing in life can ever make amends for it. *Tu interim sis laetus, et memor nostrum. Vale.*

R. H.

CXCI. [*Scott.*]

MISS ESTHER VANHOMRIGH TO SWIFT

London, *June* 6, 1713.

SIR,

NOW you are good beyond expression, in sending me that dear voluntary from St. Albans.[3] It gives me more happiness than you can imagine, or I describe, to find that your head is so much better already. I do assure you all my wishes are employed for the continuance of it. I hope the next will tell me they have been of force. Had I the power I want, every day that did not add as much to your health, till it was quite established, as Monday last, should be struck out of the calendar as useless ones. I believe you little thought to have been teased by me so soon; but when Mr. Lewis told me if I would write to you, that he would take care of my letter, I must needs own I had not self-denial enough to forbear. Pray why did not you remember me at Dunstable,[4] as well as Moll? Lord! what a

---

[1] *I.e.*, the chiefs.

[2] Presumably the reference is to the part played by Polydore in Otway's " Orphan."

[3] It appears from the following letter that John Barber accompanied Swift on his journey to Ireland as far as St. Albans, and that Swift gave him when returning a letter for Vanessa.

[4] Swift stayed evidently at Dunstable on the first night of his journey. Thence he sent another letter to Vanessa (*infra*, p. 44).

monster is Moll grown since. But nothing of poor Hess, except that the mark will be in the same place of Davila[1] where you left it. Indeed, it is not much advanced yet, for I have been studying of Rochefoucauld[2] to see if he described as much of love as I found in myself a Sunday, and I find he falls very short of it. How does Bolingbroke perform?[3] You have not kept your promise of riding but a little every day: thirty miles I take to be a very great journey.[4] I am very impatient to hear from you at Chester. It is impossible to tell you how often I have wished you a cup of coffee and an orange at your inn.

CXCII. [Scott.]

SWIFT TO MRS. VANHOMRIGH

Chester, *June* 6, 1713.

MADAM,

YOU heard of me from Dunstable, by the way of Hessy.[5] I have had a sad time since. If Moll's " even so " had been there, she would have none left.[6] Now Hessy grumbles that I talk of Moll. I have resolved upon the direction of my letter already, for I reckon Hessy and Moll are widows as well as you, or at least half widows. Davila[7] goes off rarely now. I have often wished for a little of your ratsbane;[8] what I met on the road does not deserve the name

---

[1] Of the " Historia delle Guerre Civile di Francia," by Henrico Caterino Davila, there were both French and English translations. Swift mentions Davila in the " Battle of the Books," and quotes from his work in the " Examiner " (" Prose Works," i, 173; ix, 209).

[2] "Reflexions ou Sentences et Maximes morales de M. le Duc de la Rochefoucauld."

[3] Swift had apparently been given a horse for the purpose of his journey, and had conferred on him the name of the great statesman.

[4] Dunstable is thirty-three miles from London. As Swift reached Chester, which is nearly a hundred and ninety miles from London, in six days, this must have been his average rate of progress.

[5] *Supra*, p. 43, n. 4.

[6] The entry in his account-book, under the same date as that of this letter, of "apothecary's bill 16/11" (Forster Collection, No. 509) indicates that Swift must have been then very far from well. Probably he and Vanessa's delicate sister had been wont to compare notes about their illnesses.

[7] *Supra*, n. 1.

[8] Ratsbane no doubt signified coffee.

of ratsbane. I have told Mr. Lewis the circumstances of my journey, and the curious may consult him upon it. Who will Hessy get now to chide, or Moll to tell her stories, and bring her sugar-plums? We never know anything enough till we want it. I design to send Hessy a letter in print from Ireland, because she cannot read writing-hand, except from Mr. Partinton.[1] I hope you have heard again from the Colonel,[2] and that he is fully cured of ———, I do not know what, I forget. It was under cover to Mr. Lewis that I wrote to you from Dunstable. I writ to Hessy, by Barber, from St. Albans. I left London without taking leave of Sir John. I fear a person of his civility will never pardon me.

I met no adventures in all my travels, only my horse fell under me, for which reason I will not ride him to Holyhead, I can assure him that.[3] I could not see any marks in the chimney at Dunstable, of the coffee Hessy spilt there, and I had no diamond-ring about me, to write any of your names in the windows. But I saw written, " Dearest Lady Betty Hamilton," and hard by, " Middleton Walker," whom I take to be an Irish man-midwife, which was a plain omen of her getting a husband.[4] I hear Moore, the handsome parson, came over with the Archbishop of Dublin. Did he not marry one Mrs. Devenish?[5] Lord Lanesborough has been here lately in his way to Ireland, and has got the good-will of all the folks in our town.[6] He had something

---

[1] *Supra*, vol. i, p. 390, n. 2.

[2] Mrs. Vanhomrigh's son, who was still in Paris (*supra*, p. 18).

[3] The letters for Ireland were always sent by Holyhead, but in order to escape the journey through Wales (*supra*, vol. i, p. 61, n. 3) passengers usually crossed from Parkgate near Chester. "Bolingbroke" (*supra*, p. 44, n. 3) was sent to Ireland from the latter port. The expense of sending the horse from Chester to Dublin is included in Swift's accounts, as well as the cost of a saddle and the hire of a horse for his servant from London to Chester (Forster Collection, No. 509).

[4] Lady Elizabeth Hamilton, the eldest daughter of James, sixth Earl of Abercorn, had married in the previous year William Brownlow, an ancestor of the Lords Lurgan.

[5] The Honourable and Reverend John Moore, the fourth son of the third Earl of Drogheda, had been first chaplain to the Earl of Pembroke when Lord Lieutenant, and had been appointed by that viceroy incumbent of St. Catherine's in Dublin. He married a daughter of Sir Charles Porter, who had been Lord Chancellor of Ireland in the reign of William III. She had been previously married to Edward Devenish.

[6] The Lord Lanesborough referred to was the second Viscount of the first creation. As Sir George Lane, his father is frequently mentioned

to say to every little boy he met in the streets. Well, he is the courteousest man, and nothing is so fine in the quality as to be courteous. Now Moll laughs because I speak wisely, and now Hessy murmurs again. Well, I had a charming handsome cousin here twenty years ago.[1] I was to see her to-night, and, in my conscience, she is not handsome at all; I wonder how it comes about; but she is very good-natured, and you know, Moll, good-nature is better than beauty.

I desire you will let me know what fellows Hessy has got to come to her bed-side in a morning, and when you design again to hobble to Chelsea, if you did not tell me a lie, as I must suspect. My head is something better, though not so well as I expected by my journey. I think I have said enough for a poor weary traveller. I will conclude without ceremony, and go to bed. And, if you cannot guess who is the writer, consult your pillow, and the first fine gentleman you dream of is the man. So adieu.

Addressed—To Madam Van at the Sign of the Three Widows in Pom-roy Alley. With care and speed. Present.

CXCIII. [*Scott.*]

Miss Esther Vanhomrigh to Swift

London, *June* 23, 1713.

HERE is now three long weeks passed since you wrote to me.[2] Oh! happy Dublin, that can employ all your thoughts, and happy Mrs. Emerson, that could hear from you the moment you landed.[3] Had it not been for her, I should be yet more uneasy than I am. I really believe, before you leave Ireland, I shall give you just reason to

in connection with the great Duke of Ormond, to whom he was secretary and a much attached friend. The site of the second Viscount's house in London is now occupied by St. George's Hospital.

[1] Writing to Stella from Chester three years before, when on his journey to London, Swift had said: "my cousin Abigail is grown prodigiously old" ("Prose Works," ii, 4).

[2] From Dunstable (*supra*, p. 44).

[3] Swift had arrived in Dublin on Wednesday, 10 June.

wish I did not know my letters, or at least that I could not write; and I had rather you should wish so than entirely forget me. Confess; have you once thought of me since you wrote to my mother at Chester,[1] which letter, I assure you, I take very ill? My mother and I have counted the Molls and the Hessys; it is true, the number is equal, but you talk to Moll, and only say, "now Hessy grumbles." How can you, indeed, possibly be so ill-natured, to make me either quarrel or grumble when you are at so great a distance that it is impossible for me to gain by doing so? Besides, you proposed the letter should be directed to me; but I will say no more of that, but keep my temper till we meet. Pray, have you received the letter I wrote you to Chester?[2] I hear you had a very quick passage.[3] I hope it was a pleasant one, and that you have no reason to complain of your health. We have had a vast deal of thunder for this week past.

I wish you had been here last Thursday, I am sure you could have prevented the Bills[4] being lost. Are not you prodigiously surprised at Sir Thomas Hanmer and Lord Anglesey?[5] Lord! how much we differ from the ancients, who used to sacrifice everything for the good of the commonwealth; but now our greatest men will, at any time, give up their country out of pique, and that for nothing. It is impossible to describe the rejoicings that are amongst the Whigs since that day, and I fear the elections will add to them.[6] Lord Treasurer has been extremely to blame, for all his friends advised him to let it be dropped, by consent,

---

[1] *Supra*, p. 44.   [2] *Supra*, p. 43.
[3] Swift reached Holyhead on the 10th, and landed at nine o'clock that evening at Dublin (Forster Collection, No. 509).
[4] To make effectual the eighth and ninth articles of the Treaty of Peace, by which it was proposed to establish what amounted to free trade with France.
[5] Hanmer (*supra*, p. 30, n. 2) is said by an eloquent speech to have been instrumental in securing the Tory desertion which led to the rejection of the Bills by a majority of nine. He was not only a Tory but a personal friend of the Ministers, and one of those employed in the negotiations for the treaty; and had voted for the introduction of the Bills, but at the last moment he changed his mind and declared himself against them. Lord Anglesey, who, as has been mentioned, held government office (*supra*, vol. i, p. 271, n. 2), and was a member of the British as well as of the Irish House of Lords, was prominent amongst the Whimsical or Hanover Tories.
[6] Parliament was dissolved that autumn.

till next session; but [he] would not, depending on the same success he had on the malt-tax. I know you will say: "What, does the slut mean to talk all this stuff to me? If I was there, I had as lief hear it as anything they could say; but to pursue me with her nonsense is intolerable. I will read no more. Will,[1] go to the post-office and see if there be more letters for me. What, will this packet only serve to tease me?" I can tell you, you will have none from Lady Orkney by the post, whatever you may by any other carriage.[2]

I have strictly observed your commands as to reading and walking. Mr. Ford[3] can witness the latter, for he has paddled with us several nights. I have a vast deal to tell you about him when I see you. Mr. Lewis has given me "Les Dialogues des Morts,"[4] and I am so charmed with them, that I am resolved to quit my [body,] let the consequence be what it will, except you will talk to me, for I find no conversation on earth comparable but yours; so, if you care I should stay, do but talk, and you will keep me with pleasure.

CXCIV. [*Scott.*]

Miss Esther Vanhomrigh to Swift

London, *June* [27] 1713.

It is inexpressible the concern I am in ever since I heard from Mr. Lewis, that your head is so much out of order. Who is your physician? For God sake do not be persuaded to take many slops. Satisfy me so much as to tell me what medicines you have taken, and do take. How did you find yourself while a ship-board? I fear it is your

¹ Swift's servant at that time. On 8 April, 1712, his servant Patrick (*supra*, vol. i, p. 198, n. 1) left him, and three days later William came (Forster Collection, No. 508).

² Lady Orkney and Swift had evidently continued to see much of one another until Swift left London; but as Scott observes ("Works," xix, 333) that astute lady probably considered the post office of that time a too "suspicious channel of communication" by which to carry on correspondence. In Appendix II there will be found a curious character of Oxford written by her with remarks upon it by Swift.

³ *Supra*, vol. i, p. 339, n. 2.

⁴ A translation into English of "Les Dialogues des Mortes," by Bernard le Bonyn de Fontenelle, had been published in 1708, but Vanessa probably read the work in the original.

TRIM

From a photograph by Mr. Thomas J. Westropp, M.A. Dubl.

voyage has discomposed you, and then so much business following so immediately before you had time to recruit— it was too much. I beg you make all the haste imaginable to the country, for I firmly believe that air and rest will do you more good than anything in the world besides. If I talk impertinently, I know you have goodness enough to forgive me, when you consider how great an ease it is to me to ask these questions, though I know it will be a great while before I can be answered—I am sure I shall think it so. Oh! what would I give to know how you do at this instant. My fortune is too hard, your absence was enough without this cruel addition. Sure the powers above are envious of your thinking so well, which makes them at some times strive to interrupt you; but I must confine my thoughts, or at least stop from telling them to you, or you will chide, which will still add to my uneasiness. I have done all that was possible to hinder myself from writing to you, till I heard you were better, for fear of breaking my promise, but it is all in vain, for had I vowed neither to touch pen, ink, nor paper, I certainly should have had some other invention; therefore I beg you will not be angry with me, for doing what is not in my power to avoid. Pray make Parvisol [1] write me word what I desire to know, for I would not for the world have you hold down your head. I am impatient to the last degree to hear how you are. I hope I shall soon have you here.

CXCV. [*Original.*[2]]

SWIFT TO JOSHUA DAWSON

Trim, *June* 29, 1713.[3]

SIR,[4]

DR. RAYMOND just now tells me he has received an account that Mr. Browne, your clerk, said the Doctor's

---

[1] *Supra*, vol. i, p. 118, n. 3.
[2] In the Public Record Office, Ireland; Church Miscellaneous Papers, No. 59.
[3] As Swift records in his account-book, he was installed as Dean of St. Patrick's on Saturday the 13th, and left Dublin for Laracor a fortnight after his arrival on Thursday the 25th (Forster Collection, No. 509).
[4] Dawson has been already noticed (*supra*, vol. i, p. 178, n. 4).

warrant[1] was not signed yet, and that the Lords Justices[2] designed to consider of it. This gives the Doctor some uneasiness and you the trouble of this letter. I can assure you that the day before I left London I laid the whole matter before my Lord Duke of Ormond in so plain a manner that he immediately complied with it, and I gave his Grace the Bishop of Meath's memorial, which showed how hard it would be not only upon the Doctor, but upon the church of Trim, if that small rectory, only of forty pounds a year, were disposed of any other way.[3] If any difficulty should yet remain, I must make it my request to you to present my duty to my Lord Chancellor, and let him know what I now tell you, and assure him that if it were not for the good of the Church, and that I knew every circumstance of the Bishop's memorial to be true, I would never have moved one step in it, though Dr. Raymond is a gentleman wholly unexceptionable, and very much in my esteem.

My health has been so ill that I was forced to steal away without waiting on my Lord Chancellor or anybody else, and here I am riding for life, but hope to be in town in a week or two. I am, Sir,

Your most obedient humble servant,

J. SWIFT.

You will consider what it is to keep an honest gentleman in suspense and put him out of pain as soon as you can.

[1] Presenting Raymond to the living of Moymet (*supra*, p. 25).

[2] The Lords Justices at that time were Sir Constantine Phipps, the Lord Chancellor, and Dr. John Vesey, the Archbishop of Tuam.

[3] On 13 May Swift wrote to Stella that he had failed to obtain the living of Moymet for Raymond, but some weeks later told her that as a result of further efforts he hoped Raymond might yet be given it (" Prose Works," ii, 462, 464). A letter from Secretary Southwell to the Lords Justices, written on 16 May, gives a curious account of the contradictory statements made on behalf of various applicants for this desirable piece of viceregal patronage: " His Grace in his last letter wrote to your Lordships to give the living of Moymet, near Trim, to Dr. Dunbar, the blind clergyman, his Grace supposing at that time he had no bread or subsistence. By the last packets Dr. Raymond sends over a certificate that Dunbar has a living. Some inform his Grace that Moymet is a sinecure, others say not. Some tell his Grace that Dr. Raymond has above £200 a year without this, and others say he cannot live if he has it not. His Grace therefore orders me to desire of your Lordships to a strict enquiry into this matter and your answer thereupon, and in the mean time to stop the disposal thereof" (Departmental Correspondence in P.R.O. of Ireland).

CXCVI. [*Scott.*]

Miss Esther Vanhomrigh to Swift

London, *June* [30] 1713.

Mr. Lewis assures me that you are now well, but will not tell me what authority he has for it. I hope he is rightly informed. Though it is not my usual custom, when a thing of consequence is in doubt, to fix on what I earnestly wish, but I have already suffered so much by knowing that you were ill, and fearing that you were worse than you have been, that I will strive to change that thought, if possible, that I may have a little ease, and more, that I may not write you a splenetic letter. Pray, why would not you make Parvisol write me word how you did, when I begged it so much? And if you were able yourself, how could you be so cruel to defer telling me the thing of the which I wished the most to know? If you think I write too often, your only way is to tell me so, or at least to write to me again, that I may know you do not quite forget me; for I very much fear that I never employ a thought of yours now, except when you are reading my letters, which makes me ply you with them—Mr. Lewis complains of you too. If you are very happy, it is ill-natured of you not to tell me so, except it is what is inconsistent with mine. But why do not you talk to me that you know will please me. I have often heard you say, that you would willingly suffer a little uneasiness, provided it gave another a vast deal of pleasure. Pray remember this maxim, because it makes for me. This is now the fourth letter I have wrote to you: they could not miscarry, for they were all under Mr. Lewis's cover, nor could you avoid opening them, for the same reason. Pray what have you done about the two livings?[1] Have you re-

---

[1] The livings were those of St. Nicholas Without and St. Luke's in Dublin, which were in the gift of the Dean and Chapter of St. Patrick's Cathedral, and during Stearne's tenure of the deanery were held by him. The parishioners of St. Nicholas Without were provided with church accommodation in the north transept of the Cathedral, but the parishioners of St. Luke's were without a church, and, as already stated (*supra*, vol. i, p. 72, n. 1), Stearne retained the livings himself in order to devote the revenues from them to supplying the want. On the announcement of his appointment to the bishopric of Dromore Stearne

covered them or no? You know I love law-business. I have been with lawyers since I saw you, but have not yet had their answers, therefore will not trouble you with what I have done, till I can tell you all. Pray let me know when you design coming over; for I must beg you to talk to Mr. P[artinton] and settle some affairs for me. Pray let me hear from you soon, which will be an inexpressible joy to her that is always————

CXCVII. [*Scott.*]

SWIFT TO MISS ESTHER VANHOMRIGH

Laracor, *July* 8, 1713.

I STAYED but a fortnight in Dublin, very sick, and returned not one visit of a hundred that were made me;[1] but all to the Dean and none to the Doctor. I am riding here for life, and think I am something better, and hate the

and the Chapter had, however, nominated incumbents to both parishes, fearing the Crown might claim the presentation to them as well as to the deanery. Before that time Swift had requested Stearne to leave "those livings to his disposal," and wrote to Stella that her new Bishop had acted very ungratefully in not doing so ("Prose Works," ii, 462). Swift's intention was to bestow one of the parishes on Parnell; but as appears from Archbishop King's Correspondence (June 24, 27, and July 11) the Crown actually issued patents to nominees of its own for the parishes, and only for the haste with which Stearne and the Chapter had acted would certainly have secured the presentation.

[1] In the opinion of Sir Henry Craik ("Life," i, 344), Swift's reception in Dublin had been of an unpleasant kind. "He had been hooted in the streets," says Sir Henry, "and libels had been fixed on the door of his own Cathedral." But under the circumstances mentioned in this letter, his short stay in Dublin (which Swift left on 25 June for Laracor) and his ill state of health, there can have been little opportunity for hostile greetings in public. In taking the view which he has done, Sir Henry has relied upon Lord Orrery ("Remarks," p. 49), who does not write with attention to chronological sequence, and when what Lord Orrery says is taken in conjunction with the comments of Delany ("Observations," p. 60) and Deane Swift ("Essay," p. 191), it seems probable that the mob vented their spite upon Swift after the downfall of the Tory party. There is certainly more ground for thinking that the famous verses by Dean Smedley were posted on the Cathedral door at the time of Swift's installation, but it is to be recollected that the only authority is an unfriendly one (see Mason's "Hist. of St. Patrick's," p. 269).

thoughts of Dublin, and prefer a field-bed and an earthen floor [1] before the great house there which they say is mine.[2] I had your last splenetic letter.[3] I told you when I left England, I would endeavour to forget everything there, and would write as seldom as I could. I did, indeed, design one general round of letters to my friends, but my health has not yet suffered me. I design to pass the greatest part of the time I stay in Ireland here in the cabin where I am now writing; neither will I leave the kingdom till I am sent for; and if they have no further service for me, I will never see England again. At my first coming I thought I should have died with discontent, and was horribly melancholy while they were installing me; but it begins to wear off, and change to dulness. My river walk is extremely pretty, and my canal in great beauty, and I see trout playing in it.

I know not anything in Dublin, but Mr. Ford [4] is very kind, and writes to me constantly what passes among you. I find you are likewise a good politician, and I will say so much to you that I verily think, if the thing you know of had been published just upon the peace, the Ministry might have avoided what hath since happened.[5] But I am now

---

[1] As Swift told Varina (*supra*, vol. i, p. 33), there was no house on the glebe at Laracor when he was given the benefice. The dwelling, which he erected on his " half acre of Irish bog," was evidently a very humble dwelling, and is described in a contemporary record as " a neat cabin." The knowledge of horticulture acquired at Moor Park had, however, been used by Swift to good purpose, and the fact that his demesne was " exceedingly well enclosed" and contained "a good garden," was doubtless taken into account in assessing upon it a valuation of £60 (Forster's " Life," p. 121).

[2] Of the deanery house built by Stearne (*supra*, vol. i, p. 82, n. 3) there is little known, except that one of its features was a large room on the upper storey, with " a fireplace at each end," which he designed for his books. On a visitor to Ireland twenty years after Swift's death the house, as seen from the Archbishop of Dublin's then adjacent palace, made a most depressing impression, and after reference to " the many remains of Swift's wit " to be seen in the house, he adds, " I don't wonder he disliked the situation, for from what appeared from the Archbishop's window, it was enough to turn a stronger wit than his to dulness or madness " (Hist. MSS. Com., Rept. 8, pt. ii, p. 114).

[3] See preceding letter (*supra*, p. 51, line 9).

[4] *Supra*, p. 48.

[5] This reference is to the " Four Last Years of the Queen," and is further confirmation of the partiality which Swift entertained for that work (*supra*, p. 16, n. 2).

fitter to look after willows, and to cut hedges, than to meddle with affairs of state. I must order one of the work-men to drive those cows out of my island, and make up the ditch again; a work much more proper for a country vicar, than driving out factions, and fencing against them. And I must go and take my bitter draught to cure my head, which is spoilt by the bitter draughts the public hath given me.

How does Davila[1] go on? Johnny Clark is chosen port-reeve of our town of Trim,[2] and we shall have the assizes there next week,[3] and fine doings, and I must go and borrow a horse to meet the judges, and Joe Beaumont,[4] and all the boys that can get horses will go too. Mr. War-burton has but a thin school.[5] Mr. Percival[6] has built up the other side of his house, but people whisper that it is but scurvily built. Mr. Steers is come to live in Mr. Mel-thorp's house, and it is thought the widow Melthorp will remove to Dublin. Nay, if you do not like this sort of news, I have no better, so go to your Dukes and Duchesses, and leave me to Goodman Bomford,[7] and Patrick Dollan of Clondoogan. Adieu.

[1] *Supra*, p. 44, n. 1.

[2] Clark appears to have been a gentleman of independent means, a class of resident then found in Irish towns like Trim, but, owing to facility of communication, now unknown. His will was proved in the Consistorial Court in 1732.

[3] Trim is the assize town of Meath. It was then on the north-west, and is now on the north-east circuit.

[4] Beaumont, who owned a business establishment in Trim and seems to have dealt in commodities of every kind, is described by Deane Swift ("Letters," i, 1) as "a venerable, handsome, grey-headed man, of quick and various natural abilities." According to the same amusing authority, an unfortunate propensity on Beaumont's part for abstruse mathematics led to mental derangement and the termina-tion of his life by his own hand.

[5] The Rev. Thomas Warburton, who acted then as Swift's curate, kept, probably, a school in Trim.

[6] *Supra*, vol. i, p. 57, n. 3.

[7] Probably Lawrence Bomford, of Clonmahon, in the parish of Laracor, a member of a well-known Meath family, who is said to have died in 1720 at the age of a hundred and three.

CXCVIII. [*Original.*[1]]

ERASMUS LEWIS TO SWIFT

Whitehall, *July* 9, 1713.

WE are all running headlong into the greatest confusion imaginable. Sir Thomas Hanmer is gone into the country this morning, I believe much discontented; and I am very apprehensive, neither Lord Anglesey nor he will continue long with us.[2] I heartily wish you were here; for you might certainly be of great use to us, by your endeavours to reconcile, and by representing to them the infallible consequences of these divisions. We had letters this morning from Ireland. What is the reason I had none from you? Adieu. I hope your want of health is not the cause.

Addressed—To the Reverend Dr. Swift, Dean of St. Patrick's, at Dublin, Ireland.

CXCIX. [*Sheridan.*]

SWIFT TO ARCHBISHOP KING

Trim, *July* 16, 1713.

MY LORD,

I HAVE been about five weeks in this kingdom, but so extremely ill with the return of an old disorder in my head, that I was not able to write to your Grace. I have been the greatest part of that time at my country parish, riding every day for my health. I can tell your Grace nothing from Dublin, having spent the days I was there between business and physic, and paid no visits, nor received any but one day; and I reckon it no great loss, for I hear they are all party mad, and it is one felicity of being among willows, that one is not troubled with faction. I hope you have as little of it at the Bath;[3] for I cannot fancy it does

---

[1] In the British Museum. See Preface.
[2] *Supra,* p. 47, n. 5.   [3] *Supra,* p. 35.

well with the waters. If your Grace goes to London from
the Bath, I believe I may have the honour of waiting on
you; although I shall do all in my power to save the
trouble of such a journey, which neither my fortune nor
my health will very well bear. I hope you feel the good
effects of the place you are in, and I pray God continue
your life, for the good of his Church.

The other day, Mr. Theaker, Prebendary of Saggart and
Vicar of Rathcoole, died;[1] and it would be a great mark of
goodness in your Grace, as well as a personal favour to me,
if you would please to dispose of his livings in favour of
Mr. Thomas Warburton, who has been many years my assistant in the cure of Laracor, has behaved himself altogether unblameably, and is a gentleman of very good
learning and sense. If I knew anyone more deserving, I
would not recommend him; neither would I do it, however,
because I know your Grace has a great many dependants,
but that it will be a great use to me to have a vicar in one
of my rectories, and upon my deanery,[2] in whom I can confide. I am told the livings amount to a hundred and twenty
pounds a year at most; and it may probably happen in my
way to be able to oblige some friend of yours in a greater
matter, which I shall very readily do.[3] I am, with the greatest respect, my Lord,

Your Grace's most obedient, and most humble servant,

JON. SWIFT.

[1] The parishes of Saggart and Rathcoole, which are united, lie in
the southern part of the county of Dublin adjacent to the counties of
Wicklow and Kildare, and are connected traditionally with Swift and
Vanessa, whose bower near the village of Saggart is still pointed out.
As the site of a Celtic monastery, Saggart has ecclesiastically the pre-
eminence, but in Swift's time the parishes were served as they are
to-day by the church of Rathcoole, which stands in a village of that
name on the coach road from Dublin to Cork. The parishes had been
held for more than ten years by the Rev. Thomas Theaker, a graduate
and scholar of Dublin University.
[2] The possessions of the Dean of St. Patrick's included the tithes of
Rathcoole and land within that parish as well as in the immediate
vicinity.
[3] Swift was not successful in his application for his curate, whom he
designates in his list of friends as an ungrateful person.

CC. [*Original.*[1]]

ERASMUS LEWIS TO SWIFT

Whitehall, *July* 30, 1713.

THIS day sennight the Queen goes to Hampton Court, and the Monday following to Windsor. I fancy by that time Mr. Bromley will be Secretary of State, in the room of my Lord.[2] Lord Treasurer was abroad this evening, for the first time after a fortnight's illness. I hear there came a dozen of letters from you by the same post to your friends here. My Lord Treasurer desires you will make all possible haste over, for we want you extremely.

CCI. [*Scott.*]

SWIFT TO BISHOP ATTERBURY

The Country in Ireland, *August* 3, 1713.[3]

MY LORD,

IT is with the greatest pleasure I heard of your Lordship's promotion, I mean that particular promotion, which I believe is agreeable to you, though it does not mend your fortune.[4] There is but one other change I could wish you,

---

[1] In the British Museum. See Preface.

[2] Lewis's chief, the Earl of Dartmouth (*supra*, vol. i, p. 248, n. 4), was at that time promoted to the office of Lord Privy Seal, and William Bromley, who had been Speaker of the House of Commons, was appointed in his room.

[3] In an article entitled " Inedited Letters of Dean Swift," and signed B. in the " New Monthly Magazine " for 1842 (vol. lxiv, pp. 116-120), a theory is put forward that Swift was in England at that time. It is founded on three letters in the possession of the Duke of Buccleuch which are signed Jonathan Swift, and were written from Northamptonshire in the months of July, August, and September of that year. There can be no doubt, however, that the letters were not written by Swift, whose name was adopted by another person as a fictitious signature, and that Swift did not return to England until the end of August (see Introduction, vol. i, p. xxii, and Appendix III in this volume).

[4] The bishopric of Rochester, to which Atterbury had succeeded, was united then with the deanery of Westminster, and Swift selects his

because I have heard you prefer it before all the rest; and
that likewise is now ready, unless it be thought too soon,
and that you are made to wait till another person has used
it for a step to cross the water.[1] Though I am here in a
way of sinking into utter oblivion, for *hæ latebræ nec
dulces, nec, si mihi credis, amœnæ*, yet I shall challenge the
continuance of your Lordship's favour, and whenever I
come to London, shall with great assurance cross the Park
to your Lordship's house at Westminster, as if it were no
more than crossing the street at Chelsea.[2] I talked at this
threatening rate so often to you about two years past, that
you are not now to forget it.

Pray, my Lord, do not let your being made a Bishop
hinder you from cultivating the politer studies, which your
heart was set upon when you went to govern Christ Church.
Providence has made you successor to a person, who,
though of a much inferior genius,[3] turned all his thoughts
that way; and, I have been told, with great success, by his
countenance to those who deserved. I envy Dr. Freind
that he has you for his inspector;[4] and I envy you for
having such a person in your district, and whom you love
so well. Shall not I have liberty to be sometimes a third
among you, though I am an Irish Dean? *Vervecum in
patriâ, crassoque sub aëre natus.*

A very disordered head hindered me from writing early
to your Lordship, when I first heard of your preferment;
and I have reproached myself of ingratitude, when I remembered your kindness in sending me a letter[5] upon the
deanery they thought fit to throw me into; to which I am
yet a stranger, being forced into the country, in one of my
old parishes, to ride about for a little health. I hope to
have the honour of asking your Lordship's blessing some
time in October. In the mean while, I desire your Lord-

friend's elevation to the latter peculiar dignity as the special subject
for congratulation.

[1] The bishopric of London, which has so often proved a stage on
the way to the Archbishop of Canterbury's palace at Lambeth, was
then vacant.

[2] *Supra*, vol. i, p. 287, n. 1.

[3] Swift resents, however, Burnet's severe criticisms on the style of
Atterbury's predecessor, Thomas Sprat ("Prose Works," x, 348).

[4] Dr. Robert Freind (*supra*, vol. i, p. 257, n. 1) was then the head
master of Westminster School.

[5] *Supra*, p. 21.

ship to believe me to be, with very great respect and truth, my Lord,

Your Lordship's most dutiful and most humble servant,

JON. SWIFT.

CCII. [*Original.*[1]]

MATTHEW PRIOR TO SWIFT

Paris, *August* 16 [O.S. 5], 1713.

As I did not expect, my good friend Jonathan, to have received a letter from you at Dublin, so I am sure I did not intend to write one thither to you; but Mr. Roseingrave thinks it may do him a service, in recommending him to you.[2] If so, I am very glad of it; for it can be of no other use imaginable. I have writ letters now above twenty-two years. I have taken towns, destroyed fleets, made treaties, and settled commerce in letters. And what of all this? Why, nothing; but that I have had some subject to write upon. But to write a letter only because Mr. Roseingrave has a mind to carry one in his pocket, to tell you that you are sure of a friendship, which can never do you threepence of good, and wish you well in England very soon, when I do not know when I am likely to be there myself: all this, I say, is very absurd for a letter, especially when I have this day written a dozen much more to the

---

¹ In the British Museum. See Preface.

² Several members of the Roseingrave family, to one of whom Prior refers, are still remembered as talented musicians and composers. They were at that time much identified with Dublin, where, at the close of the seventeenth century, Daniel Roseingrave had settled as organist to the two cathedrals which Dublin possesses. He had previously filled a similar position successively at Winchester and Salisbury, and it is not without interest to observe that he found in Dublin a more congenial atmosphere for his profession. It was probably his eldest son, Thomas Roseingrave, that Prior had met in Paris on his return from Italy, where three years before his father had sent him to study ("D. N. B.," xlix, 246). He seems to have been a learned as well as skilled musician, but his career was clouded by eccentricities which at times amounted to madness. In Delany's "Observations," p. 149, there is an amusing account of Swift disconcerting his friend, Provost Pratt, who was "far gone in the Italian taste," by a ridiculous imitation of Thomas Roseingrave's playing.

purpose. If I had seen your manuscript,[1] if I had received Dr. Parnell's poem,[2] if I had any news of Landau being taken,[3] why well and good; but as I know no more than that the Duke of Shrewsbury designs for England within three weeks, that I must stay here till somebody else comes,[4] and then—brings me necessarily to say, good Mr. Dean, that I am like the fellow in the Rehearsal, who did not know if he was to be merry or serious, or in what way or mood to act his part.[5] One thing only I am assured of, that I love you very well; and am, most sincerely and faithfully, dear Sir,

Your servant and brother,
M. PRIOR.

Lord and Lady Shrewsbury give their service to you. Vanhomrigh has run terribly here in debt,[6] and, being in durance, has sent to his mother upon pecuniary concerns. Adieu once more. What we are doing, or what is to become of us, I know not:

> *Prudens futuri temporis exitum*
> *Caliginosâ nocte premit Deus,*
> *Ridetque——*

This is all the Latin and writing I can at present spare you. Pray give my service to your Chancellor, and be much acquainted with Judge Nutley, and love him very well for my sake.[7] Adieu. Once more, find out my cousin

---

[1] The " Four Last Years of the Queen."   [2] *Supra*, p. 23.

[3] That town was then besieged by the French.

[4] Prior remained in sole charge of English interests at Paris until the accession of George I.

[5] "I can't guess for my life what humour I'm to be in: whether angry, melancholy, merry, or in love. I don't know what to make on't." The "Rehearsal" by George Villiers, Duke of Buckingham, Act I.

[6] *Supra*, p. 45.

[7] Lord Chancellor Phipps, whose display of party spirit brought great disrepute on the Tory administration in Ireland, found a willing assistant in Richard Nutley, who, soon after Phipps's arrival, was appointed a Justice of the Queen's Bench. In Whig opinion they were fellow conspirators in the cause of the Pretender. Nutley, who was the son of a citizen of London and a graduate of Oxford, had transferred his practice from the English to the Irish Bar about the close of the seventeenth century, and when Phipps came to Ireland occupied a seat in the Irish Parliament as member for Lisburn. His elevation to the Bench was obtained by the removal of a political opponent, and on the accession of George I, a similar fate attended him. He returned to the Bar and continued to practise until 1729,

Pennefather[1] and Nutley, if he is not too grave for you; and according to the laudable custom of your country, drink this Louis out, for a token of my generosity and your sobriety. And now, I think, I have furnished out a very pretty letter.

CCIII. [*Copy.*[2]]

ARCHBISHOP KING TO SWIFT

Bath, *August* 5, 1713.

REVEREND SIR,

I HAVE had the favour of yours of the 16th of July and am sorry to find by it that you are not in a good state of health, especially that you complain of any disorder in the head, for though such are not very mortal, yet they make one uneasy in company or in business, and effect not only the body, but the mind. An odd thought came into my mind on reading that you were among willows, imagining that perhaps your mistress had forsaken you, and that was the cause of your malady. If that be the case, cheer up, the loss may be repaired, and I hope the remedy easy.

I retired here for my health, and hoped to find a recess

when his death took place from an attack, apparently, of appendicitis. The inscription on a tablet to Nutley's memory in St. Mary's Church, Dublin, ascribes to him every attainment as well as virtue, but in "The Swan Tripe Club," a poem that has been attributed to Swift, doubt is thrown on his legal ability:

> "Nutbrain, a daggle gown of large renown,
> For small support to needy client known."

In an elegy on his death he is said to have been of Milesian descent, and is held up as an example to other English settlers as a land purchaser and owner:

> "He fairly purchas'd those large tracts he bought,
> And no man's property unjustly sought;
> What numbers of poor labourers he fed,
> And greatest artizans by him got bread."

[1] Probably Colonel Matthew Pennefather, a favourite of the Duchess of Marlborough, who had been appointed in 1709 Commissary-General of Ireland. He belonged to an Irish family, some of the more recent members of which occupy a distinguished place in the legal annals of their country, and may have been related to Prior through his mother, who was a Kingsmill.

[2] In King's Correspondence. See Preface.

from faction and business, but now I find that is a happiness reserved for heaven. I have received just a hundred and three letters, most long ones, and most of them concerning business, since I came here, and wrote near as many. Judge if this be agreeable to waters drinking. As to faction, though you had much of it in London, and it had its centre there, yet the outskirts reached here, and I believe everywhere else, but I kept myself pretty well out of its reach by conversing with few but the company I brought with me.

I leave this, God willing, to-morrow and go to Chester, and so to Ireland, leaving the parties to struggle for elections as they please. If I cannot avoid hearing of them in Dublin it is not my fault being hurried to that place by duty. As to Mr. Theaker's benefices, I have twelve or fourteen letters about them, but shall not dispose of them till I get to Ireland, and will discourse you before I do anything in that, and several other matters.

I intend to go through Northamptonshire to recruit my set with fresh horses, if I can find them.[1] I hope to be at Holyhead about the 23rd instant. I pray God send us a good meeting in Dublin, where we will study to be as easy as we can in spite of faction and business. I recommend you, etc.   W. D[UBLIN].

    Dr. Swift.

CCIV. [Original.[2]]

ERASMUS LEWIS TO SWIFT

Whitehall, *August* 6, 1713.

I HAVE so often, and in so pressing a manner, desired you to come over, that, if what I have already said has no

---

[1] When going to Bath, Archbishop King used to travel in his own coach. It was drawn by eight horses, which he took also with him. On one occasion his horses, owing to their being "faded and spoiled" by a stormy passage of four days, and tried by "burning and intolerable heat," broke down—one dropped dead on the road, another had to be left behind, and five had to be led—and horses had to be hired to complete the journey. To supply those which he had lost, the Archbishop bought two horses on that occasion at Bath (King's Correspondence, 30 May, 18 June, 13 July, 1726).

[2] In the British Museum. See Preface.

effect, I shall despair of better success by any farther arguments. If I were to recapitulate the several reasons you
offer to the contrary, and answer them separately, I should
grow peevish; which I have no way to avoid, but by telling you in general, it is all wrong. You and I have already
laid it down for a maxim, that we must serve Lord Treasurer,
without receiving orders or particular instructions; and I
do not yet see a reason for changing that rule. His mind
has been communicated more freely to you than any
other;[1] but you will not understand it. The desires of
great men are commands, at least the only ones, I hope,
they ever will be able to use. You have a mind to stay in
Ireland till October, and desire me to give my opinion
whether you should come sooner? I answer, yes. Then
you bid me consider again; that is, you would have me
say I am of opinion you should stay till October. When
judges would have a jury change their verdict, they bid
them consider again: when a man is determined to marry
a woman, and his friend advises him against it, he asks his
opinion again, and if his friend is so silly as not to alter
his advice, he marries without it. I am as much in the
spleen now I am answering your letter, as you were when
you writ it. Come over; you will cure yourself and me
too. Adieu.

CCV. [*Original.*[2]]

SWIFT TO ARCHDEACON WALLS

Trim, *August* 7, 1713.

SIR,

I RECEIVED your notification relating to one Dorothy
and her new productions, which, like other second parts,
are seldom so good as the first. I shall be in town I hope by
the time appointed, and contribute as far towards making
your new inhabitant a Christian as one of that sex can be.[3]
You are mistaken in your conjectures about Mother

---

[1] Although Oxford may have told more to Swift than to others, it is
now clear from his letters that he was far from confiding to him all
that took place or disclosing to him his whole policy.

[2] In the possession of Mr. John Murray. See Preface.

[3] It appears from a subsequent letter that Swift had been asked by
the Archdeacon and his wife (*supra*, vol. i, p. 69, n. 3; p. 70, n. 4) to

Midnight,[1] with whom I have not the least acquaintance, or with her works of darkness, and if she tells you she has been with me on a broomstick, she lies egregiously, though by the moon's paleness of late one would think some such Hecates have been abroad ; and I take their spite to Diana to be owing to her interfering in their office.

The old fellow you are pleased to be so free with is a very honest gentleman, though he has not your faculty of increasing the Queen's subjects. He has told no tales but what he can make good; and I do not doubt but he will do justice to himself and his friends ; and he has drunk so much claret of late, that it has hardened his tallow too much for you to melt it.[2]

Since the thoughts of your girl raised your fancy, it is but just that her noise should disturb it. Joe[3] says all your spite to him arises from your jealousy and that you dare not trust him with Dorothy; and truly his poor wife here is as jealous of him as yourself, and has been lately told that the girl you vapour about very much resembles him, and that a fortune-teller has foretold she will take after him in never being father of a child.

Your melancholy story of the cask is not new to me. I have known it very frequent to have empty wooden vessels stuffed with books.

Joe bids me say he defies you and that his grease has been melted down long ago. Pray say nothing of Dorothy's jealousy, for if one Johnny Clark[4] of Trim should hear it there would be no living for poor Joe. But I promise you one thing that Joe will stand to nothing he says. Joe says that women do not like him because they cannot abide ridges nor hills.[5] I cannot tell the meaning of this.

be godfather to one of their daughters. There had been previously some idea of his acting in that capacity to one of their sons, whom Swift wished to be called Harley ("Prose Works," ii, 136, 140, 151). In his accounts there is the following entry on the 12th of that month, "Christening, Mrs. Walls, £2 2s. 5d." (Forster Collection, No. 509).

[1] *I.e.*, the midwife.

[2] Swift was then staying for a day or two in Trim, probably with his friend Raymond, the Rector (*supra*, vol. i, p. 120, n. 2). In the preceding month he had paid many similar visits, and on these occasions the purchase of wine is an item in his accounts (Forster Collection, No. 509).

[3] Joe Beaumont, *supra*, p. 54.   [4] *Supra*, p. 54.

[5] A play upon Beaumont's name.

Postscript in another handwriting.—I wish you joy; ***
*** **** **** ** **** ******* *** *** * *******.   A.
R[aymond].

Postscript in Swift's handwriting.—Joe says he never
was cut out to be a father; take care he fathers nothing
upon you.

Postscript in a third handwriting.—Joe says Parson[1] upon
Dorothy is good old country dance, *** ******* *** ***
*** **** *** ****** ****.   T. W[arburton].[2]

Addressed—To Dorothy's young girl's father.   Sent by
hand.

CCVI. [*Manuscripts of the Earl of Dartmouth.*[3]]

SWIFT TO THE EARL OF DARTMOUTH

The Country, *August* 8, 1713.

MY LORD,

THE way I take of showing my duty and gratitude to
those I owe most of both, is by troubling them as seldom
as I can. This made me hitherto contradict the violent
inclinations I had to write to your Lordship, which now
I can resist no longer, especially since I begin to hold up
my head after a long disorder it has suffered by the ill life
I led, and the ill company I kept among you. And I am
not altogether in jest, for God knows I kept some very ill
company every Saturday, worse than any of my neighbouring justices here;[4] but I hope that will be mended at my
return. And now, my Lord, you are to know that I will not
obey your commands of waiting on you in Staffordshire[5]
in my way to London; neither do I think it seasonable or
safe for me to be on that side of the Channel while you are
on this side the Thames. Your Lordship, who has the
honour to be one of my brother cowards (as you know who
calls four of us), will pardon me if my heart begins to ache

---

[1] *I.e.* Raymond.   [2] *Supra*, p. 54.

[3] Hist. MSS. Com., Rept. 11, App., pt. v, p. 316.

[4] The Earl of Dartmouth was one of those admitted to the later
Cabinet dinners (" Prose Works," v, 384).

[5] The principal seat of the Earls of Dartmouth, Sandwell, is in
Staffordshire.

II   F

when I look about at Court and cannot find you. Therefore, pray give timely warning to Mr. Lewis and me, that
he may trot down to Wales, and I gallop to Holyhead.
But, my Lord, we, the common people, who have the care
of your preferment, are resolved not to take away the seals
from you,[1] till we have given you another, much more easy
and honourable, though perhaps not altogether so rich. And
I, who am much older than your Lordship,[2] can assure you,
that whenever you change your station your enemies will
be able to produce very few examples in the memory of
man, of a Minister who has served with so much honour
and integrity. My Lord, I am preparing myself to come
over and demand the dinner you owe me, and hope to find
your Lordship in your Turret at Windsor. In the mean
time I desire you to believe that I am, with the greatest
respect and truth, etc.

J. SWIFT.

CCVII. [Original.[3]]

SWIFT TO ARCHDEACON WALLS

London, September 17, 1713.

OUR St. Mary friends, I suppose, have told you I got well
here.[4] It is an empty town, and I believe I shall go to
Windsor for some time. I protest I am less fond of Eng-

---

[1] A reference to his appointment as Lord Privy Seal (*supra*, p. 57,
n. 2).
[2] The Earl of Dartmouth was born in 1672, and was therefore only
five years younger than Swift.
[3] In the possession of Mr. John Murray. See Preface.
[4] Swift set sail from Dublin on Saturday, 29 August, and landed at
Parkgate (*supra*, vol. i, p. 61, n. 3) on the following Monday. On his
way to London he spent four days with one of the Irish judges, Sir
Gilbert Dolben, at his seat in Northamptonshire. He stayed also for
a night at Chester, Newport in Shropshire, Coventry, and Market
Street in Hertfordshire, through which his route lay. On some days
he travelled nearly fifty miles, and arrived in London on Tuesday,
9 September. For the hire of horses he notes a payment of £2 10s.
As appears from a fragmentary list of letters kept by him that year
(see Appendix IV), Swift on his return to England began another
journalistic correspondence with the ladies of St. Mary's. The first of
his letters to them was written from Chester on 1 September.

land than ever. The ladies tell me they are going to live
at Trim, I hope they will pass their Christmas at Dublin.
Our club is strangely broke; the Bishop at Dromore, I
here, and none but you and Stoyte left.[1] Our Goody Walls,
my gossip, will die of the spleen. Pray write to me when
you have leisure, I care not five pence for the Dublin news,
but of our friends and of my own affairs, and give my service to my commissioner Forbes. You will have the Duke
of Shrewsbury soon over with you ; and Sir John Stanley,
his Secretary.[2] I have not yet seen the Duke nor Duchess,
for they are at Windsor with the Court. My service to the
Alderman and Goody and Catherine[3] and Mr. Manley and
lady;[4] I think I know no others. Enclose your letters to
me under a cover, which cover you must direct to Erasmus
Lewis, Esq., at Mr. Secretary Bromley's office at Whitehall.[5] My service to Parnell.[6] I have lazily deferred this
letter till the post is going. Pray God bless my little goddaughter,[7] I hope to breed her up to be good for something,
if her mother will let me.

                    Yours, etc.

Addressed—To the Reverend Mr. Archdeacon Walls, at
    his house, over against the Hospital in Queen Street,
    Dublin.[8]

[1] There has been previous reference to this club, of which Bishop
Stearne and Alderman John Stoyte, sometime a parliamentary representative of Dublin city, were prominent members, and to the card
parties for which it existed (*supra*, vol. i, p. 121).
[2] It was not until then that the Duke of Ormond resigned the
viceroyalty, and the Duke of Shrewsbury was appointed in his room
(*supra*, vol. i, p. 320, n. 3). Sir John Stanley, from whose family
Viscount Monck is descended, was connected with Ireland, and is
well known to readers of Mrs. Delany's Correspondence as the uncle
by marriage of that famous lady.
[3] Alderman Stoyte, who was a brother of Sir Francis Stoyte, an
ancestor of the Earls of Darnley, was married to a Welsh lady, a Miss
Lloyd, and Catherine was her unmarried sister. The Alderman lived
in a large Jacobean house near the green on which Donnybrook Fair
was held. It may be observed that he was a Whig.
[4] *Supra*, vol. i, p. 274, n. 3.
[5] Through his appointment as Secretary of State, Bromley had
become Lewis's chief (*supra*, p. 57, n. 2).
[6] *Supra*, p. 23.   [7] *Supra*, p. 63, n. 3.
[8] Before that time Walls had resigned the mastership of the Cathedral school and was incumbent of Castleknock, the church immortalized by Swift in his verses " On the Little House " (" Poetical Works," i,

CCVIII. [*Original.*[1]]

Dean Smalridge to Swift

Christ Church, *September* 27, 1713.

MR. DEAN,[2]

WHEN you was so kind as to favour the Master of the Temple[3] and me with your company at the chaplain's table at Kensington, there dined with us one Mr. Fiddes, a well deserving clergyman, whose circumstances, we told you, were not at all suitable to his merits.[4] You expressed on that occasion so generous a concern for him, and so great a readiness to do him any good offices, which might lie in your way, that he seems to think he should be wanting to himself, if he did not endeavour to cultivate an interest with one so willing and so able to serve him. He has therefore made repeated instances to me, that I would remind you of him, which I should not have hearkened to,

81). The King's Hospital (commonly known as the Blue Coat School) in Dublin, which now stands in Blackhall Place, was then situated in Queen Street, a short distance from its present site.

[1] In the British Museum. See Preface.

[2] The tone of this letter is not a little striking when it is recollected that the writer is "the famous Dr. Smalridge" who disclaimed the ascription to him of the "Tale of a Tub" in terms that reflected with severity on the author. He had succeeded Atterbury as Dean of Christ Church, and his appointment had been desired, according to Swift, by that college when his predecessor had been sent as its head. In the following year he became Bishop of Bristol (see "Prose Works," *passim*).

[3] Thomas Sherlock, who was prominent in the Bangorian controversy, was then Master of the Temple and a chaplain to Queen Anne. His appointment successively as Bishop of Bangor and London did not interrupt his tenure of the mastership which he held for half a century.

[4] As a theological writer, and as author of a "Life of Cardinal Wolsey," Richard Fiddes made subsequently some reputation. In his description of Swift at that time—"the most vivid picture of Swift in all his glory"—Bishop Kennett describes him in the Queen's antechamber soliciting the place of chaplain to the garrison at Hull for Fiddes, "a clergyman in that neighbourhood who had lately been in jail and published sermons to pay fees" (see Appendix V). Owing to ill-health, Fiddes was then in distressed circumstances, but there is no certainty as to the truth of Kennett's statements ("D. N. B.," xviii, 398).

were I not well assured that you would excuse, if not thank me, for furnishing you with an opportunity of doing a generous and good-natured thing. You will not, I fancy, think a formal application to any great man in his behalf either proper or requisite; but if you should, upon the perusal of one or two of his sermons, think as well of them as I do, and should in conversation with my Lord Treasurer express a good opinion of the author, one kind word from you, seasonably dropped, might determine his fortunes, and give you the satisfaction of having made him and his family as happy as they can wish to be. I am, Sir,

Your most humble servant,
GEO. SMALRIDGE.

Addressed—For the Reverend the Dean of St. Patrick's.

CCIX. [*Sheridan.*]

SWIFT TO ARCHDEACON WALLS

Windsor Castle, October 1, 1713.

I HAD just now a letter from you, wherein you mention the design of making me Prolocutor.[1] I will confess to you, there are two reasons why I should comply with it; one is, that I am heartily weary of Courts and Ministers, and politics, for several reasons impossible to tell you, and I have a mind to be at home, since the Queen has been pleased that Ireland should be my home; the other reason is, that I think somebody educated in Dublin College should be Prolocutor, and I hear there are designs of turning it another way. But, if you find it will not do, I hope you will quit the design in proper season.

I condole with you for the loss of your companions this winter; and I was always of opinion they should be in town, unless they find their health better at Trim.[2] I am a

---

[1] The immediate cause of the Duke of Shrewsbury's appointment as Lord Lieutenant (*supra*, p. 67) had been the necessity of calling a meeting of the Irish Parliament that autumn, and following precedent during Queen Anne's reign, Convocation was to be summoned at the same time. The vacancy which existed in the office of Prolocutor had been caused by Stearne's elevation to the episcopal bench.

[2] *Supra*, p. 67.

little disappointed in Parvisol's [1] return. I hoped it would have amounted to near five hundred pounds in the tithes; I doubt not the cause, and beg you will have no sort of tenderness for him, farther than it regards my interest; as to the land-rents, they are one hundred and seventy-four pounds a year in the country, besides some small things in town; and I am in no pain about them, because they are sure, nor do I desire him to concern himself about them.

I hoped, and was told, my license would be under six pounds, though all was paid, and I heard, if Lord Chancellor had taken his fees, it would have been eight pounds. Tell Mr. Fetherston, I have spoken to Baron Scrope about his affair, who promises to dispatch it with the first opportunity.[2] I am now with some Ministers and Lords, and other company, and withdrawn to a table, and hardly know what I write, they are so loud. My humble service to your Dorothy, and Alderman Stoyte, his wife, and Cellarius;[3] and duty to the Bishop of Dromore.

Yours,

J. S.

CCX. [*Original.*[4]]

SIR CONSTANTINE PHIPPS TO SWIFT

Dublin, October 10, 1713.

SIR,

I HAD the favour of your kind letter of the 22nd of September, and had sooner acknowledged it, if I had not been prevented by the constant hurry we have been in, with relation to the city and Parliament affairs.[5] I heartily

---

[1] *Supra*, p. 49.

[2] Mr. Fetherston was probably the Rev. Thomas Fetherston, who became a prebendary of St. Patrick's Cathedral, and the judge to whom Swift had spoken about Fetherston's affairs was John Scrope, a member of the English Bar, who had been sent after the Union to Scotland as a Baron of the Exchequer. In later times Scrope was known as a follower and intimate of Walpole, but as he had acted for the Tories as a Commissioner of the Great Seal before Harcourt's appointment as Lord Keeper, he would appear to have been at one time not unfriendly to Harley's Ministry.

[3] *I.e.*, Stoyte's sister-in-law (*supra*, p. 67, n. 3).

[4] In the British Museum. See Preface.

[5] Since Ormond returned to England two years before, Ireland had been ruled by Lord Chancellor Phipps. Whether the restoration of the

congratulate your safe arrival in London, and return you, with all the gratitude imaginable, my thanks for the great trouble you have given yourself, as well on behalf of my son [1] in particular, as of this kingdom in general; and I am sorry you should venture so far as to burn your fingers, but you prove such misfortunes often happen to gentlemen who have a hearty zeal for the interest of their friends. But this comfort attends them, that the burning goes off soon; whereas the credit and honour of serving one's friend last always. The account you sent me of Mr. Worsley's being an envoy was new, and had not reached us before your letter came.[2] I know not how sufficiently to acknowledge the obligations you have laid on me; but assure you, if you have any commands of this side the water, there is no one will be more proud of being honoured with them, than he, who is, with very great respect,

Your most obedient humble servant,

CON. PHIPPS.

Stuart dynasty was, as has been alleged, his aim is open to question, but it does not admit of doubt that he sought by every means in his power to establish and perpetuate the rule of his party in Ireland. At the time this letter was written a general election was impending in Ireland, and as a consequence the dispute between the Irish executive and the Corporation of Dublin as to the choice of a mayor (*supra*, vol. i, pp. 259, 281) had become more than ever a burning one. An administrator like Phipps was not inclined to lose without an effort the advantage to his party of securing a Tory returning-officer in the Irish metropolis, while the Whig Corporation, on the other hand, were more than ever determined to resist pressure from Dublin Castle, convinced as they were that Toryism and Jacobitism had become synonymous terms.

[1] Phipps desired to obtain "the place of Register of the Forfeited Estates" for him. The only son of whom anything is known is one called William, from whom the Marquess of Normanby is descended. He was then a youth about to enter Trinity College, Dublin, where a piece of plate presented by him is still to be seen.

[2] Henry Worsley, brother of Sir Robert Worsley (*supra*, vol. i, p. 144, n. 3) and member for Newtown in the Isle of Wight. He was appointed about that time envoy to the court of Portugal, and was subsequently governor of the Barbadoes.

CCXI. [*Sheridan.*]

SWIFT TO ARCHDEACON WALLS

London, *October* 13, 1713.

I HAVE two letters of yours to acknowledge—no, I mistake, it is but one, for I answered the former of September 22nd, some time ago; your other is of the 1st instant, with an account of your mayor squabble, which we regard as much here as if you sent us an account of your little son playing at cherry stones. I told your Lord Chancellor, that the best thing the government there could do, would be never to trouble us with your affairs, but do the best you can, for we will neither support nor regard you. I have received the Lords Justices' representation, just now sent to the Queen.[1] I have said more upon it than anybody else would; and I hope my Lord Lieutenant will put a good end to the dispute.

I am heartily sorry for poor Hawley, and doubt such a shake at his age will not be well recovered. Of your four candidates to succeed him, I dislike all but the first, which is Bolton.[2] As to the chair of Prolocutor, I said to you in my former all I thought necessary. I dislike the thing for myself; but I would keep a wrong man out, and would be glad of an honest excuse to leave Courts and public thoughts; but it would vex me to be proposed and not succeed.[3]

As for Williams, I am an old courtier, and will think of it; but, if we want a singer, and I can get a better, that better one shall be preferred, although my father were competitor.[4] I have spoken to Baron Scrope about Mr. Fether-

---

[1] The Alderman who had filled the civic chair for the previous year was in sympathy with the Government. The Corporation had refused to elect his successor from a select list prepared by him, and under these circumstances the Irish executive contended that he had the right to continue in office for another year (*supra*, p. 70, n. 5).

[2] Thomas Hawley, to whom Swift refers, was Archdeacon of Dublin. He died two years later at the age of sixty-eight. The successor favoured by Swift was Theophilus Bolton, afterwards Archbishop of Cashel.

[3] *Supra*, p. 69.

[4] Edward Williams, who had been previously a half vicar, was three years later appointed a Vicar Choral of St. Patrick's Cathedral.

ston's affair, and hope to get him a good account of it.[1]
You very artificially bring in your friend, Mrs. South;[2] I
have spoke to her, and heard from her, and spoke to the
Duke of Ormond; I will do her what service I can. My
service to Gossip Doll, and God bless my goddaughter.

I think you need not inquire about the land-rents of the
deanery, they are secure enough; and I believe I shall not
trouble Mr. Parvisol about them. There is one farm set
for one hundred and twenty pounds a-year, another for
fifty-four pounds. Rents adjoining to the deanery, about
two pounds ten shillings, and duties about eight pounds,
or something under; and a small lease of tithes, about four
or five pounds; which last I would be glad you would ask
Parvisol whether it be included among the tithes he has
set. You see all the rents together are under two hundred
pounds. I forgot five pounds a-year for the verger's house.
Service to Stoyte and Manley,[3] and duty to Bishop of
Dromore.

CCXII. [*Original.*[4]]

BISHOP ELLIS TO SWIFT

Dublin, *October* 20, 1713.

REVEREND SIR,[5]

I HAVE the favour of yours relating to Garencieres. I
thank you for the trouble you have been at. I do not

---

[1] *Supra*, p. 70.
[2] She was probably the widow of John South, who was a brother
commissioner of Bartholomew Vanhomrigh in the Irish revenue de-
partment.
[3] *Supra*, p. 67.
[4] Preserved amongst the State Papers relating to Ireland in the
Public Record Office. It was evidently left by Swift, as well as the
originals of several other letters in this Correspondence, either in the
office of his friend Erasmus Lewis, or in the office of his friend Charles
Ford the Gazetteer, and became merged in the official papers.
[5] Bishop Welbore Ellis held, as has been already stated (*supra*,
vol. i, p. 83), the bishopric of Kildare, to which the deanery of the
cathedral of Christ Church in Dublin was then always united. The
almost unique position of that city in possessing two cathedrals led,
until the disestablishment of the Church of Ireland, to extraordinary
relations between them, and as will be seen from this letter, the same
choir served both, and the dignitaries of St. Patrick's preached at
stated times in the sister cathedral.

doubt but he will be liked very well, having pleased so good judges. He may be admitted at St. Patrick's as soon as he comes by your order to your sub-dean.[1] Your vacancy is a vicarage, ours a stipendiary, but both together may be worth about eighty pounds a year. There is another stipendiary's place void with us, which I take to be worth at least thirty pounds a year; if the person you have your eye on will accept that at present, it would be a service to the choir to send him over too, and you may, if you please, give him some allowance from the economy of St. Patrick's, which is sometimes done, till a vacancy happens there. I have given your directions to Mr. Worrall,[2] for a list of the anthems we have here, which I shall continue to put him in mind of, till it is done. I think what you propose will be for the honour of both churches, and ours will readily concur with you in so good a design.

You went away without giving order about supplying your preaching turns at Christ Church, you know they have been annexed to the station many years; the usage can be traced, at least as far as Queen Elizabeth's reign, which is a long prescription, whatever opinion you may entertain of it. I suppose scarce any usage the Dean and Chapter of St. Patrick's, at their admission sware to observe, is of much longer continuance; and the members of that Cathedral think themselves hitherto under the influence of that obligation. I have sent you a precedent of one of your predecessors upon a neglect of this kind, who has left behind him the character of a very good governor,[3] and this transaction happened whilst his Grace, the present Archbishop of Dublin, was a member of that church. You having farther considered of this matter, will, I presume, give such directions in it as have been usual.

All here at present are very busy about elections, some for Parliament, others for Convocation. Sir William Fownes,

[1] John Garencieres was installed as a Vicar Choral of St. Patrick's on 11 January following.

[2] The Rev. John Worrall, who became so closely connected with Swift in later life, held the position of Dean's Vicar in St. Patrick's Cathedral and that of a Vicar Choral in Christ Church Cathedral.

[3] John Worth who held the deanery in the reign of James II. His father had been Bishop of Killaloe, and his brother, whose line of conduct at the time of the Revolution was somewhat tortuous, was a Baron of the Exchequer in Ireland in the reigns of Charles II and James II.

the Recorder, Mr. Burton and Mr. Tucker appear for this city.[1] On Saturday night last a mob attacked the Archbishop of Tuam's house, and hurt one of the sentinels with a brickbat, but upon a reinforcement they soon got off. They were for pulling the old Prelate out of his house for a Whig: the pretence as well as the thing was somewhat extraordinary.[2] You could not have sent any news to me so acceptable as the health of the Queen; pray God continue it. I am, Reverend Sir,

Your very humble servant,

W. KILDARE.

I just now got the list of the anthems from Mr. Worrall.

CCXIII. [*Sheridan.*]

SWIFT TO ARCHDEACON WALLS

London, *October* 20, 1713.

SIR,

I WRIT to you immediately upon receiving your former, as I do now upon your last of the 10th instant. As to the business of being Prolocutor, I will tell you the short of

---

[1] There will be further reference to this election for the City of Dublin, which was accompanied by great turbulence and violence, and occasioned much debate in the Irish Parliament. The Recorder of Dublin, John Forster, who had been Speaker during the previous session of the Irish Parliament, and became Chief Justice of the Common Pleas, and Benjamin Burton, a Dublin banker, were the sitting members and Whigs; and Sir William Fownes, who appears as one of Swift's correspondents at a later period, and Martin Tucker were their Tory opponents. All of them were connected with the civic government. Both Fownes and Burton had filled the mayoral chair, and Tucker was a common-councillor.

[2] From the fact that he was co-Lord Justice with Sir Constantine Phipps (*supra*, p. 50, n. 2), Archbishop Vesey must have been ostensibly at any rate a strong supporter of Oxford's administration. Bishop Ellis evidently believed that the attack on the Archbishop's house came from a Whig quarter, and that the ground was other than the one alleged. In this it is possible he was mistaken. The Archbishop's antecedents, as the son of a clergyman who had complied with the orders of the Commonwealth as to religion, as well as his own attitude at the time of the Revolution, gave ground for suspicion that he was a moderating influence in the Irish government. He had sat in Convocation at the time of the Restoration, and had reached a great age.

my story. Although I have done more service to Ireland, and particularly to the Church, than any man of my level, I have never been able to get a good word; and I incurred the displeasure of the Bishops, by being the instrument, *sine qua non*, of procuring the first fruits; neither had I credit to be a Convocation man in the meanest diocese of the kingdom, till poor Dean Synge,[1] who happened to think well of me, got me to be chosen for St. Patrick's;[2] so that I think there will be a great change if I am chosen Prolocutor. And yet, at the same time, I am so very nice, that I will not think of moving towards Ireland till I am actually chosen. You will say, what then must the clergy do for a Prolocutor? Why, I suppose they may appoint a Vice-Prolocutor, until my coming over, which may be in ten days.

But this perhaps is not feasible: if not, you may be sure I shall not so openly declare my ambition to that post, when I am not sure to carry it; and if I fail, the comfort of *mecum certasse ferretur*, will not perhaps fall to my share. But I go on too fast; for I find in your next lines, that the Archbishop says there will be an indispensable necessity that I should be there at the election. Why, if the Bishops will all fix it, so as to give a man time to come over, with all my heart; but, if it must be struggled for at the election, I will have nothing to do with it. As for the Bishops, I have not the least interest with above three in the kingdom: and unless the thought strikes the clergy in general, that I must be their man, nothing can come of it. We always settle a Speaker here, as soon as the writs are issued out for a Parliament; if you did so for a Prolocutor, a man might have warning in time, but I should make the foolishest figure in nature, to come over hawking for an employment I no wise seek or desire, and then fail of it. Pray

---

[1] The epithet probably originated in a recollection of the *scandale* to which allusion has been made (*supra*, vol. i, p. 71, n. 5).

[2] Swift was chosen as their proctor by the Chapter of St. Patrick's Cathedral shortly before Convocation met in 1707. A protest lodged by him at the close of the proceedings in that year is referred to by Nichols ("Works," i, 125), but is not mentioned by Bishop Reeves in his "History of the Convocation of Ireland" already cited. The debates turned mainly on the propriety and truth of the statements made to the Lower House of Convocation in England by the Rev. Francis Higgins and his companion the Rev. William Percival, Archdeacon of Cashel (*supra*, vol. i, p. 202, n. 1).

communicate the sense of what I say to the Archbishop, to whom I will write by this post.

As to my private affairs, I am sure they are in good hands; but I beg you will not have the least regard or tenderness to Parvisol, farther than you shall find he deserves. I am my Gossip's very humble servant; and the like to Mr. Stoyte, his lady, and Catherine, and Mr. Manley, and his lady and daughter.[1]   I am,

Your obedient humble servant,
JON. SWIFT.

I wrote lately to Dr. Synge; twice in all. I think you should force the St. Mary ladies to town, towards Christmas. My duty to the Bishop of Dromore. Dr. Synge wrote me word a month ago, that Roseingrave, our organist,[2] was at the point of death. Is he dead or alive?

CCXIV. [*Sheridan.*]

SWIFT TO ARCHBISHOP KING

London, October 20, 1713.

MY LORD,

THE opportunity I had of a ship was so sudden, that I had not time to receive your Grace's last commands, or pay my respects, which it was my duty and inclination to do;[3] and as for writing, I have always told your Grace that I could not set about it with a good conscience, until I were provided with matter enough for your trouble of reading. We are outwardly pretty quiet during this interval of Parliament; but I will not answer what seeds are sowing to make the next spring produce better fruit. There are several reasons, impossible for me to tell at this distance, why I shall not be so good a correspondent as I have formerly been, but may probably serve to entertain you a year or two hence; for the fashion of this world passes away, and there is nothing of so little consequence as the greatest Court secrets, when once the scene is changed. I

---

[1] *Supra*, p. 67.   [2] *Supra*, p. 59, n. 2.
[3] The Archbishop had returned to Dublin from Bath (*supra*, p. 62) only twelve days before Swift sailed for England.

said to somebody, when I was last in Ireland, who talked
to me of the advantage and felicity I had in the familiarity
of great Ministers, that it was well enough while it continued a vanity; but as soon as it ceased to be a vanity, it
began to be a vexation of spirit.[1] I have some thoughts of
passing this winter at the Bath, because my health requires it, and because I shall then be a pretty equal distance
from the factions on both sides the water; for it is not impossible your Grace may have a warm winter.

I have had some letters, particularly from Dr. Synge and
Mr. Archdeacon Walls, about my being Prolocutor. I have
this post writ my thoughts upon that subject to Mr. Walls;[2]
and to save you the trouble, have desired him to communicate them to your Grace. Our elections for the city

---

[1] The struggle between Oxford and Bolingbroke (*supra*, vol. i,
p. 253, n. 1) had now reached an acute stage, and there was imminent
danger of a breach between them when Erasmus Lewis wrote to Swift
imploring him to return to England (*supra*, pp. 55, 57, 62). Oxford
was then carrying on a correspondence with Halifax, the chief of the
Whig leaders ("Portland Manuscripts," vol. v, *passim*), which can only
have had for its object, as I have already said, the formation of a
coalition ministry (*supra*, p. 15, n. 4), and it has even been suggested
that the opposition of Hanmer and his friends to the commercial
proposals in the Treaty of Peace had his secret assistance (" Robert
Harley," by E. S. Roscoe, p. 154). At the same time, on the other
hand, Bolingbroke meditated some desperate step from which he was
dissuaded at the moment by the vacillating Shrewsbury, who begged
him "to do nothing hastily that may be deferred, for what is not done
at one time may be at another, but what is once done can never be
undone" ("Letters and Correspondence of Bolingbroke," ii, 449).
That in so critical a position Swift should have been instrumental, as
he undoubtedly was, in reconciling his illustrious friends, even for a
time, is not the least remarkable proof of his great gifts. His power
lay no doubt in his ability to divert their minds from the point
at issue. Indeed the chief question, that of the succession, was
sedulously kept from him, and the *origo mali* was in his mind the
intractability of the Queen ("Prose Works," v, 449). His attainments
were equally admired by Oxford and Bolingbroke, and his society
was sought no less eagerly by the one than by the other. How anxious
Oxford was for Swift's return from Ireland is seen from Erasmus
Lewis's letters, and Bolingbroke expresses his feelings in a letter to
Prior at the beginning of September as follows : " Our friend Jonathan
is, I hear, returned from Ireland, where he has had no good health.
You will join with me in thinking he has done well to return, since I
am sure you will join with me in thinking that his health is of more
value than the good order of all the musty chapters in any kingdom"
("Bolingbroke's Letters," ii, 490).

[2] *Supra*, p. 75.

still continue: I was this afternoon at Guildhall. I find three of the old members [leading]; and Withers, who is the lowest, tells me he does not despair of carrying it for himself. There is abundance of artifice, to give it the softest word, used on both sides.[1] I came yesterday from Windsor, where I saw the Queen in very good health, which she finds there more than anywhere else, and I believe will hardly remove until December.[2] I believe my Lord Lieutenant will be landed before this letter comes to your hands.[3] He is the finest gentleman we have, and of an excellent understanding and capacity for business; if I were with your Grace, I would say more; but leave it to your own sagacity.

I will only venture to say one thing relating to Ireland, because I believe it will be of use that your Grace should know it. If your House of Commons should run into any violences disagreeable to us here, it will be of the worst consequences imaginable to that kingdom: for, I know no maxim more strongly maintained at present in our Court, than that her Majesty ought to exert her power to the utmost, upon any uneasinesses given on your side to herself or her servants; neither can I answer, that even the legislative power here may not take cognizance of anything that may pass among you, in opposition to the persons and principles that are now favoured by the Queen.[4] Perhaps

[1] The Treaty of Commerce was the chief question in this election, and Oxford's supporters, who were the sitting members, were opposed by "four eminent merchants" who disapproved of its terms. At first the latter led, but by methods "too tedious and perhaps unsafe to be mentioned," the sitting members came to the front, and when the poll closed four days after Swift's visit, Sir William Withers, as well as the other three, was found to be leading ("The Political State of Great Britain," by A. Boyer, vi, 385).

[2] During that month Swift stayed at Windsor each week from Saturday to Monday (Forster Collection, No. 509). He went down probably with Oxford. Bolingbroke spent the greater part of the month at his hunting lodge.

[3] The Duke of Shrewsbury (*supra*, p. 67) arrived in Dublin on 27 October.

[4] The dissensions between Whig and Tory in Ireland had risen to an extreme height, and Archbishop King said that he had never seen the kingdom in so great a ferment except during actual war in the time of James II. Bolingbroke was aware of its condition, and wrote to Prior of "that distracted nation, who from knowing no distinction but Protestant and Papist are come to be more madly divided about Whig and Tory, High Church and Low, than are this society of lunatics

I am gone too far, and therefore shall end, without any ceremony.

Your Grace's, etc.

Direct to me under cover to Erasmus Lewis, Esq. at Mr. Secretary Bromley's office at Whitehall.

CCXV. [*Original.*¹]

SIR CONSTANTINE PHIPPS TO SWIFT

Dublin, *October* 24, 1713.

DEAR SIR,

I AM indebted to you for your kind letters of the 8th and 10th instant, and I very heartily acknowledge the obligation. That of the 8th gave me a great many melancholy thoughts, when I reflected upon the danger our constitution is in, by the neglect and supineness of our friends, and the vigilance and unanimity of our enemies; but I hope the Parliament proving so good will awaken our friends, and unite them more firmly, and make them more active.[2]

That part of your letter of the 10th, which related to my son,[3] gave me great satisfaction; for, though the Commissioners here have heard nothing of it, yet I believed Mr. Keightly[4] might bring over full instructions in it. But he

to which you and I belong"; but Shrewsbury appears to have gone to the country under the impression that there was "no difference but Protestant and Papist" (*cf.* "Bolingbroke's Letters," ii, 490, and "Wentworth Papers," p. 356).

¹ In the British Museum. See Preface.

² In writing to Phipps, Swift had evidently referred in guarded terms to the embarrassments created at that time by Oxford's "mysterious and procrastinating" leadership, which Swift deplores in his "Enquiry into the Behaviour of the Queen's Last Ministry" ("Prose Works," v, 448). To some extent the situation may be accounted for by Oxford's subordinating the affairs of State to his schemes for the aggrandizing of his family by contracting great alliances for his children, but to my mind the explanation is to be found mainly in the habit of intemperance to which Oxford was a victim.

³ *Supra,* p. 71.

⁴ The Right Hon. Thomas Keightly, to whom Phipps alludes, was a Commissioner of the Irish Revenue, and acted at one time as a Lord Justice. He was an uncle by marriage of Queen Anne, and to this connection his distinction was no doubt attributable.

is arrived, and knows nothing of it; so that whatever good intentions my Lord Treasurer had in relation to my son, his Lordship has forgotten to give any directions concerning him; for, with him, things are just as they were when you left Dublin. If you will be so kind to put his Lordship in mind of it, you will be very obliging.

I cannot discharge the part of a friend, if I omit to let you know that your great neighbour at St. Pulcher's is very angry with you.[1] He accuseth you for going away without taking your leave of him, and intends in a little time to compel you to reside at your deanery. He lays some other things to your charge, which you shall know in a little time.[2]

We hourly expect my Lord Lieutenant.[3] The Whigs begin to be sensible they must expect no great countenance from him, and begin to be a little down in the mouth, since they find Brodrick is not to be their Speaker.[4] I am, with very great truth,

Your most obedient servant.

[1] The relations between Archbishop King, here designated Swift's great neighbour, from the contiguity of their official residences (*supra*, vol. i, p. 60, n. 2), and Lord Chancellor Phipps, can have been at no time cordial, and were then very acrimonious owing to the Archbishop's advocacy of the claims of the Dublin Corporation in the Privy Council.

[2] There is ground for thinking that Phipps's representation of the Archbishop's feelings towards Swift is tinged with exaggeration. In writing some weeks before, on 12 September, to Bishop Stearne, the Archbishop refers to Swift with much courtesy, and implies that there was some cause for resentment on Swift's part. His words are: "I think it would not be amiss to write to the Dean, for though he behaved himself with an appearance of contempt to everybody here, yet I think in justice he ought to be set right where any real cause of offence was given him, as there seems to be in this, for though your Lordship ought not to have complied with him yet he should be told the reason."

[3] *Supra*, p. 79, n. 3.

[4] Alan Brodrick had been removed from the office of Chief Justice of Ireland (*supra*, vol. i, p. 185, n. 3) soon after the Tory Government came into power, and was returning again to the House of Commons. From his long occupancy of the Speaker's chair he was naturally put forward by his party for the position, and much to the chagrin of Phipps and his friends succeeded in defeating the Court candidate, Sir Richard Levinge (*supra*, vol. i, p. 227, n. 3).

CCXVI. [*Original.*[1]]

CHARLES DAVENANT TO SWIFT

Windsor, *November* 3, 1713.

SIR,[2]

YOU have the character of employing in good offices to others the honour and happiness you have of being often with my Lord Treasurer. This use of your access to him is an uncommon instance of generosity, deserving the highest praises; for, most commonly, men are most apt to convert such advantages to their own single interest, without any regard of others, though, in my poor opinion, not so wisely. Acts of friendship create friends, even among strangers, that taste not of them, and in my experience, I hardly ever knew a man friendly in the course of his proceedings, but he was supported in the world; ingratitude being the vice, of which the generality of men are most ashamed to be thought guilty.

My son and I have reasons to return you our thanks, for what you have already done of this kind in his favour, and we beg the continuance of it.[3] Ministers of state have such multiplicity of business, that it is no wonder, if they forget low individuals; and in such a case, private persons must be beholden to some good-natured man, to put those in power in mind of them, otherwise they may lie forgotten, till old age overtakes them. Such well disposed remembrancers, deserve access, familiarity, and interest with great men, and perhaps, they are the most useful servants they can countenance in their hours of leisure.

I need not tell you, that in point of time, he is before all pretenders to foreign business; that his affairs have now

---

[1] In the British Museum. See Preface.

[2] As one of Swift's early letters shows (*supra*, vol. i, p. 367, n. 3), Dr. Charles Davenant had been long known to him through the relationship of his "little parson cousin" to that well-known political economist.

[3] Henry Molins Davenant, to whom his father here alludes, was employed in several diplomatic missions. During the reign of Queen Anne he was stationed at Frankfort, and under George I he acted as envoy extraordinary to the Princess of Italy. Davenant is one of the persons to whom Bishop Kennett pictures Swift speaking in the Queen's antechamber (see Appendix V).

depended almost three years; that in the interim, it has gone very hard with him; and that he gave a very early instance of his zeal to the present administration. But what he builds his hopes most upon, is the promise my Lord Treasurer was pleased to make to the Duke of Shrewsbury, just as his Grace left Windsor, that a provision should be made for Mr. Davenant. We must entreat you to find some lucky moment of representing to my Lord, that the young man is pressed by a nearer concern than that of making his fortune, and that lovers can hardly be persuaded to be as patient as other men. The Duke has carried his mistress from him, and will not consent to make him happy, till he sees him in some way of being settled: in which how anxious any delay must be, possession depending upon it, he leaves you to judge, who have so well studied mankind, and who know that love is a passion, in one of his age, much stronger than ambition. I beg your pardon for this long trouble, and am, Sir,

Your most humble and most obedient servant,

CHARLES DAVENANT.

CCXVII. [*Original.*[1]]

MR. JUSTICE NUTLEY TO SWIFT

November 5, 1713.

SIR,

I HAVE the honour and favour of yours of a date too long since to name, it having lain so long unanswered.[2] Had you been less complacent I could not have been so rude as I have been; for then I myself should not have thought it an excuse to tell you that I have been studying for an answer, and as it is I fear you will not allow it, for when you see my manner of doing it, you will hardly believe my performance to be the result of labour. But indeed it has cost me many a thought how I should impart to you the

---

[1] State Papers, Ireland, in P.R.O. *Supra*, p. 73, n. 4.

[2] Swift had received Prior's letter (*supra*, p. 60) too late to enable him to make Judge Nutley's acquaintance before leaving Ireland, but as appears from the present letter found a pretext after his arrival in England for inditing a communication of a very cordial character to the Judge.

pleasure and satisfaction I found in the kind tender you made me of your friendship, and at last I know no way of doing it but by bidding you fancy me as great as your imagination could make me, and then that you heard me say to you, I will do everything for you which is in my power. I sincerely thank you for this earnest of your friendship in so readily offering to comply with my request concerning Mr. Williams,[1] if I should judge it for the service of your choir. I will willingly give up the most advantageous part of the condition, and desire my request may be granted only if it suits with your just intention of bettering the economy of your church, and mending the beauty and harmony of the service to be performed in it; but as I understood the favour I was to ask was, that since you have one in your choir, who is a good performer, and as I am told, a sober reputable man, whose present stipend is but fifteen pounds per annum, that you would advance him to be a vicar in a vacancy now in your church; but since it is so that you keep that promotion for a voice which you want, I must submit my pretensions and wait for an opportunity, when they may with more reason be revived.

I am most extremely glad to hear that her Majesty and my Lord Treasurer are in so good health. May they long continue so, and like a well built arch, may that which is below support what is above, and that which is highest strengthen and establish that which is under it.

I have done myself the honour several times since our Lord Lieutenant landed [2] to wait upon his Grace, but having never been a courtier before, it did not come into my mind to consider what an awkward figure that man makes at a levee who has not been recommended to the great man in the middle of the crowd. For that reason I cannot but wish that some other great man, by himself, or his less busy friend, would intimate to his Grace that it would be kind and condescending in him if he would take some notice of ——. He is —— and would be proud to ——. Pray, Sir, try how you can fill up these blanks, and then tell me how you like the whole piece, when it is all together. You see, Sir, upon the encouragement you have given me how great a favour I venture to ask. In return for it, I will at any

---

[1] *Supra*, p. 72.   [2] *Supra*, p. 79, n. 3.

time save your blushes, and be your zealous advocate whenever I can have an interest.

His Grace the Primate died the 2nd instant, at two o'clock in the morning.[1] The poor executors I dare say, struggled hard to save a quarter's rent, and it is more than probable this good man was as much tortured to make him live, as ever criminal was to make him die. I am of opinion that the deanery of St. Patrick's is a fine preferment for a Lord Lieutenant's chaplain to jump into after one or two months service, and if you can be tempted to part with your fine house in Dublin for an ill contrived one on a country bishopric, I can easily cut out a scheme for the advancing some eminent worthy active prelate to the primacy, and so three good persons may be promoted at once.

I am much obliged to my friend Mr. Prior for his recommendation of me to you. It is placed by that he knew you well, and how good a friend you can be, but I am surprised that he should know so well that I desired, and do it before I could think of asking it. I delivered your command to my Lord Chancellor, but he had before acknowledged the receipt of your letters.

I know I am long, but I will say no worse of myself, and therefore I will conclude with assuring you that I most sincerely am, Sir,

Your most humble and very faithful servant,
R. NUTLEY.

CCXVIII. [*Original.*[2]]

SIR CONSTANTINE PHIPPS TO SWIFT

Dublin, *November* 9, 1713.

DEAR SIR,

I HAD the favour of yours of the 27th of October, and own with all the gratitude in the world, that the trouble you have given yourself in my son's affair,[3] and the many

---

[1] Although he made for a time a temporary rally, Primate Marsh's condition during the last four years of his life seems to have been well described by Swift as that of "a dying man" (*supra*, vol. i, p. 225).

[2] State Papers, Ireland, in P.R.O. *Supra*, p. 73, n. 4.

[3] *Supra*, p. 80.

other instances of your friendship to so late an acquaintance are such that I know not in what terms to express my acknowledgment: this I can assure you that your favours are not bestowed on an ungrateful person, but on one who, whenever he has an opportunity, will be glad to show how great a sense he has of the obligations.

I believe the great affairs in which my Lord Treasurer is engaged puts matters of so small a moment as my son's out of his mind, for the warrant is not yet come down to the Commissioners of the Revenue. It is probable it may be for want of somebody to pay the fees, if so and since you have done me the honour to concern yourself so far in it, I desire you would be so kind to lay out your money and let me know what it is, and I will order the payment of it to you.

Our elections of Parliament men in this kingdom prove beyond expectation, for by the nicest calculation can be made we shall have a majority of three to two,[1] and there is a great spirit of loyalty even among the mob. I am, with very great sincerity and respect,

Your most obedient humble servant,
CON. PHIPPS.

Dr. Swift.

CCXIX. [*Sheridan.*]

SWIFT TO THE EARL OF OXFORD

November 21, 1713.

MY LORD,

YOUR Lordship is the person in the world to whom everybody ought to be silent upon such an occasion as this, which is only to be supported by the greatest wisdom and strength of mind,[2] wherein, God knows, the wisest and best

---

[1] This was an extraordinary miscalculation. On the first trial of strength, the election of a Speaker, the Tories found themselves in a minority of four, and in subsequent divisions more immediately affecting the government, the majority against them was as great as forty-six.

[2] On the preceding day Oxford had lost his eldest daughter. She had married just a year before Peregrine Hyde Osborne, Marquess of Carmarthen, the eldest son of the third Duke of Leeds, a young man

of us, who would presume to offer their thoughts, are far
your inferiors. It is true, indeed, that a great misfortune is
apt to weaken the mind, and disturb the understanding.
This, indeed, might be some pretence to us to administer
our consolations, if we had been wholly strangers to the
person gone. But, my Lord, whoever had the honour to
know her, wants a comforter as much as your Lordship:
because, though their loss is not so great, yet they have not
the same firmness and prudence, to support the want of a
friend, a patroness, a benefactor, as you have to support
that of a daughter. My Lord, both religion and reason forbid me to have the least concern for that lady's death, upon
her own account, and he must be an ill Christian, or a
perfect stranger to her virtues, who would not wish himself,
with all submission to God Almighty's will, in her condition. But your Lordship who has lost such a daughter, and
we who have lost such a friend, and the world which has
lost such an example, have, in our several degrees, greater
cause to lament than, perhaps, was ever given by any
private person before: for, my Lord, I have sat down to
think of every amiable quality that could enter into the
composition of a lady, and could not single out one, which
she did not possess in as high a perfection as human nature
is capable of. But as to your Lordship's own particular, as
it is an unconceivable misfortune to have lost such a
daughter, so it is a possession which few can boast of, to
have had such a daughter. I have often said to your Lordship, that I never knew anyone by many degrees so
happy in their domestic as you, and I affirm you are so
still, though not by so many degrees; from whence it is
very obvious, that your Lordship should reflect upon what
you have left, and not upon what you have lost.

To say the truth, my Lord, you began to be too happy
for a mortal; much more happy than is usual with the dis-
pensations of Providence long to continue. You had been
the great instrument of preserving your country from foreign
and domestic ruin; you have had the felicity of establish-
ing your family in the greatest lustre, without any obligation to the bounty of your Prince, or any industry of your

of immense wealth as well as high rank ("Prose Works," ii, 402), and
left an infant son who survived and succeeded his father as the fifth
Duke of Leeds.

own; you have triumphed over the violence and treachery of your enemies, by your courage and abilities, and by the steadiness of your temper, over the inconstancy and caprice of your friends. Perhaps your Lordship has felt too much complacency within yourself, upon this universal success, and God Almighty, who would not disappoint your endeavours for the public, thought fit to punish you with a domestic loss, where he knew your heart was most exposed; and at the same time, has fulfilled his own wise purposes, by rewarding in a better life, that excellent creature he has taken from you.

I know not, my Lord, why I write this to you, nor hardly what I am writing. I am sure, it is not from any compliance with form; it is not from thinking that I can give your Lordship any ease. I think it was an impulse upon me that I should say something, and whether I shall send you what I have written, I am yet in doubt, etc.[1]

CCXX. [*Original.*[2]]

BISHOP LINDSAY TO SWIFT

November 21, 1713.

SIR,

THIS day Mr. Justice Nutley showed me a letter of yours to him, wherein I find myself much obliged to you for kind offices done me to Lord [Treasurer] by using your endeavours to promote me to a post, which my ambition could never aim at, and I am sure my merits will never come up to.[3]

---

[1] The felicitous and graceful words in which Swift conveys consolation to the bereaved father entitle this letter to be considered a model composition of the kind. As Sir Leslie Stephen says ("Swift," p. 116), it possesses "the charm which is given to such letters only by the most genuine sympathy with the feelings of the loser, and by a spontaneous selection of the only safe topic—praise of the lost, equally tender and sincere."

[2] State Papers, Ireland, in P.R.O. *Supra*, p. 73, n. 4.

[3] The post was none other than the vacant primacy (*supra*, p. 85). As the Correspondence has shown, when he first joined the Tory party Swift considered that Archbishop King possessed an indefeasible right of succession to that office, and was prepared to advance the Archbishop's claim unreservedly. But Swift cherished then the hope that

I have already received several favours from that great Lord, but the last I fear would swell my debt so high that I should never be able by any future services to discharge it.

I know not who hath represented me to you as an enemy,[1] but if you will be pleased at any time to hint to me in what, I hope I shall be able to show the contrary to satisfaction; but had there been anything of that kind, I am sure now all enmity ought to cease at least on my part, and therefore I desire leave to subscribe myself

Your friend and humble servant,

THO. RAPHOE.[2]

the Archbishop believed, like himself, that safety for the Church was not to be found under a Whig administration, and would come to be an unqualified supporter of Oxford's government. By degrees the conviction had been forced on Swift's mind that the Archbishop could not be enrolled in such a category, and even if he had a flickering flame of enthusiasm for the Archbishop when he returned to London, the letter from Lord Chancellor Phipps, which was no doubt written of set purpose, must have extinguished it (*supra*, p. 81). Once the Archbishop was out of the question Swift was free from all personal considerations, and thought only of securing as Primate the most reliable follower of Oxford on the episcopal bench, satisfied as he was that in doing so he was not only serving the Tory party, but the best interests of the Church. From such a point of view Bishop Lindsay occupied an unassailable position. As a political partisan he appears to have been little inferior to Lord Chancellor Phipps, and in addition he possessed the advantage of being an excellent speaker, some thought the best in the Irish House of Lords. As a Churchman he ranked with the highest, and in one of a series of letters addressed to Dr. Charlett, in which he records his views on Church and State with no little frankness, we find him relating with much self-satisfaction that when travelling through Wales, the people fell upon their knees before him in the streets and roads, and crowded his room to receive his blessing (Bodleian Library, MS. No. 10794, f. 80).

[1] Swift evidently regarded Bishop Lindsay as one of his chief detractors in the affair of the first fruits (cf. "Prose Works," ii, 448, and *supra*, vol. i, p. 193).

[2] Bishop Lindsay, who was brought to Ireland by Lord Capel, had been appointed successively Dean of St. Patrick's, Bishop of Killaloe and Bishop of Raphoe. The last promotion synchronized with that of Swift to the deanery of St. Patrick's.

CCXXI. [*Sheridan.*]

MR. JUSTICE NUTLEY TO SWIFT

Dublin, *November* 21, 1713.

SIR,

I CANNOT help telling you that I think you do me great wrong in charging me with being too civil, and with want of plainness in my letters to you.[1] If you will be abundant in your favours to me, how can I forbear thanking you, and if you will call that by a wrong name, that is your fault, and not mine. I hope I shall be able to convince you of your mistake, by putting you in the place of the party obliged; and then I will show you that I can be as ready as you are in doing good offices for a friend, and when I have done them, can treat you as you do me, as if you were the benefactor, and I had received the favour. I am sorry I did not keep a copy of my letter to you, that I might compare it with that which I shall have from you, whenever I shall be so happy as to receive one from you upon that subject; for I am thoroughly persuaded, you will then as much outdo me in civility of expression, as you do now in the power of conferring favours.

By this time I hope, I have satisfied you, that it is fit for me (and I am resolved) to express the sense I have of your friendship in as high a manner as I can, until I have an opportunity of making a better return; but to show you, that it is as uneasy to me to write civil things, as it can be to you to read them, I will, as often as I can, do you services, that I may not be at the trouble or bear the reproach of being complaisant. I am so much a philosopher as to know that to be great, is to be, but not to be thought, miserable; and I am of the opinion of those among them, who allow retaliation; and therefore since you have declared your intention of loading me with cares, I will, as far as I can, make you sensible of the hurt you do me, by laying a like burden upon you.

I thank you most sincerely for the clear and full information you have given me of your grand Church affair.[2] It

---

[1] *Supra*, p. 83.
[2] The proposed promotion of Bishop Lindsay to the primacy.

entirely agrees with my judgement; for I do think that
what you propose will be the best service that has been
done to this Church and kingdom since the Restoration,
and the doing it soon will be of great advantage to the
Queen's affairs at this juncture. For, it has been given out
among the party, that the Ministry have an eye toward the
Whigs, and that if they now exert themselves, they will
soon have an open declaration in their favour. We have a
remarkable proof of this; for Mr. Brodrick has engaged a
considerable number of the Parliament men, many of them
not of his party, to promise him their votes for Speaker,[1]
by telling them he has the approbation of the Ministry and
Lord Lieutenant; and since his Grace has made known her
Majesty's pleasure, a new word is given out that the liberties
of the people are in the last danger, and that the Crown is
attempting the nomination of a Speaker. I own I am no
politician; but I think I understand the posture of affairs
here, and I am assured that the Church party is so strong,
that if anything be done on your side to excite their zeal,
and discourage their adversaries, there will be but a short
struggle here. But if the Whigs are permitted to hope, or
what is as bad, to boast of their expectations, and nothing
is done to enable others to confute them, they will, it is
probable, be able to give trouble to the government, and
what is now easy to be effected, will become difficult by
delay; and I fear the want of doing this in time will occasion some uneasiness to the Duke of Shrewsbury, for to
this is owing the doubtful dispute, who shall be Speaker.

I have showed your letter to the gentleman chiefly concerned in it:[2] this I did, because I knew it would produce a
full expression of his sentiments; and I can assure you,
whatever occasion may have been given you to think what
you say in your letter, he has a true sense of your friendship to him.[3] I will be guarantee, that according to the
power he has he will be ready to serve you, and that in
kind. My Lord Chancellor will send you his own thanks.
I am, most truly and sincerely,

Yours, etc.

[1] *Supra*, p. 81.   [2] *I.e.*, Bishop Lindsay.
          [3] *Supra*, p. 88.

CCXXII. [*Original.*[1]]

JOHN ARBUTHNOT TO SWIFT

[*November*, 1713.]

DEAR FRIEND,[2]

I AM most heartily grieved for the loss of your excellent and worthy friend, and more for the affliction of another.[3] I do not love to irritate a fresh wound else I would have taken the freedom to have wrote to my Lord. I pity his case with all my heart; for whatever other affliction he has been used to, he is much a stranger to domestic calamities. I have a true sense of his present condition for which I know philosophy and religion are both too weak, and I believe it is the will of God that it should be so. I have lost six children. If I am not deceived, I believe, I could have been content to have ransomed the lives of every one of them even at the hard terms of begging their bread. I know my Lord has the sentiment of humanity and paternal affection very strong, and I should not love him so well if he had not; therefore, my dear friend, I question not but you will upon this occasion do these offices of humanity that are incumbent upon you upon many accounts, which you will find will succeed better by turning his thoughts to other objects than by the most rational reflections upon the present affliction.

[1] State Papers, Ireland, in P.R.O. *Supra*, p. 73, n. 4.

[2] Although Dr. Johnson's opinion of Arbuthnot has been often quoted it is perhaps pardonable, as an introduction to the opening letter of the correspondence between Queen Anne's celebrated physician (*supra*, p. 18, n. 2) and Swift, to mention that the great critic gave Arbuthnot a foremost place amongst the writers of Queen Anne's reign, and considered him equally "estimable for his learning, amiable for his life, and venerable for his piety." His reputation as a physician was also very high as appears from the writings of his friends:

"Arbuthnot there I see, in physic's art
As Galen learned, or famed Hippocrate;
Whose company drives sorrow from the heart
As all disease his med'cines dissipate."

[3] This letter is evidently a reply to one from Swift to Arbuthnot deploring the death of the Marchioness of Carmarthen (*supra*, p. 86). As the concluding sentence of this letter shows, the Queen, on whom Arbuthnot was always in close attendance, was still at Windsor.

Everybody here shares in his grief from her Majesty down to the meanest of his humble servants. My Lady Masham was so much surprised and grieved that we were afraid it would hurt her in her present condition.[1] I am glad I did not know my Lady Carmarthen so well as you, but I know enough to believe her a most valuable person. I have nothing left to wish for my Lord as a saving in this case, but that God would preserve the life of the poor child [2] to be some comfort to him. I believe it will not be a good way for my Lord to keep up, but to appear as soon as possible again in his business, for I know by experience that the best cure is by diverting the thoughts. I hope we may see you here next Saturday.[3] Your friends remember you kindly. I am, dear Sir,

Your affectionate brother and most humble servant,

JO. ARBUTHNOT.

Take your opportunity to make my compliments to my Lord. I am truly sorry for him, and I have the vanity to think he would be so for me upon such an occasion.

CCXXIII. [*Original.*[4]]

SWIFT TO ARCHDEACON WALLS

London, *November* 26, 1713.

SIR,

I HAVE had two letters from you very lately, the last of the 19th instant came yesterday. As to those you sent me about the prolocutorship, I reckon them for nothing.[5] I would see you all whipped before I would venture myself in any manner to come over upon a fool's errand; and for what? For a place I would rather be without, neither would I take it upon any other score but being chosen freely by a

[1] It was not the first time there had been anxiety about Lady Masham under similar circumstances (cf. " Prose Works," ii, 385).

[2] *Supra*, p. 86, n. 2.

[3] To Swift's visits to Windsor during October there has been reference in a previous note (*supra*, p. 80, n. 2). His account-book for 1713-14 is unfortunately not forthcoming.

[4] In the possession of Mr. John Murray. See Preface.

[5] *Supra*, p. 75.

vast majority, which would let the world see they thought
me a man fit to serve the Church, and since they have not
chosen me they show they do not think me such a man,
and consequently they and I do not deserve each other.[1]

Your last letter but one was full of a project of advising
our St. Mary's friends to come to town,[2] wherein I shall
not offer to interpose; you think me a very idle fellow, and
very wise. However I think if the black lady does not find
amendment in her health they had better come where
company is stirring; and so I told them in a letter I writ
to them three days ago; when, by the same token, I forgot
to send Mrs. Dingley a bill for eight pounds which I have
received of hers here on a branch of her Exchequer money;
I will therefore now send one at the end of this letter, which
you will please to tear off and have conveyed to her.

Indeed I could hardly then think of anything, having
just lost a friend I extremely loved, the poor Marchioness
of Carmarthen. She was but twenty-four years old,[3] a most
excellent person, adorned with all possible good qualities.
She was Lord Treasurer's eldest daughter and his favourite.
I have seen him but twice since, the last time was yesterday in the afternoon, and to-morrow she will have been
dead a week. He is in great affliction and so are five
hundred others.

As to the school I did not know I had any part in the
disposal of it.[4] Yet I asked amongst you when I was in

[1] The Irish Convocation did not meet until four days later, but it
was probably known beforehand that Archdeacon Percival (*supra*, p. 76,
n. 2), upon whom the choice of the Lower House fell, would receive
large support for the Prolocutor's chair. In the opinion of Sir Walter
Scott ("Life," i, 179), Archbishop King's influence, "aided by the
envy of the inferior clergy," was the obstacle to Swift's selection, but
in the opinion of Bishop Reeves (*op. cit.*) Swift's absence from Ireland
was the difficulty. It is to be noticed that King took no part in the proceedings of Convocation at that time as the Crown appointed Archbishop
Vesey President of the Upper House. "I could not appear in it,"
says King, "because the place that I did believe was due to me was
denied me."

[2] *Supra*, p. 77.

[3] The Marchioness of Carmarthen (*supra*, p. 86, n. 2) was twenty-
eight at the time of her death; she was six years older than her
husband.

[4] The Cathedral school in which Walls was interested as a former
master. His successor in the mastership, Edward Drury, was
appointed then to the vacant prebend of Saggart (*supra*, p. 56).

Dublin and thought I had no answer. I have no engagement. But I tell you one thing, I will sacrifice in everything of this kind to reputation. I take your word and judgement, and if it were a thing not liable to censure, I would do it immediately at your request, supposing it in my disposal; but I will wait, and have your person approved by others both for your sake and my own, and then your recommendation shall have the preference. But it comes this very moment into my head, that a little before I left Ireland I saw Mr. Dawson [1] with the Archbishop recommending to his Grace some other person, and the Archbishop talked as if it were a thing of his own, and talked of the person Dawson recommended as one that would stand very fair for it [2]—it is somebody that teaches Dawson's children, I know not his name—so that I believe you and I are talking of the golden tooth. [3]

Dr. Radcliffe [4] and I did three weeks ago beset Lord Treasurer about Mrs. South, and he assured us it was done. [5] I made the Duke of Ormond speak about it lately once or twice, and I spake to Lord Treasurer myself half a dozen times. I am my Gossip's most humble servant. . . . [6]

Your most obedient humble servant,

J. SWIFT.

CCXXIV. [*Elwin.*]

ALEXANDER POPE TO SWIFT

Binfield, *December* 8, 1713.

SIR,

NOT to trouble you at present with a recital of all my obligations to you, I shall only mention two things, which I take particularly kind of you—your desire that I should write to you, and your proposal of giving me twenty

---

[1] *Supra*, p. 49.

[2] It is evident from this passage that Swift had seen Archbishop King at least once after his return from Bath (*supra*, p. 77, n. 3).

[3] Possibly an allusion to the saying that a lost tooth will be replaced by a golden one if your tongue does not touch the cavity.

[4] Swift was not an admirer of that celebrated physician (" Prose Works," *passim*).

[5] *Supra*, p. 73.

[6] Several lines here have been obliterated: all that remains is: " Pray ask the Bishop of Dromore and give him my duty. I am."

guineas to change my religion, which last you must give me leave to make the subject of this letter.[1]

Sure no clergyman ever offered so much out of his own purse for the sake of any religion. It is almost as many pieces of gold as an apostle could get of silver from the priests of old, on a much more valuable consideration. I believe it will be better worth my while to propose a change of my faith by subscription than a translation of Homer,[2] and to convince you how well disposed I am to the Reformation, I shall be content, if you can prevail with my Lord Treasurer and the Ministry to rise to the same sum each of them, on this pious account, as my Lord Halifax has done on the profane one.[3] I am afraid there is no being at once a poet and a good Christian; and I am very much straitened between the two, while the Whigs seem willing to contribute as much to continue me the one, as you would to make me the other. But, if you can move every man in the Government who has above ten thousand pounds a year, to subscribe as much as yourself, I shall become a convert, as most men do, when the Lord turns it to my interest. I know they have the truth of religion so much at heart, that they would certainly

---

[1] The friendship between Swift and Pope, to which this Correspondence owes so much of its interest, had, I think, then only just begun, and originated in a discovery by Swift of the young poet's agreement with him in political opinion. Until the publication of "Windsor Forest" in the previous spring, Pope had been regarded as a possession of Addison and his circle, but the loud paean on the peace with which that poem concludes showed that Pope had not subordinated his hereditary views to those of his Whig friends. It is then for the first time that Swift mentions Pope in the Journal to Stella ("Prose Works," ii, 439), and his commendation of "Windsor Forest" as "a fine poem,' may at least be ascribed as much to approval of Pope's sentiments as to admiration of his verse. There is no further reference to Pope in the Journal, and it seems probable that it was not until his return from Ireland in September that Swift began to cultivate Pope's acquaintance. As this letter shows he did so assiduously, and was looked upon by Pope in the light of a benefactor before the poet retired for a time from London on a visit to his father at Binfield.

[2] The first volume of Pope's translation of the "Iliad" was not published until two years later, but subscriptions were then being invited. Swift was active, as Bishop Kennett tells us, in canvassing for them: "The author shall not begin to print until I have a thousand guineas for him" (Appendix V). Swift's ambition was far more than realized as the subscription list amounted to four times that sum.

[3] Halifax subscribed for ten copies.

give more to have one good subject translated from Popery
to the Church of England, than twenty heathenish authors
out of any known tongue into ours. I therefore commission you, Mr. Dean, with full authority to transact this
affair in my name, and to propose as follows. First, that
as to the head of our Church, the Pope, I may engage
to renounce his power, whensoever I shall receive any particular indulgences from the head of your church, the
Queen. As to communion in one kind, I shall also promise
to change it for communion in both, as soon as the Ministry
will allow me. For invocations to saints, mine shall be
turned to dedications to sinners, when I shall find the
great ones of this world as willing to do me any good, as I
believe those of the other are.

You see I shall not be obstinate in the main points; but
there is one article I must reserve, and which you seemed
not unwilling to allow me,—prayer for the dead. There
are people to whose souls I wish as well as to my own;
and I must crave leave, humbly to lay before them, that,
though the subscriptions above-mentioned will suffice for
myself, there are necessary perquisites and additions,
which I must demand on the score of this charitable article.
It is also to be considered, that the greater part of those,
whose souls I am most concerned for, were unfortunately
heretics, schismatics, poets, painters, or persons of such
lives and manners, as few or no churches are willing to
save. The expense will therefore be the greater to make
an effectual provision for the said souls. Old Dryden,
though a Roman Catholic, was a poet; and it is revealed
in the visions of some ancient saints, that no poet was
ever saved under some hundreds of masses. I cannot set his delivery from purgatory at less than fifty
pounds sterling. Walsh was not only a Socinian, but what
you will own is harder to be saved, a Whig.[1] He cannot
modestly be rated at less than a hundred. L'Estrange
being a Tory, we compute him but at twenty pounds,
which I hope no friend of the party can deny to give, to
keep him from damning in the next life, considering they
never gave him sixpence to keep him from starving in

---

[1]   "And knowing Walsh would tell me I could write."
To Pope's early friend, William Walsh, Dr. Johnson gives some
credit as a poet and a critic, but more recent authorities consider his
work insignificant.

this.[1] All this together amounts to one hundred and seventy pounds.

In the next place, I must desire you to represent that there are several of my friends yet living, whom I design, God willing, to outlive, in consideration of legacies; out of which it is a doctrine in the Reformed Church, that not a farthing shall be allowed to save their souls who gave them. There is one **** who will die within these few months; with *******[2] one Mr. Jervas, who has grievously offended, in making the likeness of almost all things in Heaven above and earth below; and one Mr. Gay, an unhappy youth, who writes pastorals during the time of divine service; whose case is the more deplorable, as he hath miserably lavished away all that silver he should have reserved for his soul's health, in buttons and loops for his coat.[3] I cannot pretend to have these people honestly saved under some hundred pounds, whether you consider the difficulty of such a work, or the extreme love and tenderness I bear them, which will infallibly make me push this charity as far as I am able.

There is but one more whose salvation I insist upon, and then I have done: but indeed it may prove of so much greater charge than all the rest, that I will only lay the case before you and the Ministry, and leave to their prudence and generosity what sum they shall think fit to bestow upon it. The person I mean is Dr. Swift, a dignified clergyman, but one, who, by his own confession, has composed more libels than sermons. If it be true, what I have heard often affirmed by innocent people, that too much wit is dangerous to salvation, this unfortunate gentleman must certainly be damned to all eternity. But I hope his long experience in the world, and frequent conversation with great men, will cause him, as it

[1] In his article on Sir Roger L'Estrange, who has been described as one of the founders of English journalism, Mr. Sidney Lee says (" D. N. B.," xxxiii, 126) that Pope's sneer at the generosity of the Tory party to L'Estrange does not seem wholly justifiable.

[2] The asterisks are thought by Elwin to be an accidental interpolation.

[3] Swift had long known Jervas, who had commenced to paint a portrait of him in his Whig days (" Prose Works," ii, 7). With Gay he had probably become acquainted in Pope's company. The description of Gay's sartorial embellishments is an allusion to the preface to his " Shepherd's Week."

has some others, to have less and less wit every day. Be it as it will, I should not think my own soul deserved to be saved, if I did not endeavour to save his; for I have all the obligations in nature to him. He has brought me into better company than I cared for, made me merrier when I was sick than I had a mind to be, and put me upon making poems on purpose that he might alter them, etc.

I once thought I could never have discharged my debt to his kindness; but have lately been informed, to my unspeakable comfort, that I have more than paid it all. For Monsieur de Montaigne [1] has assured me, that the person who receives a benefit obliges the giver; for, since the chief endeavour of one friend is to do good to the other, he who administers both the matter and occasion, is the man who is liberal. At this rate it is impossible Dr. Swift should be ever out of my debt, as matters stand already; and, for the future, he may expect daily more obligations from

His most faithful affectionate humble servant.

I have finished the Rape of the Lock; [2] but I believe I may stay here till Christmas, without hindrance of business.

CCXXV. [*Original.* [3]]

ARCHBISHOP KING TO SWIFT

Dublin, *December* 15, 1713.

REVEREND SIR,

I RECEIVED the favour of yours of the 20th of October last; you may perhaps reckon me an ill correspondent that have delayed my answer so long, but to deal ingenuously with you, I have been so little pleased with the noise, hustle, and unreasonable transactions here, that I had no heart to communicate to a friend things so uneasy to myself; for six weeks we had nothing but tumults, contentions, quarrels, calumnies, and drinking about elections.

---

[1] " Essais " (liv. iii, chap. ix) "de la Vanité."
[2] The second and enlarged edition.
[3] State Papers, Ireland, in P.R.O. *Supra*, p. 73, n. 4. Froude refers (*op. cit.*, i, 353) to this letter, but failed to identify the writer. There is a copy in King's Correspondence.

Our Parliament men now met have had, as the public papers will tell, a fair trial of skill for a majority; the choice of a Speaker and chairman for elections tell you who has it;[1] this I assure you is a great disappointment, for the minor party, as it proves, were assured, and declared with the greatest confidence, that they were the greater, and it is strange to me that they are not, considering the Government, Privy Council, benches, custom house, army pensioners, officers of all sorts, dependants and expectants were all for them.

I suspected this before and therefore laboured to the utmost of my power to persuade them to make up the contest with the city before the Parliament sat, foreseeing that if it were not quieted before that happened, it would come into Parliament, and God knows what turn it might take there. But they turned a deaf ear, not only to me, but to those of greater authority,[2] and plainly told their mind: that they had a majority; that they were sure of the Privy Council and House of Lords, and as to the House of Commons they had that in their pocket, as I think the expression was, and would be justified in all they did; nay, they went so far as to brand all that were for compounding and quieting matters, and keeping the Parliament from taking cognizance of what had passed before, with the odious name of Whigs, and as encouragers of the city and others in their refractoriness, factiousness, and as some termed it, rebellion. I could never persuade myself that this could be agreeable to the Ministry on your side, for I believed that

[1] *Supra*, p. 86, n. 1.

[2] Before leaving London Shrewsbury was instructed to terminate the dispute between the Castle and the city (*supra*, p. 72, n. 2) before the Irish Parliament met, but he found that every attempt on his part towards a settlement was frustrated by Sir Constantine Phipps, who had gained an extraordinary ascendancy over the majority of the Irish Privy Council, and that he was condemned "as in a Whig interest for following the orders of her Majesty and her present Ministry" ("Manuscripts of the Marquis of Bath," i, 241). Those acquainted with Irish affairs had foreseen that Shrewsbury would not be able to work harmoniously with Phipps, and had expected that he would require Phipps and his friend Judge Nutley to be removed before accepting the viceroyalty (Departmental Correspondence in P.R.O. of Ireland); but Shrewsbury appears to have been entirely ignorant of the real position in Ireland, and was evidently quite unprepared for the pandemonium which Phipps had created by his high-handed methods.

they had business enough there, without being pestered
with memorials, representations and frivolous contests
from this kingdom; and I was farther confirmed in this
opinion when I saw the report of the Attorney General
of England with whom the Solicitor General concurred on
a long representation from the Council here about the city
of Dublin.[1] That representation was drawn up when I was
in the country, and you may assure yourself if ever the
matter come to be debated in Parliament, as I doubt it now
will, it will show a different face from what it appears to
have in that paper, yet as it was, the Attorney and Solicitor
General agreed with me in every point wherein I differed
from the major part of the Council, and, as I thought, the
Council of England sending it here was a plain intimation
that it was her Majesty's pleasure that the affair should be
made up, which might have been done without any
reflection on the Council, to avoid which I imagined it was
sent in that manner, that the Council here might make it
their own act, and not seem obliged to do it by any command or determination against them from her Majesty;
but this would not be allowed to be the sense of it at all,
but a confutation of the Attorney and Solicitor's opinion is
sent from the judges here,[2] and the city continues without
any settled magistrates or government.

This, except the penning the last memorial, all happened
before the Parliament sat, and seemed to be done in confidence of a majority, and may perhaps be excused as a
mistake; but since their weakness in the House appeared
Mr. Tucker and Sir William Fownes have petitioned
against the Recorder and Alderman Burton for an undue

---

[1] *Supra*, p. 72.
[2] There was a warm debate in the Irish Privy Council on the question of adopting the opinion of the Irish judges in which the right of
the existing Lord Mayor to hold office for another year was upheld,
and finally, as a compromise, the opinion was sent to London without
ratification by the Council. Phipps impugned the conduct of Shrewsbury on that occasion and bitterly complained of "the ill-usage"
which he received from Archbishop King, who led the opposition,
without "the least check" from the Lord Lieutenant ("Manuscripts
of the Duke of Portland," v, 370); but nothing can exceed the impartiality with which Shrewsbury summed up for Bolingbroke the arguments on both sides in a debate which was carried on, as he tells
him, "with unusual heat and passion and personal reflections" (State
Papers, Ireland).

election in the city,[1] which openeth a way to many inquiries, and brings things on the carpet, that had, I am sure, much better be let alone. You can be no stranger to the riots, mobs and quarrels that happened at the city election, and that one man was killed in it,[2] now what should tempt them to bring such a matter before a House where they knew the majority was against them, I cannot imagine; they have already spent two days in the examination, and perhaps it may last two days more, and I doubt this may produce some smart votes, that may hurt both those that make them, and those against whom they are made.

I find, however, them all unanimous in professing that they will do everything that shall be for her Majesty's service, and the ease of the Government here. I wish they may say and hold. I verily believe they will not break on money matters, and the prevailing party pretend that they chiefly endeavoured to appear so, that by their zeal and forwardness to comply with her Majesty's desires they might have an opportunity to confute the false representations of their enemies, and the calumnies with which they loaded them as enemies to the constitution of Church and State, but a House of Commons is a strange thing and no mortal man can answer for them. I cannot find that they intend any such thing as an impeachment,[3] the most they seem to aim at, is to lay a representation of what they call grievances before her Majesty.

How the proceedings of the Parliament here will relish with you, I cannot tell, but I can assure you I have not failed to lay before all that I have any influence on, the hazard they ran, and the danger of provoking her Majesty, the Ministry and Parliament there, but I prove too often a prophet with Cassandra's fate, not to be believed till the event confirmeth what I say. I believe I could give twenty instances where it has so happened, but it is the misfortune

---

[1] *Supra*, p. 75, n. 1.

[2] The chief riot, in which a man was shot by some soldiers whom the Sheriffs summoned to their assistance from the guard, was occasioned by a dispute as to whether the polling should be in the Tholsel or in the King's Hospital. It is characteristic of Shrewsbury to find him proposing as an expedient, which was adopted, that the poll should be taken at the same time in both places (State Papers, Ireland).

[3] It was thought possible that the House of Commons would impeach Sir Constantine Phipps.

of mankind to prefer a present humour or view to their true interest.

I have taken your advice in relation to her Grace the Duchess of Shrewsbury, and find what you told me to be true, for which I return you my thanks.[1]

Dean Swift.

CCXXVI. [*Original.*[2]]

SWIFT TO BISHOP STEARNE

London, *December* 19, 1713.

MY LORD,

I HAVE two letters from you to acknowledge, one of the 5th, and another of the 11th instant. I am very glad it lies in my way to do any service to Mr. Worrall, and that his merits and my inclinations agree so well.[3] I write this post to Dr. Synge, to admit him. I am glad your Lordship thinks of removing your palace to the old, or some better place.[4] I wish I were near enough to give my approbation; and if you do not choose till summer, I shall, God willing, attend you. Your second letter is about Dr. Marsh, who is one I always loved, and have shown it lately, by doing everything he could desire from a brother. I should be glad for some reasons, that he would get a recommendation from the Lord Lieutenant, or at least that he be named. I cannot say more at this distance, but assure you, that all due care is taken of him.[5] I have had

---

[1] The Duchess of Shrewsbury (*supra*, vol. i, p. 315) had evidently bewitched the Archbishop by her "pretty kind eyes." One would hardly have expected that lady to find favour with the staid prelate. Not to speak of rumours as to her anti-marital relations with Shrewsbury, her "ridiculous talk" and flirtations were the wonder of London ("Wentworth Papers," *passim*).

[2] In the British Museum. See Preface.

[3] As the address on this letter shows, Bishop Stearne was residing in St. Patrick's deanery. He was evidently concerning himself about the Cathedral, and had recommended Swift to appoint Worrall (*supra*, p. 74, n. 2) to some vacant office.

[4] Stearne's predecessor in the see of Dromore had built a new episcopal house, and had deserted the site of one in which Jeremy Taylor, who held the see of Dromore as well as those of Down and Connor, is said to have resided.

[5] Dr. Jeremiah Marsh, to whom Swift alludes, was Treasurer of St. Patrick's Cathedral. The mention of his name recalls the curious

an old scheme, as your Lordship may remember, of dividing the bishoprics of Kilmore and Ardagh; I advised it many months ago, and repeated it lately; and the Queen and Ministry, I suppose, are fallen into it.[1] I did likewise lay very earnestly before proper persons the justice, and indeed necessity, of choosing to promote those of the kingdom; which advice has been hearkened to, and I hope will be followed. I would say something likewise in relation to a friend of your Lordship's;[2] but I can only venture thus much, that it was not to be done, and you may easily guess the reasons.

I know not who are named among you for the preferments;[3] and, my Lord, this is a very nice point to talk of at the distance I am. I know a person there better qualified, perhaps, than any that will succeed. But, my Lord, our thoughts here are, that your kingdom leans too much one way; and believe me, it cannot do so long, while the Queen and administration here act upon so very different a foot. This is more than I care to say. I should be thought a very vile man, if I presumed to recommend to a [Minister] my own brother, if he were the least disinclined to the present measures of her Majesty and Ministry here. Whoever is thought to do so must shake off that character, or wait for other junctures. This, my Lord, I believe you will find to be true; and I will for once venture a step farther, than

circumstance that the see of Dublin was occupied in succession by two prelates of the same surname—Francis Marsh, the father of the Treasurer, and Narcissus Marsh, so often mentioned in this Correspondence, who were, so far as is known, in no way related. From what follows it would appear that Stearne suggested that Swift should use his influence to secure Dr. Marsh's appointment to the bishoprics of Kilmore and Ardagh, which were then vacant, as well as the primacy, and to which Dr. Marsh had an ostensible claim, as he held the deanery of Kilmore as well as his other dignity.

[1] These sees had been united only forty years previously. Although not at the time this letter was written, they were subsequently disunited, and remained so for a century, when they were again united and the see of Elphin was joined to them.

[2] In this sentence Swift prepares Stearne for the appointment of another than Archbishop King to the vacant primacy, and in the following paragraph demonstrates, so far as indirect and obscure phraseology would permit, that the Archbishop had himself rendered his promotion impossible by the line which he had taken in the political questions of the day.

[3] The bishopric of Derry, as well as those already mentioned, was then vacant.

perhaps discretion should let me: that I never saw so great a firmness in the Court, as there now is, to pursue those measures, upon which this Ministry began, whatever some people may pretend to think to the contrary: and were certain objections made against some persons we both know, I believe I might have been instrumental to the service of some, whom I much esteem. Pick what you can out of all this, and believe me to be ever,

Yours, etc.

Addressed—To the Right Reverend the Lord Bishop of Dromore at his house in St. Kevin's Street, Dublin.

CCXXVII. [*Original.*[1]]

SIR GILBERT DOLBEN TO SWIFT

Finedon,[2] *December* 22, 1713.

REVEREND SIR,[3]
I TAKE the liberty on the death of Mr. Swords, late Vicar of St. Patrick's, to renew my recommendation of Mr. Williams to your favour, whose singing to the organ is very much better than to the tossing of a boat.[4] He is, in musician's language, a ready sight-man, and in my poor

---

[1] State Papers, Ireland, in P.R.O. *Supra*, p. 73, n. 4.

[2] Near Wellingborough in Northamptonshire.

[3] Sir Gilbert Dolben, with whom Swift had stayed at Finedon on his way to London (*supra*, p. 66, n. 4), occupied throughout the reign of Queen Anne what might be thought the incompatible positions of a Justice of the Common Pleas in Ireland and a member of the British House of Commons, and appears to have contrived to discharge both his judicial and legislative duties with success. As a son of that "learned, wise, stout and most worthy prelate," John Dolben, Archbishop of York, he had secured a seat in the English Parliament for the borough of Ripon at a very early age, as far back as in the reign of James II, and evidently took a moderate line in politics, as he was the only supporter of Oxford allowed to retain his seat on the Irish judicial bench under the first Hanoverian sovereign. A scholarly taste recommended him to Swift, and also to Oxford, whose library he enriched by the gift of a valuable manuscript collection (" Portland Manuscripts," v, 146).

[4] The Rev. Henry Swords, who had been buried in St. Werburgh's Church, Dublin, early that month, had been for many years one of the Vicars-Choral. Apparently Swift had met Williams (*supra*, p. 72, n. 4) when suffering from the effects of the turbulence of the Irish Channel, and was not favourably impressed by him.

judgement, both his voice and manner are agreeable. He has a salary as supernumary, which, if he be made vicar, will be saved; he so distinguished himself by his diligence that your predecessor thought fit to give him an extra-ordinary gratuity for it. I must not omit this opportunity of expressing my thankful acknowledgments of your great friendship in pleading my cause effectually with Philippus. I doubt not but, in due time, I shall find the benefit of having so good an advocate.[1] My spouse presents her respectful services,[2] and bids me say, if you be disposed to play a Christmas gambol with the lion—he is now mounted on a tankard burnished without and unctuous within—I hope the mildness of the weather, and passableness of the ways, and *super omnia* the heartiness of the invitation may tempt you to think this as good a place to spend a month of leisure in, as even Lingerland itself. I am, Reverend Sir,

Your obliged and most humble servant,

G. DOLBEN.

CCXXVIII. [*Original.*[3]]

DEAN SMALRIDGE TO SWIFT

Christ Church, *December* 26, 1713.

MR. DEAN,

I SHOULD long before this time have acknowledged the favour of your letter, and the kind offices you were pleased at my request[4] to do Mr. Fiddes, but that when I received yours I had some thoughts of quickly going up to town, and there paying my thanks in person. These should not have been put off with my journey, but that I knew you were not in half so much haste to receive thanks, as you

---

[1] The reference is no doubt to a Captain Phillips, who is frequently mentioned in the "Correspondence of Sir Thomas Hanmer" as an *attaché* of the Speaker. Dolben was then seeking the position of Chairman of the Committee of Elections in the House of Commons, an office for which he had been suggested as a candidate three years previously, and was anxious to secure Hanmer's interest. It had been engaged for another on the previous occasion and possibly led to the success which attended his candidature on the present one (Departmental Correspondence in P.R.O. of Ireland).

[2] It was through his wife, a Miss Mulso, that Dolben had succeeded to Finedon.

[3] State Papers, Ireland, in P.R.O. *Supra*, p. 73, n. 4.

[4] *Supra*, p. 68.

were to deserve them.   You aim at much better things
for Mr. Fiddes, than he, I fancy, in his utmost ambition
ever aspired to, and although I doubt not but your interest
will be able to compass all which you propose, yet I am
confident his modesty is such, that he will be thankful
even for less.   You was extremely kind in introducing
him to my Lord Treasurer; but I am afraid he would
make as awkward a figure there as your good friend
Horace[1] did when he first waited on his Lord M[aecenas].
My Lord has done the poor man a great deal of honour
in admitting him to be his chaplain, and suffering him to
dedicate a volume of sermons to his Lordship; and I hope
he will take care not to disgrace his patron in either of
those capacities.   I am only afraid lest in the overflowings
of his gratitude he should lay his colours on with too
liberal an hand, and use the trowel instead of the pencil.
But I will take an opportunity of giving him a friendly
hint how apt his Lordship will be to wince if stroked in a
clumsy manner, or in a wrong place.   If I am not much
mistaken in his Lordship he would choose rather to be
treated as he is by John Dunton,[2] than fall into the hands
of some dedicators.   But such is the unhappy lot of some
men, that they can neither escape libels, nor penknives,
nor panegyrics.   But I hope my friend Fiddes will make a
discreet use of the power which is put into his hands, and
will in that respect as well as in others [show] himself
not altogether unworthy of the favours you have done
him at my instance, whereby you have not more obliged
him than you have, Sir,

Your most humble servant,
GEORGE SMALRIDGE.

Addressed—For the Reverend Dr. Swift, Dean of St.
   Patrick's, to be left with Mr. Thomas at the Lord
   Treasurer's in York Buildings, Westminster.

[1] Smalridge had in his mind Swift's address to Oxford in imitation
of the seventh epistle of the first book of Horace, in which Swift reminds Oxford that the promised *douceur* (*supra*, p. 32, n. 2) would not
be unwelcome ("Poetical Works," ii, 159).   The address was published
before November, as Boyer then alluded to it in his "Political State
of Great Britain."

[2] In his pamphlet "Neck or Nothing," which Swift holds up to
ridicule in the "Public Spirit of the Whigs" ("Prose Works," v, 316).

CCXXIX. [*Original.*[1]]

BISHOP LINDSAY TO SWIFT

December 26, 1713.

SIR,

YOURS of December the 8th I received, and have obeyed your commands; but am much troubled to find that the trade of doing ill offices is still continued.[2] As for my part, I can entirely clear myself from either writing or saying anything to anyone's prejudice upon this occasion; and if others have wounded me in the dark, it is no more than they have done before; for Archbishop Tillotson formerly remarked, that if he should hearken to what the Irish clergy said of one another, there was not a man in the whole country that ought to be preferred.

We are now adjourned for a fortnight, and the Commons for three weeks.[3] I hear our Lord Lieutenant is not well pleased, that we have adjourned short of them;[4] and I fancy the Queen will not be well pleased, that the Commons have had so little regard to the dispatch of public business, as to make so long an adjournment as three weeks; and indeed they hereby seem to intimate, that if the Lord Chancellor is not removed by that time, they will give her

---

[1] In the British Museum. See Preface.

[2] There must have been many cross-currents in regard to the appointment to the primacy (*supra*, p. 88, n. 3). Shrewsbury had recommended that the place should be filled by some one sent from England, and had suggested two bishops on the English episcopal bench and Dr. Smalridge as persons from whom a suitable selection might be made ("Manuscripts of the Marquis of Bath," i, 245).

[3] The second Irish Parliament of Queen Anne's reign had adjourned on Christmas Eve, and did not meet again. During the four weeks it had been in session Sir Constantine Phipps was the pivot round which every debate revolved. By the Commons he was denounced as a tyrant and a traitor, and by the Lords he was applauded as a benefactor and a saviour. The case for him is set out in a remarkable pamphlet entitled, "A Long History of a Short Session of a Certain Parliament in a Certain Kingdom," which, according to a manuscript note on a copy in the possession of the Royal Irish Academy, was written by Swift's friend, Dr. Delany, who was Phipps's chaplain, while the case against him is to be found in a pamphlet entitled, "The Conduct of the Purse in Ireland."

[4] In the "Long History" Shrewsbury is represented as always in opposition to his own party.

Majesty no more money;[1] and indeed some of them do not stick to say as much, and think it a duty incumbent on the Crown, to turn out that Minister, how innocent soever he be, whom the Commons have addressed against.[2]

I think it is as plain to any who know the state of affairs here, that no party hath strength enough directly to oppose a money bill in this kingdom, when the government thinks fit to exert itself, as to be sure it always will do upon such occasions: and the half-pay officers, no doubt, will readily come in to that supply, out of which they are to receive their pay. But should all fail, yet the Queen still may make herself easy, by disbanding two or three regiments, and striking off some unnecessary pensions.

Hobbes, in his Behemoth, talks of a height in time as well as place;[3] and if ever there was a height in time here, it is certainly now; for some men seem to carry things higher, according to their poor power, than they did in England in 1641. And now they threaten, and I am pretty well assured, have resolved upon it, that if the Chancellor is not discarded, they will impeach him before the Lords in England. But if they have no more to say against him, than what their address contains, I think they will go upon no very wise errand.

I question not but that you will receive the votes, addresses, and representations of both Houses from other hands, and therefore I have not troubled you with them; but if the Parliament should continue to sit, you may expect a greater product of that kind; for the Commons have taken upon themselves to be a court of judicature,[4] have taken examinations out of the judges' hands about murder, which is treason here, without ever applying to the government for them, and before trial have voted the sheriffs and officers to have done their duty, and acquitted

---

[1] The Commons had only voted supplies for three months.

[2] Five days before Parliament adjourned the House of Commons had voted an address to the Queen representing the hardships and oppressions Ireland groaned under, "through the evil administration of Sir Constantine Phipps," and beseeching her Majesty "for the peace and safety of her Protestant subjects" to remove him from the place of Lord Chancellor.

[3] "Behemoth, or The Long Parliament," by Thomas Hobbes, edited by Ferdinand Tonnies, p. 1.

[4] In regard to the right of the Sheriffs to call in the military to repress the riot during the election in Dublin (*supra*, p. 102, n. 2).

themselves well, when possibly the time may yet come, that some may be still hanged for that fact; which, in my poor opinion, is entirely destructive of liberty, and the freedom of elections. I am,

Your most humble servant, etc.

CCXXX. [*Sheridan.*]

SWIFT TO ARCHBISHOP KING

London, December 31, 1713.

MY LORD,

YOUR Grace's letter,[1] which I received but last post, is of an earlier date than what have since arrived. We have received the addresses for removing the Chancellor, and the counter-addresses from the Lords and Convocation; and you will know, before this reaches you, our sentiments of them here. I am at a loss what to say in this whole affair. When I writ to you before, I dropped a word on purpose for you to take notice of, that our Court seemed resolved to be very firm in their resolutions about Ireland.[2] I think it impossible for the two kingdoms to proceed long upon a different scheme of politics. The controversy with the city I am not master of: it took its rise before I ever concerned myself in the affairs of Ireland, farther than to be an instrument of doing some services to the kingdom, for which I have been ill requited. But, my Lord, the question with us here is, whether there was a necessity that the other party should be a majority? There was put into my hands a list of your House of Commons by some who know the kingdom well. I desired they would, as they often do here, set a mark on the names of those who would be for the Ministry, who I found amounted to one hundred and forty-three, which I think comes within an equality; twenty names besides they could not determine upon, so that, suppose eight to be of the same side, there would be a majority by one, but besides, we reckon that the first number, one hundred and forty-three, would easily rise to a great majority, by the influence of the government, if that had been thought fit. This is demonstration to us; for, the

<hr>

[1] *Supra*, p. 99.   [2] *Supra*, p. 79.

government there has more influence than the Court here, and yet our Court carried it for many years against a natural majority, and a much greater one.

I shall not examine the reasons among you for proceeding otherwise, but your Grace will find that we are determined upon the conclusion, which is, that Ireland must proceed on the same foot with England. I am of opinion, my Lord, that nothing could do more hurt to the Whig party in both kingdoms, than their manner of proceeding in your House of Commons. It will confirm the Crown and Ministry that there can be no safety while those people are able to give disturbance, and indeed the effects it has already produced here, are hardly to be believed; neither do we here think it worth our while to be opposed, and encourage our enemies, only for seventy thousand pounds a year, to supply which it may not be hard to find other expedients; and when there shall be occasion for a Parliament, we are confident a new one may be called, with a majority of men in the interest of the Queen and Church;[1] for when the present majority pretends to regard either, we look upon such professions to signify no more than if they were penned by my Lord Wharton,[2] or Mr. Molesworth.[3] I have suffered very much for my tenderness to some persons of that party, which I still preserve; but I believe it will not be long in my power to serve those who may want it. It would be endless to recount to your Grace the reproaches that have been made me, on account of your neighbour.[4]

It is but true, my Lord, we do not care to be troubled

[1] Shrewsbury took at that time a more correct view and wrote to Oxford: "I shall only say that the heats on both sides are such that little is to be expected from this session, nor at present from this Parliament; and what is worse, if a new one were chosen I am confident the humour of the House of Commons would not mend" ("Manuscripts of the Marquis of Bath," i, 243).

[2] A correspondent had written to Oxford a year before from Ireland that Wharton was "the tutelary God whom our Whigs invoke and adore as the sole preserver of their country and their cursed principles" ("Manuscripts of the Duke of Portland," v, 211).

[3] Mr. Robert Molesworth, afterwards first Viscount Molesworth, was one of the most active leaders of the opposition during that session, and was subsequently removed from the Privy Council of which he was then a member. See "Prose Works," v, 322.

[4] *I.e.*, Bishop Stearne, who was still residing in St. Patrick's deanery (*supra*, p. 103, n. 3), and had voted against the Government.

with the affairs of Ireland; but, there being no war, nor meeting of Parliament, we have leisure at present; besides, we look upon ourselves as touched in the tenderest part. We know the Whig party are preparing to attack us next sessions, and their prevailing in Ireland would, we think, be a great strength and encouragement to them here; besides, our remissness would dishearten our friends, and make them think we acted a trimming game. There are some things which we much wonder at, as they are represented. The address for removing the Chancellor[1] is grounded upon two facts, in the former of which he was only concerned with several others, the criminal was poor and penitent, and a *nolle prosequi* was no illegal thing;[2] as to Moore's business, the Chancellor's speech on that occasion has been transmitted hither, and seems to clear him from the imputation of prejudging.[3] Another thing we wonder at, is, to find the Commons in their votes approve the sending for the guards, by whom a man was killed.[4] Such a thing would, they say, look monstrous in England. Your Grace seems to think they would not break on money matters; but we are taught another opinion, that they will not pass the great bill until they have satisfaction about the Chancellor; and what the consequence of that will be, I suppose you may guess from what you know by this time.

My Lord, we can judge no otherwise here than by the representations made to us. I sincerely look upon your Grace to be master of as much wisdom and sagacity, as any person I have known; and from my particular respect to you and your abilities, shall never presume to censure your proceedings, until I am fully apprised of the matter. Your Grace is looked upon here as altogether in the other

[1] As has been indicated (*supra*, p. 109, n. 2) the address was a most inflated performance, and from its want of argument was calculated to defeat rather than to serve its purpose.

[2] The first charge against Phipps was that he had caused the prosecution of a bookseller, who had sold a pamphlet "impeaching her Majesty's title to the Crown," to be dropped.

[3] The second charge against Phipps was that in a speech to the Corporation of Dublin "he had inflamed and prepossessed the minds of the aldermen" against one Dudley Moore, who was about to be prosecuted for riot on the occasion when Garth's prologue was called for in the Dublin theatre (*supra*, p. 8, n. 1).

[4] *Supra*, p. 109.

party, which I do not allow when it is said to me. I conceive you to follow the dictates of your reason and conscience; and whoever does that will, in public management, often differ as well from one side as another.

As to myself, I take Ireland to be the worst place to be in while the Parliament sits, and probably I may think the same of England in a month or two. I have few obligations, farther than personal friendship and civilities, to any party; I have nothing to ask for but a little money to pay my debts, which I doubt they never will give me;[1] and wanting wisdom to judge better, I follow those who, I think, are most for preserving the Church and State, without examining whether they do so from a principle of virtue or of interest.

CCXXXI. [*Original.*[2]]

SWIFT TO THE REV. JOHN WORRALL

London, *December* 31, 1713.

SIR,

I RECEIVED last post your letter relating to a lease to be made to my Lord Abercorn[3] by the Vicars Choral.[4] I desire you will let the Vicars know that I shall to the utmost resent their presuming to make any lease without the consent of the Dean and Chapter, which they are bound to have by their own subscriptions.[5] Let them know further that I am very well instructed in my own power both from

---

[1] *Supra*, p. 32, n. 2.

[2] In the possession of Mr. Thomas P. Le Fanu, of Abington, Bray, co. Wicklow, through whose kind permission it is reproduced here.

[3] The Earl of Abercorn had been known to Swift in his Whig days (*supra*, vol. i, p. 382, n. 14) and according to Swift was indebted to him for an introduction to the Tory Ministers ("Prose Works," ii, *passim*). The Earl had, however, not recognized him of late, and resentment against "the whelp" may have had some part in the angry tone of this letter (*infra*, p. 121).

[4] As Dean's Vicar (*supra*, p. 74, n. 2) Worrall was their head.

[5] The land which it was proposed to lease was already held by the Earl of Abercorn, and lay behind his Dublin residence which was situated on the western side of St. Stephen's Green; *cf.* Mason's "Hist. of St. Patrick's," p. 97, and "The Georgian Society Records," ii, 99.

II   I

the late Dean and from Dr. Synge,[1] and that I will immediately deprive every man of them who consents to any lease without the approbation aforesaid, and shall think the Church well rid of such men who to gratify their unreasonable avarice would starve their successors. I shall write this post to Dr. Synge to take proper measures on this occasion. I desire you will read this letter to the Vicars, and let them count upon it that I will be as good as my word. I am, Sir,

Your most humble servant,

JONATH: SWIFT.

CCXXXII. [*Original.*[2]]

PRIMATE LINDSAY TO SWIFT

January 5, 1713-14.

SIR,

YOURS I received the 2nd instant,[3] and immediately got Mr. Justice Nutley to write to the Bishop of Killala,[4] at Kells, to know of him, whether, if we could get him translated to the bishopric of Raphoe, he would accept of it; and this day we received his answer, that it was not worth his while to carry his family so far northwards, for so little advantage as that bishopric would bring him, his own being upward of a thousand a year, and Raphoe not much above eleven hundred.[5] The reason why I got Judge Nutley to write, was, because I apprehended it might seem

---

[1] *Supra*, p. 76.   [2] In the British Museum. See Preface.

[3] The Queen's letter appointing Bishop Lindsay to the primacy (*supra*, p. 108) had been signed a fortnight before, and the patent had been issued on the preceding day.

[4] The Bishop of Killala at that time, William Lloyd, has been already mentioned as one of the Ashe coterie and as the recipient of a letter from Swift on some question of the day (*supra*, vol. i, p. 186, n. 1). In writing to Stella, Swift refers occasionally to Lloyd, who was amongst those of "the graver sort" that frequented her lodgings, and his anxiety to publish the letter to Lloyd was with the intention of doing honour to him ("Prose Works," *passim*).

[5] The bishopric of Raphoe (now united to the see of Derry) was, however, considered far more important than that of Killala, which has been called "the first rung in the ladder of episcopal promotion." Of thirteen bishops who held Killala in the eighteenth century, only three failed to obtain translation to a more fruitful field, and one cannot marvel at their desire to escape from a diocese which em-

irksome to him to be persuaded by myself to accept of
what I left; though at the same time I can assure you, I
have done little more than saved myself whole by that
bishopric, and he might, if he pleased, in a little time have
received sixteen or seventeen hundred pounds for fines; so
that if this comes time enough to your hands, you will
prevent any farther motion that way. But if Meath drops,
I believe it would be an acceptable post;[1] and the truth
is, he has always, in the worst of times, voted honestly, and
behaved himself as a true son of the Church. In the mean
time, be assured, the Judge knows not that you are concerned in this affair.

There is a gentleman, whom I believe you must have
heard of, Dr. Andrew Hamilton, Archdeacon of Raphoe, a
man of good learning and abilities, and one of great interest
in that country,[2] whom I could wish you would move for,
since the Bishop of Killala refuses, to succeed me in Raphoe, as one that is the most likely to do good in that part
of the country, of any man I know.

And now be pleased to accept my thanks for the great
services you have done me; and as you have contributed
much to my advancement, so I must desire you, upon
occasion, to give me your farther assistance for the service
of the Church. The Parliament is prorogued to the 18th
instant; but the Whigs continuing obstinate, and deaf to

braced country like the vast barony of Erris on the shores of the
Atlantic. "Secure in its wild fastnesses of rock, torrent, and bog,
guarded on its outer borders by a stormy and inhospitable coast, and
to the south and east by a chain of wild mountains and wilder lakes,
it remained," says Litton Falkiner ("Studies in Irish History," p. 268),
"almost to our own day remote and unvisited, untravelled and track-
less as the wilds of Lyonesse,

> 'a waste land where no one comes,
> Or hath come, since the making of the world.'"

[1] The Bishop of Meath, who is styled the Most Reverend, takes
precedence of the other suffragans in Ireland. The see is also attractive on account of its proximity to the metropolis. Lloyd possibly had
some connection with the diocese, as Kells, where he was staying, is
one of the chief towns in it.

[2] Dr. Hamilton, who was a native of that part of Ireland, and probably related to the Earl of Abercorn (*supra*, p. 113), remained Archdeacon of Raphoe until his death. He had been appointed to that
dignity when only twenty-one years of age, and held it during the un-
precedented period of sixty-four years.

all persuasions to carry on the Queen's business with peace and gentleness,[1] we conclude it must be dissolved.

If this should not come time enough to your hands, to prevent the Bishop of Killala's letter for a translation to Raphoe, I will labour all I can to make him easy.

Addressed—For the Reverend Dr. Swift, Dean of St. Patrick's in Dublin, to be left at Mr. Erasmus Lewis's at Mr. Bromley's Office, London.

CCXXXIII. [*Copy.*[2]]

ARCHBISHOP KING TO SWIFT

Dublin, *January* 13, 1713/14.

SIR,

I HAVE before me yours of the 31st of December last, which came not to my hands till yesterday. I am heartily obliged to you for the frankness and plainness of it.

As to the first thing, that it is impossible for the two kingdoms to proceed long upon a different scheme of politics, I believe it is true, but withal I think it impossible to set the two parties on the same foot in Ireland as in England; for our division is founded on the right of our estates, which are all claimed by the forfeiters, and nothing can restore them but the Pretender, nor anything take them from us but bringing him in; whereas all your contests so far as I understand them have no other foundation but who shall have the ministry and employments; the gaining these has no connection with the Pretender, you may have them without him or under him. But you see the case is widely different with us, and here is the true source of the zeal and violence of the Protestants of Ireland. Remove the fear of the Pretender, and you may lead them like a dog in a string. I know you will say there is no danger of him, but you must allow people whose all is at stake to be jealous of every step made to their ruin. I must not tell you what they reckon steps towards this, but

---

[1] The Government had sought unsuccessfully a promise from the Whig leaders that if Parliament was allowed to meet again the attack on Phipps would be dropped.

[2] In King's Correspondence. See Preface.

they have lists of them, such I mean as they want steps and such as put them out of their wits.

As to your computation of the House of Commons, I do not wonder you computed wrong, for so did everybody here, and I amongst the rest. But many of those that I reckoned on as Tories prove on this occasion Whigs, and let me tell you, that if the weight of the government were not on them many more would declare themselves on that side. I myself can count near thirty. One when they lost the Speaker, being asked how the matter went, answered with an air of pleasure: "As God would have it, the vote went against us"; and I never saw men better pleased by being worsted. I took some pains in the matter of the Speaker and had by connivance half a dozen of the chief of them at my chamber, where I represented to them the great hazard and danger they run, and with more arguments than I have yet heard from any other.[1] They could not answer me, but only told me that if they could have any assurance, or hopes, that their grievances would be removed they would drop their Speaker and insist on nothing but the removal of my Lord Chancellor and quieting the city of Dublin. I could say nothing to these, and then they said they would proceed their own way, and if undone they had rather it should be the act of others than their own. However I found this effect, that six or seven deserted, and either absented themselves or voted for Sir Richard Levinge.[2] There are in the Parliament about seventy officers, about nine or ten converts, and as many more expectants or dependents as make up a hundred. I believe as much art and as many methods have been used to make a Parliament as well could be, and this is the effect. I do not think it difficult to get a Parliament that will be in the interest of the Church and Queen, but it will not be so easy to get one that will come into all measures as desired. I remembered when you assisted to procure the first fruits

[1] One of the chief arguments of which the Government made use was that the Speaker had always been nominated by the Court, and that the defeat of Sir Richard Levinge would be "a disrespect to the Queen and the Lord Lieutenant" (State Papers Ireland).

[2] In the "Long History of a Short Session of a Certain Parliament," it is alleged that Shrewsbury secretly favoured the election of Brodrick to the Speaker's chair, but as this letter shows with no foundation, for the Archbishop would not have concerned himself for Levinge except at the request of Shrewsbury.

and twentieth parts and gave us some hope of getting the crown rents, I thought you greatly in the interest of the Church; but the highest Tories were of another opinion. You are well aware from this and many more examples that the interest of the Church is very different from that of particular persons, as is that of the Government from particular servants.

As to our representations from hence, I suppose you have seen that of the Convocation and of the House of Lords concerning Mr. Molesworth.[1] The fact was thus, being in the Presence Chamber when the Convocation made their addresses, he saw Mr. Percival[2] with others at the head of the Lower House, who a few days before had appeared at the head of a riotous and mutinous mob with laurels in their hats;[3] this moved the spleen of the peevish man, and he whispered to one by him that "those that have turned the world upside down are likewise come hither"; some overheard him, and you see what a turn is given it.[4]

As to myself, I heartily opposed and protested against some votes in the House of Lords, particularly their sending two Lords to bring away the Council books without asking leave of the government,[5] which I called rapparee-

---

[1] *Supra*, p. 111, n. 3.   [2] *Supra*, p. 94, n. 1.

[3] According to the Whigs, Archdeacon Percival was one of "the principal fomenters and ringleaders" of the disastrous riot during the Dublin election (*supra*, p. 102). It is said that with several other clergymen he marched through the streets at the head of "a vast mob composed of Papists and the scum of the people," to whom he distributed laurels to be worn "as tokens of victory," and by his influence animated "a party already influenced by hot liquors and rage, to all the excesses that countenanced rioters armed with swords, clubs and staves could possibly proceed to" ("Mr. Molesworth's Preface, with Historical and Political Remarks, to which is added a True State of his Case with respect to the Irish Convocation," Lond., 1714).

[4] The Lower House of Convocation were successful in convincing the House of Lords that the words uttered by Molesworth were "an intolerable prophanation of the Holy Scriptures," and were used with a design of representing Convocation as "a turbulent and seditious body," but the adjournment of Parliament prevented the Lords doing justice to "that venerable assembly" for "a crime of this deep dye" (State Papers Ireland).

[5] When the proceedings with regard to the election of civic officers in the city of Dublin was under consideration in the House of Lords, two peers were sent while the House sat to bring the minute books from the Privy Council Chamber.

ing them and reckoned to be a great insult on the government and Crown, and an ill precedent. I likewise dissented
from their voting my Lord Chancellor to have acquitted himself with honour and integrity, in the several stations he
had been in;[1] because the Commons were then examining
into his management, and we had actually before us the
city business, and it seemed to me a prejudicing the matter
which we were to examine, and on which for ought we
knew an impeachment might come up the next day; nor
could I come into an address to her Majesty to continue
him, lest it might give a precedent to the Commons to address against him, as it actually did; for before they seemed
and indeed promised only to make a representation of their
grievances, and humbly lay them before her Majesty, and
refer themselves to her goodness for redress; but the Lords'
proceedings put them out of all patience, and made them
conclude, that it was no more a fault in them to address to
remove him, than in the Lords to continue him. Neither
did I like the handle taken to bring this matter before the
Lords. It was thus, one Crow, as I think his name is, was
by motion called before the House and gave evidence that
sometime in August last, one Nuttall, discoursing and indeed bantering with a child, spoke to the child scandalous
words of the Lord Chancellor, which I suppose you have
seen.[2] It appeared by the man's confession that he owed

---

[1] In an address conveying this vote to the Queen the Lords spoke
of Phipps as "a discerning and vigilant governor, an equal administerer
of justice, and a zealous assertor of the Prerogative," and asked her
Majesty not to suffer any evil report against him "to make an impression on her royal heart in his disfavour."

[2] The provincialism of the Irish Parliament at that period was very
marked, but was never more displayed than on the occasion to which
the Archbishop refers. From the Journals of the House of Lords it
appears that this august assembly sat for many hours in solemn state
hearing evidence respecting a conversation carried on between a
certain Richard Nuttall and an infant of three years, the son of one
Joseph Cooper. As various witnesses affirmed, the conversation opened
by Nuttall asking the infant prodigy whether he was a Whig or a
Tory, to which there was no response. Nuttall then inquired whether
he loved Dr. Sacheverell and the Lord Chancellor, to which the ex-
asperated infant replied that he did, and that Nuttall might be assured
he was a good churchman and true Protestant. Whereupon the re-
doubtable Nuttall committed the heinous offence of saying that the
infant was a prevaricating rascal, and that the Lord Chancellor was a
canary-bird and ought to be hanged for setting Ireland by the ears.

money to this Nuttall, and that he had a suit, then depending before my Lord Chancellor. In my own opinion these circumstances were such that they could not justly found such votes, besides I thought Nuttall ought to have been called and heard what he could say for himself, which could not be obtained. For my own part I know no wisdom, but truth and honesty; if these support me, well and good, but if not it will be my wisdom patiently to submit to the will of God, which has been the method I have taken all my life, and I hope no temptation shall ever prevail with me to forsake it in my old age. I could never understand the policy of governors taking on themselves the faults or odium of their servants, and there are many examples where it has produced ill consequences.

As to the Sheriffs calling in the guard to assist them when oppressed by a mob,[1] I am not lawyer enough to say anything to it, but I think there was something like it done in suppressing a mob when I was last in London; only not thirteen soldiers were wounded before they shot, and a great part of the crowd were [not] Papists, that had nothing to do there.

If you have a mind to see the depositions taken in the Lords' House, or the votes, let me know, and those and such other papers as I think may be for your diversion shall be sent you. I told you nobody can answer for a House of Commons, nor can I now engage they will give money. I believe if they sit again, which I do not expect, they will make a more regular, and, I hope, more mannerly representation of their grievances, but hope likewise they will not be so far enemies to themselves as to deny money. If you had seen what I have done, you would not wonder that what is done here is imputed to one man.[2]

CCXXXIV. [*Sheridan.*]

SIR CONSTANTINE PHIPPS TO SWIFT

Dublin, *January* 15, 1713-14.

DEAR SIR,

MANY of my letters from London tell me how much I am obliged to you for your friendly solicitation on my

---

[1] *Supra*, p. 102, n. 2.   [2] *I.e.*, to Lord Chancellor Phipps.

son's behalf, which will be always remembered by us both, with the same gratitude, as if it had succeeded.[1] I had congratulations from the Duke of Ormond, my Lord Bolingbroke, and others, on account of my son's having the place, for they sent me word it was actually done, and several other persons had letters of it, and our friends were extremely rejoiced at the well timing of it, and it was a great addition to the mortification of the Whigs, and the disappointment will be a cause of great joy to them. But in this, and in all other things, I submit to the judgement of my superiors, who know best what is fit to be done. As to looking out for anything else for my son, there is nothing else here, that I know is fit for him; and if anything worth his having falls in England, it will be disposed of before I can have notice of it.

We are told by everybody, that the rest of our vacant bishoprics[2] will be filled to our satisfaction; if they are, you must be one of them. But if you are resolved, that you will not yet *episcopari* there, give me leave to recommend to you an affair of my Lord Abercorn's, which is, that you would consent to the agreement the Vicars Choral have made with him for renewing his lease.[3] I am informed there are some misunderstandings between you. It is very unhappy there should be any difference between two such sure and great friends to the common cause. I do assure you, we are very much obliged to my Lord Abercorn for his great service in these times of difficulty; he is as good a friend as any in the world, and as bad an enemy; and I am very sure, if you would make him a compliment, and oblige him in this matter, you would gain an entire true friend of him for the future, and oblige a great many of your friends here, who have all a great value and esteem for him.

I heartily congratulate you on her Majesty's recovery, and the good effect it has had in uniting our friends.[4]

---

[1] *Supra*, p. 85.   [2] *Supra*, p. 104.   [3] *Supra*, p. 113.
[4] The Queen's life had been in great danger at Christmas. She was then at Windsor, and Bolingbroke, who was in attendance on her, evidently expected a fatal result, and wrote to Oxford in an imploring strain begging him to come there and share the responsibility ("Portland Manuscripts," v, 374). A week later Bolingbroke said that the Queen recovered "as fast and as well as an honest heart can wish," but the improvement, as Arbuthnot foresaw, was only a temporary rally (*ibid.*, pp. 376, 381).

That, together with the resolution that is taken to support
the Church interest,[1] will, without doubt, in a little time
render all things easy and quiet in both kingdoms; though
as yet our Whigs here are as obstinate and perverse as
ever. The Commons are resolved they will give no money
till I am removed;[2] and the aldermen will not own my
Lord Mayor, nor proceed to any election, notwithstanding
the opinion of all the judges here, and of the Attorney General,
and all the Queen's counsel, except Sir Joseph Jekyll,[3] in
England.[4]

I wish you many happy new years, and should be very
proud to receive your commands here, being, with the
utmost sincerity and esteem,

Your most obedient humble servant,

CON. PHIPPS.

CCXXXV. [*Sheridan.*]

THE EARL OF ANGLESEY TO SWIFT

Dublin, *January* 16, 1713-14.

MR. DEAN,[5]

YOU judged extremely right of me that I should with
great pleasure receive what you tell me, that my endeavours
to serve her Majesty in this kingdom are agreeable to my
Lord Treasurer, and the rest of the Ministers. I have
formerly so freely expressed to you the honour I must
always have for his Lordship, that I think I cannot explain

---

[1] This was the policy of which the outcome was the Schism Act,
and which resulted in the breach between Oxford and Bolingbroke.
To it Bolingbroke doubtless refers in writing to Oxford some weeks
previously when he says: " I see an opportunity of giving new strength,
new spirit to your administration, and of cementing a firmer union
between us, and between us and those who must support us " (*ibid.*,
p. 373).

[2] Beyond the temporary grant already made (*supra*, p. 109, n. 1).

[3]
" odd old Whig,
Who never changed his principles or wig."

[4] On a fresh representation (*supra*, p. 101) the English law officers
had agreed in the opinion of the Government's legal advisers in Ireland
that the Lord Mayor of Dublin could continue in office for another
year.

[5] The writer of this letter, Arthur, fifth Earl of Anglesey, to whom
there has been already more than one reference (*supra*, p. 55), was a
grandson of the first Earl, the minister and favourite of the Restoration Court. His father and two elder brothers had followed his grand-

myself more fully on that subject. But, what his Lordship has already done for the Church and the Church interest here, and what we have assurance will soon be done, will give his Lordship so entire a command in the affections of all honest men here, which are not a few, that I am persuaded, he will soon find Ireland an easy part of the administration. For, it is my firm opinion, that steady and vigorous measures will so strengthen the hands of our friends in both kingdoms, that after the efforts of despair, which never last long, are over, her Majesty and her Ministers will receive but little trouble from the faction, either on this or on your side of the water.

You are very kind to us in your good offices for Mr. Phipps, because a mark of favour so seasonably, as at this time, conferred on Lord Chancellor's son, will have a much greater influence, and reach farther than his Lordship's person.[1] I am preparing for my journey, and I hope I shall be able to lay such a state of this kingdom before my Lord Treasurer, as may prevent future disappointments when it shall be thought necessary to hold a Parliament. If this Parliament is not to sit after the present prorogation, I do think, were I with you, I could offer some reasons why the filling the vacant bishoprics should be deferred for a little time.[2] I praise God for his great goodness in restoring her

father in rapid succession, and the title had come to him unexpectedly three years before, shortly after the formation of the Tory Ministry. With Ireland the holders of the Anglesey title were connected as descendants of Lord Mountnorris, the victim of Strafford's imperious rule, and while visiting that country not long before his death, the fourth Earl, who is spoken of in the Journal to Stella as "the great support of the Tories," had made advances to Swift with the object apparently of inducing him to join that party ("Prose Works," ii, 11). This friendship served to introduce Swift to his successor. As the fifth Earl took soon a prominent place in the debates of the peers, who began to regard him as likely to be viceroy of Ireland, and was much in the counsels of the Tory leaders, Swift was frequently brought in contact with him, and was drawn towards him especially by his zealous churchmanship which a close connection with Cambridge University, as a fellow of Magdalene College and as a parliamentary representative, had fostered. In the previous autumn Anglesey had employed Swift to make his peace with Oxford for his defection in the summer ("Portland Manuscripts," v, 361), and now Swift had conveyed to him that Minister's appreciation of his exertions to further the interests of their party in Ireland, where Anglesey not only occupied a seat in the House of Lords but also held office as a Vice-Treasurer.

[1] *Supra*, p. 120.   [2] *Supra*, p. 121.

Majesty to her health: the blessing of which, if we had no other way of knowing, we might learn from the mortification it has given a certain set of men here.

I shall trouble you with no compliments, because I hope soon to tell you how much I am, dear Sir,

Yours,

ANGLESEY.

CCXXXVI. [*Original.*]

SWIFT TO ARCHDEACON WALLS

London, *February* 2, 1713-14.

SIR,

I HAVE some letters of yours to acknowledge, and a great deal of thanks to give you for your great care of my affairs. I shall be glad if you think it convenient, to begin paying my firstfruits, for the sooner I am out of debt, the better, and if you paid the Bishop of Dromore one hundred pounds to begin with, I should be pleased to think I had but two hundred pounds more to pay him till next year.

I came yesterday from Windsor with Lord Treasurer and thought the four bishoprics[2] would have been then disposed of; but he said nothing to me, so I conceive other business stopped it. We are here in odd circumstances. Few of the Whigs will allow the Queen to be alive, or at best that she can live a month. She yesterday writ a letter to the Lord Mayor concerning these reports[3] which I suppose will be printed in the Gazette of to-day; for I write this in the morning. Our stocks are fallen six or seven per cent., and it is a plain argument, how much they would fall if she really had died. She is now very well, sat in Council long on Sunday, and signed above forty papers yesterday for Lord Treasurer, and I hope she will be in town by the 16th at the opening of the Parliament.[4]

---

[1] In the possession of Mr. John Murray. See Preface.

[2] Raphoe, Derry, Kilmore, and Ardagh (*supra*, p. 123).

[3] In this letter the Queen announced her intention of opening Parliament in person, and expressed her hope that the citizens of London would put a stop to those malicious rumours which prejudiced the public credit and tranquillity. In writing to the Queen, Bolingbroke informed her that the conduct of the Whigs at that time displayed "the ingratitude and disloyalty" that "they always had at heart."

[4] Parliament met on the date named for the election of a Speaker, but the formal opening by the Queen did not take place until 2 March.

I have done all I could for Mr. Manley.[1] I have had abundance of ill-will by being his friend. I durst not ask directly to continue him but that he and his family might not starve. I said a great deal of this to Lord Treasurer a fortnight ago when I was with him alone in his coach going to Windsor, insomuch that when at supper there several were wishing to have him out, Lord Treasurer said openly the Dean is not of your opinion, etc. I have staved it off, as I believe, but it is impossible, I think, that he can hold it, and he would have been out two years ago, if I had not battled for him. Your arguments are pure ones: "He has lost a kind brother, etc." Why his brother was a beast and did him ten times more harm than good.[2] You know Mr. Manley has been the most violent party-man in Ireland, and what can be said in behalf of such a man.

My service to Gossip Doll. I hope my godchild is well. . . .[3]

Addressed—To the Reverend Mr. Archdeacon Walls at his house in Queen Street over against the Hospital, Dublin, Ireland.

[1] As Isaac Manley, the Postmaster of Ireland (*supra*, p. 67, n. 4), was like most of Stella's friends a Whig, the Tories naturally felt anxious in those days of post office inquisitiveness, as to the safety of such letters as passed through his hands. On the day this letter is dated, Shrewsbury, in writing to Oxford, refers to the fact that two letters from Oxford had not reached him, and observes that "it is new that two letters together from a Lord Treasurer of Great Britain to a Chief Governor of Ireland should miscarry when every private man's letter is safely delivered" ("Bath Manuscripts," i, 244). If we are to believe the author of "A Long History of a Short Session of a Certain Parliament," Manley was, however, the last person whom Shrewsbury was likely to suspect, since it is made a great grievance that Manley was chosen by the Viceroy to accompany him "to the Park, to the Strand, and to the Country," and was the "Controller of his Grace's Household and of his Closet Council."

[2] When telling Stella a year before that John Manley (*supra*, vol. i, p. 274, n. 3) could not "live a month," Swift had added that he would be a great loss to her friend, as he was one of his chief supports, and on several other occasions writes to the same effect ("Prose Works," ii, 19, 74, 191, 403). Possibly in the interval John Manley's relations with the fair editress of the "Examiner" had come to Swift's knowledge.

[3] Two lines are torn off here.

CCXXXVII. [*Original.*[1]]

SWIFT TO JOSHUA DAWSON

London, *February* 11, 1713-14.

SIR,

MY affairs not suffering me to return to Ireland as soon as I intended, I must desire the favour of you to renew my letters of absence for half a year longer, and I will order my agent, Mr. Parvisol, to attend you with the charges of it.[2] I think you told me that England was not expressed in the letters of absence, of which I am glad, because I would not be limited in point of place.[3]

The Queen was very well on Monday now last, and on her birthday entertained company above three hours. We are all doing as well as we can, and I hope the efforts will make you approve our management. Derry and Ossory[4] were disposed of last Monday, as I suppose you must know; the rest are yet deferred, though expected every week, but there are some difficulties, which I may tell you six months hence. I wish our friends of Ireland, both here and there, would be a little more unanimous in their characters, and some of them more charitable. It is impossible to please them all. You see I write in a most cursory style, but you may guess the reasons. I hope the Queen will be in town in a week. I am,

Your most obedient humble servant,

J. SWIFT.

Pray burn this, and let me know you have received it.

Addressed—To Joshua Dawson, Esq., at the Castle of Dublin, Ireland.

[1] In the possession of Mrs. Lambart of 66, Park Mansions, Knightsbridge, by whose kind permission it has been used for the purposes of this edition of the Correspondence.

[2] Dignitaries of the Church, as well as civil officials, were obliged then to obtain license from the chief governor for absence from Ireland, the most essential proceeding on the part of the applicant being the payment of fees to Dawson as permanent secretary (*supra*, p. 49, n. 4). When leaving Ireland Swift had paid £5 19s. 1d. for his license.

[3] Possibly Swift had in his mind the need of refuge if the authorship of the "Public Spirit of the Whigs," which was published on the opening of Parliament, became known.

[4] The bishopric of Derry (*supra*, p. 104, n. 3) was filled by the transla-

CCXXXVIII. [*Original.*[1]]

THE EARL OF PETERBOROUGH TO SWIFT

March 5 [O.S. *February* 22], 1713-14.

QUERIES for Dr. Swift, next Saturday, at dinner:

Whether any great man, or minister, has favoured the Earl of Peterborough with one single line since he left England;[2] for, as yet, he has not received one word from any of them, nor his friend of St. Patrick?

Whether, if they do not write till they know what to write, he shall ever hear from them?

Whether anything can be more unfortunate, than to be overcome when strongest, outwitted having more wit, and baffled having most money?[3]

Whether betwixt two stools the **** to the ground, Reverend Dean, be not a good old proverb, which may give subject for daily meditation and mortification?

I send thee lazy scribbler a letter from the extremities of the earth,[4] where I pass my time, admiring the humility and patience of that power heretofore so terrible; and the new scene which we see, to wit, the most Christian King

tion of the Bishop of Ossory (*supra*, vol. i, p. 192, n. 2), and in his room the Bishop of Killaloe, the eldest son of Archbishop Vesey, was appointed.

[1] In the British Museum. See Preface.

[2] During the short time Peterborough remained in England in 1711 (*supra*, vol. i, pp. 262-264) Swift had enjoyed his hospitality and revelled in the fine gardens at Parson's Green with their hot walls for grapes, but did not write to him during a subsequent long absence abroad, for which on his return Peterborough "chid him terribly," and Swift excused himself on the ground that a letter could not overtake the hangdog, so rapid were his movements. Peterborough made then a stay of unwonted length in England, and was one of the rabble who began to intrude at the Saturday dinners, to Swift's great disgust ("Prose Works," ii, *passim*). In the previous November Peterborough had been sent off again on a mission of compliment to the Duke of Savoy, who had become a King "by the help of Sicily" as Swift predicted (*supra*, vol. i, p. 347), and in the quiet of the Sicilian kingdom began to long for one of Swift's sallies to relieve the *ennui* of his situation.

[3] The peace of Rastadt, terminating the war between France and Germany, was concluded on 24 February, and to the situation between those countries and England, "the world of the moon," prior to that event Peterborough refers in this and the following paragraphs.

[4] *I.e.*, Sicily.

waiting with so great resignation and respect, to know the
Emperor's pleasure as to peace or war.

Where I reflect with admiration upon the politics of
those, who, breaking with the old allies, dare not make use
of the new ones; who, pulling down the old rubbish and
structure, do not erect a new fabric upon solid foundations.
But this is not so much to the purpose; for, in the world of
the moon, provided toasting continue, the Church and
State can be in no danger.

But, alas! in this unmerry country, where we have time
to .think, and are under the necessity of thinking, where
impiously we make use of reason, without a blind resignation to Providence, the bottle, or chance, what opinion
think you we have of the present management in the refined parts of the world, where there are just motives of
fear? When neither steadiness nor conduct appears, and
when the evil seems to come on apace, can it be believed,
that extraordinary remedies are not thought of?

Heavens! what is our fate? What might have been our
portion, and what do we see in the age we live in? France
and England, the Kings of Spain and Sicily, perplexed and
confounded by a headstrong youth;[1] one, who has lost so
many kingdoms by pride and folly; and all these powerful
nations at a gaze, ignorant of their destiny; not capable
of forming a scheme, which they can maintain, against a
Prince, who has neither ships, money, nor conduct. Some
of the ministers assisted and supported with absolute
power, others with a Parliament at their disposal, and the
most inconsiderable of them with the Indies at their tail.

And what do I see in the centre, as it were, of ignorance
and bigotry? The first request of a Parliament to their
King is to employ effectual means against the increase of
priests; the idle devourers of the fat of the land.[2] We see
churches, shut up by the order of the Pope,[3] set open by
dragoons, to the general content of the people. To con-

---

[1] The conqueror of the North, Charles XII of Sweden, who emerged
from his retreat in Turkey some months later.

[2] King Amadeus Victor revived the *Monarchia Sicula*, an ancient
tribunal which claimed supreme control over ecclesiastical affairs and
practically excluded the Pope from any authority over the church in
Sicily.

[3] Pope Clement XI answered the King's establishment of the *Monarchia* by bann and interdict.

clude, it fell out, that one of your acquaintance [1] found himself, at a great table, the only unexcommunicated person by his Holiness; the rest of the company eating and toasting, under anathemas, with the courage of a hardened heretic.

Look upon the piece I send you. See, nevertheless, what a sneaking figure he [2] makes at the foot of the parson. [3] Who could expect this from him? But he thinks, resolves, and executes.

If you can guess from whence this comes, address your letter to him, "à Messieurs Raffnel et Fretti Sacerdotti, Genoa."

Addressed—For the Reverend Dr. Swift, Dean of St. Patrick.

CCXXXIX. [*Original.*[4]]

THE EARL OF OXFORD TO SWIFT

Wednesday Night [*March* 3, 1713-14].

I HAVE heard, that some honest men, who are very innocent, are under trouble, touching a printed pamphlet. [5] A

---

[1] Berkeley, whom, on the recommendation of Swift, Peterborough had taken with him as chaplain, is said to have been the person indicated, but he remained in Italy while Peterborough went to Sicily and the allusion is probably to Peterborough himself.

[2] *I.e.*, the King of Sicily.

[3] This was apparently a cartoon upon the King's declining papal investiture on ascending the throne.

[4] In the British Museum. See Preface.

[5] Since his return from Ireland, Swift's irritation at the dissensions in the Ministry had been reflected in his writings, and after provoking violent outbursts against Burnet and Steele ("Prose Works," iii, 129; v, 283), had led him into a breach of the privileges of Parliament in his attack upon the Scotch peers in the "Public Spirit of the Whigs" (*ibid.*, v, 313), which had been published just a week before this letter was written. When the House of Lords had met on the preceding day (*supra*, p. 124, n. 4) the peers had voted the pamphlet, on the motion of Lord Wharton, to be "a false, malicious, and factious libel," and had made an order for the attachment of John Morphew the publisher, which had been followed that day by a further order for the attachment of John Barber the printer (see "Journals of the House of Lords"). In the course of the debate Oxford had protested that he

II   K

friend of mine, an obscure person, but charitable, puts the
enclosed bill in your hands, to answer such exigencies as
their case may immediately require. And I find he will do
more, this being only for the present. If this comes safe to
your hands, it is enough.

Endorsed by Swift—Lord Treasurer Oxford to me in a
  counterfeit hand with the bill when the printers were
  prosecuted by the House of Lords.[1]

CCXL. [*Original.*[2]]

SWIFT TO ARCHDEACON WALLS

London, *March* 6, 1713-14.

I THINK I writ to you since I heard from you. I am now
under a great deal of uneasy business which I hope to get
over;[3] in the mean time I must desire you to step to

knew nothing of the pamphlet, and, although the contrary has been
assumed, it is probable that none of Swift's political friends had read
the pamphlet before it was published. Apart from the fact that the
Ministers depended on the Scotch peers for their majority in the
House of Lords, and were more anxious to propitiate than to alienate
them, it seems to have been at once recognized that a breach of parliamentary privileges had been committed. Steps were immediately
taken to withdraw the first edition, and to substitute one in which the
reflections on the Scotch peers were omitted, which greatly discon-
certed Wharton when making his speech, as a copy, which, according
to his own account, had only just been put into his hand, and was the
first that he had seen, was found not to contain the objectionable
passages. In addition, in order to prevent his being subjected to inconvenient questioning by the peers, Barber was arrested by order of
the Secretary of State for Scotland, the Earl of Mar, and bound over by
Swift's friend, Erasmus Lewis, to answer his offence in a court of law,
and "if the worst came to the worst," the gossiping Peter Wentworth
tells us, a man had been secured to own the authorship and "to save
the Doctor's bacon" ("Wentworth Papers," p. 358, and "Portland
Manuscripts," v, 389).
  [1] Other endorsements state that the bill was for £100, that the letter
was received on 14 March, and that Swift was in London at the time.
The date is doubtless a mistake for 4 March.
  [2] In the possession of Mr. John Murray. See Preface.
  [3] On the previous day Morphew and Barber had been before the
House of Lords (*supra*, p. 129, n. 5), and on the motion of Lord
Wharton the examination of Barber had been adjourned to the next

Mr. Dawson at the Castle and let him know I writ to him above three weeks ago to renew my letter of absence,[1] which ends just about the end of February, the half year being then just out. I desired he would let me know he had received my letter, and had taken out a new licence for another half year; but I have not heard from him. I likewise writ to Parvisol with orders to pay Mr. Dawson the charges of the licence. Parvisol has writ to me this post but said nothing of that affair. Pray if it be not done already get it done now, and pay Mr. Dawson. I had a short letter from Dr. Raymond just now; I will write to him soon. I am in mighty haste but however give my service to our Doll and my godchild.

Yours

JONATH. SWIFT.

Addressed—To the Reverend Mr. Archdeacon Walls at his house in Queen Street over against the Hospital, Dublin, Ireland.

CCXLI. [*Original.*[2]]

SWIFT TO ARCHDEACON WALLS

London, *March* 27, 1714.[3]

I HAD yours of the 6th instant, and am much obliged to you for your care with Parvisol. As for the Bishop's

day, when nine of his employees were ordered to be in attendance. The proceedings were, however, then abruptly closed on the Earl of Mar informing the House that he had instituted criminal proceedings against Barber (" Journals of the House of Lords " and " Parliamentary History," vi, 1262). It is to this incident that Swift alludes in the lines :

> "While innocent he scorns ignoble flight,
> His watchful friends preserve him by a sleight."
> ("Poetical Works," ii, 165.)

[1] *Supra*, p. 126.
[2] In the possession of Mr. John Murray. See Preface.
[3] On the 9th of that month the Lords, after ordering Morphew and Barber to be discharged (*supra*, p. 130, n. 3), had resolved that the Queen should be asked to issue a proclamation offering a reward for the discovery of the author of "the scandalous libel." In order that " nothing might be wanting on their parts towards the discovery and

goods,[1] I can say nothing; if our Doll and Goody Stoyte and the St. Mary ladies would consult about what I should take and the price, I would be content, and leave it to them, but the St. Mary ladies being not in town, if our Doll and Stoyte would do it alone, I am satisfied. What can I do more at this distance; I am teasing about the bishoprics, but you rail at one another so, that it is hard to settle;[2] and besides we are not in a humour now to mind you, we are in a confounded situation at present; fit only to talk of some years hence by the fireside.[3] Your schemes about yourself are all splendid; is there no place on earth to fit you but Mala—what do you call it?[4] I know not whether Jephson will be dropped or no. . . .[5] My service to Gossip Doll, Goody Stoyte and Catherine.

Addressed—To the Reverend Mr. Archdeacon Walls over against the Blue Coat Hospital in Dublin.

punishing of so great a criminal," an address to that effect was approved by them two days later, but a proposition was negatived by a large majority that one of the grounds of the request should be the author's assumption of being in the secrets of the administration ("Wentworth Papers," p. 360). A proclamation offering a reward of £300 was in due course issued. The only response was a letter which will be found in Appendix VI, and which appears to have been a hoax.

[1] As already noticed (*supra*, p. 111, n. 4) Stearne had not yet surrendered the deanery house to Swift.

[2] *Supra*, p. 124, n. 2.

[3] A great crisis in the existence of the Ministry then took place. It was only bridged over by the spirit of the Queen, who refused to accept from Oxford his resignation. In a very remarkable letter, which it is possible was prompted by Swift, Oxford's brother implored him at that time to change his mode of living, and gives much ground for the view already taken by me (*supra*, p. 80, n. 2). He reminds his brother that "the indulgence that some very great men have shown in little passions or habits, scarce discerned by themselves till it was too late, has proved very fatal to them" ("Portland Manuscripts," v, 405).

[4] The reference is to Malahidert or Mulhuddert, as it is generally called, a parish adjoining that of Castleknock (*supra*, p. 67, n. 8), the rectory of which formed the corpse of a prebend in St. Patrick's Cathedral. The prebend was then held by the Hon. John Moore (*supra*, p. 45, n. 5), and Walls apparently hoped that in the ecclesiastical changes then pending, Moore might be promoted, and he might succeed to his stall.

[5] William Jephson, who held the deanery of Lismore for twenty years, was one of the persons suggested for elevation to the episcopal bench, but his promotion was opposed by Lord Anglesey, who alleged that he was deficient in learning and morals ("Portland Manuscripts,"

CCXLII. [*Original.*[1]]

THE DUCHESS OF ORMOND TO SWIFT

April 24, 1714.

BROTHER,[2]

I SHOULD sooner have thanked you for your letter, but that I hoped to have seen you here by this time.[3] You cannot imagine how much I am grieved, when I find some people I wish well to, run counter to their own interest, and give their enemies such advantages, by being so hard upon their friends as to conclude, if they are not without fault, they are not to be supported, or scarce conversed with.[4] Fortune is a very pretty gentlewoman; but how soon she may be changed, nobody can tell. Fretting her with the seeing all she does for people only makes them despise her, may make her so sick as to alter her complexion; but I hope our friends will find her constant, in spite of all they do to shock her; and remember the story of the arrows, that were very easily broke singly, but when tied up close together, no strength of man could hurt them.[5] But that you may never feel any ill consequences from whatever may happen, are the sincere wishes of, Brother,

Yours, with all sisterly affection.

v, 403). Portion of the sentence has been struck out, but words which remain, "as Meath, Tuam, etc., but we must divide the bishoprics," show that it had reference to Swift's scheme of severing Ardagh from Kilmore (*supra*, p. 104).

[1] In the British Museum. See Preface.

[2] This friendly mode of address, reminiscent of Ormond's connection with the Brothers' Club, shows that Swift's regard for the Duchess was fully reciprocated by her (*supra*, vol. i, p. 358).

[3] The Duchess may have been in attendance on the Queen at Kensington, or possibly was writing from Richmond, where Ormond owned then the Lodge which became subsequently a royal residence. In the Journal to Stella ("Prose Works," ii, 371) Swift alludes to dining at Richmond with the Duchess, and tells that he made the journey from London by boat.

[4] Swift was of opinion that the existence of the Ministry depended then on a good understanding between Oxford and Ormond ("Prose Works," v, 451), and no doubt plotted with the Duchess the best means to preserve it.

[5] To this suggestion the poem of the "Fagot" is attributed ("Poetical Works," ii, 166).

CCXLIII. [*Original*.[1]]

THE REV. JOHN GEREE TO SWIFT

Letcombe, *April* 24, 1714.

MR. DEAN,[2]

YESTERDAY was sennight arrived here very safe the noble present of wine you were pleased to make us, in a flask of which my wife[3] and I drank your health, after it was a little settled, and think it to be so extraordinary good, that we shall readily comply with your orders not to be too prodigal of it, nor produce it to any but our best friends.

We return you our most humble thanks for it; and wish you would give us leave to take it for an earnest, that you intend yourself to follow in a little time, and honour our poor habitation with your presence, where you will have a horse, and garden, and pretty good study of books, and the master and mistress entirely at your service; though I doubt that at last the happiness of entertaining such a guest as Mr. Dean must be owing to, what I dare not wish for, the divisions and misunderstandings at Court, which may drive him into these parts.

I am, Sir, extremely obliged to you for so frankly repeating the assurances you formerly gave me of your readiness and desire to do me some good offices with the Lord Chancellor; though I purposely declined any solicitations of this kind, for fear of being troublesome, especially since I was very well assured, that whenever a favourable opportunity should offer itself you would not be wanting to my interests.[4] In the mean time, Sir, I should be much obliged to you, if you would please to encourage my school, by

[1] State Papers, Ireland, in P.R.O. *Supra*, p. 73, n. 4.

[2] Geree, with whom Swift stayed that summer for many weeks, was a native of the town of Farnham, near Moor Park, and is said to have lived "in Sir William Temple's family" ("Portland Manuscripts," vii, 186). He was a graduate of Oxford, and had been given by Corpus Christi College, of which he had been a fellow, the living of Letcombe Bassett, near Wantage in Berkshire.

[3] Swift's advice had been asked about the marriage "when it was too late to break off" ("Prose Works," ii, 368).

[4] Harcourt, to whom Swift had spoken about Geree, had promised to give him "the first convenient living" (*ibid.*, p. 403).

LETCOMBE BASSETT RECTORY
From a photograph by Mr. T. Reveley

recommending some young gentlemen hither. I would certainly take all the care of them I could, and I think I might undertake to further them more in their learning for the time, than others do at the common, or even the great schools; partly on account of the method I take with them, and partly, of the small number I propose to have the charge of, which being but ten or twelve at the most, I shall have leisure to consider every one's capacity, and apply myself to it accordingly, making things plain to slower apprehensions, and setting forward those of more quick and pregnant parts, as fast as their genius will carry them.

I hope the mention of my taking young gentlemen to board will not frighten you from making this the place of your residence, whenever you think fit to retire, since I am confident you would find no manner of inconvenience from those I have already, which are only four, besides a nephew of mine, and those very orderly and good, and I want only the revenue, which more would supply me with, to make such conveniences about me, that my number when completed should not be offensive; and therefore I hope that this consideration will be no bar to the happiness of seeing you here, and that no other may be so, is the hearty wish of, Sir,

Your most obedient, most obliged, and most humble servant,

JOHN GEREE.

My wife, Sir, presents her humble service to you.

Addressed—To the Reverend the Dean of St. Patrick's present.

CCXLIV. [*Sheridan*.]

SWIFT TO THE EARL OF PETERBOROUGH

London, *May* 18, 1714.

MY LORD,

I HAD done myself the honour of writing to your Excellency, above a month before yours of March the 5th[1] came

[1] *Supra*, p. 127.

to my hands. The Saturdays' dinners have not been re-
sumed since the Queen's return from Windsor; and I am
not sorry, since it became so mingled an assembly, and of
so little use either to business or conversation;[1] so that I
was content to read your queries to our two great friends.
The Treasurer stuck at them all; but the Secretary acquitted
himself of the first, by assuring me he had often written to
your Excellency.

I was told, the other day, of an answer you made to
somebody abroad, who inquired of you the state and dispositions of our Court: that you could not tell, for you had
been out of England a fortnight. In your letter, you mention the world of the moon, and apply it to England; but
the moon changes but once in four weeks. By both these
instances, it appears you have a better opinion of our
steadiness than we deserve; for I do not remember, since
you left us, that we have continued above four days in the
same view, or four minutes with any manner of concert. I
assure you, my Lord, for the concern I have for the
common cause, with relation to affairs both at home and
abroad, and from the personal love I bear to our friends in
power, I never led a life so thoroughly uneasy as I do at
present.[2] Our situation is so bad, that our enemies could
not, without abundance of invention and ability, have
placed us so ill, if we had left it entirely to their management. For my own part, my head turns round; and after
every conversation, I come away just one degree worse
informed than I went. I am glad, for the honour of our
nation, to find by your Excellency's letter, that some other
Courts have a share of frenzy, though not equal, nor of the
same nature with ours. The height of honest men's wishes
at present is, to rub off this session, after which, nobody
has the impudence to expect, that we shall not immediately

---

[1] From the "Memoirs relating to that Change in the Queen's
Ministry" ("Prose Works," v, 384) it may be gathered that wine flowed
freely at Oxford's later "cabinet" dinners. It seems to be implied here,
and is definitely stated in the "Memoirs," that Peterborough was one
of the small number who originally formed the company at those
dinners, but elsewhere Swift says that the guests were at first confined
to Harcourt, Bolingbroke, Rivers, and himself (*cf. supra*, vol. i, p. 256,
and "Prose Works," ii, 413).

[2] Oxford had before that time found his credit with the Queen
"wholly at an end" (*ibid.*, v, 456), and distrusted almost every member
of his own Ministry.

fall to pieces; nor is anything I write the least secret, even to a Whig footman.

The Queen is pretty well at present, but the least disorder she has puts all in alarm; and when it is over we act as if she were immortal.[1] Neither is it possible to persuade people to make any preparations against an evil day. There is a negotiation now in hand, which, I hope, will not be abortive: the States-General are willing to declare themselves fully satisfied with the peace and the Queen's measures, etc., and that is too popular a matter to slight. It is impossible to tell you whether the Prince of Hanover intends to come over or not. I should think the latter, by the accounts I have seen; yet our adversaries continue strenuously to assert otherwise, and very industriously give out, that the Lord Treasurer is at the bottom; which has given some jealousies not only to his best friends, but to some I shall not name; yet I am confident they do him wrong.[2] This formidable journey is the perpetual subject both of Court and coffee-house chat.

Our mysterious and unconcerted ways of proceeding have, as it is natural, taught every body to be refiners, and to reason themselves into a thousand various conjectures. Even I, who converse most with people in power, am not free from this evil; and particularly, I thought myself twenty times in the right, by drawing conclusions very regularly from premises which have proved wholly wrong. I think this, however, to be a plain proof that we act altogether by chance; and that the game, such as it is, plays itself.

By the present enclosed in your Excellency's letter, I find the Sicilians to be bad delineators, and worse poets.[3]

---

[1] This phrase had been used some months before by Oxford in a conversation with Swift (" Prose Works," v, 451).

[2] The application made in the previous month by the Hanoverian minister for the writ, enabling the Electoral Prince to take his seat in the House of Lords in right of his dukedom of Cambridge had, to use his own expression, driven Oxford to the wall (" Portland Manuscripts," v, 440). If he gave the slightest encouragement to the Prince's visit his dismissal by Queen Anne was certain, while any sign of opposition would be interpreted at Hanover as proof of his adherence to the Pretender. According to his usual practice he sought the aid of his opponents to rescue him from his difficulty (*ibid.*, pp. 437, 440), and left it open to Bolingbroke and his friends to represent to the Queen that he was secretly favouring the project.

[3] *Supra*, p. 129.

As sneakingly as the Prince looks at the Bishop's foot, I
could have made him look ten times worse, and have done
more right to the piece, by placing your Excellency there,
representing your mistress the Queen, and delivering the
crown to the Bishop, with orders where to place it. I
should like your new King very well, if he would make
Sicily his constant residence, and use Savoy only as a
commendam. Old books have given me great ideas of that
island. I imagine every acre there worth three in England;
and that a wise prince, in such a situation, would, after
some years, be able to make what figure he pleased in the
Mediterranean.

The Duke of Shrewsbury, not liking the weather on our
side the water, continues in Ireland, although he formally
took his leave there six weeks ago.[1] Tom Harley is every
hour expected here, and writes me word, he has succeeded
at Hanover to his wishes. Lord Strafford writes the same,
and gives himself no little merit upon it.[2]

Barber, the printer, was, some time ago, in great distress,
upon printing a pamphlet, of which evil tongues would
needs call me the author: he was brought before your
House, which addressed the Queen in a body, who kindly
published a proclamation with three hundred pounds to
discover.[3] The fault was, calling the Scots "a fierce poor
northern people." So well protected are those who scribble
for the Government; upon which, I now put one query to
your Excellency: What has a man without employment to
do among Ministers, when he can neither serve himself, his
friends, nor the public?

In my former letter, which I suppose was sent to Paris
to meet you there, I gave you joy of the government of
Minorca.[4] One advantage you have of being abroad, that
you keep your friends; and I can name almost a dozen
great men, who thoroughly hate one another, yet all love
your Lordship. If you have a mind to preserve their friend-

---

[1] Adverse winds are alleged in the official correspondence to have
been the cause of Shrewsbury's delay in returning.

[2] Oxford's cousin, Thomas Harley, had been sent to Hanover in
the spring to assure that Court of the Government's good faith with
respect to the succession, and the Earl of Strafford was at the Hague.

[3] *Supra*, p. 131, n. 3.

[4] Peterborough's appointment as Governor of Minorca had been
announced in April. Owing to the death of Queen Anne he never
assumed the office.

ship, keep at a distance; or come over, and show your power, by reconciling at least two of them; and remember, at the same time, that this last is an impossibility. If your Excellency were here, I would speak to you without any constraint; but the fear of accidents in the conveyance of the letter, makes me keep to generals. I am sure you would have prevented a great deal of ill, if you had continued among us; but people of my level must be content to have their opinion asked, and to see it not followed; although I have always given it with the utmost freedom and impartiality. I have troubled you too much; and as a long letter from you is the most agreeable thing one can receive, so the most agreeable return would be a short one. I am ever, with the greatest respect and truth, my Lord,

Your Excellency's most obedient, and most humble servant.

CCXLV. [*Original.*[1]]

CHIVERTON CHARLETON TO SWIFT

May 22, 1714.

SIR,[2]

HEARING from honest John,[3] that you still persist in your resolution of retiring into the country,[4] I cannot but give you my thoughts of it, at the same time that I am sensible how intruding it may appear in me to trouble you with what I think; but you have an unlucky quality, which exposes you to the forwardness of those who love you, I mean good-nature, from which, though I did not always suspect you guilty of it, I now promise myself an easy

---

[1] In the British Museum. See Preface.
[2] Charleton held the office of Lieutenant of the Yeomen of the Guard. It would appear from the postscript that he had a connection with the Ormonds, and possibly he was writing from their Lodge at Richmond (*supra*, p. 133, n. 3).
[3] *I.e.*, John Barber.
[4] It is probable that in the interval between writing the letter to Peterborough and receiving the present one Swift had announced to Oxford and Bolingbroke at their last meeting in Lady Masham's rooms, his despair of any reconciliation between them and determination to leave London ("Prose Works," v, 456).

pardon. So that without being in much pain as to the censure you may pass upon my assurance, I shall go on gravely to tell you I am entirely against your design.

I confess a just indignation at several things, and particularly at the returns your services have met with, may give you a disgust to the Court; and that retirement may afford a pleasing prospect to you, who have lived so long in the hurry, and have borne so great a share of the load of business; and the more so at this juncture, when the distraction among your friends is enough to make any one sick of a courtier's life. But on these very accounts you should choose to stay, and convince the world that you are as much above private resentment, where the public is concerned, as you are incapable of being tired out in the service of your country; and that you are neither afraid nor unwilling to face a storm in a good cause.

It is true, you have less reason than any one I know, to regard what the world says of you; for I know none, to whom the world has been more unjust. Yet, since the most generous revenge is to make the ungrateful appear yet more ungrateful, you should still persecute the public with fresh obligations; and the rather, because some there are of a temper to acknowledge benefits; and it is to be hoped the rest may not always continue stupid. At least, suppose the worst, the attempt to do good carries along with it a secret satisfaction, with which if you are not sensibly affected, I am at a loss how to account for many of your actions. I remember very well, what you have sometimes said upon this subject, as if you were now grown useless, etc.; to which I have this to answer, that though your efforts are in vain to-day, some unforeseen incident may make them otherwise to-morrow; and that, should you by your absence lose any happy opportunity, you will be the first to reproach yourself with running away, and be the last man in the world to pardon it.

If I denied self-interest to be at the bottom of all I have said, I know you would think I lied villanously, and perhaps not think amiss neither; for I still flatter myself with the continuance of that favour you have on many occasions been pleased to show me; and am vain enough to fancy I should be a considerable loser, if you were where I could not have an opportunity of clubbing my shilling with you now and then at good eating. But as much as I am con-

cerned on this account, I am not so selfish to say what I
have done, if it were not my real opinion; which, whether
you regard or not, I could not deny myself the satisfaction
of speaking it, and of assuring you, that I am, with the
utmost sincerity and respect, Sir,
Your most obliged, and most faithful humble servant,
CH. CHARLETON.

My Lady Duchess, I can answer for her, is very much
your servant, though I have not her commands to say so.
She is gone to see the Duke of Beaufort, who is so ill it is
feared he cannot recover.[1] She went away this morning so
early, I have had no particular account how he is; but am
told, he does nothing but doze. The messenger came to
her at three in the morning; and she went away immediately afterwards. Lady Betty[2] desires me to thank you
for your letter, and would be glad, since the Provost is
graciously pleased to stay her Majesty's time,[3] to know
where it is he designs to stay. Honest Townshend and I
have the satisfaction to drink your health as often as we do
drink together. Whether you approve of your being toasted
with the Bishop of London,[4] and such people, I cannot tell;
but at present we have disposed you in the first list of rank
Tories. A servant is just now come from the Duchess of
Ormond, and gives such an account of the Duke of Beaufort,
that it is thought he cannot possibly recover.[5]

---

[1] Henry, second Duke of Beaufort, who was the Duchess of
Ormond's nephew, died two days later. Although he had been married
no less than three times, he was only thirty years of age at the time of
his death. He had been ordered abroad for his health some years
before by the great Radcliffe, and Lady Strafford, who attributed his
illness to self-indulgence, holds his fate up to her husband as an awful
warning ("Wentworth Papers," *passim*). In opposition to the wishes
of Swift, who had an antipathy to "boys," he had been elected a
member of the Brothers' Club ("Prose Works," ii, 349).
[2] Ormond's only surviving child.
[3] Provost Pratt had been promised one of the vacant bishoprics and
had evidently determined not to leave London until it was given to him.
[4] Bishop Robinson, the Utrecht plenipotentiary (*supra*, vol. i, p. 315),
had been translated from Bristol to London.
[5] The Duke of Beaufort is said to have died at Badminton, but this
seems improbable, as that seat is over a hundred miles from London,
and the journey there and back can hardly have been made in one day.

CCXLVI. [*Scott.*]

Swift to Miss Esther Vanhomrigh

Upper Letcombe, near Wantage, in Berkshire,
June 8, 1714.[1]

You see I am better than my word, and write to you
before I have been a week settled in the house where I
am.[2] I have not much news to tell you from hence, nor
have I had one line from any body since I left London, of
which I am very glad. But, to say the truth, I believe I
shall not stay here so long as I intended. I am at a clergyman's house, an old friend and an acquaintance, whom I
love very well; but he is such a melancholy thoughtful
man, partly from nature, and partly by a solitary life, that
I shall soon catch the spleen from him.[3] Out of ease and
complaisance, I desire him not to alter any of his methods
for me; so we dine exactly between twelve and one, at

---

[1] Swift had taken the plunge that he had meditated for many weeks,
and had retired to the quiet of Geree's rectory (*supra*, p. 134). On that
day week, Monday, 1 June, he had left London and had travelled by
coach as far as Oxford, where he stayed several days. As one of the
Canons of Christ Church wrote to Oxford's son, Lord Harley ("Portland
Manuscripts," vii, 186), there was great mystery about Swift's movements while in Oxford, and little was known about them except that
he had set out for Letcombe on Thursday morning attended by his
servant "with a portmanteau big enough to contain his library as
well as his equipage."

[2] During Swift's absence in Ireland Vanessa's passion for him
became uncontrollable. The suspicion that he enjoyed there a happiness inconsistent with her own (*supra*, p. 51), and the coldness of his
reply to her ardent letters, drove her to distraction, and evoked on his
return to London the declaration of her love as described in "Cadenus
and Vanessa," which was written during one of his visits to Windsor
in the preceding autumn. Although

> "What success Vanessa met,
> Is to the world a secret yet,"

there can be no question from the tone of this letter that their intimacy had not become less.

[3] "By what I hear the Dean will be at full liberty to converse with
himself and to sort his papers without any interruption from his landlord," says Lord Harley's friend ("Portland Manuscripts," vii, 186), "and
will be obliged for his entertainment to his own reflections."

eight we have some bread and butter and a glass of ale, and at ten he goes to bed. Wine is a stranger, except a little I sent him, of which, one evening in two, we have a pint between us. His wife has been this month twenty miles off, at her father's, and will not return these ten days. I never saw her, and perhaps the house will be worse when she comes. I read all day, or walk, and do not speak as many words as I have now writ, in three days; so that, in short, I have a mind to steal to Ireland, unless I feel myself take more to this way of living, so different, in every circumstance, from what I left.[1] This is the first syllable I have writ to anybody since you saw me. I shall be glad to hear from you, not as you are a Londoner, but a friend; for I care not threepence for news, nor have heard one syllable since I came here. The Pretender, or Duke of Cambridge,[2] may both be landed, and I never the wiser. But if this place were ten times worse, nothing shall make me return to town while things are in the situation I left them. I give a guinea a week for my board, and can eat anything. I hope you are in good health and humour. My service to Moll. My cold is quite gone.

A vous, etc.

Addressed—To Mrs. Esther Vanhomrigh, at her lodgings over against the Surgeon's in Great Rider Street, near St. James's Street.

---

[1] The rectory house at Letcombe Bassett, which lies near the Vale of the White Horse, dates from the seventeenth century, and according to tradition "Some Free Thoughts upon the Present State of Affairs" was composed under the shade of a superb mulberry tree which overhangs the garden. As I learn from the Rev. E. M. Walker, Fellow of Queen's College, Oxford, and Rector of the parish of Besselsleigh in Berkshire, a portion of the garden wall is a fine specimen of early eighteenth century brickwork; in a later addition there is a brick with the initials D. G. and the date 1756. The church, he says, is of Norman architecture, and consisted originally of a nave with a chancel half its size, and a low tower. About fifty years ago a south aisle and vestry were added, and the tower was raised. There is a tradition at Letcombe, where the recollection of Swift's residence is still cherished, that Swift used to ride into Oxford almost every day, but his letters show that this was not the case.

[2] *Supra*, p. 137, n. 2.

CCXLVII. [*Original.*[1]]

JOHN GAY TO SWIFT

London, *June* 8, 1714.

SIR,[2]

SINCE you went out of the town, my Lord Clarendon was appointed Envoy Extraordinary to Hanover in the room of Lord Paget;[3] and by making use of those friends, which I entirely owe to you, he has accepted me for his secretary. This day, by appointment, I met his Lordship at Mr. Secretary Bromley's office;[4] he then ordered me to be ready by Saturday. I am quite off from the Duchess of Monmouth.[5] Mr. Lewis was very ready to serve me upon this occasion, as were Dr. Arbuthnot and Mr. Ford.[6] I am every day attending my Lord Treasurer for his bounty, in order to set me out; which he has promised me upon the following petition, which I sent him by Dr. Arbuthnot:

The epigrammatical petition of John Gay.

I'm no more to converse with the swains,
But go where fine people resort:

---

[1] In the British Museum. See Preface.

[2] Although he had only lately become acquainted with Swift (*supra*, p. 98, n. 3), Gay had been for some years one of his admirers, and, in "The State of Wit," had commended his conduct of the "Examiner," praise which was not appreciated by Swift, as he was under the impression it came from a Whig (" Prose Works," ii, 176).

[3] The substitution of Lord Clarendon for Lord Paget was supposed at the time to have been connected with the dissensions at Court, and to have been a stroke of Bolingbroke's to ingratiate himself with the Queen by preferring one who was her relation (" Wentworth Papers," p. 387). The real reason of the change was that Paget was unwilling to go to Hanover until he had received a step in the peerage, for which he had to wait the advent of George I, who created him Earl of Uxbridge ("Portland Manuscripts," v, *passim*). Clarendon, who was the third of his line, did not inherit the ability of his predecessors, and while holding the governorship of New York, in which he had preceded Hunter, had made himself ridiculous by assuming the dress of a woman in order to represent the Queen more exactly.

[4] *Supra*, p. 67.

[5] Gay had held the position of secretary to the widow of the Duke of Monmouth, who persisted apparently in using that forfeited honour instead of the title of Duchess of Buccleuch, which she held in her own right.

[6] *Supra*, p. 53.

> One can live without money on plains,
> But never without it at Court.
> If, when with the swains I did gamble,
> I array'd me in silver and blue;[1]
> When abroad, and in Courts I shall ramble,
> Pray, my Lord, how much money will do?

We had the honour of the Treasurer's company last Saturday, when we sat upon Scriblerus.[2] Pope is in town, and has brought with him the first book of Homer.

I am this evening to be at Mr. Lewis's with the Provost, Mr. Ford, Parnell, and Pope.[3] It is thought my Lord Clarendon will make but a short stay at Hanover. If it was possible, that any recommendation could be procured to make me more distinguished than ordinary, during my stay at that Court, I should think myself very happy, if you could contrive any method to procure it; for I am told, that their civilities very rarely descend so low as to the secretary. I have all the reason in the world to acknowledge this as wholly owing to you. And the many favours I have received from you purely out of your love for doing good, assures me you will not forget me in my absence. As for myself, whether I am at home or abroad, gratitude will always put me in mind of the man, to whom I owe so many benefits. I am

Your most obliged humble servant,

J. GAY.

Addressed—For the Reverend Dr. Swift, Dean of St. Patrick's.

[1] *Supra*, p. 98.

[2] The club, which was formed to write the memoirs of Martinus Scriblerus, used to meet in St. James's Palace, and must have come into existence subsequent to the Queen's arrival there in February to open Parliament. The members were Arbuthnot, Gay, Parnell, Pope, and Swift, and Oxford attended sometimes as a guest. See Appendix VII.

[3] As appears from this and subsequent letters, since December Swift had seen much of Pope and Gay, as well as of Parnell, who had soon followed him from Ireland (*supra*, p. 67), and of Provost Pratt, who was looking for a bishopric (*supra*, p. 141). But his closest friends were Arbuthnot, Lewis, and Ford. With the Duke of Ormond and his family Swift had also become much more intimate.

CCXLVIII. [*Original.*[1]]

JOHN BARBER TO SWIFT

London, *June* 8, 1714.

DEAR SIR,

I HAVE enclosed all the letters that have come to my hands. I saw my Lord Treasurer to-day, who asked me where you were gone? I told his Lordship you were in Berkshire. He answered: "It is very well; I suppose I shall hear from him." My Lord Bolingbroke was very merry with me upon your journey, and hoped the world would be the better for your retirement, and that I should soon be the midwife. The Schism Bill was read the second time yesterday, and committed for to-morrow, without a division.[2] Everybody is in the greatest consternation at your retirement, and wonders at the cause. I tell them, it is for your health's sake. Mr. Gay is made secretary to my Lord Clarendon, and is well pleased with his promotion. The Queen is so well, that the Sicilian ambassador has his audience to-night. She can walk, thank God, and is well recovered. . . .[3]

Your most obedient humble servant,

TYRANT.[4]

I forgot to tell you that I saw Mr. Harley,[5] who told me he would instantly send for the horse from Herefordshire,

---

[1] In the British Museum. See Preface.

[2] This famous act, which excluded anyone not professing the doctrines of the Church of England from the calling of a teacher, had passed the House of Commons by a large majority, but was only carried in the House of Lords on the third reading by five votes. It was in the debate on the second reading that the Earl of Nottingham spoke of Swift "as a divine who is hardly suspected of being a Christian," and gave expression to his horror at the idea of giving unlimited power over education to such a man.

[3] A sentence has been obliterated; the only words that remain are "as does Sir." Over this sentence some other words have been written, all that can be read are, "consent, I will appoint the happy day."

[4] Sir Walter Scott is responsible for the following note: "most persons who have had to do with the press, can assign good reasons for distinguishing its directors by the tremendous epithet assumed by Barber."

[5] Oxford's cousin, Thomas Harley (*infra*, p. 155, n. 5).

but that, being at grass, he had ordered his man not to ride hard; but that you should have him with all convenient speed.

CCXLIX. [*Original.*[1]]

SWIFT TO ARCHDEACON WALLS

June 11, 1714.

I THINK it is long since I wrote to you[2] or you to me; I am now retired into the country, weary to death of Courts and Ministers and business and politics; I hope to be in Ireland if possible by the end of the summer, sooner I cannot having many papers to look over and settle while I am here. I was six weeks compassing the great work of leaving London and did it at last abruptly enough; but go I would, the reasons I may live to tell you or perhaps you will guess them by their effects before I see you. I shall say no more but that I care not to live in storms when I can no longer do service in the ship and am able to get out of it. I have gone through my share of malice and danger, and will be as quiet the rest of my days as I can, so much for politics.

I should hope Parvisol might have paid in enough to discharge the Bishop of Dromore three hundred pounds. He set the tithes of the deanery for four hundred and thirty pounds, of which I had thirty pounds. My other livings cannot be much less, I hope, than two hundred pounds, of which one hundred and forty or one hundred and fifty pounds may come to my share after paying Warburton and other things, and he had large arrears upon Laracor, of which I think you sent me word he had brought in some part.[3] Here is above five hundred pounds besides the arrears; and I never had one bill from him since I came here, but have lived upon some other money I brought over with me, upon a little principal I melted, and some interest I received and money I have borrowed; and the rest upon the revenues of our two friends at Trim

---

[1] In the possession of Mr. John Murray. See Preface.
[2] *Supra*, p. 131.
[3]   "And Parvisol discounts arrears
        By bills, for taxes and repairs."
            ("Poetical Works," ii, 162.)

which I received here and gave them bills on Parvisol,
which article (with twenty pounds I now give them bills
for in the enclosed, though I have not yet received the
money out of the Exchequer) will not amount I am sure
to one hundred pounds. So that he ought to have paid you
in above four hundred pounds, unless he hath suffered the
farmers of the deanery to run in arrear, which under the
late Dean they never used to do. As for the land-rents of
the deanery I have ordered Parvisol not to receive them,
nor design to do it till I examine into the leases which
shall be as soon as I come over.

I have in the [South Sea Stock one thousand pounds]
which belongs to three friends but left to my management;
it is worth now about . . . English, for it has fallen of late,
and that returned to Ireland with a little addition would
make. . . . To tell you a secret, I think as times are like to
be, I should be glad to have my money in another place,
and would willingly make some purchase in Ireland if I
could hear of any between Dublin and Trim or near thereabouts; and if you would join with me, we would purchase
together and you should either have the land for security
or be a joint purchaser as you pleased. This I say because I
think you have told me that your money lies in several
hands at interest which is liable to accidents; if you approve
of this, pray enquire; if not do it for me, and I will purchase
for myself as far as one thousand or fifteen hundred pounds;
because I could borrow money on the land and pay it by
degrees or pay the interest as I pleased. But when you
enquire name no names.

I have sent over six boxes with books by long sea; I
suppose they will come in a little time; pray be so kind to
leave word for them at the Custom House; your neighbour
Craven will do me that good office. You must pay the
freight of them, but let them lie in the Custom House till
I come over, because I will wrangle hard about the custom,
for they are all old books and half of them very bad ones,
bought at auctions, only to make a show as a Dean of
St. Patrick's should. My service to Gossip Doll. I hope
my godchild is well, and pray give my service to Alderman Stoyte, and Goody, and Catherine, and Mr. Manley
and lady.[1]

[1] *Supra*, p. 67.

Tell Dr. Synge[1] I have his letter of May 24th just now come to me. I will answer it in some time. At present you may let him know that I am fully resolved to call the Vicars to account to the utmost I am able.[2] He wants to see the books belonging to the Dean and Chapter. I know not who has the key of the cabinet, in which cabinet I suppose is the key of some chest of drawers where the books are; I believe either you or Mrs. Brent[3] has it, pray see. He tells me Mr. Fetherston[4] is gone to Lusk, and that my sermons cost twenty shillings every five weeks; very dear that. Doll and you shall pay for it.

Yours, etc.

Addressed—To the Reverend Mr. Archdeacon Walls, over against the Hospital in Queen Street, Dublin.

CCL. [*Aitken's Life of Arbuthnot.*[5]]

SWIFT TO JOHN GAY

June 12, 1714.

I WONDER how you could have the impudence to know where I am.[6] I have this post writ to Mr. Harley, who is just come from Hanover,[7] to desire he would give you a letter. I have described you to him, and told him I would write to you to wait on him, which will do you no hurt neither about your affair in the Treasury. You begin to be an able courtier, which I know from two instances: first for giving me thanks for your preferment, to which I only contributed by saying to Dr. Arbuthnot and Mr. Lewis

---

[1] *Supra*, p. 76.   [2] *Supra*, p. 113.
[3] Swift's factotum in Dublin.

[4] Fetherston (*supra*, p. 70, n. 2) had apparently preached in Swift's place, and his absence necessitated the employment of a more expensive substitute. Lusk lies in the northern part of the County of Dublin, on the coast, and is notable for a round tower and the remains of an Early English church.

[5] For permission to include this letter, and others from the same source, the editor is indebted to the Oxford University Press, and to Mr. George A. Aitken, to whose valuable edition of the Journal to Stella there has been more than one reference.

[6] *Supra*, p. 144.

[7] *I.e.*, Oxford's cousin, Thomas Harley (*infra*, p. 155, n. 5).

that I wished it; secondly for wheedling my Lord Treasurer with an epigram, which I like very well, and so I am sure will he, and I reckon you will succeed. But pray learn to be a manager, and pick up language as fast as you can, and get Aristotle upon politics, and read other books upon government, Grotius de Jure Belli et Pacis, and accounts of negotiations and treaties, etc.; and be a perfect master of the Latin, and be able to learn everything of the Court where you go; and keep correspondence with Mr. Lewis, who if you write letters worth showing, will make them serviceable to you with Lord Treasurer; and take Mr. Lewis's advice in all things, and do not despise mine, and so God bless you, and make you able to make my fortunes. I am glad Mr. Pope has made so much despatch. My service to him and the Parnellian.[1]

CCLI. [*Original.*[2]]

JOHN ARBUTHNOT TO SWIFT

St. James's, *June* 12, 1714.

DEAR BROTHER,

I AM glad your proud stomach is come down, and that you submit to write to your friends. I was of opinion, that if they managed you right, they might bring you to be fond even of an article of the Post-boy or Flying Post.[3] As for the present state of our Court affairs, I thank God, I am almost as ignorant as you are to my great ease and comfort. I have never inquired about anything, since my Lady Masham told the Dragon,[4] that she would carry no

---

[1] *I.e.*, the poet Parnell (*supra*, p. 145).

[2] In the British Museum. See Preface.

[3] These newspapers were doubtless regarded by Swift with equal contempt, but as the organ of his own party the "Post-boy" had to be tolerated, and anathemas reserved for the "Flying Post." In the "Dunciad" the editors are bracketed:

> "There Ridpath, Roper, cudgelled might ye view;
> The very worsted look black and blue."

[4] *I.e.*, Oxford. In a note in Swift's handwriting on a later letter, Oxford is said to have been "so called by the Dean by contraries, for he was the mildest, wisest, and best Minister that ever served a Prince."

more messages, nor meddle nor make, etc.[1] I do not know whether things were quite so bad when you went. The Dragon manages this Bill pretty well, for you know that it is his *forte*;[2] and I believe, at the rate they go on, they will do mischief to themselves, and good to nobody else.

You know that Gay goes to Hanover, and my Lord Treasurer has promised to equip him. Monday is the day of departure; and he is now dancing attendance for money to buy him shoes, stockings, and linen.[3] The Duchess has turned him off,[4] which, I am afraid, will make the poor man's condition worse, instead of better.

The Dragon was with us on Saturday night last,[5] after having sent us really a most excellent copy of verses. I really believe when he lays down, he will prove a very good poet. I remember the first part of his verses was complaining of ill usage, and at last he concludes:

> He that cares not to rule, will be sure to obey,
> When summon'd by Arbuthnot, Pope, Parnell, and Gay.

Parnell has been thinking of going chaplain to my Lord Clarendon; but they will not say whether he should or not. I am to meet our club at the Pall Mall coffee-house, about one to-day, where we cannot fail to remember you. The Queen is in good health; much in the same circumstances with the gentleman I mentioned, in attendance upon her Ministers for something she cannot obtain. My Lord and

---

[1] Swift attributes Oxford's loss of favour with the Queen chiefly to that Minister's disregard of Lady Masham, whose influence with the Queen he sought rather to lessen than "to cultivate or preserve" ("Prose Works," v, 449). In spite of her relationship to Oxford, Lady Masham had by degrees become alienated from him, and during the cabinet crisis in March (*supra*, p. 132, n. 3) had been very indignant with Oxford for asking her to convey his threat of resignation to the Queen ("Portland Papers," v, 403).

[2] On the following day the Schism Bill (*supra*, p. 146, n. 2) was read a third time in the Lords. Oxford abstained from voting. His conduct with respect to that measure, highly ambiguous and irresolute as it was, has received from posterity a very different judgement to that of Arbuthnot, and has been said to have "sealed his political ruin" (Stanhope's "Hist. of England," i, 119).

[3] The date of Arbuthnot's letter fell on a Saturday. On Thursday Gay had written to Oxford reminding him of "his Shepherd's petition" (*supra*, p. 144), and of the short time before his departure ("Portland Manuscripts," v, 457).

[4] *Supra*, p. 144.

[5] At a meeting of the Scriblerus Club (*supra*, p. 145).

my Lady Masham, and Lady Fair,[1] remember you kindly; and none with more sincere respect than
Your affectionate brother and humble servant,
JO. ARBUTHNOT.

Addressed—For the Reverend the Dean of St. Patrick's.

CCLII. [*Aitken's Life of Arbuthnot.*[2]]

SWIFT TO JOHN ARBUTHNOT

June 16, 1714.

DEAR BROTHER,

MY stomach is prouder than you imagine, and I scorned to write till I was writ to. I have already half lost the ideas of Courts and Ministers. I dine between twelve and one, and the whole house is abed by ten and up at six. I drink no wine, and see but one dish of meat. I pay a guinea a week for dieting and lodging myself and man with an honest clergyman of my old acquaintance, and my paying is forced, for he has long invited me. I did not know till last night that the Princess Sophia was dead,[3] when my landlord and I chanced to pay a visit to a farmer in a neighbouring village, and was told so over a mug of ale, by a brisk young fellow just come from London, who talked big and looked on us with great contempt. I thank you for your kindness to poor Gay. Was the money paid, or put off till the day after he went?[4] I reckon by what you tell me that it is now a high season to be very merry in Lady Fair's[5] lodgings. I heartily pity you in particular. Look after your mistress and yourself, grow rich, and since nothing better can be done, let the world *vadere*.

I have a mind to live in Yorkshire for a year,[6] in order to put myself out of memory and debt. The fashion of this

---

[1] *I.e.*, Lady Masham's sister, Alice Hill (*supra*, vol. i, p. 350).
[2] It is also printed in Peter Cunningham's edition of Johnson's "Lives of the Poets," iii, 203, but the version given by Mr. Aitken (*supra*, p. 149, n. 5), who had access to the original, is far more accurate.
[3] The Electress died on 28 May.   [4] *Supra*, p. 144.
[5] *I.e.*, Lady Masham's sister, *supra*, n. 1.
[6] This idea had probably its origin in his knowledge of the connection of his family with that county (" Prose Works," xi, 367).

world passeth away: however, I am angry at those who disperse us sooner than there was need. I have a mind to be very angry, and to let my anger break out in some manner that will not please them at the end of a pen.[1] I wish you could get Lady M[asham] to give you those hints [2] we have often spoke of, and to muster up your own; for the Dragon,[3] I despair he will do that any more than anything else, and indeed you are all of you Dragons more or less, for I am sure it is above three years since I have spoke to Lady M[asham] and you about this. My humble service to my Lord and her, whom I love as much as you do, though I have greater obligations to them, and my humble services and thanks to the Qu[een] of Prudes [4] for remembering me.

You are a set of people drawn almost to the dregs; you must try another game; this is at an end. Your Ministry is fourscore and ten years old, and all you can endeavour at is an euthanasia, or rather it is in a deep consumption at five-and-twenty. I approve Lady M[asham]'s conduct, and think all she can now do in relation to the Dragon is to be passive; for the rest to cultivate her own credit to the utmost. Writing to you much would make me stark mad; judge his condition who has nothing to keep him from being miserable but endeavouring to forget those for whom he has the greatest value, love, and friendship. But you are a philosopher and a physician, and can overcome by your wisdom and your faculty those weaknesses which other men are forced to reduce by not thinking on them. Adieu, and love me half so well as I do you.

---

[1] His "Free Thoughts upon the Present State of Affairs" ("Prose Works," v, 396) was then contemplated if not actually begun, and this passage is worthy of notice as showing the spirit in which it was written.

[2] With respect to the circumstances which attended "the great change of employments" while he was in Ireland (*ibid.*, v, 364-366). This information Swift desired not for the "Free Thoughts," but for the history of the reign of Queen Anne, which he proposed also to write at that time.

[3] *I.e.*, Oxford (*supra*, p. 150, n. 4).

[4] *I.e.*, Lady Masham's sister (*supra*, p. 152, n. 1).

CCLIII. [*Elwin.*]

ALEXANDER POPE TO SWIFT

June 18, 1714.

WHATEVER apologies it might become me to make at any other time for writing to you, I shall use none now, to a man who has owned himself as splenetic as a cat in the country. In that circumstance, I know by experience, a letter is a very useful, as well as amusing thing. If you are too busied in state affairs to read it, yet you may find entertainment in folding it into divers figures, either doubling it into a pyramidical, or twisting it into a serpentine form, to light a pipe; or if your disposition should not be so mathematical, in taking it with you to that place where men of studious minds are apt to sit longer than ordinary, where, after an abrupt division of the paper, it may not be unpleasant to try to fit and rejoin the broken lines together. All these amusements I am no stranger to in the country, and doubt not but by this time you begin to relish them, in your present contemplative situation.

I remember a man, who was thought to have some knowledge in the world, used to affirm, that no people in town ever complained they were forgotten by their friends in the country: but my increasing experience convinces me he was mistaken, for I find a great many here grievously complaining of you upon this score. I am told farther, that you treat the few you correspond with in a very arrogant style, and tell them you admire at their insolence in disturbing your meditations, or even inquiring of your retreat: but this I will not positively assert, because I never received any such insulting epistle from you. My Lord Oxford says you have not written to him once since you went; but this perhaps may be only policy, in him or you; and I, who am half a Whig, must not entirely credit anything he affirms. At Button's [1] it is reported you are gone to Hanover, and that Gay goes only on an embassy to you. Others apprehend some dangerous state treatise from your retirement,

---

[1] The coffee-house to which Addison and his "little senate" resorted.

and a wit who affects to imitate Balzac,[1] says, that the Ministry now are like those heathens of old who received their oracles from the woods. The gentlemen of the Roman Catholic persuasion are not unwilling to credit me, when I whisper that you are gone to meet some Jesuits commissioned from the Court of Rome in order to settle the most convenient methods to be taken for the coming of the Pretender. Dr. Arbuthnot is singular in his opinion, and imagines your only design is to attend at full leisure to the life and adventures of Scriblerus.[2] This, indeed, must be granted of greater importance than all the rest, and I wish I could promise so well of you. The top of my own ambition is to contribute to that great work, and I shall translate Homer by the by. Mr. Gay has acquainted you what progress I have made in it.[3] I cannot name Mr. Gay, without all the acknowledgments which I shall ever owe you on his account. If I writ this in verse, I would tell you, you are like the sun, and while men imagine you to be retired or absent, are hourly exerting your indulgence, and bringing things to maturity for their advantage. Of all the world, you are the man, without flattery, who serve your friends with the least ostentation; it is almost ingratitude to thank you, considering your temper; and this is the period of all my letter: which I fear you will think the most impertinent. I am, with the truest affection,

Yours, etc.

CCLIV. [*Original.*[4]]

THOMAS HARLEY TO SWIFT

June 19, 1714.

SIR,[5]

YOUR letter gave me a great deal of pleasure. I do not mean only the satisfaction one must always find in hearing

---

[1] Whose grandiose phrases had probably excited Swift's ridicule. *Cf.* the "Hue and Cry after Dean Swift" ("Prose Works," v, 481), which there is reason to suppose was written by Steele.

[2] *Supra*, p. 145, n. 2.   [3] *Supra*, p. 145.

[4] In the British Museum. See Preface.

[5] The writer of this letter, "the Secretary of the Treasury and Lord Treasurer's cousin german," is referred to by Swift as his very good friend, and was even pardoned for such "gross neglect" of the Brothers' Club as led to his expulsion ("Prose Works," ii, *passim*).

from so good a friend, who has distinguished himself in the world, and formed a new character, which nobody is vain enough to pretend to imitate.[1] But you must know the moment after you disappeared, I found it was to no purpose to be unconcerned, and to slight, as I really have done, all the silly stories and schemes I met with every day; the effects of self-conceit, and a frightened, hasty desire of gain. They asked me: "Has not the Dean left the town? Is not Dr. Swift gone into the country?" Yes; and I would have gone into the country too, if I had not learned, one cannot be hurt till one turns one's back, for which reason I will go no more on their errands. But, seriously, you never heard such bellowing about the town of the state of the nation, especially among the sharpers, sellers of bear-skins,[2] and the rest of that kind: nor such crying ******* and squalling among the ladies; insomuch that it has at last reached the House of Commons; which I am sorry for, because it is hot and uneasy sitting there in this season of the year.[3] But I was told to-day, that in some countries, people are forced to watch day and night to keep wild beasts out of their corn. Do you not pity me, for yielding to such grave sayings, to be stifled every day in the House of Commons?

When I was out of England, I used to receive five or six letters each post, with this passage: "As for what passes here, you will be informed by others much better; therefore I shall not trouble you with anything of that sort." You will give me leave to use it now, as my excuse to you for not writing news. I hope, honest Gay will be better supplied by some friend or other. Before I received your direction, I had ordered my servant, who comes next Monday out of Herefordshire, to leave your horse[4] at the Crown in Farringdon,[5] where you can easily send for him.

---

[1] As Sir Walter Scott says ("Works," xvi, 124), this allusion to the disinterested part which Swift played during the ministerial feuds is very happy.

[2] Or as they would now be called "bears." According to the Oxford Dictionary the phrase originated in the proverb, "to sell the bear's skin before one has caught the bear."

[3] Thomas Harley represented Radnorshire throughout the reign of Queen Anne.

[4] *Supra*, p. 146.

[5] About nine miles from Letcombe. Oxford used to stay at this inn when travelling from his seat in Herefordshire.

I hear he was so fat, they could not travel him till he was
taken down; and I ordered he should go short journeys.
He is of a good breed, and therefore I hope will prove
well; if not, use him like a bastard, and I will choose
another for you.   I am, Sir,

Your most faithful humble servant,

T. HARLEY.

Addressed—For the Reverend the Dean of St. Patrick's.

CCLV. [*Original.*[1]]

WILLIAM THOMAS TO SWIFT

June 22, 1714.

REVEREND SIR,[2]

IT was with some difficulty, that I prevailed with myself
to forbear acknowledging your very kind letter. I can
only tell you, it shall be the business of my life to endeavour to deserve the opinion you express of me, and
thereby to recommend myself to the continuance of your
friendship.

My Lord Treasurer does, upon all occasions, do justice
to your merit, and has expressed to all his friends the
great esteem he has for so hearty and honest a friend,
and particularly on occasion of the letter you mention to
have lately writ to him, and all his friends can inform you
with what pleasure he communicated it to them.[3]

And now for business; I am to acquaint you, that last
Thursday I received the fifty pounds, which now waits
your orders, and dated your receipt accordingly, which I
delivered to Mr. Whetham, who paid me the money.[4]

I do not pretend to tell you how matters go. Our friend

[1] In the British Museum. See Preface.

[2] As appears from an endorsement the writer was secretary to
Oxford.

[3] So far as is known Swift had not written to Oxford since leaving
London. The sentence is somewhat vague, and it seems possible that
Swift may have postponed writing for a fortnight, when a letter was
sent by him to Oxford which is still in existence (*infra*, p. 160).

[4] The reference is to the business between Mr. Fetherston and
Baron Scrope (*supra*, p. 70). Whetham, who was first commissioner of
excise, appears to have been connected by marriage with the Baron.

says very bad. I am sanguine enough to hope not worse. I am, with all possible esteem,

Ever yours.

CCLVI. [*Original.*[1]]

JOHN ARBUTHNOT TO SWIFT

Kensington, *June* 26, 1714.

DEAR BROTHER,

I HAD almost resolved not to write to you, for fear of disturbing so happy a state as you describe.[2] On the other hand, a little of the devil, that cannot endure anybody should enjoy a paradise, almost provoked me to give you a long and melancholy state of our affairs. For you must know, that it is just my own case. I have with great industry endeavoured to live in ignorance; but at the same time would enjoy Kensington Garden,[3] and then some busy discontented body or another comes just cross me, and begins a dismal story, and before I go to supper, I am as full of grievances as the most knowing of them.

I will plague you a little, by telling you that the Dragon[4] dies hard. He is now kicking and cuffing about him like the devil; and you know parliamentary management is the *forte*, but no hopes of any settlement between the two champions. The Dragon said last night to my Lady Masham and me, that it is with great industry he keeps his friends, who are very numerous, from pulling all to pieces. Gay had a hundred pounds in due time, [and] went away a happy man. I have solicited both Lord Treasurer and Lord Bolingbroke strongly for the Parnellian,[5] and gave them a memorial the other day. Lord Treasurer speaks mighty affectionately of him, which you know is an ill sign in ecclesiastical preferments. Witness some, that you and I know, when the contrary was the best sign in the world.

Pray, remember Martin,[6] who is an innocent fellow and

---

[1] In the British Museum. See Preface.   [2] *Supra*, p. 152.
[3] The Queen was then residing in Kensington Palace.
[4] *I.e.*, Oxford (*supra*, p. 150, n. 4).
[5] *I.e.*, the poet Parnell (*supra*, p. 145).
[6] The first book of the " Memoirs of Martinus Scriblerus," which is all that has been printed, had probably been written before Swift left

will not disturb your solitude. The ridicule of medicine is so copious a subject that I must only here and there touch it. I have made him study physic from the apothecary's bill, where there is a good plentiful field for a satire upon the present practice. One of his projects was, by a stamp upon blistering-plasters, and melilot by the yard, to raise money for the Government, and to give it to Radcliffe and others to farm.[1] But there was likely to be a petition from the inhabitants of London and Westminster, who had no mind to be flayed. There was a problem about the doses of purging medicines published four years ago, showing that they ought to be in proportion to the bulk of the patient. From thence Martin endeavours to determine the question about the weight of the ancient men, by the doses of physic that were given them.[2] One of his best inventions was a map of diseases for the three cavities, and one for the external parts; just like the four quarters of the world. Then the great diseases are like capital cities, with their symptoms all like streets and suburbs, with the roads that lead to other diseases. It is thicker set with towns than any Flanders map you ever saw. Radcliffe is painted at the corner of the map, contending for the universal empire of this world, and the rest of the physicians opposing his ambitious designs, with a project of a treaty of partition to settle peace.

There is an excellent subject of ridicule from some of the German physicians, who set up a sensitive soul as a sort of a first Minister to the rational. Helmont[3] calls him Archaeus. Dolaeus[4] calls him Microcosmetor. He has under him several other genii, that reside in the particular parts of the body, particularly Prince Cardimelech in the heart; Gasteronax in the stomach; and the plastic Prince

London, and part of his scheme for its continuation is here outlined by Arbuthnot.

[1] While acquiring the great fortune, which he bequeathed for public uses, Radcliffe (*supra*, p. 95, n. 4) did not escape charges of venality from his contemporaries, and especially from his professional brethren who looked upon him as an empiric.

[2] A contributor to "Notes and Queries" (2, vi, 123), who argues that Swift obtained Arbuthnot's assistance in the calculations of the proportions in "Gulliver's Travels," sees in this sentence "a faint resemblance to the leading idea of the travels."

[3] Jan Baptista van Helmont, author of "Ortus Medicinae," etc.

[4] Johann Dolaeus, author of numerous medical works.

in the organs of generation. I believe I could make you laugh at the explication of distempers from the wars and alliances of those Princes, and how the first Minister gets the better of his mistress *Anima Rationalis*. The best is, that it is making a reprisal upon the politicians, who are sure to allegorize all the animal economy into state affairs. Pope has been collecting high flights of poetry, which are very good; they are to be solemn nonsense.[1]

I thought upon the following the other day, as I was going into my coach, the dust being troublesome:

> The dust in smaller particles arose,
> Than those which fluid bodies do compose:
> Contraries in extremes do often meet,
> 'Twas now so dry, that you might call it wet.

I do not give you these hints to divert you, but that you may have your thoughts, and work upon them.

I know you love me heartily, and yet I will not own that you love me better than I love you. My Lord and Lady Masham love you too, and read your letter to me with pleasure. My Lady says she will write to you, whether you write to her or not. Dear friend, adieu.

CCLVII. [*Original.*[2]]

SWIFT TO THE EARL OF OXFORD

July 3, 1714.

WHEN I was with you, I have said more than once, that I would never allow quality or station made any real difference between men.[3] Being now absent and forgotten,

---

[1] Material which was afterwards used in his essay, "Περὶ Βάθους, or the Art of Sinking in Poetry."

[2] In the possession of the Duke of Portland (see Preface), who has granted permission for its use in the preparation of this edition of the Correspondence. To his Grace's librarian, Mr. Richard W. Goulding, I am indebted not only for the benefit of his knowledge of the great collection in his charge, but also for much assistance rendered necessary by my residence in Ireland.

[3] This letter was evidently intended as an apology to Oxford for "Some Free Thoughts upon the Present State of Affairs" (*supra*, p. 153, n. 1) which Swift sent at the same time to London for publication, and knew that Oxford would recognize as his work. As there is

I have changed my mind. You have a thousand people who can pretend they love you, with as much appearance of sincerity as I, so that according to common justice I can have but a thousandth part in return of what I give. And this difference is wholly owing to your station. And the misfortune is still the greater, because I always loved you just so much the worse for your station. For in your public capacity you have often angered me to the heart, but, as a private man, never once. So that if I only looked towards myself, I could wish you a private man to-morrow. For I have nothing to ask, at least nothing that you will give, which is the same thing, and then you would see whether I should not with much more willingness attend you in a retirement,[1] whenever you pleased to give me leave, than ever I did at London or Windsor. From these sentiments I will never write to you, if I can help it, otherwise than as to a private person, nor allow myself to have been obliged by you in any other capacity.

The memory of one great instance of your candour and justice, I will carry to my grave, that having been in a manner domestic with you for almost four years, it was never in the power of any public or concealed enemy, to make you think ill of me, though malice and envy were often employed to that end. If I live, posterity shall know that and more, which, though you, and somebody that shall be nameless, seem to value less than I could wish,[2] is all the return I can make you. Will you give me leave to say how I would desire to stand in your memory; as one, who was truly sensible of the honour you did him, though he was too proud to be vain upon it; as one, who was neither assuming, officious, nor teasing, who never wilfully misrepresented persons or facts to you, nor consulted his passions when he gave a character; and lastly, as one whose indiscretions proceeded altogether from a

---

reason to believe that the treatise was printed from a copy revised by Bolingbroke (*infra*, p. 170), it is possible that there was even plainer speaking about Oxford's administration in the treatise when it came from Swift's pen than there is at present.

[1] Before leaving London Swift had advised Oxford to retire at the close of the parliamentary session (*infra*, p. 223).

[2] Swift is referring to his application for the office of Historiographer ("Prose Works," v, 477), which then lay before "somebody that shall be nameless," or in other words the Queen.

weak head, and not an ill heart? I will add one thing more, which is the highest compliment I can make, that I never was afraid of offending you, nor am now in any pain for the manner I write to you in. I have said enough; and, like one at your levee, having made my bow, I shrink back into the crowd.

CCLVIII. [*Original.*[1]]

SWIFT TO JOHN ARBUTHNOT

July 3, 1714.

I RECKONED you would have held up for one letter and so have given over; this is the usual way I treat my best absent friends when I am in London. Did I describe myself in a happy state here?[2] Upon my faith you read wrong: I have no happiness but being so far out of the way of the Dragon[3] and the rest. Lewis reproaches me as one who has still an itch to the Court, only because I asked him how the *summa rerum* went. Was not that unjust? And quotes upon me, *quae lucis miseris tam dira cupido*. I do assert that living near a Court with some circumstances is a most happy life, and would be so still if the Dragon did not spoil it. I find the triumvirate of honest counsellors is at an end; I am gone, Lewis says he lives in ignorance in his castle, and you meddle as little as you can. One thing still lies upon you, which is to be a constant adviser to Lady Masham. The game will of course be played into her hand. She has very good sense, but may be imposed upon. And I had a whisper, that the Squire[4] plies there again. It is as you say, if the Dragon speaks kindly of Parnell, he is gone. It is the Ossorys that get the Derrys[5] and the Chesters the Yorks.[6]

To talk of Martin in any hands but yours, is a folly. You every day give better hints than all of us together could do in a twelvemonth; and to say the truth, Pope who

---

[1] In the Forster Collection, No. 540.   [2] *Supra*, p. 158.
[3] *I.e.*, Oxford (*supra*, p. 150, n. 4).   [4] *I.e.*, Bolingbroke.
[5] *Supra*, p. 126, n. 4.
[6] Sir William Dawes had been recently translated from Chester to York on the death of Archbishop Sharp.

first thought of the hint has no genius at all to it, in my mind. Gay is too young; Parnell has some ideas of it, but is idle; I could put together, and lard, and strike out well enough, but all that relates to the sciences must be from you. I am a vexed unsettled vagabond, and my thoughts are turned towards some papers I have, and some other things I would fain get from you and Lady Masham and would have had from the Dragon, but that is impossible till he is out and then I will go to him to Herefordshire and make him give me hints.[1] I have got my History[2] from Secretary Bromley; and they shall never have it again; and it shall be an altered thing if I live.

The hints you mention relating to medicine are admirable; I wonder how you can have a mind so *degagé* in a Court where there is so many million of things to vex you. You must understand, I have writ this post to the Dragon, but you must not take notice of it, nor I fancy will he; for what I writ is very odd and serious. I think to go and ramble for a month about Herefordshire and those parts.[3] Ask the Dragon whether he will order his people at his castle to receive me. Why do you not send your Parliament a grazing? What do you mean by your proclamation and five thousand pounds? Till I hear reasons I dislike your politics. Why do I talk of it say you? Why did that puppy Barber write it to me? But the Commons offer a hundred thousand pounds. If I was the Pretender, I would come over myself and take the money to help to pay my troops.[4] They had better put out a proclamation that whoever discovers the Pretender or the longitude[5] shall have a

---

[1] For Swift's proposed history of Queen Anne's reign (*supra*, p. 153, n. 2).

[2] Of the "Four Last Years of the Queen" (*supra*, p. 53, n. 5).

[3] The wish to visit Herefordshire had probably originated, like the idea of residing in Yorkshire, from the connection of his family with that county ("Prose Works," xi, 370) as well as from the fact that it was Oxford's home.

[4] In April the Lords had presented an address to the Queen praying that a reward might be offered for the apprehension of the Pretender in the event of his landing in England, and had been told that they would be better employed in bringing to a close "the groundless fears and jealousies which were so industriously promoted." On 23 June a proclamation was, however, issued, offering a reward of £500, which the House of Commons thought insufficient and proposed should be increased to one of £100,000.

[5] A reward for the discovery of the longitude was offered at that time.

hundred thousand pounds. This strain is a sacrifice to Hanover, the Whigs, and the Queen's state of health. It will neither satisfy Hanover, silence the Whigs, nor cure the gout. Give him a pension, and oblige him to live beyond the Alps. What is become of your project to make it high treason to bring over foreign troops? [1] I wish a little care was taken for securing the kingdom as well as the succession.

But country politics are doubly insupportable, and so I have done, and retire to lament with my neighbours the want of rain, and dryness of hay. Farmer Tyler says, the white mead at Chawdry has not been so bad in the memory of man, and the summer barley is quite dried up; but we hope to have a pretty good crop of wheat. Parson Hunsdon [2] it is thought must stick to his bargain, but all the neighbours say the attorney was an arrant rogue. We cannot get a bit of good butter for love or money. I could tell you more of the state of our affairs, but doubt your taste is not refined enough for it.

Addressed—To Dr. Arbuthnot.

CCLIX. [*Original.*[3]]

SWIFT TO ARCHDEACON WALLS

July 3, 1714.

I RECEIVED yours of June 24th [4] just now, and heartily thank you for it, and for the pains you and Mr. Forbes are at about my rotten affairs. I have made that Parvisol a rogue by my own carelessness and trusting to his accounts; and have denied myself many a necessary thing, hoping to

---

[1] Three months before Oxford had asked leave to introduce a bill for that purpose, but nothing more had been heard of his proposal. As it would have been contrary to the interests of the house of Hanover, as well as to those of the Pretender, that such a bill should pass, Oxford's object has proved inexplicable.

[2] The adjoining parish of Letcombe Regis had been held for many years by the Rev. John Hunsdon, a native of Wantage, and a graduate of Oxford.

[3] In the possession of Mr. John Murray. See Preface.

[4] Which was evidently a reply to Swift's letter of 11 June (*supra*, p. 147).

have some money in bank against I wanted it. I look upon
him as a knave and I beg you will do so too; and if you
are of opinion to take a new manager for my deanery and
livings this year, I believe the power I left you will suffice,
for as I remember it was as large as I could make it. I
leave it all to you; his sinking the thirty-five pounds odd
moneys of this last year is insupportable. He never was
allowed above twelve pence per pound in all for my other
livings both setting and receiving. He always gets setting
money besides which is a considerable perquisite, and that
twelve pence is never allowed by me, but by the tenant;
except in Rathbeggan,[1] where by an old custom, I think,
the minister pays it. In the deanery and Laracor etc., the
tenant always pays it.

For his quantums and his merit, he is a rascal; he knows
how much I have remitted to him and given to him several
years. Must I be a loser by giving him the deanery to set?
Can I not hire a hundred would be glad to be employed?
If he takes journeys are they above a dozen miles and is he
not paid for them by his place? Let him give me a clear
account and then talk of merit. For my own part, I think
the best way would be to seize on himself and all his bonds
and force him to the best account we can, and employ
somebody else this coming year. But I leave it to you. I
am in no fear of being thought a hard master, and if you
think it the wisest way, I will take the blame of the un-
merciful part. For I think such a rascal deserves nothing
more than rigorous justice. He has imposed upon my easi-
ness; and that is what I never will forgive; and therefore
I beg you will not do the least thing in regard to him, but
merely for my interest, as if I were a Jew, and let who will
censure me. I have been often told I have been too easy
with that fellow and was led by him; but yet nobody
would positively advise me to shake him off or recommend
me to another. I must be a blind puppy indeed to be led
by him. Pize on it, you talk so mealy mouthed of a scoundrel whom I kept with his family a dozen years from
starving, as if you fear getting ill-will by complaining.
What you would do in your own case, do in mine; only be
something less merciful, because he deserves no other

[1] The outlying parish included in the union of Laracor (*supra,*
vol. i, p. 32, n. 2).

mercy than what is for my interest. So again, "tender of doing him ill-offices"; I am sure you are tenderer of doing them to me. I shall hate you if you talk at that rate; tender of a rascal, that by his pride, vanity, and carelessness is ruining me, when I am loaden with debts and the Court will not give me a penny to pay them. I am above a hundred and fifty pounds in debt in London since I came.

I have been in the country these five weeks and probably shall return to town no more. I design to be in Ireland I hope by the end of summer. I am weary of Ministers: I stole from them all and have here a little quiet, and have somewhat recovered my health, which I had sufficiently shaken among them. I set abundance of people at a gaze by my going away; but I laid it all on my health and now the nine days' wonder is over. They expect I will return, but I mean to balk them, and take a ramble for some weeks about Herefordshire[1] etc., and so to Ireland. I would be with you sooner but that I wait the issue of some things. My service to your Trim ladies when you write to them. I intend to write to them in some time. Lord Kingston's[2] affairs are all chimeras; besides I hope I have done with Courts for ever. My service to Gossip and Stoytes and Manleys; I hope my godchild is well.

I think by the account Parvisol's arrears are greater than when I left Ireland. Why should I give him allowances for journeys, when I can have a manager in Dublin or on the spot, who will do it for the common perquisites, as the late Dean had? In short he is a cursed villain; and if it will not hurt my interest, I shall be glad to be rid of him, which if you and Forbes agree to do, there must be some concert with Mr. Warburton who is his broker[3] [at] Laracor, and I think Dr. Raymond, I have forgot. Do as you please, but let no regard to him influence you; I will take all the blame of hardship on myself, and lay it on me as strong as you please.

Addressed—To the Reverend Mr. Archdeacon Walls over against the Hospital in Queen Street, Dublin.

---

[1] *Supra*, p. 163.

[2] John, third Lord Kingston, of the first creation, who had for a time followed the fortunes of James II, but who had returned to Ireland and been granted a free pardon.

[3] *I.e.*, agent or middleman.

CCLX. [*Original.*[1]]

WILLIAM THOMAS TO SWIFT

July 6, 1714.

REVEREND SIR,

I SHOULD not have presumed to break in upon your retirement, nor so much as inquire for your address, had not the enclosed given me a fair occasion to ask after your health.[2] I need not add anything to what the papers will inform you touching that affair. The person mentioned in the Baron's letter has not yet called upon me. When you have endorsed the letter of attorney, please to return that and the Baron's letter, that I may punctually follow his directions. I dare not mention anything of politics to one that has purposely withdrawn himself from the din of it. I shall only tell you, that your friends applaud your conduct with relation to your own ease; but they think it hard you should abdicate at a juncture your friendship seems to be of most use to them. I am sure some of them want your advice, as well as assistance. You will forgive this digression from business, when I tell you I shall not repeat this trouble, not having so much as kept a copy of your direction. You may direct your commands to me, under cover, to our common friend.[3] I hope you believe me too sensible of obligations to need formal assurances of the sincere respect, wherewith I am, Reverend Sir,

Your most obedient and most humble servant,

WM. THOMAS.

CCLXI. [*Original.*[4]]

ERASMUS LEWIS TO SWIFT

Whitehall, *July* 6, 1714.

SIR,

YOU give me such good reasons for your desire of knowing what becomes of our grand affair, that to oblige you,

---

[1] In the British Museum. See Preface.

[2] This letter had evidently reference, like the writer's preceding one (*supra*, p. 157), to the business between Fetherston and Baron Scrope.

[3] *I.e.*, Erasmus Lewis.

[4] In the British Museum. See Preface.

and perhaps to give myself vent, I will tell you what I think on it. The two ladies [1] seem to have determined the fall of the Dragon,[2] and to entertain a chimerical notion, that there shall be no *Monsieur le Premier*, but that all power shall reside in one, and profit in the other. The man of Mercury [3] soothes them in this notion with great dexterity and reason, for he will be *Monsieur le Premier* then of course, by virtue of the little seal. His character is too bad to carry the great ensigns; therefore he takes another method, and I think it very artful, viz. to continue his present station, to which the power may altogether be as properly attached as to the wand. In this brangle I am no otherwise concerned, than that I must lose part of the pleasure I had in the conversation of my friends. And that I am really apprehensive the two ladies may suffer by the undertaking; for the man of Mercury's bottom is too narrow, his faults of the first magnitude; and we cannot find, that there is any scheme in the world how to proceed. Mercurialis complains, that the Dragon has used him barbarously; that he is in with the democraticals, and never conferred a single obligation upon him since he had the wand. *Le temps nous éclaircira.*

I propose to move on the 2nd of August to Bath, and to stay there, or go from thence, according as our chaos settles here. I believe I shall not go to Abercothy,[4] otherwise I would attend you. Shall not we meet at Bath? Before I began this paragraph, I should have added something to the former, which is, that the Dragon is accused of having betrayed his friends yesterday upon the matter of the three explanatory articles of the Spanish treaty of

[1] At that crisis in Oxford's fortunes the Duchess of Somerset, who was still Mistress of the Robes, as well as Lady Masham (*supra*, p. 151, n. 1), exercised at Court an influence hostile to him. He had played the one against the other, in order that neither might gain too much power over the Queen, until at last he found that they had both deserted him and ranged themselves on the side of his rival Bolingbroke, or Mercurialis as Lewis calls him in this letter. The Duchess was probably at heart no more friendly to Bolingbroke than she had been three years before (*supra*, vol. i, p. 279), and only gave her support to him because she foresaw that in the event of the Queen's death his administration was certain to be superseded by a Whig one, and could not feel so confident that a similar fate would attend a Ministry of which Oxford was the head.

[2] *I.e.*, Oxford (*supra*, p. 150, n. 4).   [3] *I.e.*, Bolingbroke.
[4] Lewis's birthplace near Caermarthen.

commerce,[1] which he allowed not to be beneficial, and that the Queen might better press for their being changed, if it was the sense of the House they ought to be so. The address then passed without a negative.

I thank you for the account you give me of the farm in Buckinghamshire. I could like the thing, and the price too very well; but when it comes to a point, I own my weakness to you : I cannot work myself up to a resolution whilst I have any hope of the two hundred pounds a year I told you of in my own parish; it lies now at sale; if I miss, I would catch greedily at the other. When I am at the Bath I will set down the hints you desire.

CCLXII. [*Original.*[2]]

CHARLES FORD TO SWIFT

London, *July* 6 [1714].

IF Barber be not a very great blockhead, I shall soon send you a letter in print, in answer to your last: I hope it may be next post, for he had it on Sunday.[3] I took care to blot the *e*s out of on*e*ly,[4] and the *a*s out of sche*a*me, which I suppose is the meaning of your question, whether I corrected it? I do not know any other alteration it wanted; and I made none except in one paragraph, that I changed the present to the past tense four times, and I am not sure I did right in it neither. There is so great a

---

[1] By those articles the duties which were imposed under the Treaty made at Utrecht were abandoned, and as it was alleged that the alterations were prejudicial to English interests, and had not been obtained honestly, a motion was carried in the Lords that the Queen should be asked to lay before Parliament all the papers relating to the negotiations. These had been entirely in Bolingbroke's hands so far as England was concerned, and it has been suggested that the motion in the Lords was instigated by Oxford to retaliate on Bolingbroke for forcing on him the Schism Bill (Leadam, *op. cit.*, p. 218).

[2] In the British Museum. See Preface.

[3] Swift had sent a few days before the date of this letter, which fell upon Tuesday, a copy of his "Free Thoughts upon the present State of Affairs" to Ford (*supra*, p. 160, n. 3) with directions to convey it to Barber for publication without disclosing the name of the author.

[4] Unlike Addison and other writers of that time, Swift used invariably the older spelling of *only*.

tenderness and regard shown all along to the [Queen], that I could have wished this expression had been out:—" the uncertain timorous nature of the [Queen]." [1] But there was no striking it out without quite spoiling the beauty of the passage: and, as if I had been the author myself, I preferred beauty to discretion. I really think it is at least equal to any thing you have writ; and I dare say it will do great services as matters stand at present.

The Colonel [2] and his friends give the game for lost on their side; and I believe by next week we shall see Lord Bolingbroke at the head of affairs. The Bishop of Rochester is to be Lord Privy Seal. They talk of several other alterations, as that my Lord Trevor is to be President of the Council; Lord Abingdon, Chamberlain; Lord Anglesey, Lord Lieutenant of Ireland; [3] that Mr. Bromley is to go out, [4] and a great many more in lesser employments. I fancy these reports are spread to draw in as many as they can to oppose the new scheme. I can hardly think anybody will be turned out of the cabinet, except the Treasurer and the Privy Seal. [5] Perhaps my Lord Poulett may lay down. [6] Certainly the Secretary [7] may continue in, if he pleases, and I do not hear that he is disposed to resign, or that he is so attached to any Minister, as to enter into

---

[1] These words do not occur in the tract. Their exclusion was probably due to Bolingbroke who, as will subsequently appear, altered the text (*infra*, p. 180, n. 2).

[2] *I.e.*, Oxford.

[3] This forecast of Bolingbroke's ministry indicates no belief in his adherence to the cause of the Pretender. Anglesey, as we have seen (*supra*, p. 47, n. 5), was leader of the Hanoverian Tories; Abingdon and Trevor were also of that number; and Bishop Atterbury alone could have been privy to a design for the restoration of the Stuarts. Trevor was then Chief Justice of the Common Pleas. He is said by Swift, in the "Enquiry into the Behaviour of the Queen's Last Ministry" ("Prose Works," v, 453), to have been at that time one of the few friends left to Oxford, whose schoolfellow he had been and by whom he had been raised to the peerage two years before as one of the famous twelve, but a subsequent letter (*infra*, p. 197) shows that there was ground to believe that his sympathy was with Bolingbroke.

[4] Bromley is said by Swift to have been on Oxford's side (*ibid.*).

[5] There had been much discord between Lord Dartmouth, who still held the Privy Seal (*supra*, p. 57, n. 2), and Bolingbroke when they were co-Secretaries of State.

[6] The office of Lord Steward, which he still held (*supra*, p. 15, n. 3).

[7] *I.e.*, Bromley.

their resentments. What has John of Bucks done,[1] and yet
the report is very strong, that he is to be succeeded by my
Lord Trevor. The Duke of Shrewsbury was one out of
eight or nine Lords, that stood by my Lord Bolingbroke
yesterday, in the debate about the Spanish treaty,[2] and
spoke with a good deal of spirit. Is it likely he is to be
turned out of all?[3]

The Lords have made a representation to the Queen, in
which they desire her to surmount the insurmountable
difficulties the Spanish trade lies under by the last treaty.
It is thought there was a majority in the House to have
prevented such reflection upon the treaty, if they had
come to a division. The clamour of the merchants, Whig
and Tory, has been too great to have passed a vote in
vindication of it, as it stands ratified. But my Lord Anglesey
and his squadron seemed willing to oppose any censure of
it; and yet this representation was suffered to pass, nobody
knows how. To-day they are to take into consideration the
Queen's answer to their address, desiring to know who
advised her to ratify the explanation of three articles?
She sent them word she thought there was little difference
between that and what was signed at Utrecht. When they
rise I will tell you what they have done. The last money
bill was sent up yesterday; so that in all probability the
Parliament will be up in two or three days, and then we
shall be entertained with Court affairs. I hope you got
mine last post, and one a fortnight ago. Will the change o
the Ministry affect Elwood?[4] He is in pain about it, and I
am told the people of Ireland are making a strong opposition against the present Provost.

The consideration of the Queen's answer is deferred till
to-morrow. I am now with my Lord Guilford[5] and three
other Commissioners of Trade, who were examined to-day
at the bar of the House of Lords. They are prodigiously
pleased with what has been done. But I do not understand

---

[1] The Duke of Buckingham (*supra*, vol. i, p. 239, n. 2) had become
President of the Council.
[2] *Supra*, p. 169, n. 1.
[3] *I.e.*, the chamberlainship and the viceroyalty of Ireland.
[4] Elwood (*supra*, vol. i, p. 56, n. 3) was evidently designated as
Pratt's successor in the provostship (*supra*, p. 141, n. 3).
[5] In Swift's opinion "a mighty silly fellow" ("Prose Works," x,
280).

it well [enough] to give you an account of it; for the rapture they are in hinders them from explaining themselves clearly. I can only gather from their manner of discourse, that they are come off without censure.[1]

CCLXIII. [*Original.*[2]]

JOHN BARBER TO SWIFT

London, *July* 6, 1714.

HONOURED SIR,

I HAD yours of the 3rd instant, and am heartily glad of your being in health, which I hope will continue. Pray draw what bills you please: I will pay them at demand. I will take care of Mrs. Rolt's[3] affair; I wish you would write to her. I had a visit from Mrs. Brackley[4] to-day; she gives her humble service, and desired my assistance with General Hill. I told her it was best to stay till there was a master;[5] and I did not doubt but something would be done.

I fortunately met Lord Bolingbroke yesterday, the minute I had your letter. I attacked him for some wine, and he immediately ordered you two dozen of red French wine, and one dozen of strong Aaziana white wine. The hamper will be sent to-morrow by Robert Stone the Wantage carrier, and will be there on Friday. I am afraid it will cost you five shillings to George, my Lord's butler; but I would do nothing without order. My Lord bid me tell you this morning, that he will write to you, and let you know that as great a philosopher as you are, you have had the pip; that the public affairs are carried on with the same zeal and quick dispatch as when you was here; nay, that they are improved in several particulars; that the same

---

[1] In a subsequent letter from Charles Ford (*infra*, p. 176) further reference will be found to the examination of the Commissioners of Trade.

[2] In the British Museum. See Preface.

[3] Swift's favourite cousin (*supra*, vol. i, p. 382, n. 11).

[4] She is probably a lady who is mentioned several times in the Journal to Stella, under the name of Bradley, and who appears to have been a friend of the Moor Park days.

[5] *I.e.*, until Oxford was dismissed.

good understanding continues; that he hopes the world will be the better for your retirement; that your inimitable pen was never more wanted than now; and more, which I cannot remember. I believe he expects you should write to him. He spoke many affectionate and handsome things in your favour. I told him your story of the spaniel, which made him laugh heartily.

CCLXIV. [*Scott.*]

SWIFT TO MISS ESTHER VANHOMRIGH

July 8, 1714.

I FIND you take heavily that touch upon your shoulder.[1] I would not have writ to you so soon, if it were not to tell you, that, if you want to borrow any money, I would have you to send to Mr. Barber, or Ben Tooke,[2] which you please, and let them know it, and the sum, and that I will stand bound for it, and send them my bond. I did not know our posts went on Tuesday, else I would have writ two days ago to tell you this.[3] I do not see how you can be uneasy when the year is out, for you can pay only what you receive;—you are answerable for no more, and I suppose you have not given bonds to pay your mother's debts. As for your two pounds, five shillings that you gave your note for, if that be all, it is a trifle, and your owning it with so much apology looks affected. If you have no more secret debts than that, I shall be glad. But still, I cannot understand how any of those creditors of your mother can give you any trouble, unless there be some circumstances that I do not know the bottom of. I believe I shall not stay here much longer, and, therefore, if you want to borrow money, I would have you do it soon, and of the two, rather of Ben Tooke; because I have just drawn a note upon Barber for thirty guineas for my own expenses. I believe

[1] Vanessa's mother, who had died before that time, left, as will be seen from this letter, her affairs in an embarrassed state, and the encounter to which Swift alludes is supposed to have been with a bailiff.
[2] Swift had secured his old friend Tooke's (*supra*, vol. i, p. 183) appointment as publisher of the Gazette, and refers to him frequently in the Journal to Stella.
[3] Swift was writing on Thursday.

a bond had better be sent to me down to sign, and I will
send it back to you, and you may give it Ben. You may
speak freely to Ben of this, and if he has no money by
him, we must apply to Barber. I am forced to conclude in
haste, because the post-house is two miles off, and it will
be late if I stay longer. Adieu. My service to Molkin.

CCLXV. [*Original.*[1]]

John Arbuthnot to Swift

Kensington, *July* 10, 1714.

DEAR BROTHER,

I HAVE talked of your affairs to nobody but my Lady
Masham. She tells me, that she has it very much at heart,
and would gladly do it for her own sake, and that of her
friends; but thinks it not a fit season to speak about it.[2]
We are indeed in such a strange condition as to politics,
that nobody can tell now who is for who. It were really
worth the while to be here for four-and-twenty hours only,
to consider the oddness of the scene. I am sure it would
make you relish your country life better.

The Dragon[3] holds fast with a dead gripe the little
machine.[4] If he would have taken but half so much pains
to have done other things as he has of late to exert himself
against the Esquire,[5] he might have been a Dragon instead
of a Dagon. I would no more have suffered and done what
he has, than I would have sold myself to the galleys.
Haec inter nos. However, they have got now rid of the
Parliament, and may have time to think of a scheme: perhaps they may have one already. I know nothing, but it is
fit to rally the broken forces under some head or another.
They really did very well the last day but one in the
House of Lords; but yesterday they were in a flame about
the Queen's answer, till the Queen came in and put an
end to it.[6]

[1] In the British Museum. See Preface.
[2] The reference is apparently to Swift's application for the office of
Historiographer (*supra,* p. 161, n. 2).
[3] *I.e.,* Oxford (*supra,* p. 150, n. 4).
[4] The Lord Treasurer's emblem of office.   [5] *I.e.,* Bolingbroke.
[6] Parliament had been prorogued on the previous day.

The Dragon showed me your letter,[1] and seemed mightily pleased with it. He has paid ten pounds for a manuscript of which I believe there are several in town. It is a history of the last invasion of Scotland,[2] wrote just as plain, though not so well, as another history which you and I know,[3] with characters of all the men now living, the very names, and invitation that was sent to the Pretender. This by a flaming Jacobite, that wonders that all the world are not so. Perhaps it may be a Whig, that personates a Jacobite. I saw two sheets of the beginning, which was treason every line. If it goes on at the same rate of plain dealing, it is a very extraordinary piece, and worth your while to come up to see it only. Mr. Lockhart, they say, owns it. It is no more his than it is mine.[4] Do not be so dogged; but after the first shower, come up to town for a week or so. It is worth your while. Your friends will be glad to see you, and none more than myself. Adieu.

Addressed—For the Reverend the Dean of St. Patrick's.

CCLXVI. [*Original.*[5]]

CHARLES FORD TO SWIFT

London, *July* 10, 1714.

WHAT answer shall I send?[6] I am against any alteration; but additions, I think, ought by no means to be allowed. I wish I had called sooner at St. Dunstan's; but I did not expect it would have come out till Thursday,

---

[1] *Supra*, p. 160.

[2] "Memoirs concerning the Affairs of Scotland from Queen Anne's Accession to the Throne to the Commencement of the Union of the two Kingdoms of Scotland and England in May 1707, with an Account of the Origine and Progress of the Designed Invasion from France in March 1708," by George Lockhart of Carnwath.

[3] The "Four Last Years of the Queen," to which Lockhart's Memoirs are not comparable.

[4] As appears above Arbuthnot was mistaken.

[5] In the British Museum. See Preface.

[6] To a letter from Barber which Ford enclosed (*infra*, p. 177) with respect to the "Free Thoughts upon the Present State of Affairs" (*supra*, p. 169, n. 3). As will be seen, in order to preserve its anonymity Ford had sent the tract to Barber under an assumed name.

and therefore did not go there till yesterday. Pray let me know what you would have done. Barber was a blockhead to show it all; but who can help that? Write an answer either for yourself or me; but I beg of you to make no condescensions.

Yesterday put an end to the session, and to your pain. We gained a glorious victory in the House of Lords the day before: the attack was made immediately against Arthur Moore,[1] who appeared at the bar, with the other Commissioners of Trade. The South Sea Company had prepared the way by voting him guilty of a breach of trust,[2] and incapable of serving them in any office for the future. This passed without hearing what he had to say in his defence, and had the usual fate of such unreasonable reflections. Those, who proposed the resolutions, were blamed for their violence: and the person accused, appearing to be less guilty than they made him, was thought to be more innocent than I doubt he is. The Whigs proposed two questions in the House of Lords against him, and lost both, one by twelve, and the other, I think, by eighteen votes.

Court affairs go on as they did. The cry is still on the Captain's[3] side. Is not he the person Barber means by one of the best pens in England? It is only my own conjecture, but I can think of nobody else. Have you the Queen's speech, the Lords' address, etc., or shall I send them to you? And do you want a comment? Have Pope and Parnell been to visit you as they intended?[4]

I had a letter yesterday from Gay,[5] who is at the Hague, and presents his humble service to you. He has writ to Mr. Lewis too; but his respect makes him keep greater distance with him, and I think mine is the pleasanter letter, which I am sorry for.

[1] Moore, who was a favourite political lieutenant of Bolingbroke, and is said to have been a financial genius (Sichel's "Bolingbroke and his Times" *passim*), had been deeply concerned in the negotiations about the explanatory articles (*supra*, p. 171), and was made the scapegoat.

[2] In having been privy to a clandestine trade.

[3] *I.e.*, Bolingbroke.

[4] Pope and Parnell had ridden over to Letcombe from Binfield on the preceding Sunday, and had stayed with Swift for some days. (See Appendix VIII.)

[5] *Supra*, p. 151.

We were alarmed by B[arber] two days ago: he sent Tooke word our friend was ill in the country, which we did not know how to interpret, till he explained it. It was Mrs. M[anley[1]] he meant; but she is in no danger. Pray, write immediately, that there may be no farther delay to what we ought to have had a week ago.

Enclosure—

JOHN BARBER TO "SAMUEL BRIDGES"

Lambeth Hill, *July* 6, 1714.

SIR,

I THANKFULLY acknowledge the receipt of a packet sent last Sunday. I have shown it only to one person, who is charmed with it, and will make some small alterations and additions to it, with your leave. You will the easier give leave, when I tell you, that it is one of the best pens in England. Pray favour me with a line. I am, Sir,

Your most obedient servant,
JOHN BARBER.

Addressed—To Samuel Bridges, Esq., at St. Dunstan's Coffee-house, Fleet Street.

CCLXVII. [*Original.*[2]]

VISCOUNT BOLINGBROKE TO SWIFT

July 13, 1714.

I NEVER laughed, my dear Dean, at your leaving the town: on the contrary, I thought the resolution of doing so, at the time when you took it, a very wise one.[3] But I confess, I laughed, and very heartily too, when I heard that you affected to find, within the village of Letcombe, all your heart desired. In a word, I judged of you, just as

---

[1] Swift's understudy in the "Examiner" (*supra*, p. 125, n. 2) was then living at Finchley in great poverty ("Portland Manuscripts," v, 458, 491).
[2] In the British Museum. See Preface.
[3] Probably Swift had written to Bolingbroke on receiving the message through Barber (*supra*, p. 172).

II N

you tell me in your letter that I should judge. If my grooms did not live a happier life than I have done this great while, I am sure they would quit my service. Be pleased to apply this reflection. Indeed I wish I had been with you, with Pope and Parnell,[1] *quibus neque animi candidiores.* In a little time, perhaps, I may have leisure to be happy. I continue in the same opinions and resolutions as you left me in; I will stand or fall by them. Adieu. No alteration in my fortune or circumstances can even alter that sincere friendship with which I am, dear Dean, yours.

I fancy you will have a visit from that great politician and casuist, the Duke.[2] He is at Oxford with Mr. Clarke.[3]

CCLXVIII. [*Original.*[4]]

SWIFT TO JOHN ARBUTHNOT

July 13, 1714.

CCLXIX. [*Deane Swift.*]

CHARLES FORD TO SWIFT

London, *July* 15, 1714.

YOU see I was in the right; but I could wish the booby had not convinced me by naming my Lord Bolingbroke,[5]

[1] *Supra*, p. 176, n. 4.
[2] *I.e.*, the Duke of Ormond, who was Chancellor of Oxford as well as Dublin University.
[3] George Clarke, who combined academic and political distinction, was then one of the Commissioners of the Admiralty as well as a Fellow of Brasenose College, Oxford. He had been long known to Ormond, and while attending King William's army in Ireland as Secretary at War had made the Duke's castle at Kilkenny his chief abode. Although as a statesman and virtuoso he has received lengthy notice ("D. N. B.," x, 424), that episode in Clarke's life is not mentioned, nor is any reference given to voluminous correspondence of his at that time which is preserved in the Library of Trinity College, Dublin.
[4] This letter was a few years ago in the possession of Mr. Sabin of 172, New Bond Street.
[5] Evidently Ford again enclosed a letter from Barber (*supra*, p. 177) in which it was clearly stated that Bolingbroke was the person who

and then I should have dealt well enough with him. Since
it has happened so, the best remedy I could think of, was
to write him a very civil answer; in which, however, I have
desired to see the alterations: this is mentioned with great
respect to my Lord. Though he is promised to have it
again to-morrow, it is probable he may be disappointed,
and there may be time enough for me to receive your
directions what I shall do, when I get it into my hands. If
the alterations are material, shall I send it to some other
printer as it was first written? Reflect upon everything you
think likely to happen, and tell me beforehand what is
proper to be done, that no more time may be lost. I hate
the dog for making his court in such a manner.

I am very sorry you have had occasion to remove your
premier minister.[1] We are told now, we shall have no
change in ours, and that the Duke of Shrewsbury[2] will
perfectly reconcile all matters. I am sure you will not
believe this any more than I do; but the Dragon[3] has been
more cheerful than usual for three or four days; and therefore people conclude the breaches are healed. I rather
incline to the opinion of those who say he is to be made a
Duke, and to have a pension. Another reason given why
there is to be no change is, because the Parliament was not
adjourned to issue new writs in the room of those who
were to come in upon the new scheme, that they might
sit in the House at the next meeting. But I cannot see
why an adjournment may not do as well at the beginning,
as at the end of a session; and certainly it will displease
less in January or February, than it would have done in
July. The Whigs give out the Duke of Marlborough is
coming over, and his house is now actually fitting up at
St. James's.[4] We have had more variety of lies of late
than ever I remember. The history we were formerly
talking of, would swell to a prodigious size, if it was carried
on.[5] There was a fire last night on Tower-hill, that burnt

was making the alteration in the "Free Thoughts upon the Present
State of Affairs" (*supra*, p. 176).

[1] The allusion is apparently to Parvisol (*supra*, p. 164).

[2] Shrewsbury had returned from Ireland early in June (*supra*, p.
138).

[3] *I.e.*, Oxford (*supra*, p. 150, n. 4).

[4] Marlborough, who had been for some time abroad, returned to
England on the day Queen Anne died.

[5] *Supra*, p. 153, n. 2.

down forty or fifty houses. You say nothing of coming to town. I hope you do not mean to steal away to Ireland without seeing us.

CCLXX. [*Deane Swift.*]

CHARLES FORD TO SWIFT

London, *July* 17, 1714.

A SECOND to-morrow is almost past,[1] and nothing has been yet left at St. Dunstan's. B[arber] will lose by his prodigious cunning; but that is nothing to the punishment he deserves. Had it been only his fear, he would have chosen somebody else to consult with; but the rogue found it was well written, and saw the passages that galled.[2] I am heartily vexed at the other person,[3] from whom one might have expected a more honourable proceeding. There is something very mean in his desiring to make alterations, when I am sure he has no reason to complain, and is at least as fairly dealt with as his competitor.[4] Besides, a great part of it is as much for his service as if he had given directions himself to have it done. What relates to the Pretender is of the utmost use to him;[5] and therefore I am

[1] *Supra,* p. 179.

[2] It is probable that these were removed by Bolingbroke and do not appear in the only version of the "Free Thoughts upon the Present State of Affairs" that is known to us (*supra,* p. 160, n. 3). There seems no ground for doubt that the existing version is Swift's text as revised by Bolingbroke. Sir Walter Scott was under the impression (" Life," p. 207) that Barber had returned the copy sent to him to Swift, but from the advertisement appended to the tract when it was first published in 1741 (" Prose Works," v, 395) it appears that this was not so, and that the tract was printed from the copy which was for many weeks in Bolingbroke's hands.

[3] *I.e.,* Bolingbroke.

[4] The only reference of a personal kind to Bolingbroke in the text of the "Free Thoughts" known to us, occurs where Swift likens the Ministers to "a ship's crew quarrelling in a storm or while their enemies are within gunshot." In that passage he speaks of " very great resentment" on Bolingbroke's part contributing, in even a larger degree than reserve on the part of Oxford, to the dissensions between them, and dwells upon the " lesson of humiliation to mankind" their animosities afford (" Prose Works," v, 405).

[5] Swift's vindication of the Ministry from the charges of disloyalty to the Hanoverian succession is extremely forcible, and no one who

as much surprised at this delay, as at his ungenerous manner of treating an unknown author, to whom he is so much obliged. But perhaps I may wrong him, and he would not desire to turn the whole to his own advantage. If it had come to me yesterday, or to-day, I was resolved to have sent it to some other printer without any amendment; but now I shall wait till I have your directions. I wish you had employed somebody else at first; but what signifies wishing now? After what B[arber] writ in his last, I can hardly think he will be such a —— as not to let me have it; and in my answer I have given him all manner of encouragement to do it. He has as much assurance as he can well desire, that the alterations shall be complied with, and a positive promise that it shall be returned to him the same day he leaves it at St. Dunstan's.

I cannot imagine why we have no mischief yet. Sure we are not to be disappointed at last, after the bustle that has been made. It is impossible they [1] can ever agree, and I want something to make my letters still entertaining. I doubt you will hardly thank me for them, now the Parliament is up; but as soon as anything happens you shall know it.

The Queen has not yet appointed the time for removing to Windsor. My Lord Chief Baron Ward is dead,[2] and we have already named seven successors, among whom is our Lord Chancellor Phipps. Frank Annesley was to have had his place under my Lord Anglesey,[3] so that it is well for him [4] we have provided him with another for life.

---

reads it can for a moment believe that the slightest suspicion ever crossed Swift's mind that the Ministers were in communication with the Pretender's court at St. Germains (*ibid.*, p. 408).

[1] *I.e.*, Oxford and Bolingbroke.

[2] Sir Edward Ward, who had died the preceding day, had been appointed Chief Baron by William III. In his early years Ward had been distinguished for Whig sympathies, and had held his own in conflict with Jeffreys; but at the time of his death he was regarded as a follower of Oxford, and a Tory newsletter, in announcing his illness, remarks that "when his Lordship departs this life the world will miss him, not only for his great ability in the law, but for his politeness in politics" ("Portland Manuscripts," v, 472).

[3] The rumour that Francis Annesley (*supra*, p. 15) was to be Lord Chancellor of Ireland in the event of the Earl of Anglesey becoming Lord Lieutenant, originated no doubt in the fact that they were kinsmen.

[4] *I.e.*, Phipps.

CCLXXI. [*Original.*[1]]

ERASMUS LEWIS TO SWIFT

July 17, 1714.

I AM sorry to find by those [that] have fresher advices from you than yours of the 11th instant to me, that Parvisol's conduct puts you under a necessity of changing the administration;[2] for it will probably draw you to Ireland whether you will or no. However, I hope to see you at Bath three weeks hence, whatever happens. I meet with no man or woman, who pretend upon any probable grounds to judge who will carry the great point. Our female friend[3] told the Dragon[4] in her own house, last Thursday morning,[5] these words: "You never did the [Queen] any service, nor are you capable of doing her any." He made no reply, but supped with her and Mercurialis[6] that night, at her own house.[7] His revenge is not the less meditated for that. He tells the words clearly and distinctly to all mankind. Those, who range under his banner, call her ten thousand bitches and kitchen-wenches. Those who hate him do the same. And from my heart, I grieve that she should give such a loose to her passion; for she is susceptible of true friendship, and has many social and domestic virtues.[8] The great Attorney,[9] who made you a sham offer of the Yorkshire living, had a long conference with the Dragon on Thursday, kissed him at parting, and cursed him at night.[10]

---

[1] In the British Museum. See Preface.   [2] *Supra,* p. 179.

[3] Swift notes on the margin: " Mrs. Masham [who] was the Queen's favourite, fell out in a rage, reproaching Lord Treasurer very injuriously."

[4] *I.e.,* Oxford. Here Swift inserts the note which has been already given (*supra,* p. 150, n. 4).

[5] The 15th.   [6] *I.e.,* Bolingbroke.

[7] Until about that time there is no indication in their correspondence of the strained relations between Oxford and Bolingbroke; indeed not many months before Bolingbroke had written to Oxford in terms almost of affection (" Portland Manuscripts," v, 324, 360, 454).

[8] Swift entertained the same opinion, but others did not form so favourable a judgement, and speaks of her as revengeful and exceptious (" Prose Works," v, 365).

[9] *I.e.,* Lord Chancellor Harcourt.

[10] Whatever part he may have taken at that moment, there is evidence (" Portland Manuscripts," v, *passim*) that until a short time before

He went to the country yesterday; from whence some conjecture nothing considerable will be done soon.

Lord Harley and Lady Harriot[1] went this morning to Oxford. He has finished all matters with Lord Pelham,[2] as far as can be done without an Act of Parliament. The composition was signed by the Auditor,[3] and Naylor, brother-in-law to Lord Pelham.[4] This day sevennight Lord Harley is to have the whole Cavendish estate,[5] which is valued at ten thousand per annum, and has upon it forty thousand pounds worth of timber. But three of this ten thousand a year he had by the will. He remits to Lord Pelham the twenty thousand pounds charged for Lady Harriot's fortune on the Holles estate; and gives him some patches of land, that lie convenient to him, to the value of about twenty thousand pounds more. According to my computation, Lord Harley gets by the agreement, if the timber is worth forty thousand pounds, a hundred and forty thousand pounds; and when the jointures fall in to him, will have sixteen thousand a year. But the cant is, twenty-six thousand. Lord Pelham will really have twenty-six thousand pounds a year from the Newcastle family, which, with

Harcourt had continued to act the part of a mediator (*supra*, p. 31, n. 2).

[1] The great alliance between Oxford's son and the only child of John Holles, Duke of Newcastle, who had acted as Lord Privy Seal during the first year of Oxford's administration, had taken place while Swift was in Ireland in the preceding year ("Portland Manuscripts," v, 324). The negotiations had been prolonged. A few months after the Duke's death, which occurred by a fall from his horse in July, 1711, Swift had mentioned to Stella a rumour that Lord Harley had married the Duke's daughter, and said that although it was not true he hoped that it soon might be, as a union between them had been "privately managing this long time" ("Prose Works," ii, 277). The homely phrases in which the couple are described to Stella as "a very valuable young gentleman" and a handsome girl with "good sense but red hair," are amusing when compared with the seraphic allusions in the lines addressed "To Lord Harley on his Marriage" ("Poetical Works," i, 87).

[2] To his nephew Thomas, second Baron Pelham, the future Duke of Newcastle and Prime Minister, Lord Harley's father-in-law bequeathed the greater part of his possessions, which were very vast.

[3] Oxford's brother, Edward Harley, who represented Leominster in Parliament.

[4] George Naylor, who sat for Seaford.

[5] To which John Holles, Duke of Newcastle, had succeeded through his wife, one of the daughters of Henry Cavendish, second Duke of Newcastle of the first creation.

his paternal estate, will be twice as much as Lord Harley's.[1]
The estate of the latter is judged to be in the best condition; and some vain-glorious friends of ours say, it is
worth more than the other's; but let that pass. Adieu.

CCLXXII. [*Original.*[2]]

LORD HARLEY TO SWIFT

July 17, 1714.

BROTHER SWIFT,[3]
    YOUR sister has at last got rid of her lawyers. We are
just setting out for Oxford, where we hope to see you.
I am,

Your affectionate brother,
HARLEY.

CCLXXIII. [*Original.*[4]]

JOHN ARBUTHNOT TO SWIFT

London, *July* 17, 1714.

DEAR BROTHER,
    I THOUGHT it necessary to speak to Lady Masham about
that affair, because I believe it will be necessary to give
her Majesty the same notion of it, which the memorial does,
and not that you are asking a little scandalous salary for a
sinecure.[6] Lewis despairs of it, and thinks it quite over
since a certain affair. I will not think so. I gave your

---

    [1] It has been suggested that Swift assisted in the negotiations for
Lord Harley's marriage and in the arrangements which followed for
the division of the property of Lady Harley's father, but I cannot agree
with Sir Walter Scott ("Life," p. 192) in thinking this supposition
highly probable.
    [2] In the British Museum. See Preface.
    [3] Lord Harley was an original member of the Brothers' Club.
    [4] In the British Museum. See Preface.
    [5] The office of Historiographer (*supra*, p. 174). As will subsequently
appear (*infra*, p. 188), it had been given to another before this letter
was written.
    [6] The salary was £200 a year.

letter, with the enclosed memorial,[1] *cavalièrement*, to Lord
Bolingbroke. He read it, and seemed concerned at some
part of it, expressing himself thus: that it would be among
the eternal scandals of the Government to suffer a man of
your character, that had so well deserved of them, to have
the least uneasy thought about those matters. As to the
fifty pounds, he was ready to pay it; and if he had had it
about him, would have given it me.[2] The Dragon[3] all the
while was walking with the Duke of Shrewsbury. So my
Lord Bolingbroke told me:—"I would immediately stir in
this matter, but I know not how I stand with some folks"
—for the Duke of Shrewsbury is taken himself to the
Dragon in appearance—"I know how I stand with that
man"—pointing to the Dragon—"but as to the other I cannot tell; however, I will claim his promise:"[4] and so he
took the memorial.

Do not think I make you a bare compliment in what I
am going to say; for I can assure you I am in earnest. I
am in hopes to have two hundred pounds before I go out
of town, and you may command all or any part of it you
please, as long as you have occasion for it. I know what
you will say: "To see a scoundrel pretend to offer to lend
me money." Our situation at present is in short thus: they
have *rompu en visière* with the Dragon, and yet do not
know how to do without him. My Lady Masham has in a
manner bid him defiance, without any scheme, or likeness
of it in any form or shape, as far as I can see. Notwithstanding he visits, cringes, flatters, etc. which is beyond my
comprehension.

I have a very comical account of Letcombe, and the
Dean of St. Patrick's, from Pope, with an episode of the
burning-glass.[5] I was going to make an epigram upon the
imagination of your burning your own history with the

---

[1] Swift apparently enclosed a copy of the Memorial to the Queen
which he had drawn up in April ("Prose Works," v, 477).

[2] Swift appears to have been then in urgent need of money, and
to have been obliged to make use of the £50 which he had received
for Fetherston (*supra*, p. 157, and *infra*, p. 227).

[3] *I.e.*, Oxford (*supra*, p. 150, n. 4).

[4] Bolingbroke had written in January to the Duke of Shrewsbury,
who, as Lord Chamberlain, had some part in the disposal of the office
of Historiographer, on behalf of Swift, and had evidently received a
favourable reply (see Bolingbroke's letter in Appendix IX).

[5] *Supra*, p. 176, and Appendix VIII.

burning-glass. I wish Pope or Parnell would put it into rhyme. The thought is this: Apollo speaks, that since he had inspired you to reveal those things which were hid, even from his own light, such as the feeble springs of some great events; and perceiving that a faction who could not bear their deeds to be brought to light, had condemned it to an ignominious flame, that it might not perish so, he was resolved to consume it with his own—a celestial one. And then you must conclude with some simile; thus, etc. There are two or three that will fit it.

Whiston has at last published his project of the longitude; the most ridiculous thing that ever was thought on.[1] But a pox on him! he has spoiled one of my papers of Scriblerus, which was a proposal for the longitude, not very unlike his, to this purpose: that since there was no pole for East and West, that all the Princes of Europe should join and build two prodigious poles, upon high mountains, with a vast light-house to serve for a pole-star. I was thinking of a calculation of the time, charges, and dimensions. Now you must understand, his project is by light-houses, and explosion of bombs at a certain hour.

Lewis invited me to dinner to-day, and has disappointed me. I thought to have said something more about you. I have nothing more to add, but, my dear friend, adieu.

CCLXXIV. [*Sheridan.*]

SWIFT TO THE DUKE OF ORMOND

July 17, 1714.

MY LORD,[2]
I NEVER expected that a great man should remember me in absence, because I knew it was unreasonable, and that your Grace is too much troubled with persons about you, to think of those who are out of the way. But,

---

[1] The scheme for which the Rev. William Whiston (" Prose Works," iv, 274) was responsible was, it is said, obviously chimerical (" D. N. B.," lxi, 12).
[2] As previously mentioned (*supra*, p. 133, n. 4) Swift had looked upon the influence of Ormond as the one hope of saving the Ministry.

if Dr. Pratt[1] has done me right, I am mistaken, and your Grace has almost declared that you expected a letter from me; which you should never have had, if the Ministry had been like you, for then I should have always been near enough to have carried my own messages. But I was heartily weary of them, and your Grace will be my witness, that I despaired of any good success, from their manner of proceeding, some months before I left town, where I thought it became me to continue no longer, when I could do no service either to myself, my friends, or the public. By the accounts I have from particular friends, I find the animosity between the two great men does not at all diminish, though I hear it is given out that your Grace's successor[2] has undertaken a general reconcilement. If it be true, this will succeed like the rest of his late undertakings.[3]

I must beg your Grace's pardon, if I entreat you for several reasons to see Lady Masham as often as you conveniently can; and I must likewise desire you to exert yourself in the disposal of the bishoprics in Ireland.[4] It is a scandal to the Crown, and an injury to the Church, that they should be so long delayed. There are some hot-headed people on the other side the water, who understand nothing of our Court, and would confound everything; always employed to raise themselves upon the ruins of those characters they have blasted. I wish their intermeddling may not occasion a worse choice than your Grace approved of last winter. However, I beg you will take care that no injury be done to Dr. Pratt, or Dr. Elwood,[5] who have more merit and candour than a hundred of their detractors. I am, with the greatest respect, my Lord,

Your Grace's most obedient and most obliged humble servant,

JON. SWIFT.

[1] Who was evidently still in London (*supra*, p. 145).
[2] *I.e.*, the Duke of Shrewsbury, Ormond's successor in the office of Lord Lieutenant.
[3] To reconcile the party differences in Ireland (*supra*, p. 116).
[4] *Supra*, p. 132.   [5] *Supra*, p. 171.

CCLXXV. [*Original.*[1]]

SWIFT TO JOHN GRIGSBY

July 20, 1714.

MR. GRIGSBY,[2]

PRAY pay to Mr. John Barber my dividend on one thousand pounds being all my stock in the South Sea Company's books[3] for half a year's interest due at midsummer last, and this shall be your sufficient warrant.

JONATH. SWIFT.

CCLXXVI. [*Original.*[4]]

CHARLES FORD TO SWIFT

London, *July* 20, 1714.

WHO would ever do anything for them, when they are so negligent of their own interest? The Captain[5] must see what use it[6] would be to him to have it published, and yet he has not returned it. You have another copy by you: I wish you would send it, and if you do not care it should appear in your own hand, I will get it transcribed. My secretary is a boy of ten or eleven years old, and no discovery can be made by him. I do not know what my Lord Bolingbroke may do, but I dare say Barber does not suspect from whence it comes. However, I wonder he has not mentioned it to you.

I thought you had heard the Historiographer's place[7] had been disposed of this fortnight. I know no more of him who has it, than that his name is Madox.[8] It would be im-

---

[1] In the Forster Collection.

[2] The accountant of the South Sea Company.   [3] *Supra*, p. 148.

[4] In the British Museum. See Preface.   [5] *I.e.*, Bolingbroke.

[6] *I.e.*, the " Free Thoughts on the Present State of Affairs " (*supra*, p. 180).

[7] *Supra*, p. 184.

[8] Thomas Madox, who was sworn on 12 July into the office of Historiographer, presented a great contrast to Swift, and may be described, to use a phrase of the late Mr. Litton Falkiner, as an antiquary of the dryasdust type (" D. N. B.," xxxv, 305).

pudence in them to send for you; but I hope you will come. A reconcilement is impossible, and I can guess no reason why matters are delayed, unless it be to gain over some Lords, who stick firm to the Dragon,[1] and others that are averse to the Captain. The Duke of Shrewsbury declares against him in private conversation; I suppose because he is against every chief minister, for it is known he has no kindness for the Colonel.[2] Lord Anglesey rails at the Chancellor, for some opinion the Attorney and Solicitor General have given relating to Ireland.[3] Who can act, when they have so much caprice to deal with?

Mr. Lewis says, he will speak to Mr. Bromley for his part, and will engage it shall be paid as soon as Lord Bolingbroke has given his.[4] But it was mentioned before my Lord Treasurer, and he immediately took the whole upon himself. If they lived near one another, and a house between them was on fire, I fancy they would contend who should put it out, till the whole street were burned. Mr. Lewis goes into Wales the week after next.[5] I shall have the whole town to myself. Now it is my own, I begin not to value it. Pope and Parnell tell me, you design them a visit. When do you go? If you are with them in the middle of a week, I should be glad to meet you there. Let me know where you are to be in Herefordshire,[6] and I will send you some claret. It is no compliment, for I am over-stocked, and it will decay before I drink it. You shall have either old or new; I have too much of both. I paid the woman for your handkerchiefs; but should not have given her so much, if she had not assured me you agreed with her. I think you may very well strike off the old debt, and she will have no reason to complain; so I told her, but if you would have me, I will pay her. Pray send me the other copy,[7] or put me in a way of recovering the former. I am, etc.

---

[1] *I.e.*, Oxford (*supra*, p. 150, n. 4). [2] *I.e.*, Oxford.
[3] The opinions of six counsel, besides the Attorney and Solicitor-General, were then taken on the civic dispute in Dublin (*supra*, p. 101), and four were found in favour of the Irish executive and four in favour of the Dublin Corporation ("Portland Manuscripts," v, 473).
[4] This is presumably a reference to the grant of £1,000 to pay his induction expenses (*supra*, p. 107, n. 1).
[5] *Supra*, p. 168. [6] *Supra*, p. 166.
[7] *I.e.*, of the " Free Thoughts."

CCLXXVII. [*Aitken's Life of Arbuthnot.*[1]]

SWIFT TO JOHN ARBUTHNOT

Oxford, *July* 22, 1714.

How came I here? Why, Lord Harley wrote to me,[2] and so I came to have his company and his lady's two or three days.[3] They go to-morrow, and I return to my country place, where I will not stay a fortnight, and then I will ramble somewhere else. The language spoken to me now is that the Dragon[4] will be out in a few days; and perhaps is already, because Lord Chancellor was summoned from his country house two days ago by Lord Bolingbroke in great haste, and they conceive it may be to put a finishing stroke. I cannot heartily pardon your giving over to advise Lady Masham, who in my opinion is going on upon a very dangerous adventure without one creature to direct her. I am told that Lady Masham is as much taken with the Dragon as Lord Bolingbroke, and what she said to the Dragon a week ago is of so desperate a strain,[5] that I cannot think her in a temper to be at the head or the bottom of a change; nor do I believe a change accompanied with such fusions can ever succeed. For God sake do not leave her to herself; your post keeps you always near her, and she cannot but think you her friend. I am quite struck by the accounts given me by those I am now with. What can be your new scheme? What are your new provocations? Are you surer of a majority? Will not the Dragon when he is out, be able to draw off your friends? Lord Bolingbroke's language to me was quite contrary to his proceedings. Therefore I do not approve the last. I know not what to say; but if I were to be of necessity always at Court like you, I could never let people run mad without telling

---

[1] *Supra,* p. 149, n. 5.   [2] *Supra,* p. 184.

[3] Lord Harley stayed while in Oxford with Dr. William Stratford, the Canon of Christ Church, to whom there has been already allusion (*supra,* p. 142, n. 1). He had been Oxford's chaplain, and watched over Harley during his college course. From that time he carried on an incessant correspondence with Harley, and his letters have been printed by the Hist. MSS. Com. amongst the Portland Manuscripts, filling an entire volume.

[4] *I.e.,* Oxford (*supra,* p. 150, n. 4).   [5] *Supra,* p. 182.

and warning them sufficiently. You acted a great part four
years ago under the first change, and will you not hinder
men from kicking down all if you can. Pray write to me
soon, and excuse yourself and tell me how things are.
Adieu.

CCLXXVIII. [*Original.*[1]]

THE DUKE OF ORMOND TO SWIFT

July 22, 1714.

SIR,

I AM very glad to hear from you.[2] I thought you had hid
yourself from the world, and given over all thoughts of
your friends. I am very sorry for the reason of your retirement. I am a witness to your endeavours to have made up,
what I believe the great man you mention will hardly
compass. I am of your opinion, that it is shameful that
the vacant bishoprics are not disposed of. I shall do all
that lies in my power, to serve the gentlemen that I have
already mentioned to the Queen, and hope with good
success.

For the lady you mention I shall endeavour to see her
as often as I can. She is one that I have a very great
esteem for. I send you some Burgundy, which I hope you
will like. It is very good to cure the spleen. Believe me,
with great truth, Sir,

Your most affectionate friend and humble servant,

ORMOND.

CCLXXIX. [*Original.*[3]]

ERASMUS LEWIS TO SWIFT

Whitehall, *July* 22, 1714.

SIR,

I RECEIVED a letter from you last Monday,[4] for my Lord
Treasurer, in a blank cover. Last Friday Lord Chancellor

---

[1] In the British Museum. See Preface.   [2] *Supra*, p. 186.
[3] In the British Museum. See Preface.   [4] The 19th.

went into the country, with a design to stay there to the
10th of August; but last Tuesday he was sent for express
by Lord Bolingbroke. Next Tuesday the Queen goes to
Windsor. What changes we are to have, will probably appear before she goes. Dr. Arbuthnot dines with me to-day,
and in the evening we go to Kensington.

CCLXXX. [*Original.*[1]]

CHARLES FORD TO SWIFT

London, *July* 22, 1714.

PRAY send me the other copy,[2] and let us have the benefit
of it, since you have been at the trouble of writing. Unless
[Lord Bolingbroke [3]] be served against his will, it is not
likely to be done at all, but I think you used to take a
pleasure in good offices of that kind, and I hope you would
not let the cause suffer; though I must own, in this particular, the person who has the management of it, does not
deserve any favour. Nothing being left for me at St. Dunstan's, I sent to B[arber] for an answer to my last.[4] He
says, it is not yet restored to him; as soon as it is, I shall
have it. This delay begins to make me think all ministers
are alike: and as soon as the Captain[5] is a Colonel,[6] he will
act as his predecessors have done.

The Queen goes to Windsor next Tuesday, and we expect all matters will be settled before that time. We have
had a report, that my Lord Privy Seal[7] is to go out alone;
but the learned only laugh at it. The Captain's friends
think themselves secure; and the Colonel's are so much of
the same opinion, that they only drink his health while he
is yet alive. However it is thought he will fall easy, with a
pension of four thousand pounds a year, and a dukedom.
Most of the staunch Tories are pleased with the alteration,

---

[1] In the British Museum. See Preface.

[2] Of the " Free Thoughts " (*supra*, p. 188).

[3] Other editors have suggested "Lord Treasurer" as the words to
be supplied, but so far as appears Oxford had never seen the "Free
Thoughts," and from the context it seems clear that the reference is
to Bolingbroke.

[4] *Supra*, p. 188.   [5] *I.e.*, Bolingbroke.

[6] *I.e.*, chief minister.   [7] Lord Dartmouth (*supra*, p. 170).

and the Whimsicals pretend the cause of their disgust was, because the Whigs were too much favoured.

In short, we propose very happy days to ourselves as long as this reign lasts; and if the "uncertain timorous nature of [the Queen]"[1] does not disappoint us, we have a very fair prospect. The Dragon[2] and his antagonist meet every day at the cabinet. They often eat, and drink, and walk together, as if there was no sort of disagreement,[3] and when they part, I hear they give one another such names, as nobody but Ministers of State could bear, without cutting throats. The Duke of Marlborough is expected here every day.[4] Dr. Garth[5] says, he comes only to drink the Bristol waters for a diabetes. The Whigs are making great preparations to receive him. But yesterday I was offered considerable odds, that not one of those who go out to meet him, will visit him in half a year. I durst not lay, though I can hardly think it. My Lord Mar is married to Lady Frances Pierrepoint;[6] and my Lord Dorchester,[7] her father, is to be married next week to Lady Bell Bentinck. Let me know if you go to Pope's, that I may endeavour to meet you there. I am, etc.

CCLXXXI. [*Original.*[8]]

CHARLES FORD TO SWIFT

London, *July* 24, 1714.

WE expected the great affair[9] would have been done yesterday, and now everybody agrees it will be to-night. The Bishop of London,[10] Lord Bathurst,[11] Mr. Brydges,[12] Sir

---

[1] *Supra*, p. 170.   [2] *I.e.*, Oxford (*supra*, p. 150, n. 4).
[3] *Supra*, p. 182.   [4] *Supra*, p. 179.
[5] In his Whig days Swift was often in Garth's company ("Prose Works," ii, *passim*).
[6] According to G. E. C. ("Complete Peerage," v, 237), the Scotch Secretary (*supra*, p. 129, n. 5) was married on 26 July to the Marquess of Dorchester's daughter.
[7] He was created Duke of Kingston-upon-Hull by George I.
[8] In the British Museum. See Preface.
[9] *I.e.*, the dismissal of Oxford.   [10] *Supra*, p. 141, n. 4.
[11] He was one of the twelve peers created two years previously.
[12] *Supra*, vol. i, p. 253, n. 1.

II   O

William Wyndham,[1] and Campion,[2] are named for Commissioners of the Treasury; but I have not sufficient authority for you to depend upon it. They talk of the Duke of Ormond for our Lord Lieutenant. I cannot get the pamphlet[3] back. What shall I do? I wish you would send me the other copy. My Lord Anglesey goes next Monday to Ireland. I hear he is only angry with the Chancellor, and not at all with the Captain.[4]

Addressed—To the Rev. Dr. Swift, Dean of St. Patrick's.

CCLXXXII. [*Original.*[5]]

ERASMUS LEWIS TO SWIFT

Whitehall, *July* 24, 1714.

I SAW Lord Harley this morning. He tells me, that he left you horridly in the dumps.[6] I wish you were here; for after giving a quarter of an hour's vent to our grief for the departure of our Don Quixote,[7] we should recover ourselves, and receive consolation from each other. The triumph of the enemy makes me mad. I feel a strange tenderness within myself, and scarce bear the thoughts of dating letters from this place, when my old friend is out, whose fortune I have shared for so many years. But *fiat voluntas tua*. The damned thing is, we are to do all dirty work. We are to turn out Monckton,[8] and I hear we are to pass the new commission of the Treasury. For God's sake write to Lady Masham, in favour of poor Thomas, to preserve him from ruin.[9] I will second it. I intended

---

[1] The Chancellor of the Exchequer.

[2] Henry Campion, who represented Sussex in Parliament, and was a member of the October Club (*supra*, vol. i, p. 236).

[3] *I.e.*, the "Free Thoughts."   [4] *I.e.*, Bolingbroke.

[5] In the British Museum. See Preface.

[6] *Supra*, p. 190.   [7] *I.e.*, Oxford.

[8] It was through revelations made by Robert Monckton, one of the Commissioners for Trade, that the proceedings with respect to the explanatory articles with Spain (*supra*, p. 171) became a subject of inquiry.

[9] The Lord Treasurer's secretary (*supra*, p. 167). He is said to have written to Swift "by the same post, for a recommendation to Lady Masham, either to be continued in the same office under the

to have writ you a long letter: but the moment I had turned this page, I had intelligence that the Dragon[1] has broke out in a fiery passion with my Lord Chancellor, sworn a thousand oaths that he would be revenged, etc. This impotent, womanish behaviour, vexes me more than his being out. This last stroke shows, *quantula sint hominum corpuscula*. I am determined for the Bath on the 2nd or the 9th of August at farthest.

CCLXXXIII. [*Original.*[2]]

JOHN ARBUTHNOT TO SWIFT

[*July* 24, 1714.]

DEAR BROTHER,
I SUPPOSE you have received the account of St. Kilda. There is an officer there, who is a sort of *tribunus plebis,* whose office it is to represent the grievances of the people to the Laird of M'Leod, who is supposed to be their oppressor. He is bound to contradict the Laird, till he gives him three strokes with a cane over the head, and then he is at liberty to submit.[3] This I have done, and so has your friend Lewis.[4] It has been said that we and the Dean were the authors of all that has since happened, by keeping the Dragon[5] in, when there was an offer to lay down.[6] I was told to my face,[7] that what I said in this case went for

Commissioners, or to be considered in some other manner by way of compensation"; and to have urged "a precedent for this in the case of his predecessor, who, being removed from his post of secretary, got the office of controller of the lotteries, worth £500 per annum for thirty-two years" (Hawkesworth "Letters," ii, 85).

[1] *I.e.*, Oxford (*supra*, p. 150, n. 4).
[2] In the British Museum. See Preface.
[3] It was to the steward of the Laird of Macleod that the *tribunus plebis* represented the grievances of the people. He was expected to press the request until the steward either granted it, or in exasperation struck him "three strokes with his cudgel upon the crown of his head," and in the event of the steward giving him only one stroke instead of the legitimate number, he was obliged to continue to plead until the steward gave him "both a second and a third" (Scott, "Works," xvi, 163).
[4] To Lady Masham.   [5] *I.e.*, Oxford (*supra*, p. 150, n. 4).
[6] The reference must be to the ministerial crisis in March (*supra*, p. 132, n. 3).
[7] Evidently by Lady Masham.

nothing; that I did not care, if the great person's [1] affairs went to entire ruin, so I could support the interests of the Dragon; that I did not know the half of his proceedings. Particularly it was said, though I am confident it was a mistake, that he had attempted the removing her [2] from the favour of a great person. In short, the fall of the Dragon does not proceed altogether from his old friend, but from the great person, whom I perceive to be highly offended, by little hints that I have received. In short, the Dragon has been so ill used, and must serve upon such terms for the future, if he should, that I swear I would not advise Turk, Jew, nor infidel, to be in that state. Come up to town, and I can tell you more. I have been but indifferently treated myself, by somebody at court, in small concerns. I cannot tell who it is. But mum for that. Adieu.

CCLXXXIV. [*Aitken's Life of Arbuthnot.*[3]]

SWIFT TO JOHN ARBUTHNOT

July 25, 1714.

YOU are every way too kind.[4] As to the Historiographer's place, I now hear it has been disposed of these three weeks to one Madox.[5] I wonder Lord Bolingbroke knew nothing of it. So there is an end of that, and of twenty reflections one might make upon it. If the Queen is indifferent in those matters, I may well be so too.[6] I was three days last week in Oxford with Lord and Lady Harley, and Dr. Stratford.[7] Our talk was of the Dragon's being out, as a thing done; so no more reflections on that neither. *Qu'est que l'homme.*

And so you will lend me all your money. The mischief is, I never borrow money of a friend. You are mightily mistaken: all your honour, generosity, good nature, good

---

[1] *I.e.*, the Queen.   [2] *I.e.*, Lady Masham (*supra*, p. 151, n. 1).
[3] *Supra*, p. 149, n. 5.   [4] *Supra*, p. 184.   [5] *Supra*, p. 188.
[6] Swift attributes elsewhere (" Prose Works," v, 366, 367) the Queen's neglect of his proposal to write a history of her reign to procrastination rather than to indifference, and on the authority of Lady Masham says that her Majesty was " as desirous of preserving her reputation with posterity, as might justly become a great Prince to be."
[7] *Supra*, p. 190.

sense, wit, and every other praiseworthy quality, will never make me think one jot the better of you. That time is now some years past, and you will never mend in my opinion. But really, Brother, you have a sort of shuffle in your gait; and now I have said the worst that your most mortal enemy could say of you with truth. I defy Pope and his burning glasses; a man cannot amuse himself fifty miles from London, after four years jading himself with Ministers of State, but all the town must hear of it. However, if Pope makes the right use of your hint for an epigram, or a longer copy, I shall not be angry. It was a malicious satire of yours upon Whiston, that what you intended as a ridicule, should be any way struck upon by him for a reality. Go on for the sake of wit and humour, and cultivate that vein which no man alive possesses but yourself, and which lay like a mine in the earth, which the owner for a long time never knew of.

Lady Masham, who talked of writing to me first has not answered my letter; put her not in mind, I beg you. I believe she has heard of my letter to the Dragon,[1] and dislikes it as partial. I hear he has shown it to every living soul, and I believe has done so in malice, as the French understand that word. My humble services to Lord and Lady Masham and Mrs. Hill. By what I heard at Oxford Lord Trevor is fallen off with the rest;[2] and indeed the circle of the Dragon's friends seemed very narrow, by the loss they were at for healths: we came to yours six glasses before the usual time. Adieu.

CCLXXXV. [*Sheridan.*]

Swift to the Earl of Oxford

July 25, 1714.

My Lord,

To-morrow sevennight I shall set out from hence to Ireland: my license for absence[3] being so near out, that I can

---

[1] *Supra*, p. 160.
[2] An idea that Trevor (*supra*, p. 170) would have had more influence than Bolingbroke, if the Queen had lived, afterwards gained some credence ("Wentworth Papers," p. 412).
    Supra, p. 126.

stay no longer without taking another. I say this, that if you have any commands, I shall have just time enough to receive them before I go. And if you resign in a few days, as I am told you design to do, you may possibly retire to Herefordshire,[1] where I shall readily attend you, if you soon withdraw; or, after a few months stay in Ireland, I will return at the beginning of winter, if you please to command me. I speak in the dark, because I am altogether so, and what I say may be absurd. You will please to pardon me; for, as I am wholly ignorant, so I have none of your composure of mind. I pray God Almighty direct and defend you, etc.

CCLXXXVI. [*Original.*[2]]

THE EARL OF OXFORD TO SWIFT

July 27, 1714.

IF I tell my dear friend the value I put upon his undeserved friendship, it will look like suspecting you or myself. Though I have had no power since July 25, 1713,[3] I believe now, as a private man, I may prevail to renew your license of absence, conditionally you will be present with me; for to-morrow morning I shall be a private person. When I have settled my domestic affairs here, I go to Wimpole;[4] thence alone, to Herefordshire.[5] If I have not

[1] To his own seat, Brampton Castle.
[2] In the British Museum. See Preface.
[3] At that time there was a correspondence between Oxford, who was ill in London, and Bolingbroke, who was in attendance on the Queen at Windsor, about their future policy and the reconstruction of the Ministry which then took place (*supra*, p. 57). On the day named Oxford addressed a letter to Bolingbroke in which he gave an account of "the pretences for giving disturbance to the Queen's servants," proposed the remedy and what was necessary to be done by Bolingbroke, and finally put Bolingbroke in mind of "the several particulars which then required attention" ("Parliamentary History," vi, App.). Bolingbroke's reply was most loyal in its tone and much to the point ("Portland Manuscripts," v, 311), but Oxford believed that at the moment Bolingbroke was intriguing "to have terms put upon him and a junto" (*ibid.*, p. 467), and said that from that day Bolingbroke did not pay the slightest attention to his opinion.
[4] His son's seat in Cambridgeshire, afterwards the residence of the Earls of Hardwicke.
[5] *Supra*, n. 1.

tired you *tête-à-tête*, fling away so much time upon one who loves you. And I believe, in the mass of souls, ours were placed near each other. I send you an imitation of Dryden, as I went to Kensington:

> To serve with love,
>   And shed your blood,
> Approved is above.
>   But here below,
>   Th' examples show,
> 'Tis fatal to be good.

CCLXXXVII. [*Original.*[1]]

ERASMUS LEWIS TO SWIFT

Whitehall, *July* 27, 1714.

SIR,

I HAVE yours of the 25th. You judge very right; it is not the going out, but the manner, that enrages me. The Queen has told all the Lords the reasons of her parting with him,[2] viz. that he neglected all business; that he was seldom to be understood; that when he did explain him-self, she could not depend upon the truth of what he said; that he never came to her at the time she appointed; that he often came drunk; that lastly, to crown all, he behaved himself toward her with ill manner, indecency, and dis-respect.[3] *Pudet haec opprobria nobis*, etc.

I am distracted with the thoughts of this, and the pride of the conqueror.[4] I would give the world I could go out of town to-morrow; but the Secretary[5] saith I must not go till he returns, which will not be till the 16th of August, or perhaps the 23rd; but I am in hopes I may go toward Bath the 16th. The runners are already employed to go to all the coffee-houses. They rail to the pit of hell. I am ready to burst for want of vent. The stick is yet in his hand, because they cannot agree who shall be the new Commissioners. We suppose the blow will be given to-night

---

[1] In the British Museum. See Preface.   [2] *I.e.*, Oxford.
[3] It is suggested by Leadam (*op. cit.*, p. 219) that these remarks were made by the Queen at the Council table after Oxford had sur-rendered the staff, but Lewis was writing before that event, and the sentences seem rather a summary of what was said by the Queen in private conversation than in public.
[4] *I.e.*, Bolingbroke.   [5] *I.e.*, Bromley.

or to-morrow morning. The sterility of good and able men is incredible.

When the matter is over, I will wait upon our she friend.[1] If she receives me as usual, I will propose to her, that I will serve where I do, provided I may be countenanced, and at full liberty to pay my duty to all the Harleian family in the same manner I used to do. If that is not allowed me in the utmost extent, consistent with my trust here, I will propose an employment in the revenues, or to go out without anything; for I will not be debarred going to him. If she does not receive me as she used to do, I will never go again. I flatter myself she will be so friendly as to enter into the consideration of my private circumstances, and preserve her old goodness to me.

There is no seeing the Dragon till he is out, and then I will know his thoughts about your coming to Brampton.[2] I hear he goes out of town instantly to Wimpole, and my lady to Brampton; that he will join her there, after a few days stay at Wimpole. Adieu.

CCLXXXVIII. [*Original.*[3]]

Lady Masham to Swift

July 29, 1714.

My good Friend,

I own it looks unkind in me not to thank you, in all this time, for your sincere kind letter;[4] but I was resolved to stay till I could tell you the Queen had got so far the better of the Dragon,[5] as to take her power out of his hands. He has been the most ungrateful man to her, and to all his best friends, that ever was born. I cannot have so much time now to write all my mind, because my dear mistress is not well, and I think I may lay her illness to the charge of the Treasurer, who, for three weeks together, was teas-

---

[1] *I.e.*, Lady Masham.   [2] *Supra*, p. 198.

[3] In the British Museum. See Preface.

[4] Writing on the 24th of that month to Lord Harley, Dr. Strafford (*supra*, p. 190, n. 3) says: "The reverend person who was with you here will certainly behave decently to your father, but he will adhere to Lady Masham" ("Portland Manuscripts," vii, 196).

[5] *I.e.*, Oxford (*supra*, p. 150, n. 4).

ing and vexing her without intermission, and she could not get rid of him till Tuesday last.[1]

I must put you in mind of one passage in your letter to me, which is: "I pray God send you wise and faithful friends to advise you at this time, when there are so great difficulties to struggle with." That is very plain and true; therefore will you, who have gone through so much, and taken more than anybody pains, and given wise advice, if that wretched man had had sense enough and honesty to have taken it, I say, will you leave us and go into Ireland? No, it is impossible; your goodness is still the same, your charity and compassion for this poor lady, who has been barbarously used, would not let you do it. I know you take delight to help the distressed; and there cannot be a greater object than this good lady, who deserves pity. Pray, dear friend, stay here; and do not believe us all alike to throw away good advice, and despise everybody's understanding but their own. I could say a great deal upon the subject, but I must go to her, for she is not well.

This comes to you by a safe hand,[2] so that neither of us need be in any pain about it. My Lord and brother are in the country. My sister and girls are your humble servants.

CCLXXXIX. [*Original.*[3]]

ERASMUS LEWIS TO SWIFT

July 29, 1714.

SIR,

I HAVE yours of the 27th. I write this in the morning, for I go in the evening to Kensington.[4] If I am well re-

---

[1] The 27th. After Oxford had given up his staff on that day the Council proceeded to consider the appointment of Commissioners (*supra*, p. 193) to take his place, but although their debate was prolonged until two o'clock the next morning they could not agree as to the persons to be nominated. The Queen remained to the end, and her fatal illness dates from that time. Oxford's enemies attributed it to agitation caused by a violent speech which he had made before his withdrawal, and his friends to her "trouble and concern" on parting from him (*cf.* Leadam, *op. cit.*, p. 219 and "Portland Manuscripts," v, 480).

[2] That of John Barber, who then intended to visit Swift at Letcombe (*infra*, p. 205).

[3] In the British Museum. See Preface.

[4] To see Lady Masham (*supra*, p. 200).

ceived, I will continue my homage, if not, they shall hear
of me no more. Where shall I write to you again?
For I cannot stir from hence, till the 16th of August
at soonest. Nothing could please me more than to pass a
few months with you at Abercothy;[1] but I am yet uncertain whether I shall go there at all. All I am sure of is,
that I will go out of town to some place for some time;
first to the Bath, for I cannot bear staying in this room. I
want physic to help my digestion of these things, though
the Esquire[2] is kinder to me than before. I am not mortified
at what you tell me of Mercurialis:[3] only I would know,
whether any disrespectful conduct of mine has brought it
upon me, or whether it is only a general dislike of me,
because I am not a man of parts, or because I am in other
interests? They would not give the Dragon[4] the least
quarter, excepting only a pension, if he will work journey-
work by the quarter. I have long thought his parts decayed,
and am more of that opinion than ever. The new commission is not yet named. Would not the world have roared
against the Dragon for such a thing? Mercurialis entertained Stanhope, Craggs, Pulteney, and Walpole.[5] What if
the Dragon had done so? The Duke of Somerset dines
to-day with the fraternity at Greenwich, with Withers.[6]
Nobody goes out with the Dragon; but many will sit very
loose. Some say the new men[7] will be Lexington,[8] Wyndham,[9] Strangways,[10] Sir John Stonhouse,[11] and Campion.[12]

---

[1] *Supra*, p. 168, n. 4.

[2] Whether the reference is to Bromley or Bolingbroke seems
doubtful.

[3] *I.e.*, Bolingbroke.

[4] *I.e.*, Oxford (*supra*, p. 150, n. 4).

[5] The future Whig ministers.

[6] Sir William Withers, one of the Tory members for the City of
London (*supra*, p. 79).

[7] *I.e.*, the Commissioners of the Treasury (*supra*, p. 201, n. 1).

[8] Robert Sutton, second Baron Lexington, who had been Ambassador to Madrid, and is said by Swift to have had only "a very
moderate degree of understanding" ("Prose Works," *passim*).

[9] *Supra*, p. 194.

[10] Thomas Strangways, who sat for Dorsetshire.

[11] He was Controller of the Household, and one of the parliamentary
representatives for Berkshire.

[12] *Supra*, p. 194, n. 2.

CCXC. [*Original.*[1]]

SWIFT TO ARCHDEACON WALLS

July 29, 1714.

THIS day I received yours of the 20th instant. You know, I suppose, that two months ago, I retired to the place where I now am, above fifty miles from London, foreseeing the storm that would happen. This day I had a letter from my Lord Treasurer to let me know he was just going to give up the staff,[2] which I suppose he did yesterday. He says he is going in a week or two to retire to his house in Herefordshire, and begs I would stay with him some time there. I cannot possibly refuse his request; therefore I must intreat you to go to Mr. Dawson, and desire him to renew my license, when the last is expired, which will be at the end of August. I have writ to him this post to the same purpose.[3] I had fixed my journey for Ireland to the 2nd of August four days hence, and my trunk with all my clothes and linen was sent last week to Chester, and I am almost in rags. I hope to be in Ireland by the end of autumn. Pray direct your letters no more to Mr. Lewis, who is retiring upon this occasion, but to Charles Ford Esquire at his office at Whitehall. You may let Parvisol still expect me in Ireland, till he hear to the contrary, or tell him as you please.[4] And for the rest I leave the whole to you and Mr. Forbes; turn him out, keep him, hang him, save him, just as you please. I am ashamed to give you all this trouble, and I am now a poor cast courtier.

[Tell] Mr. ——, the young parson, I forget his name, that gave me the Sacrament at, I do not know where, the Sunday after I was installed, I have received his fifty pounds; it is in a friend's hand and shall be paid to his order, when he pleases—oh! Mr. Fetherston, that is his name,[5] pray tell him this when you see him. Service to our Doll; I thought to have been so merry with you a fortnight hence. Service to Goody Stoyte, Catherine and the

---

[1] In the possession of Mr. John Murray. See Preface.
[2] *Supra*, p. 198.   [3] *Infra*, p. 204.   [4] *Supra*, p. 164.
[5] Fetherston (*supra*, p. 185) was then Vicar of Crumlin, a village three miles to the south-west of Dublin.

Manleys.[1] I served Manley while I was able; I said to Lord Treasurer I would not let him turn him out without a pension, and so it stuck, and so he has lingered on:[2] he should now I believe look out for some other friends, and if you are great there you should hint it to him. I shall lose all favour with those now in power by following Lord Oxford in his retreat. I am hitherto very fair with them, but that will be at an end.

Addressed—To the Reverend Mr. Archdeacon Walls over against the Hospital in Queen Street, Dublin.

CCXCI. [*Scott*.]

SWIFT TO JOSHUA DAWSON

July 29, 1714.

SIR,[3]

I HAVE been these two months fifty miles from London, to avoid the storm that has happened at Court. The news will tell you a post or two before this of my Lord Oxford's laying down; he was to do it yesterday. He has sent to desire I would stay some time with him at his house in Herefordshire,[4] which I am not likely to refuse, though I may probably suffer a good deal in my little affairs in Ireland by my absence. This makes it necessary for me to desire you would please to renew my license of absence, which expires about the end of August. As soon as it is expired, I should hope so much from your friendship, that, though any accident might happen to prevent your timely notice, you would do me such a favour whenever there is occasion. I had fixed my journey to Ireland to be on the 2nd of August, when this incident changed it. I think it is about this time two years[5] that you came to my lodgings with Mr. Pratt,[6] to tell me the news of Lord Godolphin's going out, which was as joyful to me as this is otherwise. I believe you will reckon me an ill courtier to follow a discarded statesman to his retirement, especially when I have been always well with those now in power, as

---

[1] *Supra*, p. 67.   [2] *Supra*, p. 125.   [3] *Supra*, p. 126.
[4] *Supra*, p. 198.   [5] *Recte*, four years.
[6] The Provost's brother (*supra*, vol. i, p. 188, n. 2).

I was with him. But to answer that would require talking,
and I have already troubled you so much who are a man
of business. I am Sir,
            Your most obedient humble servant.

Pray let the absence be general as before. I was very
near wanting it some months ago with a witness.[1] I know
not what alterations this change may make in the scheme
for Irish promotions. I hear Dr. Pratt and Elwood are
secure.[2]

CCXCII. [*Original.*[3]]

JOHN BARBER TO SWIFT

July 31, 1714.
Six at night.

DEAR SIR,
    I AM heartily sorry I should be the messenger of so ill
news, as to tell you the Queen is dead, or dying: if alive,
it is said, she cannot live till morning. You may easily
imagine the confusion we are all in on this sad occasion.
I had set out yesterday to wait on you, but for this sad
accident, and should have brought letters from Lord
Bolingbroke and Lady Masham, to have prevented your
going.[4] Pray do not go, for I will come to you when I see
how things stand. My Lord Shrewsbury is made Lord
Treasurer,[5] and everything is ready for the proclaiming the
Duke of Brunswick King of England. The Parliament will
sit to-morrow, and choose a new Speaker; for Sir Thomas
is in Wales.[6] For God's sake do not go; but either come to
London, or stay till I come to you.

Addressed—To the Rev. Mr. Geree at Upper Letcombe,
    near Wantage in Berks.

---

[1] When the Public Spirit of the Whigs was under discussion, and
the thought of retiring abroad occurred to Swift (*supra,* p. 126, n. 3).
[2] *Supra,* p. 171.   [3] In the British Museum. See Preface.
[4] To Ireland (*supra,* p. 197).
[5] The circumstances of his appointment will be subsequently seen
(*infra,* p. 207).
[6] Hanmer was, however, sent for (*infra,* p. 208), and the House of
Commons adjourned on meeting after the Queen's death until he
came.

CCXCIII. [*Original.*[1]]

ERASMUS LEWIS TO SWIFT

Kensington, Saturday, *July* 31 [1714],
Six in the Evening.

SIR,

AT the time I am writing, the breath is said to be in the Queen's nostrils; but that is all. No hope left of her recovery. Lord Oxford is in Council; so are the Whigs.[2] We expect the demise to-night. There is a prospect that the Elector will meet with no opposition; the French having no fleet, nor being able to put one out soon. Lady Masham did receive me kindly.[3] Poor woman, I heartily pity her. Now, is not the Dragon[4] born under a happy planet, to be out of the scrape? Dr. Arbuthnot thinks you should come up. You will not wonder if all my country resolutions are in suspense. Pray come up, to see how things go.

CCXCIV. [*Original.*[5]]

CHARLES FORD TO SWIFT

London, *July* 31, 1714.
Three in the afternoon.

I DO not doubt but you have heard the Queen is dead, and perhaps we may be so unfortunate before this comes to you, but at present she is alive, and much better than could have been expected. I am just come from Kensington, where I have spent almost these two whole days. I am in great haste; but, till dinner comes up, I will write to you, and give you as full an account as I can of her illness.

[1] In the British Museum. See Preface.
[2] On the morning of the preceding day the Duke of Argyll and the Duke of Somerset, although not summoned, had appeared at the Council, and subsequently the attendance of all Privy Councillors was requested.
[3] *Supra*, p. 201.   [4] *I.e.*, Oxford (*supra*, p. 150, n. 4).
[5] In the British Museum. See Preface.

Her disorder began between eight and nine yesterday morning.[1] The doctors ordered her head to be shaved, and while it was doing, she fell into a fit of convulsion, or as they thought an apoplexy. This lasted near two hours, and she was speechless, and showed little sign of life during that time; but came to herself upon being blooded. As soon as she recovered, my Lord Bolingbroke went to her, and told her the Privy Council was of opinion, it would be for the public service to have the Duke of Shrewsbury made Lord Treasurer. She immediately consented, and gave the staff into the Duke's hands.[2] The great seal was put to the patent by four o'clock. She continued ill the whole day. In the evening I spoke to Dr. Arbuthnot, and he told me he did not think her distemper was desperate.[3] Radcliffe was sent for to Carshalton [4] about noon, by order of the Council; but said he had taken physic, and could not come.[5] In all probability he had saved her life; for I

[1] The Queen had, however, shown symptoms of illness for two days. One of her physicians, Shadwell, told Peter Wentworth and "all the world," that on feeling her pulse on Wednesday the 28th before dinner "he did not like it," and so informed her and the Duke of Shrewsbury, but that Arbuthnot said that "her pulse was well," an assertion that may have originated as much from consideration for the patient as from a desire to keep her illness a secret, which is attributed to him by Wentworth ("Wentworth Papers," p. 408). According to a letter supposed to be written by Oxford's brother, "the Queen slept very little on Tuesday night, on Wednesday was much indisposed, and on Thursday was seized with a lethargic fit" ("Portland Manuscripts," v, 480).

[2] "The Queen to-day about one o'clock," writes Peter Wentworth (*op. cit.*, p. 408), "gave the Treasurer's staff to the Duke of Shrewsbury, my Lord Chancellor holding her hand to direct it to the Duke. When he took it he told her he would keep it to resign to her again when she was better."

[3] Peter Wentworth, who was one of the Queen's equerries, overheard, however, much to his dismay, Arbuthnot whisper to some one else that "it was ten thousand to one if she recovered" (*op. cit.*, p. 407).

[4] Near Croydon.

[5] Radcliffe's conduct was discussed in the House of Commons, and gave rise to much popular indignation, his dread of which is said to have hastened his own death. His excuse was that he had not been summoned by "her Majesty or those in commission next to her" (see his letter in Hawkesworth's "Letters," ii, 100). The Queen's aversion to him was very great, and Peter Wentworth (*op. cit.*, p. 410), who had no more love for Radcliffe than had Swift (*supra*, p. 95, n. 4), thought this excuse not an unreasonable one. By whom Radcliffe was summoned is not certain: both Lady Masham and the Duchess of Ormond have been named.

am told the late Lord Gower[1] had been often in the same condition with the gout in his head, and Radcliffe kept him alive many years after.

This morning, when I went there before nine, they told me she was just expiring. That account continued above three hours, and a report was carried to town, that she was actually dead. She was not prayed for, even at her own chapel at St. James's, and what is more infamous, stocks arose three per cent. upon it in the city. Before I came away, she had recovered a warmth in her breast and one of her arms, and all the doctors agreed she would in all probability hold out till to-morrow, except Mead,[2] who pronounced several hours before, she could not live two minutes, and seems uneasy it did not happen so. I did not care to talk much to Arbuthnot, because I heard him cautious in his answers to other people; but by his manner, I fancy he does not yet absolutely despair.

The Council sat yesterday all day and night, taking it by turns to go out and refresh themselves. They have now adjourned, upon what the doctors said, till five. Last night the Speaker[3] and my Lord Chief Justice Parker[4] were sent for, and the troops from Flanders.[5] This morning the Hanoverian envoy was ordered to attend with the black box,[6] and the herald to be in a readiness to proclaim the new King. Some of the Whigs were at Council yesterday but not one failed to-day; and most of the members of that party, in each House, are already come to town. If any change happens before the post goes out, I will send you word in a postscript; and you may conclude her alive, if you hear no more from me, and have no better authority than post-letters to inform you of the contrary. For God's

---

[1] John, first Baron Gower, who died in 1709.

[2] Richard Mead, who as Sir Frederick Falkiner says ("Prose Works," xii, 54) was "one of the most eminent of the eminent of his day," was a great favourite of Radcliffe, and is said by the latter to have omitted nothing for the Queen's preservation.

[3] *Supra*, p. 205.

[4] Better known as Earl of Macclesfield, the title under which he was subsequently promoted to the Woolsack, and became the subject of an historic impeachment.

[5] Ten battalions of the English army, which were then in Flanders, were recalled.

[6] Containing the names of the Lords Justices nominated by the Elector.

sake do not think of removing from the place where you are, till matters are a little settled. Ireland is the last retreat you ought to think of; but you can never be better than you are now, till we see how things go.

I had yours with the printed pamphlet, as well as the other, and should have sent it away to-morrow.[1] Pray let me hear from you. . . .[2] Have you had all mine? I have failed you but one post, I think it was the last, for a fortnight or more.

Eleven at night.

The Queen is something better, and the Council is again adjourned till eight in the morning.

CCXCV. [*Scott.*]

SWIFT TO MISS ESTHER VANHOMRIGH

August 1, 1714.

I HAVE had now two letters of yours to answer. I am pleased to see you piqued about my dearness to Ben and John.[3] They are worthy subjects; there are some words I never use to some people, let that satisfy. How many gentlemen, says you, and fine young gentlemen truly, would be proud to have you desire so much of them. Who told you I was going to Bath?[4] No such thing. I had fixed to set out to-morrow for Ireland; but poor Lord Oxford desires I will go with him to Herefordshire; and I only

---

[1] Evidently Ford had received from Swift another copy of the " Free Thoughts," and only for the Queen's illness would have before then sent it to another printer (*supra*, p. 194).

[2] Five lines are obliterated; the reason is subsequently explained (*infra*, p. 217).

[3] *I.e.*, Benjamin Tooke and John Barber. It is probable, as Sir Walter Scott suggests (" Works," xix, 339), that Swift was wont to address them when writing as " dear Ben " and " dear John," and that Vanessa had seen letters from Swift to them in connection with the subject of his previous letter to her (*supra*, p. 173). That mode of address was, however, an unusual one at that period, and so far as I am aware not used by Swift to other persons.

[4] Erasmus Lewis had no doubt mentioned to Vanessa his wish that Swift should accompany him to Bath (*supra*, p. 168). Possibly Swift had given him reason to expect that he would do so.

expect his answer, whether I shall go there before, or meet him hereabouts, or go to Wimpole, his son's house, and to go with him down;[1] and I expect to leave this in two or three days, one way or other. I will stay with him till the Parliament meets again, if he desires it. I am not of your opinion about Lord Bolingbroke; perhaps he may get the staff, but I cannot rely on his love to me. He knew I had a mind to be Historiographer, though I valued it not but for the public service, yet it is gone to a worthless rogue that nobody knows.[2] I am writ to earnestly by somebody to come to town, and join with these people now in power, but I will not do it. Say nothing of this, but guess the person. I told Lord Oxford I would go with him when he was out, and now he begs it of me, and I cannot refuse him. I meddle not with his faults, as he was a Minister of State; but you know his personal kindness to me was excessive. He distinguished and chose me above all other men while he was great, and his letter to me the other day was the most moving imaginable.

The knife-handles should surely be done up in silver, and strong. I believe Brandeth, my toyman, in Exchange Alley, would deal most honestly by me. Barber knows him. Where is your discretion in desiring to travel with that body, who, I believe, would not do it for a thousand pounds, except it were to Italy.[3] Pray God send you a good deliverance through your accounts. It is well you have been a lawyer so long. You will be two hours reading this letter, it is writ so ill. When I am fixed anywhere, perhaps I may be so gracious as to let you know: but I will not promise. Service to Moll. Adieu.

---

[1] *Supra*, p. 198.

[2] As a previous reference has shown (*supra*, p. 185, n. 4), Swift wronged Bolingbroke in thinking him indifferent to his ambition. He had many months before solicited the office of Historiographer for him. See Appendix IX. There is also reason to believe that Bolingbroke did not neglect Swift's interest in regard to the more important matter of the pecuniary grant (*supra*, p. 189), and caused an order to be signed in Swift's favour for £1,000, which the Queen's death only prevented being paid (see Scott's "Life," p. 208).

[3] Vanessa had no doubt expressed her desire to accompany Barber when he went to Letcombe (*supra*, p. 205), and appears subsequently to have invaded Swift's retirement (*infra*, p. 234).

CCXCVI. [*Original.*[1]]

THE REV. JOHN BIRCH TO SWIFT

Wantage, *August* 1, 1714.
One o'clock.
MR. DEAN,[2]
AT twelve o'clock Lord Bolingbroke's man rid through
Wantage, to call Mr. Packer[3] to London, the Queen being
dead.[4] I am confounded at the melancholy news; yet
could not forbear sending it to you.
Your truly humble servant,
JO. BIRCH.

Addressed—To the Reverend the Dean of St. Patrick's,
Letcombe.

CCXCVII. [*Original.*[5]]

ERASMUS LEWIS TO SWIFT

Tuesday, *August* 3, 1714.
I AM overwhelmed with business, and therefore have only
time to tell you I received yours of August the 1st, and
think you should come to town, to see how the world goes:
for all old schemes, designs, projects, journeys, etc. are
broke by the great event. We are ill prognosticators.
Everything goes on with a tranquillity we durst not hope
for. Earl Berkeley commands the fleet;[6] Lord Dorset

---

[1] In the British Museum. See Preface.
[2] The writer had been Vicar of Wantage for more than twenty
years.
[3] Packer was one of the knights of the shire for Berkshire. He
was related to Lady Bolingbroke, and his family succeeded on her
death to Bucklebury in that shire, which had been, in right of his
wife, Bolingbroke's country seat.
[4] The Queen died that morning between seven and seven thirty
o'clock. As Wantage is fifty-nine miles from London, the messenger
had made an extraordinarily rapid journey.
[5] In the British Museum. See Preface.
[6] James, third Earl of Berkeley, the son of Swift's old patron. He
had seen much service with Rooke and Shovell, whose fate he narrowly

compliments the King;[1] Duke of Bolton, Lord Lieutenant of Southampton;[2] Addison, secretary to the Regents.[3]

Addressed—To the Revd. the Dean of St. Patrick's at Mr. Geree's at Upper Letcombe, near Wantage, Berks.

CCXCVIII. [*Original.*[4]]

JOHN BARBER TO SWIFT

August 3, 1714.

HONOURED SIR,

YOU may easily imagine the concern we were all in on the sudden surprise of the Queen's death. I have hardly recovered it yet. Lord Bolingbroke told me last Friday,[5] that he would reconcile you to Lady Somerset, and then it would be easy to set you right with the Queen, and that you should be made easy here, and not go over.[6] He said

---

escaped. Swift appears to have had no high opinion of him ("Prose Works," ii, 122).

[1] There has been already mention of Lord Dorset (*supra*, vol. i, p. 110, n. 1), and further information about him will be given in later years when he was Lord Lieutenant of Ireland and one of Swift's correspondents.

[2] Charles Paulett, second Duke of Bolton, whom Swift pronounced to be "a great booby" ("Prose Works," x, 274).

[3] As the Whigs were in a majority amongst the Regents, none but members of their party were selected for the duties mentioned. The Earl of Berkeley has been sometimes confounded with Lord Berkeley of Stratton, who was a Tory.

[4] In the British Museum. See Preface.   [5] The 30th of July.

[6] This conversation between Bolingbroke and Barber shows the truth of what Swift says as to the Queen's disinclination to give him preferment in England. In the lines "Upon Himself" ("Poetical Works," ii, 163), which were evidently written while he was at Letcombe, Swift attributes his disfavour with the Queen, or the "royal prude" as he calls her, to the influence of Archbishop Sharp, who had told her of Swift's connection with the "Tale of a Tub," as well as to that of the Duchess of Somerset. But the Archbishop was dead and had been reconciled before his death to Swift:

"Poor York! the harmless tool of others' hate,
He sues for pardon, and repents too late;"

and at all times the Duchess, with the recollection of the terrible "Windsor Prophecy" (*supra*, vol. i, p. 310, n. 8) in her mind, must have been far the more dangerous foe. This Swift felt, and even twenty things in your favour, and commanded me to bring you up, whatever was the consequence. He said further, he would make clear work with them. But all vanished in a minute; and he is now threatened and abused every day by the party, who publicly rejoice, and swear they will turn out every Tory in England. Enclosed you have a letter from my Lord: he desires you would come up, and be anywhere *incognito*.[1]

The Earl of Berkeley is to command the fleet to fetch over the King;[2] and the Duke of Argyll is to go to Scotland. I send you the list of the twenty-five Kings.[3] Poor Lady Masham is almost dead with grief.[4] . . . The Parliament meets to-morrow, which will hinder me from coming down for three or four days; but if you resolve to go in the country farther,[5] I will certainly come down, for I must needs see you. Pray favour me with a line. I am, Sir,
Your most obedient humble servant.

Pray come up. When my Lord gave me the letter,[6] he said, he hoped you would come up, and help to save the constitution, which, with a little good management, might be kept in Tory hands.

in the calm of Letcombe he could not resist pouring out invectives upon her:

" Now angry Somerset her vengeance vows
On Swift's reproaches for her murder'd spouse;
From her red locks her mouth with venom fills,
And thence into the royal ear instils."

[1] " Why not at the Queen's house " is erased.   [2] *Supra*, p. 211.
[3] The Lords Justices consisted of seven officers of state, viz., the Archbishop of Canterbury, the Lord Chancellor, the Lord Treasurer, the Lord President of the Council, the Lord Privy Seal, the First Commissioner of the Admiralty, the Chief Justice of the King's Bench, and nineteen peers nominated by the Elector. Shrewsbury was one of the latter, and owing to his appointment as Lord Treasurer the number of Lords Justices was reduced to twenty-five.
[4] Some words are here obliterated. Peter Wentworth raises (*op. cit.*, p. 408) a suspicion as to the genuineness of Lady Masham's tears: " The town tell a world of stories of Lady Masham now, as that on Friday [two days before the Queen's death] she left the Queen for three hours to go and ransack for things at St. James's. I can't say if this is true or false, a Saturday I remember particularly I see her go away, but as I thought with too much grief to have any thoughts of herself."
[5] To stay with Oxford (*supra*, p. 210).   [6] *Infra*, p. 214.

CCXCIX. [*Original.*¹]

VISCOUNT BOLINGBROKE TO SWIFT

August 3, 1714.

DEAR DEAN,

THE Earl of Oxford was removed on Tuesday; the Queen died on Sunday. What a world is this, and how does Fortune banter us. John Barber tells me, you have set your face toward Ireland. Pray do not go. I am against it. But that is nothing; John is against it. Ireland will be the scene of some disorder, at least it will be the scene of mortification to your friends. Here everything is quiet, and will continue so. Beside which, as prosperity divided, misfortune may perhaps to some degree unite us.² The Tories seem to resolve not to be crushed; and that is enough to prevent them from being so. Pope has sent me a letter from Gay:³ being learned in geography, he took Binfield to be the ready way from Hanover to Whitehall. Adieu. But come to London, if you stay no longer than a fortnight. Ever yours, dear Jonathan,

Most sincerely.

I have lost all by the death of the Queen, but my spirit; and I protest to you, I feel that increase upon me. The Whigs are a pack of Jacobites; that shall be the cry in a month, if you please.⁴

CCC. [*Original.*⁵]

CHARLES FORD TO SWIFT

London, *August* 5, 1714.

I HAVE writ to Dawson for a license of absence for you;⁶ but you know you must take the oaths in Ireland within

¹ In the British Museum. See Preface.
² If Bolingbroke's famous letter to Wyndham can be relied upon this did not include union with Oxford. In that letter Bolingbroke says: "I abhorred Oxford to that degree that I could not bear to be joined with him in any case."
³ *Supra*, p. 176.
⁴ *I.e.*, if Swift would give Bolingbroke the assistance of his pen.
⁵ In the British Museum. See Preface.
⁶ In addition to writing to Dawson (*supra*, p. 204), Swift had evid-

three months. There are a great many here in the same
circumstances, and in all probability, some of them will
desire an Act of Parliament to have leave to do it here. In
that case, it will be no difficult matter to have you included.
Mr. Lewis tells me, he wrote to you to come up to town,[1]
and I see no reason why you should not. All matters go
on very quiet, and we are not apprehensive of any disturb-
ances. Stocks never rose so much in so few days. This is
imputed to the hatred of the old Treasurer, and the popu-
larity of the new one. The Whigs were not in Council
when he was recommended.[2] Lord Bolingbroke proposed
it there, as well as to the Queen;[3] and I hope they two are
upon very good terms, though Mr. Lewis seems positive of
the contrary. I never heard of any pique the Duke had to
him, but that he was to be Chief Minister; and that being
at an end, why may not they be reconciled?

The Dragon[4] was thought to show more joy upon proclaiming the King, than was consistent with the obligations
he had received from [the Queen]. He was hissed all the
way by the mob, and some of them threw halters into his
coach. This was not the effect of party; for the Duke of
Ormond was huzzaed throughout the whole city, and followed by a vast crowd to his own house, though he used
all possible endeavours to prevent it. There was an attempt

ently written to Ford to obtain a fresh licence for him. Ford's application, dated the same day as this letter, is in the P.R.O. of
Ireland.

[1] *Supra*, p. 211.

[2] The Duke of Somerset and the Duke of Argyll are said by Boyer
("Political State of Great Britain," viii, 87) to have been present when
it was decided to ask the Queen to appoint the Duke of Shrewsbury
Lord Treasurer, and the view generally taken is that this step was due
to them. Wyon has, however, not failed to note (*op. cit.*, ii, 525) the
contrary statement made by Ford. Mr. Lecky, in a very learned note
on this subject (*op. cit.*, i, 164), takes the view that Ford does not
refer to Argyll and Somerset, but to the other Whig statesmen who
were subsequently summoned (*supra*, p. 206, n. 2). It would appear
that Somerset and Argyll had never been formally struck off the list
of those entitled to attend ("Wentworth Papers," p. 408), and were
in a different position from the others.

[3] Mr. Lecky (*op. cit.*) believes this to have been the case. Bolingbroke had not much trust in Shrewsbury (*supra*, p. 185), but foresaw
that the Elector would succeed to the throne with general assent and
that the only hope of the Tory party finding favour with him lay in
their being led by Shrewsbury.

[4] *I.e.*, Oxford (*supra*, p. 150, n. 4).

to affront the Captain[1] in the cavalcade, but it did not succeed; and though a few hissed, the acclamations immediately drowned their noise. Not a single man showed the least respect to the Colonel;[2] and last night my Lord Bingley was beaten by mistake, coming out of his house.[3] I doubt he has disobliged both sides so much, that neither will ever own him; and his enemies tell stories of him, that I shall not believe till I find you allow them.

The Lords Justices made a speech to the Parliament to-day. If it comes out time enough, I will send it you; but I hear it only contains their proceedings upon the Queen's death, that they have yet received no directions from the King, and to desire the Commons to continue the funds, which are expired. I am told our Regents are already divided into four parties. The greatest use they have yet made of their power, is to appoint my Lord Berkeley to command the fleet which is to bring over the King, and to make the Duke of Bolton Lord Lieutenant of Hampshire.[4]

I send you a Gazette, though I am ashamed to have it seen. I had writ a great deal more of the Queen's illness, an account of her birth, etc. but I could not find out Mr. Lewis, and had nobody to consult with, and therefore chose rather to say too little, than anything I doubted might be improper.[5] Yesterday the Duke of Marlborough made his public entry through the city;[6] first came about two hun-

---

[1] *I.e.*, Bolingbroke.   [2] *I.e.*, Oxford.

[3] According to a newsletter of that day Lord Bingley (*supra*, vol. i, p. 323, n. 1) was "insulted" by a woollen draper named Mann, who had previously called Oxford "all to naught," and had said it was a pity Guiscard had not stabbed him "to his heart" ("Portland Manuscripts," v, 485).

[4] *Supra*, p. 211.

[5] Ford might well apologize for the announcement which was as follows: "London, August 1. This day at half an hour past seven in the morning died our late most gracious Sovereign Queen Anne, in the fiftieth year of her age and the thirteenth of her reign; a Princess of exemplary piety and virtue. Her Majesty complained on Thursday last of a pain in her head; the next day she was seized with convulsion fits, and for some time lost the use of her speech and senses, which though she afterwards recovered upon the application of proper remedies, she continued in a very weak and languishing condition till she expired."

[6] *Supra*, p. 179.

dred horsemen, three in a row, then a company of train-
bands, with drums, etc., his own chariot with himself and
his Duchess, then my Duchess's [chariot], followed by sixteen coaches with six horses, and between thirty and forty
with two horses.[1] There was no great mob when he passed
through the Pall Mall, but there was in the city; and he
was hissed by more than huzzaed. At Temple Bar, I am
assured, the noise of hissing was loudest, though they had
prepared their friends to receive him, and the gathering of
others was only accidental. You may guess how great a
favourite he is, by some old stories of his behaviour at the
camp, when [the King] was there, and afterward at Hanover; and by the share he and his family have in the
regency.[2] But to be sure, this discreet action will endear
him more than any subject in England. We had bonfires,
etc. at night. From the list of Lords Justices and some
other things, we imagine to ourselves there will not be
many changes;[3] but the vacancies for some time will be
filled up with Whigs.

What I blotted out in my last,[4] was something that
passed between the Captain and Barber, relating to you.
After I had writ, they told me all letters would be opened,
which made me blot out that passage. Barber says, he
gave you some account of it, though not a full one.[5] I
really believe Lord Bolingbroke was very sincere in the
professions he made of you, and he could have done anything. No minister was ever in that height of favour;
and Lady Masham was at least in as much credit, as she
had been in any time of her life. But these are melancholy reflections. Pray send me your poem: *Hoc erat,*

---

[1] " The Duke of Marlborough was never so much out of favour with
me as he is now at present, for the insulting manner he entered the
town," writes Peter Wentworth (*op. cit.*, p. 410); " he that used to come
so privately when in favour and with victory, to suffer himself to be
met with a train of coaches and a troop of militia with drums and
trumps. He is ashamed of it and says he begged the city to excuse
their compliment."

[2] Neither the Duke of Marlborough nor his son-in-law the Earl of
Sunderland were named as Lords Justices.

[3] The King included the Earls of Anglesey, Abingdon, and Nottingham, the Duke of Roxburghe and the Archbishop of York,
who belonged to the Hanoverian wing of the Tory party, in his
list.

[4] *Supra*, p. 209.   [5] *Supra*, p. 212.

etc.,[1] or bring it up yourself. Barber told me he had been several hours with the Captain, upon a thing that should have come out, but was now at an end.[2] He did not tell what it was; and I would not ask many questions, for fear of giving him suspicion.

CCCI. [*Original.*[3]]

JOHN GAY TO JOHN ARBUTHNOT, OR SWIFT

Hanover, *August* 16 [O.S. 5], 1714.

YOU remember, I suppose, that I was to write you abundance of letters from Hanover;[4] but as one of the most distinguishing qualities of a politician is secrecy, you must not expect from me any arcanas of state. There is another thing, that is necessary to establish the character of a politician, which is, to seem always to be full of affairs of state, to know the consultations of the cabinet council, when at the same time all his politics are collected from newspapers. Which of these two causes my secrecy is owing to, I leave you to determine. There is yet one thing more that is extremely necessary for a foreign minister, which he can no more be without than an artizan without his tools; I mean the terms of his art. I call it an art, or a science, because I think the King of France has established an academy to instruct the young Machiavelians of his country in the deep and profound science of politics. To the end that I might be qualified for an employment of this nature, and not only be qualified myself, but, to speak in the style of Sir John Falstaff, be the cause of qualifications in others,[5] I have made it my business to read memoirs, treaties, etc.[6] And

[1] The "Imitation of part of the Sixth Satire of the Second Book of Horace" beginning :

"I often wish'd that I had clear,
For life, six hundred pounds a year,"

which was afterwards extended and published by Pope (" Poetical Works," ii, 167).

[2] *I.e.*, the "Free Thoughts," *supra*, p. 209.

[3] In the British Museum. See Preface.   [4] *Supra*, p. 145.

[5] "I am not only witty in myself, but the cause that wit is in other men" (2 Hen. IV, i, 2).

[6] See Swift's advice to him (*supra*, p. 150).

as a dictionary of law-terms is thought necessary for young beginners, so I thought a dictionary of terms of state would be no less useful for young politicians. The terms of politics being not so numerous as to swell into a volume, especially in time of peace, for in time of war all the terms of fortification are included, I thought fit to extract them in the same manner, for the benefit of young practitioners, as a famous author has compiled his learned treatise of the law, called the " Doctor and Student." [1] I have not made any great progress in this piece; but, however, I will just give you a specimen of it, which will make you in the same manner a judge of the design and nature of this treatise.

Politician. What are the necessary tools for a prince to work with?

Student. Ministers of state.

Politician. What are the two great qualities of a minister of state?

Student. Secrecy and dispatch.

Politician. Into how many parts are the ministers of state divided?

Student. Into two: first, ministers of state at home; secondly, ministers of state abroad, who are called foreign ministers.

Politician. Very right. Now as I design you for the latter of these employments, I shall waive saying anything of the first of these. What are the different degrees of foreign ministers?

Student. The different degrees of foreign ministers are as follow: first, plenipotentiaries; second, ambassadors-extraordinary; third, ambassadors in ordinary; fourth, envoys-extraordinary; fifth, envoys in ordinary; sixth, residents; seventh, consuls; and eighth, secretaries.

Politician. How is a foreign minister to be known?

Student. By his credentials.

Politician. When are a foreign minister's credentials to be delivered?

Student. Upon his first admission into the presence of the prince to whom he is sent, otherwise called his first audience.

---

[1] This treatise, which was written by Christopher Saint German, and first published early in the sixteenth century, continued to be used as a handbook for legal students until the appearance of Blackstone's Commentaries.

Politician. How many kinds of audiences are there?

Student. Two, which are called a public audience, and a private audience.

Politician. What should a foreign minister's behaviour be when he has his first audience?

Student. He should bow profoundly, speak deliberately, and wear both sides of his long periwig before, etc.

By these few questions and answers you may be able to make some judgment of the usefulness of this politic treatise. Wicquefort, it is true, can never sufficiently be admired for his elaborate treatise of the conduct of an ambassador in all his negotiations;[1] but I design this only as a compendium, or the ambassador's manual, or *vade mecum.*

I have wrote so far of this letter, and do not know who to send it to; but I have now determined to send it, either to Dr. Arbuthnot, the Dean of St. Patrick's, or to both. My Lord Clarendon is very much approved of at Court,[2] and I believe is not dissatisfied with his reception. We have not much variety of diversions: what we did yesterday and to-day we shall do to-morrow, which is, go to Court, and walk in the gardens at Herrenhausen. If I write any more my letter will be just like my diversions, the same thing over and over again; so, Sirs,

Your most obliged humble servant,

J. GAY.

I would have writ this letter over again, but I had not time. Correct all erratas.

Addressed—For Dr. Arbuthnot or the Dean of St. Patrick's.

CCCII. [*Original.*[3]]

ERASMUS LEWIS TO SWIFT

Whitehall, *August* 7, 1714.

SIR,

IT is true you have nothing to do here; but what have you to do anywhere else till you go to Ireland, where you

---

[1] " L'Ambassadeur et Ses Fonctions," by Abraham de Wicquefort (La Haye, 1680).

[2] *Supra*, p. 144.   [3] In the British Museum. See Preface.

must indeed be before three months end, in order to qualify yourself?[1] The law requires it, as much as if your deanery was but now conferred upon you.

Arbuthnot is removed to Chelsea, and will settle there.[2] The town fills every moment. We are as full in the House of Commons as at any time. We are gaping and staring to see who is to rule us. The Whigs think they shall engross all. We think we shall have our share. In the mean time we have no divisions at Council, or in Parliament. I sent twice to Kensington to inquire after Lady Masham's health. Next week I will go to see her, and will keep up my acquaintance, in all events, if she thinks fit. I doubt she and her sister[3] are not perfectly easy in their affairs; but you forgot one who is worse than either, that is Mr. Hill,[4] who has not a sou.[5] I stay here till our commission is either renewed to us, or given to another. I am,

Yours, etc.

CCCIII. [*Sheridan.*]

SWIFT TO LADY MASHAM

August 7, 1714.

MADAM,

I HAD the honour of a letter from your Ladyship a week ago; and the day after, came the unfortunate news of the Queen's death, which made it altogether unseasonable, as perhaps it may be still, to give your Ladyship this kind of trouble. Although my concern be as great as that of any other good subject, for the loss of so excellent a Princess, yet I can assure you, Madam, it is little to what I suffer

---

[1] *Supra*, p. 214.
[2] From subsequent references it appears that Arbuthnot held some office in connection with Chelsea Hospital.
[3] *Supra*, p. 152.
[4] *I.e.*, Brigadier-General John Hill, *supra*, vol. i, p. 336.
[5] The apprehensions of Lady Masham's friends as to either her own circumstances or those of her family do not appear to have been well-founded. The Queen had failed to sign her will (*infra*, p. 232) under which Lady Masham was expected to benefit, but there is ground to believe that Lady Masham had not neglected to provide at least in some degree for herself and those related to her during the Queen's lifetime.

upon your Ladyship's particular account. As you excel in the several duties of a tender mother, a true friend, and a loving wife, so you have been the best and most faithful servant to your mistress, that ever any sovereign had.[1] And although you have not been rewarded suitably to your merits, I doubt not but God will make it up to you in another life, and to your children and posterity in this.[2] I cannot go about to comfort your Ladyship in your great affliction, otherwise than by begging you to make use of your own piety, and your own wisdom, of both which you have so great a share. You are no longer a servant; but you are still a wife, a mother, and a friend, and you are bound in conscience to take care of your health, in order to acquit yourself of these duties, as well as you did of the other, which is now at an end.

I pray God to support your Ladyship, under so great a share of load, in this general calamity; and remain, with the greatest respect and truth, Madam,

Your Ladyship's most obedient, and most obliged servant,

JON. SWIFT.

I most heartily thank your Ladyship for the favourable expressions and intentions in your letter, written at a time when you were at the height of favour and power.

CCCIV. [*Sheridan.*]

SWIFT TO VISCOUNT BOLINGBROKE

August 7, 1714.

MY LORD,

I HAD yours of the 3rd; and our country post is so ordered, that I could acknowledge it no sooner. It is true,

---

[1] It has been observed that opinions varied as to Lady Masham's character (*supra*, p. 182, n. 8), and that it was even suggested at that time that her grief for the Queen was assumed (*supra*, p. 213, n. 4). Peter Wentworth, who it must be admitted however was no admirer of the Queen's favourite, refers again to the latter subject in a later letter (*op. cit.*, p. 416) and says: "Lady Masham, Mrs. Hill, and Mrs. Danvers are cry out upon for their behaviour, though they roared and cried enough whilst there was life, but as soon as there was none they took care of themselves."

[2] *Supra*, p. 221, n. 5.

my Lord, the events of five days last week might furnish
morals for another volume of Seneca. As to my Lord Oxford, I told him freely my opinion before I left the town,
that he ought to resign at the end of the session. I said
the same thing often to your Lordship and my Lady Masham, although you seemed to think otherwise, for some
reasons;[1] and said so to him one afternoon, when I met
you there with my Lord Chancellor. But, I remember, one
of the last nights I saw him—it was at Lady Masham's
lodgings—I said to him, that, upon the foot your Lordship
and he then were, it was impossible you could serve together
two months; and, I think, I was just a week out in my
calculation.[2] I am only sorry, that it was not a resignation,
rather than a removal, because the personal kindness and
distinction I always received from his Lordship and you,
gave me such a love for you both, if you great men will
allow that expression in a little one, that I resolved to preserve it entire, however you differed between yourselves;
and in this I did, for some time, follow your commands and
example. I impute it more to the candour of each of you,
than to my own conduct, that having been, for two years,
almost the only man who went between you, I never observed the least alteration in either of your countenances
towards me. I will swear for no man's sincerity, much less
for that of a Minister of State: but thus much I have said,
wherever it was proper, that your Lordship's proposals were
always the fairest in the world, and I faithfully delivered
them as I was empowered, and although I am no very
skilful man at intrigue, yet I durst forfeit my head, that if
the case were mine, I could either have agreed with you,
or put you *dans votre tort*.

When I saw all reconciliation impracticable, I thought
fit to retire; and was resolved, for some reasons, not to be
mentioned at this distance, to have nothing to do with whoever was to be last in. For either I should not be needed,
or not be made use of. And let the case be what it would,
I had rather be out of the way. All I pretended was, to

---

[1] At the time of the ministerial crisis in March, and evidently from
this letter at a later period, Bolingbroke opposed Oxford's resignation,
feeling his own position not yet strong enough to justify him in taking
the reins. There has been already reference to Lady Masham's attitude
(*supra*, p. 151, n. 1).

[2] *Supra*, p. 139, n. 4.

speak my thoughts freely, to represent persons and things without any mingle of my interest or passions, and sometimes to make use of an evil instrument,[1] which was likely to cost me dear, even from those for whose service it was employed. I did believe there would be no farther occasion for me, upon any of those accounts. Besides, I had so ill an opinion of the Queen's health, that I was confident you had not a quarter of time left for the work you had to do ; having let slip the opportunity of cultivating those dispositions she had got after her sickness at Windsor.[2] I never left pressing my Lord Oxford with the utmost earnestness, and perhaps more than became me, that we might be put in such a condition, as not to lie at mercy on this great event; and I am your Lordship's witness that you have nothing to answer for in that matter.

I will, for once, talk in my trade, and tell you, that I never saw anything more resemble our proceedings, than a man of fourscore, or in a deep consumption, going on in his sins, although his physician assured him he could not live a week. Those wonderful refinements, of keeping men in expectation, and not letting your friends be too strong, might be proper in their season, *sed nunc non erat his locus*. Besides, you keep your bread and butter till it was too stale for anybody to care for it. Thus your machine of four years modelling is dashed to pieces in a moment; and, as well by the choice of the Regents as by their proceedings, I do not find there is any intention of managing you in the least. The whole nineteen[3] consist either of the highest party-men, or, which mightily mends the matter, of such who left us upon the subject of the peace, and affected jealousies about the succession.[4] It might reasonably be expected, that this quiet possession might convince the successor of the good dispositions of the Church party[5]

---

[1] *I.e.*, the press.

[2] In consequence of the reports which had reached her of the disloyalty of the Whigs during her illness in the previous winter (*supra*, p. 121, n. 4, p. 124, n. 3), the Queen was willing to agree to the supersession of all officers and officials who were opposed in political opinion to Oxford's Ministry (see " Prose Works," v, 451).

[3] *Supra*, p. 213, n. 3.   [4] *Supra*, p. 217, n. 3.

[5] In the " Free Thoughts upon the Present State of Affairs " Swift treats the support of the Church interest as one of the most valuable assets of Oxford's Ministry. Assuming that it would be continued with the same unanimity to his friends under Hanoverian rule, and

LETCOMBE BASSETT CHURCH

From a photograph by Mr. T. Reveley

towards him; and I ever thought there was a mighty failure somewhere or other, that this could not have been done in the Queen's life. But this is too much for what is past; and yet, whoever observed and disliked the causes, has some title to quarrel with the effects.

As to what is to come, your Lordship is in the prime of your years, *plein des esprits qui fournissent les espérances*; and you are now again to act that part, though in another assembly, which you formerly discharged so much to your own honour and the advantage of your cause. You set out with the wind and tide against you, yet, at last, arrived at your port, from whence you are now driven back into open sea again. But, not to involve myself in an allegory, I doubt whether, after this disappointment, you can go on with the same vigour you did in your more early youth. Experience, which has added to your wisdom, has lessened your resolution. You are now a general, who, after many victories, have lost a battle, and have not the same confidence in yourself, or your troops. Your fellow-labourers have either made their fortunes, or are past them, or will go over to seek them on the other side. Yet after all, and to resume a little courage, to be at the head of the Church interest is no mean station, and that, as I take it, is now in your Lordship's power; in order to which, I could heartily wish for that union you mention,[1] because, I need not tell you, that some are more dexterous at pulling down their enemies than, etc. We have certainly more heads and hands than our adversaries; but, it must be confessed, they have stronger shoulders and better hearts. I only doubt my friends, the rabble, are at least grown trimmers; and that, setting up the cry of "trade and wool," against "Sacheverell and the Church,"[2] has cooled their zeal.

believing that it would secure their recognition in any new ministry, he now lost no opportunity of emphasizing that the Tory party was the Church party.

[1] *Supra*, p. 214.

[2] These had been the party cries during the General Election in the previous year, when the Tories had returned to the House of Commons with a majority little diminished. "It was in vain that the Whig candidates," says Wyon (*op. cit.*, ii, 471), "wore in their hats locks of wool to remind an ungrateful people, by this display of the staple commodity, of their devotion to the trade and prosperity of the commonwealth. The oak leaf, which was sported by their rivals, appealed successfully to the hearts of thousands of rustic voters."

II   Q

I take it for granted, there will be a new Parliament against winter; and if they will retain me on the other side as their counsellor, I will engage them a majority. But since it is possible I may not be so far in their good graces, if your Lordship thinks my service may be of any use in this new world, I will be ready to attend you by the beginning of winter. For the misfortune is, that I must go to Ireland to take the oaths; which I never reflected on till I had notice from some friends in London,[1] and the sooner I go the better, to prevent accidents, for I would not willingly want a favour at present. I think to set out in a few days, but not before your Lordship's commands and instructions may reach me.[2]

I cannot conclude without offering my humblest thanks and acknowledgments, for your Lordship's kind intentions towards me, if this accident had not happened, of which I received some general hints. I pray God direct your Lordship; and I desire you will believe me to be what I am, with the utmost truth and respect,

Your Lordship's most obedient, etc.

JON. SWIFT.

CCCV. [*Sheridan.*]

SWIFT TO ARCHDEACON WALLS

Letcombe, *August* 8, 1714.

IF I had but fixed a week sooner for my journey to Ireland, I should have avoided twenty inconveniencies that have since happened to me, and been with you the time I am now writing. Upon the Earl of Oxford's removal, he desired I would go with him into Herefordshire, which I

---

[1] *Supra*, p. 220.

[2] Owing to the line which he has taken in the "Free Thoughts upon the Present State of Affairs," Swift has not escaped an imputation of disloyalty to Oxford and readiness to side with his rival (see Macknight's "Life of Bolingbroke," p. 408). But his sincerity cannot be doubted. Although Bolingbroke's policy was more in accord with his views than Oxford's, and a prospect was opened "upon the path of honour, ambition, and preferment," Swift could not forget his old friend and patron, and to "his immortal honour," as Sir Walter Scott says ("Life," p. 209), before the news of the Queen's death reached him, decided to accompany Oxford "to neglect and seclusion."

consented to, and wrote you word of it desiring you would renew my license of absence at the end of this month,[1] for I think it then expires. Two days after, I had earnest invitation from those in power, to go up to town and assist them in their new Ministry, which I resolved to excuse; but, before I could write, news came of the Queen's death,, and all our schemes broke to shatters. I am told I must take the oaths in Ireland in three months; and I think it is better travelling now than later; and although I am earnestly pressed by our broken leaders to come up to town, I shall not do it; but hope to set out on the 16th instant towards Ireland, and if it please God, be with you in nine or ten days after this comes to your hands. However, let my license be renewed before it expires.

I think I answered yours in my last.[2] I leave all things entirely to you and Mr. Forbes. My service to Gossip Doll, Goody Stoyte and Martha,[3] and Mr. Manley and lady. Mr. Manley is, I believe, now secure in his post; and it will be my turn to solicit favours from him.[4] I have taken up Mr. Fetherston's money, to pay some debts in London.[5] I desire you will pay him fifty pounds, with the usual exchange, at twenty days sight; or later, if it be inconvenient.

CCCVI. [*Original.*[6]]

ERASMUS LEWIS TO SWIFT

Whitehall, *August* 10, 1714.

I NEVER differed from you in opinion in any point so much, as in your proposal to accommodate matters between the Dragon[7] and his *quondam* friends.[8] I will venture to go

---

[1] *Supra*, p. 203.　　　　　　[2] *Supra*, p. 203.
[3] *I.e.*, Mrs. Stoyte's sister, who has been previously called Cellarius (*supra*, p. 70).
[4] *Supra*, p. 204.　　　　　　[5] *Supra*, p. 185, n. 2.
[6] In the British Museum. See Preface.
[7] *I.e.*, Oxford (*supra*, p. 150, n. 4).
[8] Evidently Swift had taken the view that Bolingbroke was alluding in his letter to the possibility of union with Oxford (*supra*, p. 214), and had written to Lewis proposing to go to London for the purpose of effecting a reconciliation between his friends.

so far with you, as to say he contributed to his own disgrace, by his petitenesses,[1] more than they did, or ever had
it in their power to do. But since they would admit of no
terms of accommodation, when he offered to serve them in
their own way,[2] I had rather see his dead carcase, than that
he should now tamely submit to those, who have loaded
him with all the obloquy malice could suggest, and tongues
utter. Have not Charteris,[3] Brinsden,[4] and all the runners,
been employed to call him dog, villain, sot, and worthless?
And shall he, after this, join them? To what end? I have
great tenderness for Lady [Masham], and think her best
way is to retire, and enjoy the comforts of a domestic life.
But sure the earth has not produced such monsters as
Mercurialis,[5] and his companion,[6] and the Prelate.[7] The
last openly avows he never had obligation to the Dragon,
and loads him with ten thousand crimes; though his
greatest, in reality, was preferring him.

But to come out of this rant. What should they be
friends for? *Cui bono?* Are we in a dream? Is the Queen
alive again? Can the lady[8] hereafter make any figure, but
a *persona muta* in the drama? If the Dragon declares
against the Man of Mercury, he may strike in with the
tertium quid, that will probably arise, but with him he can
never be otherwise than spurned and hated. The natural
result of this is, that however I may, for my private satisfaction, desire to see you here,[9] I cannot but think you
should go to Ireland to qualify yourself, then return hither,
when the chaos will be jumbled into some sort of order. If
the King keeps some Tories in employment, the notion of
Whig and Tory will be lost; but that of Court and country
will arise. The regency has declared in favour of the
Whigs in Ireland.[10] I believe Mr. Thomas will stand his

---

[1] Swift uses this word in "Gulliver's Travels."

[2] This is a remarkable corroboration of the view that in the end
Oxford clung to office with the utmost tenacity. No one was more
likely to know the real facts than Lewis.

[3] The notorious Colonel Francis Charteris ("D. N. B.," x, 135)
who comes under the lash of both Pope and Hogarth.

[4] Brinsden, who is said to have been an oculist, attended on Prince
Eugene during his visit to England (*supra*, vol. i, p. 314, n. 3).

[5] *I.e.*, Bolingbroke.   [6] *I.e.*, Lord Harcourt.

[7] *I.e.*, Bishop Atterbury.   [8] *I.e.*, Lady Masham.

[9] *Supra*, p. 220.

[10] In a newsletter of that date it is stated that the Lords Justices

ground.[1] We shall be dissolved as soon as we have settled the civil list. We have no appearance that any attempt will be formed by the Pretender.

CCCVII. [*Original.*[2]]

VISCOUNT BOLINGBROKE TO SWIFT

August 11, 1714.

I SWEAR I did not imagine, that you could have held out through two pages, even of small paper, in so grave a style.[3] Your state of late passages is right enough. I reflect upon them with indignation, and shall never forgive myself for having trusted so long to so much real pride and awkward humility, to an air of such familiar friendship and a heart so void of all tenderness, to such a temper of engrossing business and power and so perfect an incapacity to manage one, with such a tyrannical disposition to abuse the other, etc. But enough of this, I cannot load him[4] as a knave, without fixing fool on myself. For you I have a most sincere and warm affection, and in every part of my life will show it. Go into Ireland, since it must be so, to swear, and come back into Britain to bless, to bless me and those few friends who will enjoy you.

Johannes Tonsor[5] brings you this. From him you will hear what is doing. Adieu, love me, and love me the better,

had taken steps to terminate the dispute between the Corporation of Dublin and the Irish executive (*supra*, p. 189, n. 3), and had sent orders to the Corporation to proceed to the election of a Lord Mayor and Sheriffs, and to the Council to approve of whatever persons might be elected. The paralysis of civic government in Dublin during this conflict was very remarkable. Writing to a friend on 8 May Archbishop King says: "We are in the utmost confusion in this city for want of Mayor and Sheriffs; no debts can be recovered, no malefactors tried, no regulation of markets, the streets unpaved, the poor undone, and everybody suffers; the Aldermen elect and elect, but because the person the Council would have is not elected (they having the power of confirmation) will confirm none." *Cf.* also Froude, *op. cit.*, i, 351.

[1] *Supra*, p. 194.
[2] In the British Museum. See Preface.
[3] *Supra*, p. 222.   [4] *I.e.*, Oxford.
[5] *I.e.*, John Barber (*supra*, p. 213).

because after a greater blow than most men ever felt, I keep up my spirit, am neither dejected at what has passed, nor apprehensive at what is to come. *Meâ virtute me involvo.*

CCCVIII. [*Original.*[1]]

CHARLES FORD TO SWIFT

London, *August* 12, 1714.

OUR Justices sit several hours every day, without affording us the least news. I do not hear anything they have done worth mentioning, except some orders they have given about the dispute in the city of Dublin.[2] You may be sure they are not such as will please our friends; but I think you and I agreed in condemning those proceedings in our own people. My Lord Derby[3] is made Lord Lieutenant of Lancashire. That and Hampshire are the only vacant employments they have filled up; I suppose, under pretence of their being maritime counties. If the Whigs had directed the list of Regents, Marlborough, Sunderland, and Wharton had not been left out.[4] There are five Tories too, that would not have been in.[5] Though they were a little whimsical for three or four days about the succession, they seemed to recant, and own themselves in an error by the later votes. Every one of them approved the peace, and were for the address at the end of the last session, that it was safe, honourable, and advantageous. Considering what ministers were employed here by the Court of Hanover,

---

[1] In the British Museum. See Preface.

[2] *Supra*, p. 228, n. 10.

[3] James, tenth Earl of Derby, about whom Macky and Swift widely differ ("Prose Works," x, 276); in the opinion of the one he was a man of honour, in the opinion of the other an arrant scoundrel.

[4] Writing to Lord Strafford on 3 August Lord Berkeley of Stratton says: "It was a surprise to me and I fancy will not be less so to himself not to see my Lord Wharton's name in the list, and my Lord Sunderland looked very pale when the names were read" ("Wentworth Papers," p. 409). Marlborough and his son-in-law, Sunderland, are supposed to have been omitted owing to the Elector's dislike of the former, and Wharton owing to Queen Anne's aversion to him.

[5] *Supra*, p. 217, n. 3.

and that the King himself had little information but what he received from them, I think his list shows no ill disposition to the Tories; and they say he is not apt to be hasty in removing the persons he finds in employment. The Bill is brought in for granting him the old duties for the civil list. One Wykes, of Northampton, moved to tack the Place Bill to it, but nobody seconded him, and he was extremely laughed at.[1] He happens unluckily to be a Tory.

Did you receive your papers last post? The first copy[2] is not yet left at St. Dunstan's.[3] Should I send to Barber for it in Lord Bolingbroke's name? I have writ to him to bring in his bill, and as soon as he comes I will pay him. I suppose I shall see him to-morrow. I wish you a good journey to Ireland. But if I hear Saturday's post comes into Wantage on Sunday, I may trouble you again.[4] Pray let me know when you land in Ireland, that I may write to you, if anything happens worth while. I shall be very impatient for what you promise me from thence.[5] I should be very glad to hear from you while you are on the road.

Lord Anglesey came to town last Tuesday. They[6] are all here now, except Pembroke and Strafford.[7] Charles Eversfield is making his court to the Dukes of Somerset and Argyll; he declares he will keep his place, if he can, and that he will not stir for Campion's election in the

---

[1] "Hereupon John Wykes, Esq., member for the town of Northampton, proposed the tacking to it [the Civil List Bill] the bill which had so often miscarried for limiting the numbers of officers in the House of Commons, but nobody seconded the motion which, had it been carried, might have had fatal consequences" (Boyer, *op. cit.*, viii, 151).

[2] Of the "Free Thoughts." As has been already mentioned Swift had sent a second copy to Ford (*supra*, p. 209, n. 1).

[3] Ford was evidently still carrying on the correspondence with Barber under an assumed name from St. Dunstan's Coffee-house.

[4] Swift proposed to leave on the following Monday, 16 August (*supra*, p. 227).

[5] The allusion is probably to "Some Considerations upon the Consequences hoped and feared from the Death of the Queen" ("Prose Works," v, 421), which is dated 9 August in that year, and is probably the beginning of what was intended to be a pamphlet of considerable size.

[6] *I.e.*, the Lords Justices.

[7] The Earl of Strafford was at the Hague; the cause of the Earl of Pembroke's absence is not known.

county of Sussex. Campion and he have had some high words upon that account.[1] Lord Orford[2] told the Commissioners of the Admiralty, they were ignorant, negligent of their duty, and wanted zeal for the King's service.

CCCIX. [*Original.*[3]]

JOHN ARBUTHNOT TO SWIFT

London, *August* 12, 1714.

MY DEAR FRIEND,

I THANK you for your kind letter, which is very comfortable upon such a melancholy occasion. My dear mistress's days were numbered even in my imagination, and could not exceed such certain limits; but of that small number a great deal was cut off by the last troublesome scene of this contention among her servants. I believe sleep was never more welcome to a weary traveller, than death was to her; only it surprised her too suddenly before she had signed her will, which, no doubt, her being involved in so much business hindered her from finishing. It was unfortunate, that she had been persuaded, as is supposed by Lowndes,[4] that it was necessary to have it under the great seal. I have figured to myself all this melancholy scene, and even, if it be possible, worse than it has happened, twenty times; so that I was prepared for it. My case is not half so deplorable as poor Lady Masham's,[5] and several of the Queen's poor servants; some of whom have no chance for their bread but the generosity of his present Majesty, which several people, that know him, very much commend. So far is plain from what is happened in public affairs, that what one party affirmed of the settlement has proved true, that it was firm, that it was in some measure an advantage to the successor not to have been here, and so obliged to declare himself in several things, in

[1] Eversfield was member for Horsham in Sussex, the county which Campion represented (*supra*, p. 194). Campion had been a Commissioner of Accounts, and it had been thought possible would be Chancellor of the Exchequer ("Wentworth Papers," p. 391).

[2] *Supra*, vol. i, p. 177, n. 2.

[3] In the British Museum. See Preface.

[4] William Lowndes of the Treasury (*supra*, vol. i, p. 24, n. 2).

[5] *Supra*, p. 221, n. 5.

which he is now at liberty. And indeed never any Prince in this respect came to the crown with greater advantage. I can assure you, the peaceable scene that now appears, is a disappointment to more than one set of people.

I have an opportunity calmly and philosophically to consider that treasure of vileness and baseness, that I always believed to be in the heart of man; and to behold them exert their insolence and baseness; every new instance, instead of surprising and grieving me, as it does some of my friends, really diverts me, and in a manner improves my theory; though I think I have not met with it in my own case, except from one man, and he was very far mistaken, for to him I would not abate one grain of my proud spirit. Dear friend, the last sentence of your letter quite kills me. Never repeat that melancholy tender word, that you will endeavour to forget me. I am sure I never can forget you, till I meet with, what is impossible, another, whose conversation I can delight so much in as Dr. Swift's, and yet that is the smallest thing I ought to value you for. That hearty sincere friendship, that plain and open ingenuity in all your commerce, is what I am sure I never can find in another man. I shall want often a faithful monitor, one that would vindicate me behind my back, and tell me my faults to my face. God knows I write this with tears in my eyes. Yet do not be obstinate, but come up for a little time to London; and if you must needs go, we may concert a manner of correspondence wherever we are. I have a letter from Gay just before the Queen's death. Is he not a true poet, who had not one of his own books to give to the Princess, that asked for one? [1]

CCCX. [*Scott.*]

SWIFT TO MISS ESTHER VANHOMRIGH

August 12, 1714.

I HAD your letter last post; and before you can send me

---

[1] As will be seen from a later letter, the Electoral Princess, the future Queen Caroline of England, gave Gay reason to hope she would befriend him (*infra*, p. 247).

another I shall set out for Ireland. I must go and take the oaths, and the sooner the better. I think, since I have known you, I have drawn an old house upon my head. You should not have come by Wantage for a thousand pounds.[1] You used to brag you were very discreet: where is it gone? It is probable I may not stay in Ireland long, but be back by the beginning of winter. When I am there, I will write to you as soon as I can conveniently, but it shall always be under a cover; and if you write to me, let some other direct it; and I beg you will write nothing that is particular, but what may be seen; for I apprehend letters may be opened, and inconveniences will happen. If you are in Ireland while I am there, I shall see you very seldom. It is not a place for any freedom, but where everything is known in a week, and magnified a hundred degrees. These are rigorous laws that must be passed through; but it is probable we may meet in London in winter, or, if not, leave all to fate, that seldom cares to humour our inclinations. I say all this out of the perfect esteem and friendship I have for you. These public misfortunes have altered all my measures, and broke my spirits. I shall, I hope, be on horseback in a day after this comes to your hand. I would not answer your questions for a million, nor can I think of them with any ease of mind. Adieu.

CCCXI. [*Original.*[2]]

CHARLES FORD TO SWIFT

August 14, 1714.

I HOPE you did not pay the two shillings for postage. If you did, pray send me the cover, that I may inquire into the meaning of it. I suppose you expect news upon Craggs's[3] return from Hanover, but I do not hear a word more than

---

[1] There seems no doubt that Vanessa had fulfilled her wish (*supra,* p. 210, n. 3) and had paid Swift a visit. In a letter many years later he alludes to "the Berkshire surprise."

[2] In the British Museum. See Preface.

[3] George Craggs, afterwards one of the Secretaries of State, who had been sent to announce the Queen's death to the Elector.

what you have in the Lords Justices' speech. Yesterday morning after he came, the Whigs looked dejected, and our friends very much pleased, though I do not know any reason for either, unless it was expected by both sides, that he would have brought orders for alterations. It seems the Dragon's[1] entertainment was upon a family account, upon the agreement between Lord Harley and Lord Pelham,[2] and only those, who were concerned in their affairs, were invited. But slighter grounds would have served to raise a story at this time; and it was sufficient, that my Lord Townshend[3] and Lord Cowper[4] dined at his house. However, we look upon him as lost to our side; and he has certainly made advances of civility to the Whigs, which they have returned with the utmost contempt. I am told Dismal[5] begins to declare for his old friends, and protests he was really afraid for the Protestant succession, which made him act in the manner he did.

The foreign peers are certainly deprived of their right of voting by the express words of the Act of Succession, and it appears it was the intention of the legislature at that time, for Prince George of Denmark was excepted by name, but it is thought the Lords will interpret it otherwise, when it comes to be tried. They do not lose the other privileges of peerage, and their posterity born here may sit in the house. The same clause extends to the House of Commons; and no foreigner can enjoy any employment, civil or military. They may be favourable to the Lords, who are all Whigs, but I doubt poor Duke Disney will lose his regiment.[6]

I suppose Barber has given you an account of Lord Bolingbroke's pamphlet.[7] If you and he are not come to an *éclaircissement* upon it, I shall send to him for it. I long for the other. Yesterday the Commons voted *nemine contra-*

---

[1] *I.e.*, Oxford (*supra*, p. 150, n. 4).
[2] *Supra*, p. 183.
[3] Bolingbroke's successor as Secretary of State.
[4] Lord Harcourt's successor as Lord Chancellor.
[5] *I.e.*, the Earl of Nottingham (*supra*, vol. i, p. 309).
[6] Duke Disney, a member of the Brothers' Club, is frequently mentioned by Swift and was an intimate of Bolingbroke (see Sichel's "Bolingbroke and his Times," i, 288). His real name was Henry Desaulnais.
[7] *I.e.*, the "Free Thoughts" as revised by Bolingbroke.

dicente to pay the Hanover troops, that deserted us in 1712.[1]
To-day Sir William Wyndham, Campion,[2] and two or three
more, gave some opposition to it, for which they are extremely blamed.[3] I think they had acted right, if they had
spoke against it yesterday, but it seems they were not then
in the House. They had not strength enough to-day to
come to a division. Once more I wish you a good journey,
and a quick return; and I hope you will find things go
better than you expect.

CCCXII. [*Original.*[4]]

SWIFT TO THE EARL OF OXFORD

August 15, 1714.

MY LORD,
    THIS great event of the Queen's death, as it has broken
your measures of retiring, and called you back again into
affairs,[5] so it has affected me so far as to force me into
Ireland to take the oaths. I set out to-morrow morning,
and shall have no thoughts of returning, unless some juncture of affairs shall make my friends think it may be of any
use. I wish your Lordship good success in this new scene,
and that you may have credit enough with the King to set
him right in his opinions of persons and things. I am
almost tempted to think it was by the peculiar favour of
Providence that your Lordship gave up your employment

---

[1] When Ormond separated from Prince Eugene and refused to
carry on the war. There were then large arrears due to the Hanover
troops which had never been paid.

[2] *Supra*, p. 232, n. 1.

[3] Lord Stanhope says (*op. cit.*, i, 143) that Wyndham seconded the
motion.

[4] In the possession of the Duke of Portland (*supra*, p. 160, n. 2).

[5] Owing to the Queen's death Oxford had not carried out his intention of leaving London (*supra*, p. 198), and was lingering on there in
the hope that he would be recalled to office by the King. He was of
opinion that without a coalition no stable administration could be
formed, and so confident was he then that his assistance would be
found necessary that he approached some of his former colleagues in
order to secure their support when the summons came (Hist. MSS.
Com., Rept. 11, App., pt. v, p. 321).

before her Majesty's death. At least it is thus I judge at distance, from the leavings of the little I knew when I came from town. However, I conceive you have still as hard a game to play as any man now in England, and will be as much obnoxious to censure as when you were at the head of the Ministry; though perhaps less to danger, and though I know you value neither, yet I could wish to see you always exempt from both, as far as human prudence can place you. At least, a good man should only be threatened by cowards and censured by fools, and then he will be safe enough in his person and reputation. I am, with the greatest respect, your Lordship's, etc.

CCCXIII. [*Sheridan.*]

SWIFT TO VISCOUNT BOLINGBROKE

Dublin, *September* 14, 1714.[1]

MY LORD,

I HOPE your Lordship, who were always so kind to me while you were a servant, will not forget me now in your greatness.[2] I give you this caution, because I really believe you will be apt to be exalted in your new station of retirement, which was the only honourable post that those who gave it you were capable of conferring. And as, in other employments, the circumstances with which they are given, are sometimes said to be equally valuable with the gift itself, so it was in your case. The sealing up your office, and especially without any directions from the King,[3]

---

[1] Swift had presumably left Letcombe on Monday 16 August (*supra*, p. 231). Of the circumstances attending his journey to Ireland there is nothing known.

[2] Bolingbroke had been dismissed from office a fortnight before the date of this letter, but the fact was only known in Ireland on 11 September, when the "Dublin Gazette" announced that on 31 August "the Right Hon. the Lord Bolingbroke was removed from being one of his Majesty's Principal Secretaries of State, and his office sealed up."

[3] Swift may have inferred from the announcement just quoted that the Lords Justices of Great Britain acted on their own initiative, or may have been so informed by some of his correspondents, but there

discovered such sentiments of you in such persons, as would make any honest men proud to share them. I must be so free as to tell you, that this new office of retirement will be harder for you to keep, than that of Secretary; and you lie under one great disadvantage, beside your being too young, that whereas none but knaves and fools desire to deprive you of your former post, all the honest men in England will be for putting you out of this. I go on in writing, though I know not how to send you my letter. If I were sure it would be opened by the sealers of your office, I would fill it with some terms of art, that they would better deserve, than relish.

It is a point of wisdom too hard for me, not to look back with vexation upon past management. Divines tell us often from their pulpits, that half the pains which some men take to be damned, would have compassed their salvation: this, I am sure, was extremely our case. I know not what motions your Lordship intends; but, if I see the old Whig measures taken in the next elections, and that the Court, the Bank, East India, and South Sea,[1] act strenuously, and procure a majority, I shall lie down and beg of Jupiter to heave the cart out of the dirt. I would give all I am worth, for the sake of my country, that you had left your mantle with somebody in the House of Commons, or that a dozen honest men among them had only so many shreds of it. And so, having dispatched all our friends in England, off flies a splinter, and knocks two governors of Ireland dead.[2]

seems no doubt, as Boyer says (*op. cit.*, viii, 187), that Bolingbroke was dismissed under the direct order of George I sent from Hanover.

[1] "One thing I might add, as another acknowledged maxim in that party," says Swift in the "Examiner," "and in my opinion, as dangerous to the constitution as any I have mentioned, I mean, that of preferring, on all occasions, the moneyed interest before the landed" ("Prose Works," ix, 231).

[2] The Lords Justices of Ireland had taken exception to the orders sent to them with regard to the civic dispute (*supra*, p. 228, n. 10), and the Lords Justices of Great Britain had retorted by superseding Primate Lindsay and Lord Chancellor Phipps in the government of Ireland, and appointing in their room Archbishop King and the Earl of Kildare. Archbishop Vesey was still continued as a Lord Justice, which Archbishop King attributes to a feeling of compassion for Vesey's venerable age (Mant, ii, 277), but which was probably due to a knowledge of the moderation of his political opinions (*supra*, p. 75, n. 2).

I remember, we never had leisure to think of that kingdom.
The poor dead Queen is used like the giant Lougarou in
Rabelais.[1] Pantagruel took Lougarou by the heels, and
made him his weapon to kill twenty other giants; then
flung him over a river into the town, and killed two
ducks and an old cat. I could talk very wisely to you, but
you would regard me not. I could bid you, *non desperare
de republicâ*; and say, that *res nolunt diu male administrari*.
But I will cut all short, and assure you, that if you do not
save us, I will not be at the pains of racking my invention
to guess how we shall be saved; and yet I have read
Polybius.

They tell me you have a very good crop of wheat, but
the barley is bad.[2] Hay will certainly be dear, unless we
have an open winter. I hope you found your hounds in
good condition, and that Bright has not made a stirrup-
leather of your jockey-belt. I imagine you now smoking
with your humdrum squire, I forget his name, who can go
home at midnight, and open a dozen gates when he is
drunk. I beg your Lordship not to ask me to lend you
any money. If you will come and live at the deanery, and
furnish up an apartment, I will find you in victuals and
drink, which is more than ever you got by the Court: and
as proud as you are, I hope to see you accept a part of
this offer before I die. The ——— take this country; it has,
in three weeks, spoiled two as good sixpenny pamphlets,
as ever a proclamation was issued out against.[3] And since
we talk of that will there not be [many libels about me
written by the Whigs?].[4] I shall be cured of loving Eng-

[1] Book II, chap. xxix.
[2] In the "Dublin Gazette" of the same date as this letter, it is
mentioned that Bolingbroke had ten days before "set out for his seat
at Bucklebury in Berkshire" (*supra*, p. 211, n. 3), and possibly it was
on hearing this news that Swift sat down to write to him. In the
following sentences Swift recalls what he had learned of Bolingbroke's
life at Bucklebury when he had accompanied him there three years
before and found him "a perfect country gentleman," who smoked
tobacco with his neighbours, inquired about the wheat, and knew his
hounds by name ("Prose Works," ii, 218).
[3] *I.e.*, "Some Free Thoughts upon the Present State of Affairs," and
"Some Considerations upon the Consequences hoped and feared from
the Death of the Queen" (*supra*, p. 231, n. 5).
[4] The "Hue and Cry after Dean Swift" ("Prose Works," v, 480)

land, as the fellow was of his ague, by getting himself whipped through the town.

I would retire too, if I could, but my country seat, where I have an acre of ground, is gone to ruin. The wall of my own apartment is fallen down, and I want mud to rebuild it, and straw to thatch it.[1] Besides, a spiteful neighbour has seized on six feet of ground, carried off my trees, and spoiled my grove.[2] All this is literally true, and I have not fortitude enough to go and see those devastations. But, in return, I live a country life in town, see nobody, and go every day once to prayers;[3] and hope, in a few months, to grow as stupid as the present situation of affairs will require. Well, after all, parsons are not such bad company, especially when they are under subjection; and I let none but such come near me.[4] However, pray God forgive them, by whose indolence, neglect, or want of friendship, I am reduced to live with twenty leagues of salt water between your Lordship and me, etc.

had been published before Swift left England ("Wentworth Papers," p. 411), and some hint of its appearance cannot but have reached his ears and given him a foresight of the numerous satires which the press poured out about him at that time.

[1] This reference confirms what I have said (*supra*, p. 53) as to the humble character of Swift's dwelling at Laracor. It shows also that a block of masonry, six feet long by four feet broad, with considerable resemblance to a gate pier, which is exhibited as a fragment of the house, is hardly likely to have formed any portion of it. A photograph of this supposed relic of Swift's residence is reproduced in Birkbeck Hill's "Unpublished Letters of Dean Swift," together with a photograph of a well which is said to have been in the cellar of his house. Even from the photographs it may be seen that to cover the two objects the vicarage would have had to be of palatial extent.

[2] In his "Imitation of Horace" (*supra*, p. 218) Swift refers to his grove:

"A terrace-walk, and half a rood
Of land, set out to plant a wood."

The neighbour must have been Percival (*supra*, p. 54), and, according to Delany ("Observations," p. 193), the trees were "very fine elms."

[3] See the comments of the Dean of St. Patrick's on Swift's ecclesiastical life (Introduction, vol. i, p. liii).

[4] His circle of clerical friends was indeed limited at that time. So far as his correspondence shows Archdeacon Walls, Dr. Raymond, his vicar, Worrall, and his curate, Warburton, were alone allowed to come near him. See *ibid.*, p. xlv.

CCCXIV. [*Copy.*[1]]

SWIFT TO KNIGHTLEY CHETWODE

Dublin, *September* 27, 1714.

SIR,[2]

THE person who brought me your letter delivered it in such a manner that I thought I was at Court again, and that the bearer wanted a place; and when I received it, I

---

[1] This is the first letter in the correspondence between Swift and Knightley Chetwode, which formed the text for the late Dr. G. Birkbeck Hill's elaborate commentary in the volume entitled "Unpublished Letters of Dean Swift." The original letters have disappeared and are said to have been destroyed owing to exposure to damp, but two copies of the correspondence remain, preserved respectively by Chetwode's descendants and in the Forster collection. The genesis of the latter copy is explained by Forster in the preface to his "Life of Swift," where, after an allusion to the rare gifts and charm of the representative of the Chetwode family at that time, Forster tells that his accomplished friend, who treasured Swift's letters as an heirloom of honour, and would not allow them out of his keeping, made with his own hand the copy for him, and invited him subsequently to his seat in Ireland to collate it with the original letters. This copy is evidently scrupulously accurate, and has great superiority over the Chetwode copy in that respect as well as in containing some letters from Chetwode to Swift which are not found in the other. It has therefore been used for the purposes of this edition of Swift's Correspondence, and as now printed Swift's letters to Chetwode will be found at times to differ from the version given by Dr. Hill, who knew only of the copy in the possession of the Chetwode family, and believed it to have been the one made for Forster which had been returned to them after his death.

[2] It required at that time in Ireland, where Whig opinion had become completely dominant on the accession of George I, some courage to be known as a friend of the champion of the Tory Ministers, and few visitors came to the deanery on Swift's return to Dublin. But one or two devoted adherents to the Tory cause, with whom he had previously been unacquainted, waited on Swift as on an oracle to inquire the fate of their party, and to seek consolation in the hour of defeat. Chief amongst these was Knightley Chetwode. He was the owner of a considerable estate in Ireland, with two country residences, one in the county of Meath about twelve miles to the north of Laracor, and the other in the Queen's county, and was a man of abilities and acquirements above his fellows. His political views followed naturally from his antecedents. He could trace his descent from the time of William the Conqueror through a long line of ancestors who appear first as lords of the lands of Chetwode in Buckinghamshire, and afterwards as owners of the lands of Warkworth in Northamptonshire, and

had my answer ready to give him after perusal, that I
would do him what service I could. But I was easy when
I saw your hand at the bottom, and then I recollected I
was in Ireland, that the Queen was dead, the Ministry
changed, and I was only the poor Dean of St. Patrick's.
My Chapter joins with me: we have consulted a lawyer,
who, as it is usual, makes ours a very good case; my
desires in that point are very moderate, only to break the
lease, and turn out nine singing men.[1] I should have been
with you before this time, if it had been possible for me to
find a horse; I have had twenty sent to me; I have got
one, but it is good for nothing, and my English horse [2] was
so ill I was forced to send him to grass. There is another
evil, that I want a stock of hay, and I cannot get any. I
remember Prince Butler [3] used to say: "By my soul, there

could claim amongst them heroes of the Crusades and other warriors
whose eminence proud tombs in Warkworth Church commemorate.
By the alliances which they had made the Chetwodes had also added
distinction to their race, and had become heirs to the ancient barony
of Wahull. But Knightley Chetwode's more immediate progenitors fell
on evil days, and at the time of the Restoration his grandfather, who
was a graduate of Oxford, came to Ireland to retrieve their fallen
fortunes. With the aid of the first Duke of Ormond, to whom he was
introduced by Archbishop Sheldon ("Carte Papers"), he was not unsuccessful in this design, and his grandson, who was the only surviving child of his second son, appears to have been endowed with
ample means.

[1] The dispute between Swift and the Vicars Choral as to the lease
from the latter to the Earl of Abercorn (*supra*, p. 113) was evidently
not yet terminated. That nobleman is hardly likely to have been
viewed with more favour by Swift when he read a few days later that
on hearing of the King's arrival, Lady Abercorn displayed exuberant
joy, sending for a hundred of her neighbours to rejoice with her, and
presenting each of them with cake and a bottle of wine to drink the
King's health, " which was done upon their knees " (" Dublin Gazette").

[2] From a subsequent reference this would appear to have been
" Bolingbroke," the horse which Swift had brought to Ireland when he
came over for his installation (*supra*, p. 44).

[3] Otherwise Brinsley Butler, who became the second Lord Newtown-Butler and first Viscount Lanesborough. He and his elder brother
Theophilus, otherwise Ophy, on whom the barony of Newtown-Butler
was conferred by George I, were college contemporaries of Swift.
They were well known members of society, and appear to have been
equally acceptable to Whig and Tory. Theophilus is immortalized by
a bequest under which some very small loaves are displayed in some
very large cases in one of the Dublin churches before being given to the
poor, as well as by his curious collection of poems known as " The
Whimsical Medley" (Barrett's " Essay," p. 85), but Brinsley has been

is not a drop of water in the Thames for me." This is my case; I have got a fool to lend me fifty pounds, and now I can neither get hay nor horse, and the season of the former is going. However if I cannot soon get a horse, I will send for my own from grass, and in two days endeavour to reach you; for I hear October is a very good month.

Jourdain[1] has been often telling my agent of some idle pretence he has to a bit of one of my parishes worth usually about five pounds per annum, and now the Queen is dead perhaps he may talk warmer of it. But we in possession always answer in those cases, that we must not injure our successors. Those idle claims are usual in Ireland, where there has been so much confusion in parishes, but they never come to anything. I desire my humble service may be presented to Mrs. Chetwode.[2] I am,

Your most obedient humble servant,

JON. SWIFT.

September 28.

This was writ last night not knowing the post day: I now tell you that by noise and bonfires I suppose the packets are come in with account of the King's arrival.[3]

Addressed—To Knightley Chetwode Esq., at his house near Portarlington, in the Queen's County. Per post.

less fortunate, although he left money to gild the balcony of St. Paul's Cathedral, and indited a sheaf of letters to Joshua Dawson.

[1] The Rev. John Jourdain who, for more than half a century, held the parish of Dunshaughlin, adjoining Rathbeggan, the outlying parish in the union of Laracor.

[2] Chetwode's wife, to whom he had been married fourteen years previously by the famous Francis Higgins, was the daughter of Richard Brooking, a Devonshire gentleman. Her father, who had come to Ireland under the protection of Sir Richard Reynell, an illustrious member of the Irish judicial bench and a countryman of his own, had died young. Through her mother, Mrs. Chetwode was a niece of " our Justice Boate " (" Poetical Works," ii, 198), and half-sister of Swift's friend, Bishop Stopford.

[3] The King landed at Greenwich on Saturday, the 18th, but owing to contrary winds the news did not reach Dublin for ten days. " Last Tuesday night (the 28th) was received," says the " Dublin Gazette," " the joyful news of the safe arrival of his Majesty King George and his Royal Highness the Prince in England, upon which the great guns were fired and the night concluded with ringing of bells, bonfires, illuminations, and all other demonstrations of joy."

CCCXV. [*Copy.*[1]]

SWIFT TO KNIGHTLEY CHETWODE

Dublin, *October* 6, 1714.

SIR,

I ACKNOWLEDGE both your letters, and with any common fortune might have spared you the trouble of reading this by coming myself. I used to value a good revenue, because I thought it exempted a man from the little subaltern cares of life; and so it would if the master were wise, or servants had honesty and common sense. A man who is new in a house, or an office, has so many important nothings to take up his time that he cannot do what he would. I have got in hay; but my groom offended against the very letter of a proverb, and stacked it in a rainy day, so that it is now smoking like a chimney.[2] My stable is a very hospital for sick horses. A joiner who was to shelve a room for my library has employed a fortnight, and yet not finished what he promised in six days. One occasion I have to triumph, that in six weeks time I have been able to get rid of a great cat,[3] that belonged to the late Dean, and almost poisoned the house. An old woman under the same circumstances I cannot yet get rid of, or find a maid. Yet in spite of all these difficulties, I hope to share some part of October at Woodbrooke.[4] But I scorn your coach; for I find upon trial I can ride.

Indeed I am as much disquieted at the turn of public affairs as you or any men can be.[5] It concerns us spiritual

---

[1] In the Forster Collection (*supra*, p. 241, n. 1).

[2] Owing to the damp climate of Ireland hay has to be treated there in a special manner. Swift's groom, who was a Scotchman, may not have been aware of the precautions necessary.

[3] There is ground for believing, however, that Swift was not without a weakness for cats. See Appendix X.

[4] By this combination of the last syllable of his own name and the first of his wife's, Chetwode had found an appropriate name for his Queen's county residence, which still remains the seat of his descendants. The name is now spelled without the final letter, but as appears from an autograph letter (Civil Correspondence, P. R. O. of Ireland) Chetwode adopted the spelling used here.

[5] Swift had evidently entertained until the last a hope that some of his Tory friends would be retained in the Ministry, and was unprepared for the complete transfer of power to the Whigs which took

men in a tender temporal point. Everything is as bad as possible; and I think if the Pretender ever comes over, the present men in power have traced him the way. Your servant is just come for this, and I am dressing fast for Prayers.

Your most obedient, etc.

J. S.

Addressed—To Knightley Chetwode Esq.

CCCXVI. [*Original.*[1]]

JOHN ARBUTHNOT TO SWIFT

October 19, 1714.

DEAR BROTHER,

EVEN in affliction, your letter made me melancholy, and communicated some of the spleen which you had when you wrote it,[2] and made me forfeit some of my reputation of cheerfulness and temper under afflictions. However, I have so many subjects amongst my friends and fellow-servants to be grieved for, that I can easily turn it off myself with credit. The Queen's poor servants are, like so many poor orphans, exposed in the very streets, and those, whose past obligations of gratitude and honour

---

place on the King's arrival. The dismissals had extended even to Ireland, and a week before the King had superseded Chancellor Phipps (by the appointment of Brodrick), the three Common Law Chiefs, and a puisne judge in the person of Nutley.

[1] In the British Museum. See Preface.

[2] Early in September Arbuthnot wrote to Pope: "I have seen a letter from Dean Swift; he keeps up his noble spirit and though like a man knocked down, you may behold him still with a stern countenance, and aiming a blow at his adversaries." But on hearing of the final discomfiture of his political friends Swift gave way to despair; an attack of illness supervened, and as we see in the lines "In Sickness," which he then wrote, Swift prayed for death. Evidently there was no one whom he missed in his banishment more than Arbuthnot:

> "My state of health none care to learn;
> My life is here no soul's concern:
> And those with whom I now converse
> Without a tear will tend my hearse;
> Removed from kind Arbuthnot's aid,
> Who knows his art, but not his trade."
> "Poetical Works," ii, 180.

ought to have engaged them to have represented their case, pass by them like so many abandoned creatures, without the possibility of ever being able to make the least return for a favour, which has added to my theory of human virtue. I wish I did not only haunt you in the obliging and affectionate sense you are pleased to express it, but were personally present with you; and I think it were hardly in the power of fortune not to make some minutes pleasant. I dine with my Lord and Lady Masham to-day, where we will, as usually, remember you.

You have read, ere this time, the History of the White Staff,[1] which is either contrived by an enemy, or by himself, to bring down vengeance, and I have told some of his nearest friends so. All the Dragon[2] can say will not give him one single friend amongst the whole party, and therefore I even wonder at him, which you will say is a strange thing. The very great person of all[3] can hardly speak of him with patience. The Condé[4] acts like a man of spirit, makes up to the King and talks to him, and would have acted with more sense than any of them, could he have had any body to have acted along with him: *nos numerus sumus, etc.* The man you speak of is just as you describe, so I beg pardon. Shadwell says, he will have my place of Chelsea. Garth told me, his merit was, giving intelligence about his mistress's health.[5] I desired he would do me the favour to say, that I valued myself upon quite the contrary, and I hoped to live to see the day,

---

[1] "The Secret History of the White Staff, being an account of Affairs under the Conduct of some late Ministers, and of what might probably have happened if her Majesty had not died." It was written by Daniel de Foe, with knowledge which can only have been gained from Oxford. That Minister's connection with de Foe is one of the most extraordinary episodes in his life, and it would have been a source of much chagrin to Swift had he known to what an extent de Foe enjoyed the confidence of Oxford.

[2] *I.e.*, Oxford (*supra*, p. 150, n. 4).   [3] *I.e.*, the King.

[4] *I.e.*, the Earl of Peterborough, who had much similarity in his character, as well as in his career, to the great Condé. He had then just returned from Italy.

[5] The allusion is evidently to an office held by Arbuthnot in connection with Chelsea Hospital (*supra*, p. 221). Sir John Shadwell was, like Sir Samuel Garth, a Whig, but was one of Queen Anne's physicians, and, as we have seen, attended her in her last illness (*supra*, p. 207, n. 1). In their love of literature Garth and Arbuthnot forgot, doubtless, a difference in politics.

when his Majesty would value me the more for it too. I have not seen anything as yet to make me recant a certain inconvenient opinion I have, that one cannot pay too dear for peace of my mind.

Poor philosopher Berkeley has now the idea of health, which was very hard to produce in him; for he had an idea of a strange fever upon him so strong, that it was very hard to destroy it by introducing a contrary one.[1] Poor Gay is much where he was, only out of the Duchess's[2] family and service. He has some confidence in the Princess[3] and Countess of Picburgh;[4] I wish it may be significant to him. I advised him to make a poem upon the Princess before she came over, describing her to the English ladies; for it seems the Princess does not dislike that—she is really a person that I believe will give great content to everybody. But Gay was in such a grovelling condition, as to the affairs of the world, that his Muse would not stoop to visit him. I can say no more of news, than that you will find the proceedings hitherto have been comparatively gentle. Adieu.

CCCXVII. [*Copy.*[5]]

SWIFT TO KNIGHTLEY CHETWODE

Dublin, *October* 20, 1714.

SIR,

THE Bishop of Dromore is expected this night in town on purpose to restore his cat,[6] who by her perpetual noise and stink must be certainly a Whig. In compliance to your observation of old women's tenderness to each other, I have got one as old and ugly as that the Bishop left, for

[1] Berkeley had returned from Italy with Peterborough. A year before Swift, in speaking of Berkeley's philosophy, had said that he had not succeeded in making a convert of Arbuthnot (Hist. MSS. Com., Rept. 7, App., p. 239).

[2] *I.e.*, the Duchess of Monmouth (*supra*, p. 144, n. 5).

[3] *I.e.*, the future Queen Caroline, who had landed in England on 11 October.

[4] "A lady of high birth, great fortune, and superior merit," by whom the Princess was accompanied to England.

[5] In the Forster Collection (*supra*, p. 241, n. 1).

[6] *Supra*, p. 244.

the ladies of my acquaintance would not allow me one with a tolerable face though I most earnestly interceded for it. If I had considered the uncertainty of weather in our climate, I should have made better use of that short sunshine than I did; but I was amusing myself to make the public hay and neglected my own. Do you mean my Lady Jenny Forbes that was?[1] I had almost forgot her. But when love is gone, friendship continues. I thought she had not at this time of day been at a loss how to bring forth a child. I find you are readier at kindling other people's bonfires than your own. I had one last night *par manière d'acquit*, and to save my windows.[2]

Your closet of eighteen foot square is a perfect gasconade. I suppose it is the largest room in your house or rather two rooms struck out into one. I thank you for your present of it, but I have too many rooms already; I wish you had all I could spare, though I were to give you money along with them. Since you talk of your *cave de brique*, I have bought forty-six dozen bottles and want nothing but the circumstance of wine to be able to entertain a friend. You are mistaken, I am no coy beauty but rather with submission like a wench who has made an assignation and when the day comes, has not a petticoat to appear in. I am plagued to death with turning away and taking servants; my Scotch groom ran away from me ten days ago and robbed me and several of the neighbourhood. I cannot stir from hence till

---

[1] She was a daughter of the second Earl of Granard, and had married Major Josiah Champagne, who lived near Woodbrooke at Portarlington. In the "Memoirs of the Earl of Granard" she is described as "a pious, sensible, and worthy woman." Her father's political opinions were calculated to recommend her to Chetwode.

[2] Swift was writing on the day of the King's coronation, which was observed in Dublin "with great solemnity." The celebration is recorded in the "Dublin Gazette" as follows: "About eleven in the morning a very great number of the nobility, clergy, judges and gentry, and a great many ladies in very fine clothes, went to the Castle. About twelve o'clock a coronation song in honour of his Majesty was performed by the best masters; when the music ended the great guns of the Castle were fired three rounds, and answered by three volleys of small arms from the regiments that are on duty here drawn up in College Green. In the evening there was a play, and at night their Excellencies [the Lords Justices] went to a fine set of fireworks burnt on the Custom House Quay and on the water, and the night concluded with ringing of bells, bonfires, illuminations, and all other demonstrations of joy."

a great vessel of Alicant is bottled, and till my horse is in
a condition to travel and my chimneypiece made. I never
wanted so much a little country air, being plagued with
perpetual colds and twenty ailments,[1] yet I cannot stir at
present as things stand.

I am your most obedient etc.

Addressed—To Knightley Chetwode Esq., at Woodbrooke,
near Portarlington.

CCCXVIII. [*Copy.*[2]]

KNIGHTLEY CHETWODE TO SWIFT

[October 24, 1714.]

I AM favoured with your letter,[3] but not a great deal pleased
with its contents: I mean that anything should ail you
whom I so much value. If air would remove it as you say,
I am sorry you will not believe that air and prospects were
as beneficial and agreeable as those on each side your door
streetward. If it be worth while, as you pleasantly say, for
a Whig-drove Bishop to make a journey to restore his cat,
sure it will be worth his endeavour to get a day set apart
on the occasion. I will expect for the future the 20th of
October in our calendar in lieu of the 29th of May. The
ladies of your acquaintance are I confess a little hard upon
you in regard to faces to tie you down to ugliness and age.
But you know best if it be not just.[4]

The lady I mention is the veritable Lady Jenny Forbes,
your quondam acquaintance; she was more at a loss to
bring forth [than] would easily be believed, and so diffident
lest it should prove *une grossesse de vent* that nothing but
seeing and feeling could convince, even after so much pain
and so much danger. You banter your country friends
strangely; but nevertheless though your bottles do, yet my
cave de brique does not want the circumstance of wine to

---

[1] *Supra*, p. 245, n. 2.
[2] In the Forster Collection (*supra*, p. 241, n. 1).
[3] *Supra*, p. 247.
[4] The following words are struck out: " Since the world says you
may command a very agreeable one and yet defer it.

enable me to entertain a friend. You are either a great deal diffident or not at all so, otherwise you would see, judge, try if my eighteen foot square be a gasconade. I wish I could take what rooms you say you could spare; for aught I know it might not only serve you and me but both our successors. I really at first apprehended you had discovered a bit of extravagance of mine when you mention your chimneypiece; for I had sent for one of marble to my closet. I thought you [who] said so much of the Scotch could not so easily forget the thistle motto. It is plain in your case what has been often said to me by Sir Edward Seymour[1] does not hold true, that no one ever got anything from that nation but what stuck to them; [for] your groom did not stick to you though he robbed you. Pray let me know if your great vessel of Alicant be bottled. I have some in bottles which I will pretend to put in competition with it.

I am afraid your inclinations are not as good as your horse's condition to travel. Pray let me know if I may hope to see you manage these difficulties, and when; if you will let me hope for it in a reasonable time, I will delay going to my winter quarters,[2] which for a month past nothing but my expectation of you has made me defer. Mrs. Chetwode who is much your admirer and humble servant, bade me tell you, your not coming hither is owing to your fears of being upbraided with being an old bachelor. You great men never say a word of news to little ones, otherwise you would have mentioned my Lord Bolingbroke as I desired, for I am more attached to him than, I believe, you know of. I have not to add, but to desire *toujours avoir l'honneur de votre amitié*, for I am, with all imaginable respect,

Your faithful friend and obedient servant.

---

[1] Chetwode was probably acquainted with that statesman, who died in 1707, through his wife (*supra*, p. 243, n. 2). Her father mentions leases which he held from Sir Edward in his will.

[2] *I.e.*, to his residence in the county of Meath (*supra*, p. 241, n. 2).

CCCXIX. [*Hawkesworth.*]

SWIFT TO SIR ARTHUR LANGFORD

Trim, *October* 30, 1714.

SIR,[1]

I WAS to wait on you the other day, and was told by your servant that you are not to be seen till towards evening, which, at the distance I am at this time of the year,[2] cannot easily be compassed. My principal business was, to let you know, that since my last return from England many persons have complained to me, that I suffered a conventicle to be kept in my parish, and in a place where there never was any before.[3] I mentioned this to your nephew Rowley[4] in Dublin, when he came to me with this message from you; but I could not prevail with him to write to you about it. I have always looked upon you as an honest gentleman, of great charity and piety in your way; and I hope you will remember at the same time, that it becomes you to be a legal man, and that you will not promote or encourage, much less give a beginning to a thing directly contrary to the law.

You know the Dissenters in Ireland are suffered to have their conventicles only by connivance, and that only in places where they formerly used to meet. Whereas this conventicle of yours is a new thing, in a new place entirely of your own erection, and perverted to this ill use from the design you outwardly seemed to have intended it for. It has been the weakness of the Dissenters to be too sanguine and assuming upon events in the State which appeared to

---

[1] There has been already notice of Sir Arthur Langford, an ancestor of the Lords Langford, as one of Swift's parishioners at Laracor (*supra*, vol. i, p. 181, n. 1).

[2] As appears from the superscription Swift had left Dublin and come to Trim. The reference is to the greater distance of Summerhill, Sir Arthur Langford's seat, from that town than from Swift's vicarage.

[3] Of his devotion to the Presbytery Sir Arthur Langford, who died in less than two years, gives ample proof in his will, bequeathing to trustees £4,000 of his "first and readiest money" for its use as well as many smaller legacies for specific purposes.

[4] Hercules Rowley, who represented the county of Londonderry in the Irish Parliament, and was ancestor of the Lords Langford.

give them the least encouragement; and this, in other turns of affairs, has proved very much to their disadvantage. The most moderate Churchmen may be apt to resent, when they see a sect, without toleration by law, insulting the established religion. Whenever the legislator shall think fit to give them leave to build new conventicles, all good Churchmen will submit: but till then we can hardly see it without betraying our Church.

I hope, therefore, you will not think it hard if I take those methods which my duty obliges me, to prevent this growing evil as far as it lies in my power, unless you shall think fit, from your own prudence, or the advice of some understanding friends, to shut up the doors of that conventicle for the future.[1] I am, with true friendship and esteem, Sir,

Your most obedient humble servant,

B.

CCCXX. [*Scott.*]

SWIFT TO MISS ESTHER VANHOMRIGH

Philipstown, *November* 5, 1714.[2]

I MET your servant when I was a mile from Trim, and could send him no other answer than I did, for I was going abroad by appointment; besides, I would not have gone to Kildrought to see you for all the world.[3] I ever told you

[1] Swift does not appear to have succeeded in closing the conventicle, as in his will Sir Arthur Langford desires to be buried in his chapel at Summerhill, and leaves a rent charge of £30 towards the maintenance of a Presbyterian minister there.

[2] Swift had set out that morning from Trim to pay his promised visit to Chetwode (*supra*, p. 249), and was stopping on his way at Philipstown, then the assize town of the King's County.

[3] Whether there had been any communication between Swift and Vanessa since he left England does not appear, but probably she had learned that he had relinquished his idea of returning to London that winter (*supra*, p. 234), and thereupon had resolved to follow him to Ireland. She had evidently arrived after he had gone to Trim, and had taken up her abode at Kildrought, now known as Celbridge, where she is said to have inherited a house from her father (*supra*, vol. i, p. 299, n. 1). Celbridge lies about eleven miles to the west of Dublin, in the direction of, although not on the main road to, Trim.

you wanted discretion. I am going to a friend upon a promise, and shall stay with him about a fortnight, and then come to town, and I will call on you as soon as I can, supposing you lodge in Turnstile Alley,[1] as your servant told me, and that your neighbours can tell me whereabouts. Your servant said you would be in town on Monday;[2] so that I suppose this will be ready to welcome you there. I fear you had a journey full of fatigues. Pray take care of your health in this Irish air, to which you are a stranger.[3] Does not Dublin look very dirty to you, and the country very miserable? Is Kildrought as beautiful as Windsor,[4] and as agreeable to you as the Prebend's lodgings there?[5] Is there any walk about you as pleasant as the avenue, and the Marlborough Lodge?[6] I have rode a tedious journey to-day,[7] and can say no more. Nor shall you know where I am till I come, and then I will see you. A fig for your letters and messages. Adieu.

Addressed—To Mrs. Vanhomrigh, at her lodgings in Turnstile Alley, near College Green, Dublin.

---

[1] This Alley, afterwards known as Parliament Row, adjoined the Houses of Parliament in College Green, Dublin.

[2] The 9th.

[3] In the year 1711 ("Prose Works," ii, 222) Swift mentions that Vanessa was about to pay a visit to Ireland, but she had probably not done so.

[4] It is not possible to compare the stately grandeur of Windsor with the scenery round Celbridge, but the latter place is famous for its natural beauty. It is situated on the river Liffey, which is there crossed by a bridge, and was originally known as *Cilldroichid*, the church of the bridge, a name of which Kildrought and Celbridge are respectively a corruption and misinterpretation. See Joyce's "Irish Names of Places."

[5] When Vanessa had been at Windsor with Swift two years before (*supra*, vol. i, p. 344), he was occupying the residence of one of the prebendaries ("Prose Works," ii, 380).

[6] The residence of the Duchess of Marlborough in right of the rangership of Windsor Park, now known as Cumberland Lodge.

[7] The journey from Trim to Philipstown is one of twenty-five Irish miles.

CCCXXI. [*Copy.*[1]]

SWIFT TO KNIGHTLEY CHETWODE

Woodbrooke, *November* 6 [1714]
past one in the afternoon.

NOT to disturb you in the good work of a godfather nor spoil your dinner, I only design Mrs. Chetwode and you would take care not to be benighted; but come when you will you shall be heartily welcome to my house.[2] The children's tutor is gone out and so there was no pen and ink to be had.

Endorsed—A pencil note from Woodbrooke where he came in Knightley Chetwode's absence dining out.

CCCXXII. [*Original.*[3]]

JOHN ARBUTHNOT TO SWIFT

November, 1714.

DEAR BROTHER,

I SEND you the scrap of a letter begun to you by the whole Society,[4] because I suppose you even value the fragments of your friends. The honest gentleman, at whose lodgings we wrote, is gone for France. I really value your judgement extremely in choosing your friends. I think worthy Mr. Ford is an instance of it, being an honest, sensible, firm, friendly man, *et qualis ab inceptu processerat, etc.*[5] Though, by the way, praising your judgement is a

---

[1] In the Forster Collection (*supra*, p. 241, n. 1).

[2] Swift had evidently arrived early at Woodbrooke, which is only about ten Irish miles from Philipstown, and had found his host and hostess out attending a christening feast in the neighbourhood. This note was probably sent in the carriage which was to bring them home.

[3] In the British Museum. See Preface.

[4] The Scriblerus Club (*supra*, p. 145).

[5] Ford, who had been relieved of the editorship of the "Gazette" on the arrival of George I (*supra*, p. 216), was apparently "the honest gentleman" who had gone to France. This letter is, however, written

little compliment to myself, which I am apt to fall into of late, nobody now being at the trouble of doing it for me. The Parnellian, who was to have carried this letter, seems to have changed his mind by some sudden turn in his affairs;[1] but I wish his hopes may not be the effect of some accidental thing working upon his spirits, rather than any well-grounded project.

If it be any pleasure to you, I can assure you that you are remembered kindly by your friends, and I believe not altogether forgot by your enemies. I think both is for your reputation. I am told, that I am to lose my little preferment:[2] however, I hope to be able to keep a little habitation warm in town. I cannot but say, I think there is one thing in your circumstance, that must make any man happy: which is, a liberty to preach. Such a prodigious privilege, that if it did not border upon simony, I could really purchase it for a sum of money. For my part, I never imagine any man can be uneasy, that has the opportunity of venting himself to a whole congregation once a week. And you may pretend what you will, I am sure you think so too, or you do not judge right. As for news, I never inquire about any. *Fuimus Troes, etc., sed nunc ferox Jupiter transtulit omnia ad Argos.*

My present politics is to give no disturbance to the present folks in the due exercise of their power, for fear of forcing them to do very strange things, rather than part with what they love so well. Untoward reports in the country will make elections dearer, which I am sorry for. The Dragon,[3] I am afraid, will be struck at. Adieu, in haste.

I must not forget to tell you a passage of the Pretender's declaration to this purpose: that he had no reason to doubt of his sister's good intentions towards him, which made him sit quiet in her time, but was now disappointed by the deplorable accident of her sudden death.

on the same sheet as one from Arbuthnot to Ford in which he is asked to forward Swift's letter to him. Perhaps France had some hidden meaning.

[1] Parnell went, however, soon afterwards to Ireland. He had spent September at Bath with Pope (Elwin and Courthope, *op. cit.*, vii, 417, 453).

[2] His post at Chelsea (*supra*, p. 246).

[3] *I.e.*, Oxford (*supra*, p. 150, n. 4).

CCCXXIII. [*Original.*[1]]

SWIFT TO ARCHDEACON WALLS

November 23, 1714.

I WRIT to you or some of your crew the day before I left Trim; I have been here ever since at Mr. Chetwode's where I am used very well, and ride out whenever the weather will let me, and have been in tolerable health, though really I think I used more exercise in Dublin, for in the country of Ireland there is no walking in winter. I have been in three or four neighbouring towns, all better than Trim; and there is a great deal of wood and hedges, hereabouts, so that in summer it would be a sort of England only for the bogs. I have waited for good weather and opportunity to see my lands near Athy,[2] which is but ten miles off; and that, besides my laziness and welcome, has kept me so long here, and may still a week longer. Your letter to Portarlington was rightly directed if you had added in the Queen's county.

Why the whole room painted?[3] Is it not enough to have only the new panels and edges of the shelves painted? Do what you will; but pray let it be done before I come that the smell may go off. Is the chimneypiece up, or only finished at the man's house? I am sorry the Bishop[4] went out of town before I came. Read that last sentence to Mrs. Johnson and observe whether she turns up her forehead and dabs her hand on the table or on her knee.[5] I desired that Mrs. Brent[6] might be spoke to, and have the

---

[1] In the possession of Mr. John Murray. See Preface.

[2] The corps of the deanery of St. Patrick's included the rectory, and some part of the lands, of the parish of Kilberry near the town of Athy, in the county of Kildare. In a subsequent letter Swift describes them at length (*infra*, p. 266).

[3] Evidently a reference to the work then being executed for Swift in the deanery house (*supra*, p. 244).

[4] *I.e.*, Stearne, the Bishop of Dromore (*supra*, p. 247).

[5] This is doubtless an allusion to some practice of Stella when playing cards.

[6] Mrs. Brent, who is frequently mentioned in the Journal to Stella, appears to have superintended Swift's household, but did not at that time reside at the Deanery.

groom cover the wine with litter to prevent frost, and to take care not to shake the vessel; some litter should be under and over. But pray do not let him fill the whole cellar with it only just enough to keep out the frost. My service to Gossip and the ladies of St. Mary's. What does Gossip do for want of a gamester?[1] Pray give the groom and maid some board-wages. If you cannot read this your lodgers can. What news of Bolton and the living?[2]

Addressed—To the Reverend Mr. Archdeacon Walls over against the Hospital in Queen Street, Dublin.

CCCXXIV. [*Copy.*[3]]

SWIFT TO KNIGHTLEY CHETWODE

Dublin, *December* 3, 1714.

SIR,

MR. GRAVES never came to me till this morning, like a vile man as he is.[4] I had no letters from England to vex me except on the public account.[5] I am now teased by an impertinent woman, come to renew her lease; the Baron[6]

---

[1] Swift was probably Mrs. Walls's partner at cards, and provided the stakes.

[2] Theophilus Bolton (*supra*, p. 72) was appointed at that time Chancellor of St. Patrick's Cathedral. He had been Stearne's nomination to the incumbency of St. Nicholas Without (*supra*, p. 51), and as will be seen from the next letter it is to that living Swift refers.

[3] In the Forster Collection. *Supra*, p. 241, n. 1.

[4] As the superscription shows, Swift had returned from Woodbrooke to Dublin.

[5] It would appear from Chetwode's reply (*infra*, p. 260) that there had been an announcement in the newspapers about Swift, or about some matter in which he was concerned.

[6] The Baron, otherwise Robert Rochfort, whose family so often provided subjects for Swift's verse, had just been deprived of the chief seat in the Court of Exchequer in Ireland (*supra*, p. 244, n. 5). That he was then an uncompromising Tory is evident from " The Country Life " (" Poetical Works," i, 137), where we read of

> " how little weight he sets
> On all Whig papers and gazettes ;"

but his career had displayed an oscillation characteristic of his race, who trace their descent in Ireland from valiant men " of the strong and she are talking together. I have just squired her down, and there is at present nobody with me but—yes, now Mr. Walls is come in—and now another—you must stay. Now I am full of company again and the Baron is in haste;[1] I will write to you in a post or two. Manley is not Commissioner nor expects it.[2] I had a very ingenious Tory ballad sent me printed, but receiving it in a Whig house I suddenly read it, and gave it to a gentleman with a wink, and ordered him to burn it, but he threw another paper into the fire. I hope to send you a copy of it. I have seen nobody since I came. Bolton's patent for St. Werburgh's is passed,[3] and I believe I shall find difficulties with the Chapter about a successor for him. I thought to give the Baron some good coffee, and they made it so bad, that I would hardly give it Wharton.[4] I here send some snuff to

rock," in the dawn of Anglo-Norman rule, and who in their succeeding generations in that country have been found in the ranks with ancient Englishry, Cromwellians, Williamites, Jacobites, and Hanoverians. Rochfort, who was the posthumous son of an officer in Cromwell's army, the victim of a fate no less mysterious than untimely, was sufficiently established at the Irish bar on the accession of William III to be chosen by that sovereign as a Commissioner of the Great Seal of Ireland. In that capacity he accompanied William from London to the Boyne (Library of Trinity College, Dublin, MS. 1181, f. 125), but disapproving of the policy foreshadowed in the Articles of Limerick, went into opposition, and in William's first Irish Parliament joined with Brodrick in vigorous denunciation of the concession granted to Roman Catholicism by the Irish executive of that day (Froude, *op. cit.*, i, 232). In the second Parliament their appointment as the law officers, and Rochfort's election to the Speaker's chair, alone secured the passage of the necessary supplies. For twelve years Rochfort filled the office of Attorney-General, but on the accession of Queen Anne surrendered to his colleague Brodrick the Speaker's chair, and seems from that time to have thrown in his fortunes with Ormond, who secured Rochfort's promotion to the place of Chief Baron when retiring from his first viceroyalty. Of Chetwode the Baron was an intimate, and to him owed possibly his introduction to Swift.

[1] The Baron was going to Chetwode and was taking Swift's letter.

[2] There had been apparently a rumour that Postmaster Manley was to be made a Commissioner of the Revenue.

[3] The parish of St. Werburgh's, in Dublin, formed part of the corps of the Chancellorship of St. Patrick's Cathedral (*supra*, p. 257, n. 2).

[4] Swift's old enemy had been left out in the cold on the Hanoverian accession in the appointment of Lords Justices (*supra*, p. 230, n. 4), but had been made Privy Seal.

Mrs. Chetwode; the Baron will tell you by what snatches I write this paper. I am,

Yours, etc.

My humble service to Dame Pliant.[1]

Addressed—To Knightley Chetwode, Esq., per messenger.

CCCXXV. [*Scott.*]

Miss Esther Vanhomrigh to Swift

Dublin [*December*], 1714.

YOU cannot but be sensible, at least in some degree, of the many uneasinesses I am slave to: a wretch of a brother, cunning executors, and importunate creditors of my mother's, things I can no way avoid being subject to at present, and weighty enough to sink greater spirits than mine without some support.[2] Once I had a friend that would see me sometimes, and either commend what I did, or advise me what to do, which banished all my uneasiness. But now when my misfortunes are increased by being in a disagreeable place, among strange prying deceitful people, whose company is so far from an amusement, that it is a very great punishment, you fly me, and give me no reason, but that we are amongst fools, and must submit. I am very well satisfied we are amongst such, but know no reason for having my happiness sacrificed to their caprice. You once had a maxim, which was, to act what was right,

---

[1] Swift had applied evidently the character of the handsome widow in Ben Jonson's "Alchemist" to Chetwode's wife.

[2] Vanessa had found on Swift's return to Dublin that his edict from Letcombe (*supra*, p. 234) was written with purpose, and that their intercourse in Ireland was likely to be of the most formal kind. In the impassioned sentences of this letter Vanessa's character does not appear in an attractive light. There is too much reason to suspect a want of reality in the reiterations of her misfortunes, and to attribute them, as Sir Henry Craik suggests ("Life," ii, 23), to a desire "to draw the bonds of their intimacy more close." Nor are the terms in which her only brother is spoken of creditable to her heart. Little did she opine that in a will made that year he had bequeathed to his "loving sisters" a life interest in his estate, or that before many months elapsed they were to succeed to it owing to his early death.

and not mind what the world said; I wish you would keep to it now. Pray what can be wrong in seeing and advising an unhappy young woman? I cannot imagine. You cannot but know that your frowns make my life unsupportable. You have taught me to distinguish, and then you leave me miserable. Now all I beg is, that you will for once counterfeit, since you cannot otherwise, that indulgent friend you once were, till I get the better of these difficulties for my sister's sake; for were not she involved, who, I know, is not able to manage them as I am, I have a nobler soul than sit struggling with misfortunes, when at the end I cannot promise myself any real happiness. Forgive me; I beg you will believe it is not in my power to avoid complaining as I do.

CCCXXVI. [*Scott.*]

SWIFT TO MISS ESTHER VANHOMRIGH

Monday morning [*December* 6, 1714].

I WILL see you in a day or two, and believe me it goes to my soul not to see you oftener. I will give you the best advice, countenance, and assistance I can. I would have been with you sooner if a thousand impediments had not prevented me. I did not imagine you had been under difficulties. I am sure my whole fortune should go to remove them. I cannot see you, I fear, to-day, having affairs of my place to do; but pray think it not want of friendship or tenderness, which I will always continue to the utmost.

CCCXXVII. [*Copy.*[1]]

KNIGHTLEY CHETWODE TO SWIFT

Woodbrooke, *December* 8, 1714.

I RECEIVED your letter[2] by the Baron and the Pliant Dame's snuff, for both which favours we are thankful to you. I

---

[1] In the Forster Collection. *Supra*, p. 241, n. 1.
[2] *Supra*, p. 257.

stayed another day at Naas[1] and from thence went to
Mount Air. I brought the historian of that family home
with me. We had some discourse of you and drank your
health; I shall acquaint you when I see you of a good deal
passed whilst I stayed there. I am glad you received
nothing from England to vex you which regarded your
private. I can assure you my pains on that head were not a
few. Yours makes me easy in the point, though it is said
in the public Gazette which I read.[2] This place I hate since
you left it; I will go off Monday eight days. I have been
diligent for some days past to get some work done you advised; I flatter myself it is to your satisfaction.[3] I have
been this day upwards of nine hours at the same sort of
work you were at one day, am pretty much fatigued, [and]
am glad it is night to get victuals and ease.

I must let you know I have the Baron's faithful promise
about your affair; all the directions I could give was Kilberry and the lands adjoining belonging to the Dean of St.
Patrick's.[4] I know not if these instructions be sufficient; if
not I pray send me fuller, and the other denominations if
more there be. I am in great hopes of the aforesaid ballad
you mention; pray send it me. The Baron tells me I am
not longer Mr. Justice.[5] Dame Pliant and I join in our requests that you will so order your affairs to be with us at
Martry[6] this Christmas. According to what I hear from you

[1] Chetwode had apparently accompanied Swift on his journey to
Dublin as far as Naas, which is the assize town of the county of
Kildare, and lies half-way between Woodbrooke and Dublin.
[2] A search in the official Gazettes, published in London and Dublin,
has failed to disclose the subject of this allusion.
[3] The demesne at Woodbrooke, which is about nine hundred acres
in extent, comprises woodland as well as park, and is especially remarkable for its fine timber, principally beech ("Unpublished Letters,"
p. xxiv). Its design had occupied Chetwode for some time, and in a
letter written two years before to Secretary Dawson about a dishonest
mason who had absconded, he refers to a wilderness which he had
laid out, and which was approached through two entrances furnished
with stone piers (Civil Correspondence in P.R.O. of Ireland). Swift,
who considered himself an authority on such subjects, found congenial
employment in suggesting improvements, and to the present day there
is a grove of beech trees near the house which is traditionally said to
owe its origin to him.
[4] *Supra*, p. 256, n. 2.   [5] *I.e.*, in the Commission of the Peace.
[6] Chetwode's residence in the county of Meath, which took its name
from the parish in which it is situated. The latter lay not far from the
parish of Ardbraccan, of which Knightley Chetwode's father, who was

we will concert the method of getting you conveyed
thither. There is good hay [there], though wanted here. I
hear you will meet with great difficulty with your Chapter ;
I hope I am misinformed. Pray hint to me if you confide
in Manley.[1] If you see him, and believe it worth while, you
may please to let him know I am his humble servant. All
here are entirely devoted to your service, and I am with the
utmost respect and affection,

Your faithful and obedient, etc.

CCCXXVIII. [*Original.*[2]]

SWIFT TO ARCHDEACON WALLS

Belcamp, Monday Morning, December 27 [1714].

SOME business kept me in town an hour longer than I
thought, and I was forced to come back to the Deanery for
something I had forgot.[3] It was near three before I

---

in holy orders, had been rector. Martry has been in the possession of
the Tisdalls of Charlesfort since the Restoration, and the house occupied by Chetwode must have been rented from them.

  [1] Judging from the fact that his letters to Chetwode were generally
sent by private hand, it is evident that Swift did not trust Postmaster
Manley, and, as appears later on, had good reason for his suspicions.

  [2] In the possession of Mr. John Murray. See Preface.

  [3] Swift now appears for the first time as a guest in the ancestral
home of Ireland's great son, the illustrious Henry Grattan. Belcamp
was then the residence of the mother of Swift's seven famous friends.
She was the widow of the Rev. Patrick Grattan, a Senior Fellow of
Trinity College, Dublin, who on his marriage had obtained a stall in
St. Patrick's Cathedral as Prebendary of Howth, the well-known pro-
montory in the Bay of Dublin, and discharged the cure of souls in his
prebendal parish, which lies not far from Belcamp, as well as in others
adjacent to it. Of her sons the eldest, Henry, who was the grandfather
of the patriot, was seated in Cavan ; the second, William, who had
been like his father a Fellow, held a college living in the north of
Ireland ; the third, James, was a Dublin physician ; the fourth,
Robert, who was in holy orders, held his father's prebend in Swift's
Cathedral ; the fifth, John, who was also in holy orders, was Rector
of a parish adjacent to Belcamp ; the sixth, Richard, who became
Lord Mayor of Dublin and was knighted, was a merchant ; and the
seventh, Charles, to whom there has been reference in connection with
the loss of his fellowship (*supra*, p. 19, n. 5), was master of Portora, a
school of royal foundation in the north of Ireland. (See " The Family

crossed the ferry.[1] There Tom and the groom waited, and
my horses were standing at a shop where brandy is sold;
at the door of it I used to take horse. I observed the two
loobies put on my cloak the wrong side outwards and I
found Will was drunk; I rode on and found Tom did not
come up;[2] I stayed, he galloped up; I chid him, he
answered foolishly; he was drunk as a dog, tottered on his
horse, could not keep the way, sometimes into the sea[3] then
back to me; swore he was not drunk. I bid him keep on,
lashed him as well as I could, then he vowed he was
drunk, fell a crying, came back every moment to me. I
bid him keep on; at last with galloping and turning back-
wards and forwards Bolingbroke[4] grew mad, and threw
him down. I came up and called a boy and man to get
the horse from him; he resisted us all three, was stark mad
with drink. At last we got the bridle from him, the boy
mounted and away we rode, Tom following after us.
What became of him I know not, I fancied he would reel
hither.

The bearer is the boy that came with me. I beg you
would step to the Deanery, and see lest Tom should come
there, and perhaps in his desperate humour rob me. I

of Grattan," by G. D. Burtchaell, Athlone Pursuivant, in "The Irish
Builder," xxx, 225.) To his Prebendary Swift's allurement to Belcamp
was doubtless due:

> "O! were but you and I so wise,
> To see with Robert Grattan's eyes!
> Robin adores that spot of earth,
> That literal spot which gave him birth;
> And swears Belcamp is to his taste,
> As fine as Hampton Court at least."
> "Poetical Works," i, 147.

[1] Belcamp lies about five miles to the north of Dublin, a little to the
west of the road from Dublin to a seaside resort called Malahide.
From St. Patrick's Cathedral the road would now be reached by crossing the lowest bridge on the river Liffey, known as Butt Bridge, but
then the shortest way was by a ferry which crossed the Liffey at even
a lower point. To save time Swift had sent his horses round by one of
the two bridges then available, to await him at the ferry.

[2] In "The Duty of Servants at Inns" ("Prose Works," xi, 360), it
is seen how Swift loved to ride in state preceded by his groom and
followed by his valet.

[3] There has been already reference to the strand across which
Swift rode as a haunt of Archbishop King (*supra*, vol. i, p. 68, n. 4)

[4] *Supra*, p. 242, n. 2.

would have his great-coat, boots, and whip taken from him; let him have a crown in part of his wages, and the rest he shall have when I come and his account is given up. Let him leave the house immediately with a charge to the maid and Gillespy not to let him come into the doors. I was an hour going between the ferry and the Red House, but got here before it was dark. My humble service to the ladies. Tom has my quill and brush for my teeth, I believe, in his pocket, for I cannot find it among my things; get it from him and I will send for it to your house, for I want it mightily.

Pray inquire for some lad for a servant; I will also turn off Will when I come. Remember to send my letters to-night. My service to Gossip and the ladies. The bearer is the boy who came with us. I have given him a shilling. Adieu.

Addressed—To the Reverend Mr. Archdeacon Walls in Queen Street.

CCCXXIX. [*Copy*.[1]]

SWIFT TO KNIGHTLEY CHETWODE

January 3, 1714-15.

I HAVE had a letter of yours[2] by me these three weeks, which among others has lain unanswered, because I left off my old custom of answering letters before the post-day; and it happened that upon post-day I never had leisure; but besides I waited till I could hear you had got to Martry. I know not what you observed in the public Gazette about that business I was uneasy at: for I never heard of anything, and had letters since from the person chiefly concerned. I am afraid the Dean's field[3] will be quite spoiled in your absence. I had made an extract out of the lease of Kilberry, of the denominations, but feared

---

[1] In the Forster Collection. *Supra*, p. 241, n. 1.
[2] *Supra*, p. 260.
[3] Evidently Swift had allowed his name to be conferred on one of the Woodbrooke fields.

you had no correspondence with the Baron since you left the neighbourhood. However I will here annex it. Ay, the ballad; I cannot for my life tell where it is at present, but a copy shall be sent or brought to you.[1]

I had gone thus far when company came in, and I was forced to leave off, and go abroad to a Christmas dinner, where I stayed till eleven, and at coming home my maid told me that one of your servants were here to know whether I would go down to Martry, and that he will call to-morrow morning; therefore I resolve to finish this letter to-night, and am glad of the opportunity, not knowing where to direct to you better than by Navan.[2] I believe you may be out of the peace, because, I hear almost all our friends are so. I am sorry Tories are put out of the King's peace; he may live to want them in it again. My visitation is to be this day sennight, after which I soon intend for the county of Meath; I design great things at my visitation, and I believe my Chapter will join with me. I hear they think me a smart Dean; and that I am for doing good. My notion is, that if a man cannot mend the public he should mend old shoes if he can do no better; and therefore I endeavour in the little sphere I am placed to do all the good it is capable of.

As for judicious John, he is walked off. Your cursed good ale ruined him. He turned such a drunkard and swaggerer, I could bear him no longer: I reckon every visit I make you will spoil a servant. I shall come with two servants and three horses,[3] but a horse and a servant I shall leave at Trim. I hear an universal good character of Mr. Davis; but however I shall have my eye over him and the lads.[4] As for news, the d——l a bit do I ever hear, or suffer to be told me. I saw in a print that the King has

---

[1] The ballad may have been one entitled: "Britannia's Tears: A Satyrical Dirge by way of a Lamentation on the Deplorable Death of Her late Gracious Majesty Queen Anne, of Blessed Memory: and as a Chastisement to all Her Merry Mourners," which was published in Dublin in 1714 (Royal Irish Academy Pamphlets).

[2] Martry lies a few miles to the north-west of Navan, a small town in the county of Meath.

[3] *Supra*, p. 263, n. 2.

[4] Probably some of Chetwode's children had been sent to school in Dublin. Besides two who died as infants Chetwode had three sons, John born in 1706, Valentine born in 1708, and Crewe born in 1710 ("Miscellanea Genealogica et Heraldica," 2nd Ser., i, 87).

taken care to limit the clergy what they shall preach;[1] and that has given me an inclination to preach what is forbid: for I do not conceive there is any law yet for it. My humble service to Dame Pliant. You talk of your hay but say nothing of your wine. I doubt it is not so good as at Woodbrooke: and I doubt I shall not like Martry half so well as Woodbrooke.

Now for the lands at Kildare:—The manors, lordships and townships of Kilberry, Castleriddy and Cloney; also the prebend of Kilberry, with the lands, tenements and tithes whatsoever appertaining to the said prebend, rectory, churches, and towns of Kilberry, Bert, Cloney, Srowland, Kilcolman, Oldcourt, and Tullygorey, Prusselstown, Shanraheen, Tyrrellstown, Clonwannir, and Russellstown. The land without the prebend and all those cursed Irish names is seventeen hundred and odd acres; supposing the land to be a crown an acre at full rent the whole is worth

per annum £425 0 0

Supposing the prebend and tithes of all
those hard names worth   50 0 0

The whole will be worth at full rent   £475 0 0

And it pays me only   £120 0 0

There was a great deal of young wood which has been horribly abused. If the Baron could contrive that I might have some account of this land etc., he would do me a great favour.

Addressed—To Knightley Chetwode Esq., per private hand.

―――――――――

[1] The reference is to directions issued by the King on 11 December to the Archbishops and Bishops for the "preserving of unity in the Church, and the purity of the Christian Faith, concerning the Holy Trinity; and also for preserving the peace and quiet of the State."

CCCXXX. [*Original.*[1]]

ERASMUS LEWIS TO SWIFT

[*January*, 1714-15.[2]]

SIR,[3]

I HAVE one letter from you to acknowledge, which I will do very soon. In the mean time I send this to acquaint you, that if you have not already hid your papers in some private place in the hands of a trusty friend, I fear they will fall into the hands of our enemies. Sure you have already taken care in this matter, by what the public prints told you of the proceedings of the great men toward the Earl of Strafford and Mr. Prior.[4] However, for greater caution, this is sent you by ——. I am, etc.

Addressed—To the Reverend Dr. Swift, Dean of St. Patrick's, in Dublin, Ireland.

CCCXXXI. [*Draft.*[5]]

SWIFT TO MONSIEUR GIRALDI

De Dublin en Yrlande, *Fevrier* 25, 1714-15.

MONSIEUR,[6]

JE prens la liberté de vous presenter le porteur de

[1] In the British Museum. See Preface.
[2] This letter has been hitherto dated 4 November, 1714, but as the contents show incorrectly.
[3] In common with the other Tory officials Lewis had been superseded in his office of Under Secretary of State.
[4] These proceedings were the first indication of the severe course which the new Ministers intended to pursue against their predecessors. On 11 January the Earl of Strafford, who had returned from the Hague (*supra*, p. 231, n. 7) ten days before, was ordered by the Council to surrender all papers and correspondence in his possession relating to the negotiations for the peace, and soon afterwards Prior had a similar demand made upon him by the Earl of Stair, who arrived in Paris on 12 January as Prior's successor in the position of envoy to the French Court.
[5] In the British Museum. See Preface. It has seemed desirable to follow the original orthography.
[6] Giraldi was secretary to the Duke of Tuscany. How Swift knew

cellecy, Monsieur Howard,[1] gentilhomme savant et de condition de ce pais cy, qui pretend de faire le tour d'Italie, et qui etant chanoine en mon doyenné et professeur de college icy, veut en voyageant parmi les catholiques s'opiniatrer le plus dans son heresie. Et apres tout, Monsieur, ce n'est que juste, que puisque vous avez derobé notre franchise Angloise pour l'ajouter à votre politesse Italienne, que quelques-uns de nous autres tramontanes devoient en voyageant chez vous faire des reprisailles. Vous me suffrirez aussi de vous prier de presenter mes tres humbles devoirs à son altesse royale le grand Duc.

Pour mon particulier, Monsieur, je prens la liberté de vous dire, que deux mois devant la morte de la reyne, voyant, qu'il étoit tout à fait impossible de r'accommoder mes amis du ministere, je me retiré à la campagne en Berkshire, d'ou apres ce triste evenement je venois en Yrlande, ou je demeure en mon doyenné, et attens avec la resignation d'un bon Chrétien la ruine de notre cause et de mes amis, menacés tous les jours par la faction dominante. Car ces Messieurs sont tout à fait resolus de trancher une demi-douzaine de tetes des meilleures d'Angleterre, et que vous avez fort bien connus et estimé. Dieu sait quel en sera l'evenement. Pour moy j'ai quitté pour jamais la politique, et avec la permission des bonnes gens qui sont maintenant en vogue, je demeureray la reste de ma vie en mon hermitage pour songer à mon salut.

Adieu, Monsieur, et me faites la justice de croire, que je suis, avec beaucoup de respect, Monsieur, votre, etc.

him does not appear, but Giraldi was not the first minister of that Court with whom Swift had correspondence. In a copy of the third volume of Sir William Temple's Letters (published in 1703) in the British Museum there is the following inscription in Swift's handwriting: "To His Excellency Count Magalotti, Councillor of State to His Most Serene Highness the Great Duke of Tuscany, By his Excellency's most obedient and most humble Servant, Jonathan Swift."

[1] Robert Howard, who was Prebendary of Maynooth in St. Patrick's Cathedral and a Fellow of Trinity College, Dublin, was the second son of Dr. Ralph Howard (*supra*, vol. i, pp. 374, 375), and father of the first Lord Wicklow. He was raised to the episcopal bench.

CCCXXXII. [*Original.*]

SWIFT TO LORD HARLEY

Dublin, *March* 8, 1714-15.

MY LORD,[2]

SINCE I left England I have not seen a newspaper, nor have above three or four times heard anybody talk of what passes in the world. It is the only receipt I have to possess any degree of quiet. The other day I was told it was in the printed papers that the best lady in the world had lately brought one of her own sex into it,[3] for which I do most heartily congratulate with your Lordship and her, and I hope to live long enough to send you half a dozen letters of congratulation upon the same account; only my Lady must take care now and then to vary the sex. I hope her Ladyship's health is by this time quite re-established, and that she can run up to the nursery to visit her little infant. I could be almost angry that your Lordship did not consider what a part I take in everything that concerns you, at whatsoever distance I am; for then you would have contrived I might have known a thing of so much importance by a surer way than common report. But a circumstance shall not make me quarrel with what I like, and since you want no addition of fortune or honour, I shall pray God to preserve your health, and increase your family. I must say one thing more, that though these are not times for raillery, I am impatient to see my little niece.

Pray tell my Lady that I have broke my heart with breaking her snuff box. I put it in a close pocket, when I was on horseback, and forgot to remove it when I alighted, and so overlaid it, as a mother does a child she is too fond of. But the matter cannot rest thus. I tax her Ladyship with five guineas, which she must lay out on an etui, just

---

[1] In the possession of the Duke of Portland. *Supra*, p. 160, n. 2.

[2] *Supra*, p. 190.

[3] Lord Harley's only surviving child, the future wife of the second Duke of Portland, was born on 11 February in that year. The Earl of Oxford was under notice from the Crown to surrender a house near St. James's Palace, to which he had moved from York Buildings about a year before, but as Boyer records (*op. cit.*, ix, 155), "out of civility to the fair sex his Majesty gave leave to the Lady Harley to lie in there."

such a one as your Lordship's, with shagreen outside, and silver instruments. I cannot easily break that. Pray let my Lady buy it immediately with her own hands; or if she will not do that, let me have two small copies of her picture and your Lordship. They will not come to above five pounds each, for I am tender of your purse.

Another thing you must both promise me, that whenever these gentlemen in power shall think fit to destroy the Church, and abolish bishoprics and deaneries as wicked and useless, you will settle on me fifty pounds a year to live in Guernsey, for there I am determined, because wine and victuals are cheap in that island, and I promise when I am an old gentleman to come back and be a tutor to your children. Perhaps I am not so much in jest as you may believe, for there is nothing too bad to be apprehended, in my opinion, from the present face of things. I am with the greatest respect and truth, my Lord,

Your Lordship's most obedient and most humble servant
JON. SWIFT.

Will your Lordship present my most humble service to my Lord Oxford and to my Lord and Lady Dupplin.[1]

Addressed—To the Right Honorable the Lord Harley, in London.

CCCXXXIII. [*Copy.*[2]]

SWIFT TO KNIGHTLEY CHETWODE

Dublin, *March* 31, 1715.

SIR,

I HAVE been these ten weeks resolving every week to go down to Trim, and from thence to Martry;[3] and have not

---

[1] Oxford's daughter and son-in-law, who are frequently mentioned in the Journal to Stella. Lord Dupplin was heir-apparent to the earldom of Kinnoul, but as one of Oxford's famous creation (*supra*, vol. i, p. 311) had already become a peer in his own right. He was, like Lord Harley, an original member of the Brothers' Club, and was one of those who in the opinion of Swift caused its destruction by extravagant entertainment.

[2] In the Forster Collection. *Supra*, p. 241, n. 1.

[3] *Supra*, p. 261.

been able to compass it, though my country affairs much required my presence. This week I was fully determined to have been at Trim, but my Vicars hinder me, their prosecutions being just come to an issue,[1] and I cannot stir from hence till the end of April, when nothing but want of health or horses shall hinder me. I can tell you no news. I have read but one newspaper since I left you and I never suffer any to be told me. I send this by my steward,[2] who goes to Trim, to look after my rents at Laracor. Pray present my most humble service to Dame Pliant. I suppose you do not very soon intend to remove to the Queen's county. When I come to Trim I shall after a few days there, stay awhile with you, and go thence to Athy;[3] and thence if possible to Connaught and half round Ireland. I hope your little fire-side is well. I am with great truth and esteem

Your most obedient humble servant

J. S.

Is it impossible to get a plain easy sound trotting Horse?

Addressed—To Knightley Chetwode Esq (private hand).

CCCXXXIV. [*Copy.*[4]]

Knightley Chetwode to Swift

April 5, 1715.

Dear Sir,

Though I am to be yet three weeks longer without you and of consequence as long unhappy, yet did I with the greatest pleasure receive yours from Trim[5] since you think of me and with kindness. Love, which is ever jealous, made

---

[1] *Supra*, p. 242.

[2] Gillespy, who is mentioned by Swift in his last letter to Walls (*supra*, p. 264), and who resided in the deanery house (*infra*, p. 288), seems to have then superseded Parvisol (*supra*, vol. i, p. 118, n. 3) in the collection of Swift's tithes and rents. The arrangement did not last long, and later on Parvisol is again found in Swift's employment.

[3] To see his lands of Kilberry (*supra*, p. 256).

[4] In the Forster Collection. *Supra*, p. 241, n. 1.

[5] The preceding letter was no doubt sent to Chetwode by way of Trim.

me fear I had lost that share in your regards I most covet to possess; it is my greatest satisfaction you give me to know it is otherwise. I have confined myself to Martry closely, lest I should be out of the way when you should arrive, which I daily expected, till some days ago I started to Rowly Singleton and Dean Cox at Drogheda[1] where I drank your health as I do daily, but there particularly in company of Mr. Whaley, Lord Primate's chaplain.[2]

I hope nothing will divert your purpose of seeing me this month. Do you preserve health? I will procure you horses. There is a grey gelding in my neighbourhood in a mad fellow's custody—nothing the better of that you will say—which I like and have offered money for; he is strong, young, tolerably handsome, and I am told sound, trots well, has good spirit, but I think him too dear. He asks sixteen pounds for him and swears he refused twelve pounds, which I am not willing to believe the more for his swearing it, or because it is against my interest. I have broke a young mare since you left me, which abounds in mettle, trots finely, and carries tolerably well, but I fear is not comely enough for his Grace of St. Patrick's. If you like her she is yours. If this does not please, the bay mare you rode to Powerscourt[3] has got so much flesh and spirit that she has forgot to trip. Say which of these three will be most to your *goût*.[4]

I do not intend Dame Pliant and the family shall see Woodbrooke this long time, though I have sent several

---

[1] Rowland Singleton was the father of Swift's executor, Prime Serjeant Singleton, who became successively Chief Justice of the Common Pleas, and Master of the Rolls in Ireland, and Dean Cox, who enjoyed that title in right of the deanery of Ferns, was Rector of Drogheda (see the Rev. J. B. Leslie's "Armagh Clergy and Parishes," p. 239). Drogheda lies about eleven miles to the north-east of Martry.

[2] Nathaniel Whaley, who will be again mentioned in the Correspondence, was probably in Drogheda on business connected with the primatial see, within which Drogheda lies. He had no doubt become known to Primate Lindsay as a Fellow of Wadham College, of which Lindsay had also been a don (see *ibid.*, p. 114).

[3] The picturesque demesne in the county of Wicklow, from which Viscount Powerscourt takes his title.

[4] Chetwode was evidently a lover of horseflesh. In the "Dublin Gazette" of 4-8 November, 1707, there is a curious advertisement from him describing a "very handsome English mare," a "broad squat black mare," and a "well fore-hand black mare," that had been stolen off the lands of Martry.

workmen up thither and have appointed carpenters to meet
me there Passion week to agree for to prepare to build the
dwelling house which I am impatient to begin. I am now
upon taking my Lord Meath's house in this county till my
own house and deer park be finished;[1] finding this house
too small I propose to let it, and the house I am about to
take being but fifteen miles from Dublin, I the better
like it.

I heard from some friends in England since I saw you.
Upon it I postpone my journey thither till I have answers
to letters I sent by a private hand to several of my friends
there; I did not judge the messenger being a lady so proper
for you or she should have called for your commands.[2] This
bearer, my steward's son, going to Dublin with some money
to Doctor Travers,[3] I have given the Doctor the hint of
printing the second scene of the fourth act of Shakespeare's
Henry the Eighth, with no title, [as] a parallel case.[4] I will
not be out of the way the latter end of the month, by which
time I hope to have it in my power to apprise you of my
English friends' sense of my journey, and shall regulate
myself in the affair by your advice.

If you go or progress, as you hint, I shall esteem it an
honour if you take me into your train. I hope the Baron
has found means to satisfy you in a certain affair; I pressed
him again on that head but a few weeks since. If I could

[1] This house, which had been formerly known as New Hall or Tara
Hall and was then called Brabazon Lodge, was situated near the hill
of Tara, the seat of supreme sovereignty in ancient Erin. Owing to
disinclination on the part of the owner to let the house, the bargain
was not completed (see letter from Ludlow to Chetwode in Forster
Collection).

[2] From subsequent letters it will be seen that Chetwode was in
correspondence with some leading member of the Tory party in England, presumably the Duke of Ormond, to whom as well as to his
grandfather (*supra*, p. 241, n. 2) the Chetwodes were known. In the
opinion of his descendant, Forster's friend (*supra*, p. 241, n. 1). Chetwode was an ardent Jacobite, but he appears to have been a very
devoted son of the Church of England, and may to some extent have
been drawn into a Jacobite connection more by circumstances than
inclination.

[3] The Reverend John Travers, who was a member of Swift's
Chapter and Vicar of St. Andrew's, the Dublin parish in which the
Parliament House lay.

[4] Bishop Burnet had died in March, and probably the suggestion
was to apply Queen Catherine's character of Cardinal Wolsey to
him.

by any means contribute to your service or satisfaction I think myself happier than you perhaps believe, for I am *toujours jusqu'au tombeau, mon cher Monsieur et digne ami, tout à vous du meilleur de mon cœur.*

K. C.

CCCXXXV. [*Copy.*[1]]

SWIFT TO KNIGHTLEY CHETWODE

Dublin, April 6, 1715.

SIR,

YOUR messenger brought me your letter[2] when I was under a very bad barber's hands, meaning my own. I sent for him, because I heard he was something gentlemanish, and he told me he returned to-day; so that I have only time to thank you for your letter, and assure you, that bar accidents I will be in Trim in a fortnight. I detest the price of that horse you mention, and as for your mare I will never trust her. My grandmother used to say that good feeding never brings good footing. I am just going to church, and can say no more, but my humble service to Dame Pliant. I believe the fellow rather thinks me mad than is mad himself: sixteen pounds—why it is an estate; I shall not be master of it in sixteen years.

I thought that passage out of Shakespeare had been of my own starting, and that the magistrate of Martry would not have imagined it. How can you talk of going a progress of two hundred miles? I know nothing of any shoes I left.[3] I am sure they are not paid for, and so at least I shall be no loser whatever you may be. Adieu.

Addressed—To Knightley Chetwode Esq.

[1] In the Forster Collection. *Supra*, p. 241, n. 1.
[2] *Supra*, p. 271.
[3] There is no reference to shoes in Chetwode's letter. Possibly a postscript was added of which a copy was not kept.

CCCXXXVI. [*Copy.*[1]]

KNIGHTLEY CHETWODE TO SWIFT

Trim, *April* 25, 1715.
Dr. Raymond's parlour, Two o'clock.

DEAR DEAN,

I AM just alighted here from Woodbrooke where I doubted not of finding his Grace of St. Patrick's, but you are so in love with synodical bear-gardens,[2] that you would no more leave Dublin before Wednesday[3] than you would send me news-pamphlets or ballads. I bade Tom Warburton[4] tell you I said you were a sad fellow, because I durst not be so free to write it; I prevailed on him since he had a budget on each side of him, to add your letter to the bulk. If you were a great Prince you would I believe imprison half your subjects, for you have confined me to Martry near four months for so [I have been] since but expecting you.

Well now a few words *seria mixta jocis*; Tommy, little Tommy, pretty Tommy is gone like Judas *ad locum proprium suum*; Galloway also stone dead; you and Gay Mortimer have brought a rot among the wicked; as for Mortimer, I do not expect much from him, but I thought you as a churchman would allow him time to repent, which, however, upon the whole matter I saw little hope of from any but horn mad Sunderland from marrying.[5] The Baron will see you to-morrow or at the Synod, and will give you

---

[1] In the Forster Collection. *Supra,* p. 241, n. 1.

[2] In addition to Convocation, diocesan and provincial synods were held in Ireland, in accordance with a custom which, as Bishop Reeves shows in his learned history of Convocation, had existed from the earliest times. The synod to which Chetwode refers was no doubt for the Meath diocese, for which Dublin was the most convenient centre.

[3] The 28th.

[4] Swift's curate (*supra,* p. 240, n. 4), who was evidently going to Dublin to attend the synod.

[5] In this obscure passage Chetwode gives his views on the political situation at that moment. The Whigs had been weakened in March by the death of Wharton, here called Tommy, as well as Burnet (*supra,* p. 273, n. 4), here called Galloway. But the Tory party were without an efficient leader. Chetwode and Swift were agreed that Oxford, here called Mortimer, was useless. For his part Chetwode saw no hope except in Sunderland, who was dissatisfied at being relegated to the position of Lord Lieutenant of Ireland, and might possibly be detached from the influence of his wife and her father, the Duke of Marlborough.

account of his commission.[1] I am so angry with you, if it were not for offending Dame Pliant, and that I know you would have your frisk like the Berkshire acquaintance without consequence,[2] I would go to Dublin with Tom Warburton. This town since Wharton's death is like hell, nothing but weeping, wailing, and gnashing of teeth.[3] For God sake do somewhat to comfort Joe,[4] and send him back contented; tell him you will make the next his friend, keep him from melting his tallow, help him in his longitude,[5] do anything to keep him alive.

Dinner appears, I am hungry, Mrs. Raymond as prodigiously civil as ugly, and I forced to conclude, with the assurance of this truth from a good hand that I am,

Yours.

CCCXXXVII. [*Manuscripts of the Duke of Marlborough.*[6]]

THE DUKE OF ORMOND TO SWIFT

May 3, 1715.[7]

CORINNIKIN [8] and myself drink your health daily; she

---

[1] Rochfort was possibly the Bishop of Meath's vicar-general.

[2] Can this be a reference to Vanessa's visit to Letcombe (*supra*, p. 234)? Possibly Swift had written verses upon it.

[3] The allusion to the grief for Wharton is ironical. "His arbitrary proceedings about the election of a mayor in Trim," are noted in the "Short Character" ("Prose Works," v, 27).

[4] *I.e.*, Joe Beaumont (*supra*, p. 64).

[5] To the calculations about the longitude the loss of his reason is assigned (*supra*, p. 54, n. 4).

[6] Hist. MSS. Com., Rept. 8, App. i, p. 58.

[7] This letter and the following one were seized by the Irish executive. As appears from letters which will be found in Appendix XI, two packets addressed to Swift, in one of which these letters were enclosed, were given by the Duchess of Ormond's chaplain, Mr. Charleton, probably a relation of Chiverton Charleton (*supra*, p. 139), to a Mr. Jeffreys, who is described as agent to Bishop Hartstonge (*supra*, p. 126, n. 4), to bring to Ireland. On landing in Dublin Jeffreys was searched by a custom-house officer, and on the packets being found they were brought owing to "the present circumstances of affairs" to the acting Lords Justices, Archbishop King and the Earl of Kildare (*supra*, p. 238, n. 2). The Lords Justices opened the packets and sent off the letters that evening to Stanhope, the Secretary of State in charge of Irish affairs. The next day copies, from which the letters are here reproduced, were sent to Sunderland as Lord Lieutenant, who was then at Bath.

[8] *I.e.*, the Duchess of Ormond. Her real name was Mary.

is come to love a glass of wine much better than she did, with this remark, that it happens in the very worst time. We have no new favourite, nor never can; you have left so sweet a relish by your conversation upon all our pleasures that we cannot bear the thoughts of intimacy with any person.[1] A faint copy of a most agreeable original is to be found in a certain reverend divine whom you introduced to our acquaintance,[2] but it will not do even with the advantage of youth. We see him once a week. . . . Tyrant[3] has undertook to furnish you by this same hand with all the news. I hear that you desire none. . . . Corinnikin sends you her love and service. I send you her very words.

CCCXXXVIII. [*Manuscripts of the Duke of Marlborough.*[4]]

JOHN BARBER TO SWIFT

May 3, 1715.

. . . TWO days before the Captain[5] went abroad he sent for me, and, amongst other things, asked me with great earnestness if there was no possibility of sending a letter safe to your hands. I answered I knew but of one way, and that was to direct to you under cover to Mrs. Van——. He replied no way by post would do. I then said though I was lame and ill, I could go over with it myself if he pleased. He thanked me, and said I should hear from him in a day or two, but I never saw him more. Sir W. Wyndham[6] had a letter yesterday from him dated about eight days ago; he was then very well and Mr. Ford with him.[7] His motions depend upon the report from the Secret Com-

---

[1] This passage confirms the view which I have taken (*supra*, p. 145, n. 3) as to the frequent intercourse between Swift and the Ormonds during his last visit to London.
[2] Possibly Berkeley (*supra*, p. 247, n. 1).
[3] *I.e.*, John Barber (*supra*, p. 146).
[4] Hist. MSS. Com., Rept. 8, App. i, p. 59.
[5] *I.e.*, Bolingbroke, who had sailed for France on March 27.
[6] Of whom it has been said Bolingbroke was the moral as well as political mentor (" D. N. B.," lxiii, 253).
[7] Ford's letters to Swift show that his sympathies lay with Bolingbroke rather than with Oxford, but it is uncertain whether he followed Bolingbroke into the Pretender's service.

mittee, and the Brin[sde]n,[1] with the last instructions from his friends here, will go over, by which he will confirm himself. You have seen a letter which bears his name.[2] I will tell you a secret; it was written by Bishop Atterbury. It hath done a great deal of good, and we have not lost a man by his going. It was a great surprise to his friends at first, but everybody is now convinced he would have been sacrificed had he staid. . . .

Among other things I send you the Duke of Ormond's Conduct[3] which it is hoped will do that great man service. He is in the highest esteem here, and last Friday, being his birthday, two hundred of his Grace's friends dined at the Devil's at Temple Bar, and at night there were two bonfires on that occasion, one in Newgate Market, the other in the Pall Mall. Mr. P[rio]r is despised by all honest men here for giving up his letters, yours among the rest.[4] Dr. Arb[uthno]t was turned out on that score.[5] . . . Lord Wharton's death hath extremely mortified the Whigs. Sunderland is very ill, has been mad for some time, and is going to the Bath. Walpole is in a very bad way, and Stanhope is the bully.[6]

---

[1] *Supra*, p. 228.

[2] In this letter, which is dated as if written at Dover, Bolingbroke alleges as the cause of his departure his knowledge that those who had power intended to pursue him to the scaffold, and his conviction that he could not obtain a fair trial. He challenges production of any proof of criminal correspondence or corruption on his part, hopes for a favourable construction on any warm or unguarded expression which may have escaped him in his zeal for his royal mistress, and affirms his devotion to his country (Boyer, ix, 231).

[3] "The Conduct of His Grace the Duke of Ormonde in the Campagne of 1712" (Lond., 1715).

[4] Prior was distrusted by the Tories at that time. He was in great want of money, and obtained it possibly by holding out to the Whigs some hope of revelations on his part with regard to the peace negotiations.

[5] *Supra*, p. 246.

[6] Any hopes the Tories had then from the state of the Ministry (*supra*, p. 275, n. 5) were soon shattered. Sunderland's illness is supposed to have been to a great extent merely an excuse to avoid going to Ireland, and Wharton was sufficiently recovered a few weeks later to draft the report of the Committee of Secrecy, which was then sitting, and of which he was chairman.

CCCXXXIX. [*Original.*[1]]

SWIFT TO ARCHDEACON WALLS

Trim, *May* 5, 1715.[2]

SINCE your inmates[3] are so lazy and saucy that they make you their secretary I will take no notice of them. I would have Gillespy[4] come down as soon as he has put the affair of his new farm in such a way as not to suffer by his absence, and I thought that would have been by Monday next.

If your scheme of moves can be brought about, I will do my part fully in it; as for Chamberlain, or the Archbishop, or Bolton working any of theirs, they shall be deceived as far as all my power reaches, and they shall not find me altogether so great a cully as they would willingly make me.[5] Whenever you see me fail in any part relating to you, I desire I may hear of it, and if you be mealy-mouthed do it by whom you please; and whenever you think any step I can make will be for your service, tell me freely and I will either comply or show you why I cannot. Nobody is so stiff as an easy man put upon his mettle, and they shall neither fool me nor you, at least in this point. Well, but however my service to Doll and the ladies. Adieu.

Joe's[6] respects to all. Mr. Chetwode presents you his service.[7]

Addressed—To the Reverend Mr. Archdeacon Walls over against the Hospital in Queen Street, Dublin.

---

[1] In the possession of Mr. John Murray. See Preface.
[2] Swift had at length left Dublin (*supra*, p. 275).
[3] *I.e.*, Stella and Mrs. Dingley (*supra*, p. 264).
[4] *Supra*, p. 271.
[5] The reference is to a project of Walls for his own benefit in connection with the vacant cure of St. Nicholas Without (*supra*, p. 257, n. 2). The Rev. Philip Chamberlain, whom Swift mentions, had been appointed a year before to a prebend in St. Patrick's Cathedral.
[6] *I.e.*, Joe Beaumont (*supra*, p. 276).
[7] Chetwode had evidently joined Swift at Trim, whence, as appears from the next letter, they set out to pay a visit to the Rochforts.

CCCXL. [*Original.*[1]]

SWIFT TO ARCHDEACON WALLS

Woodbrooke, Mr. Chetwode's house,
Sunday, *May* 22, 1715.

[I CAME] here on Friday last from Mr. Rochfort's where I [stayed until that] day with Mr. Chetwode, very well entertained, and by a very fine place.[2] I go hence to-morrow, God willing, to the deanery lands near Athy about twelve miles off,[3] and on Wednesday night intend to be at Trim.

We have had perpetual ill-weather ever since I left you except one or two days; yet I have seldom failed being on horseback and have my health well enough. Gillespy[4] is to meet me at Athy and from thence, I suppose, will go to Dublin about Thursday; but for my own return I can say nothing. However I desire you will finish the machine for dining *sub dio*. I hope we shall have some merry dinners under it this summer. I will send Bolingbroke[5] to Clem Barry[6] if I can get another horse; he is very fat and well,

---

[1] In the possession of Mr. John Murray. See Preface.
[2] The "very fine place" was the far-famed Gaulstown, which is situated amidst the celebrated lake scenery of the county of Westmeath, and its owner was George Rochfort, the eldest son of the Chief Baron (*supra*, p. 257, n. 6), to whom his father appears to have given the property on his marriage to Lady Betty Moore:

> "At ten my Lady comes and hectors
> And kisses George, and ends our lectures;
> And when she has him by the neck fast
> Hauls him, and scolds us, down to breakfast."

Gaulstown lies, although not on the direct road, between Trim and Woodbrooke. Of the house, which has given place to a modern mansion, the seat of Lord Kilmaine, Dr. Delany sang:

> "'Tis so old and so ugly, and yet so convenient,
> You're sometimes in pleasure, though often in pain in't;
> 'Tis so large you may lodge a few friends with ease in't,
> You may turn and stretch at your length if you please in't.

(See "Poetical Works," i, 136, 137.)
[3] *Supra*, p. 256.   [4] *Supra*, p. 279.   [5] *Supra*, p. 242.
[6] The "chief favourite and governor of Gaulstown" whose arrival

but I hate riding him. As to my wine in the hogshead I would have it filled up when it wants, but I will not have it forced. Mr. Rochfort sent your letter after me. I thank you for your care about it, but no messenger has been here yet from the government,[1] nor will I hope till I get to Athy; for I should be sorry to go back till I see the land.

My humble service to Gossip Doll and the ladies. I suppose they want a third at ombre sometimes by way of stop-gap and miss me. Pray press Gillespy to get money from the deanery, and receive it from him, and let Mrs. Brent[2] go now and then into the cellar to prevent accidents in my wine. If anything happens about St. Nicholas let me know it at Trim.[3] I am,

                    Yours, etc.,

                              J. S.

Addressed—To the Reverend Mr. Archdeacon Walls over against the Hospital in Queen Street, Dublin.

CCCXLI. [*Original.*[4]]

SWIFT TO ARCHDEACON WALLS

                    Trim, *June* 15, 1715.

I AM here at the fair to buy a horse,[5] but cannot succeed. I had all your letters; as for Taylor he may go hang him-

---

there with his wife on a subsequent occasion led to the discomfiture of Swift and his satellites:

> "The Dean must with his quilt supply
> The bed in which those tyrants lie;
> George is half scared out of his wits,
> For Clem gets all the dainty bits."

Barry, who was a distant cousin of the Lord Santry of that day, lived near Dublin at Saggart, which has been already mentioned as traditionally connected with Swift and Vanessa (*supra*, p. 56, n. 1). He had inherited his residence there from his grandfather, who was for many years a government official in Ireland, and who is remarkable as having been a centenarian at the time of his death.

[1] Walls had evidently at once sent intelligence to Swift of the seizure of his letters (*supra*, p. 276, n. 7).

[2] *Supra*, p. 256.   [3] *Supra*, p. 279.

[4] In the possession of Mr. John Murray. See Preface.

[5] Swift had evidently come there with Chetwode from either Woodbrooke or Martry. See the two preceding letters.

self if he pleases; I hope he will leave us and then I will have a better; but I will not turn him out without your leave.[1] I hope Gillespy has got you some money, I wonder he has not writ to me. It is time for him to reckon the sheep and lambs; he should have done it in these livings when he was here; but it was out of my head. Pray speak to him about it. I know not whether he is used to those sort of tithes, being only practised in impropriations; but you must talk to him of it. I will not have any rents received from Smith or Benson till I give you notice. My service to Gossip Doll and your inmates. Mr. Chetwode presents his service to you; so does Dr. Raymond, Warburton and Joe to you and the ladies. Bolingbroke is very well. I have just writ to the Bishop of Clogher, who I yesterday hear is arrived.[2] I hope Mrs. Brent sees the cellar sometimes. I would have the vessel of wine filled if it wants, but by no means forced or touched by a wine-cooper.

Addressed—To the Reverend Mr. Archdeacon Walls, over against the Hospital in Queen Street, Dublin.

CCCXLII. [*Copy.*[3]]

SWIFT TO KNIGHTLEY CHETWODE

Dublin, *June* 21, 1715.

I WAS to see Jourdain,[4] who tells me something but I have forgot it; it was, that he had a letter ready and you were gone, or something of that kind. I had a terrible hot journey and dined with Forbes,[5] and got here by nine.

I have been much entertained with news of myself since I came here: it is said there was another packet directed to me, seized by the Government, but after opening several

[1] The reference is probably to one of the Vicars-Choral of St. Patrick's Cathedral—Charles Taylor, who had been a member of the choir for over twenty years.

[2] As appears from a subsequent letter (*infra*, p. 286) Bishop Ashe had been in London.

[3] In the Forster Collection. *Supra*, p. 241, n. 1.

[4] *Supra*, p. 243.

[5] The Rev. Thomas Forbes, to whom Swift has previously referred (*supra*, p. 227), was Rector of Dunboyne, a parish between Dublin and Trim.

seals it proved only plum-cake. I was this morning with
the Archbishop who told me how kind he had been in preventing my being sent to etc.[1] I said I had been a firm
friend of the last Ministry, but thought it brought me to
trouble myself in little parties without doing good, that
I therefore expected the protection of the government, and
that if I had been called before them, I would not have
answered one syllable or named one person. He said that
would have reflected on me. I answered I did not value
that, and that I would sooner suffer more than let anybody
else suffer by me, as some people did. The letter which was
sent was one from the great lady you know, and enclosed in
one from her chaplain.[2] My friends got it, and very wisely
burned it after great deliberation, for fear of being called to
swear; for which I wish them half hanged. I have been
named in many papers as proclaimed for five hundred pounds.

I want to be with you for a little good meat and cold
drink; I find nothing cold here but the reception of my
friends. I said a good deal more to the Archbishop not
worth telling at this distance. I told him I had several
papers, but was so wise to hide them some months ago.[3]
A gentleman was run through in the playhouse last night
upon a squabble of their footmen's taking places for some
ladies. My most humble service to Dame Pliant; pray
God bless her fireside. They say the Whigs do not intend
to cut off Lord Oxford's head, but that they will certainly
attaint poor Lord Bolingbroke.[4]

Addressed—To Knightley Chetwode Esq., at Martry, near
Navan, in the County of Meath.

[1] As the Dean of St Patrick's surmised (*supra*, vol. i, p. xxix), Swift
was under no obligation to Archbishop King in regard to this incident.
The letter addressed by the Archbishop and his co-Lord Justice, the
Earl of Kildare, to Mr. Secretary Stanhope (Appendix, No. XI), which
I have only recently found, shows that the Lords Justices themselves
opened Swift's letters, and affords, from its tone at least, strong pre-
sumptive evidence that no question of friendship would have prevented
Swift's prosecution if a case could have been made against him.

[2] In addition to the letters from the Duke of Ormond and John
Barber, Bishop Hartstonge's agent had evidently brought one from
the Duchess of Ormond which had escaped seizure. Swift was probably unaware what the packets which had been seized contained.

[3] *Supra*, p. 267.

[4] The impeachment of Oxford, as well as of Bolingbroke (*supra*,
p. 277, n. 5), had been voted in the House of Commons eleven days
before.

CCCXLIII. [*Copy*.[1]]

SWIFT TO KNIGHTLEY CHETWODE

Dublin, *June* 28, 1715.

I WRITE to you so soon again, contrary to my nature and custom which never suffer me to be a very exact correspondent. I find you passed your time well among ladies and lions and St. Georges and dragons. Yesterday's post brought us an account that the Duke of Ormond is voted to be impeached for high treason. You see the plot thickens.[2] I know not the present disposition of people in England, but I do not find myself disposed to be sorry at this news. However in general my spirits are disturbed, and I want to be out of this town. A Whig of this country now in England has writ to his friends, that the leaders there talk of sending for me to be examined upon these impeachments. I believe there is nothing [in] it; but I had this notice from one who said he saw the letter or saw somebody that saw it.

I write this post to Dr. Raymond to provide next Sunday for Mr. Sub,[3] so I suppose he may be at ease, and I wish I were with him. I hope Dame has established her credit with you for ever, in the point of valour and hardiness. You surprise me with the account of a disorder in your head; I know what it is too well and I think Dame does so too. You must drink less small beer, eat less salad, think less, walk and drink more, I mean wine and ale, and for the rest, emetics and bitters are certainly the best remedies. What length has the river walk to thirty foot breadth? I hope a thousand at least. If Sub had no better a taste for beef and claret than he has for improvements of land, he should provide no dinners for me. Does Madam gambol now and then to see it? How is the Dean's field? So it cost a bottle of wine, extra dry, to dry poor Sub. I hope he sometimes loses his eyes to please Dame.

---

[1] In the Forster Collection. *Supra*, p. 241, n. 1.

[2] In addition to the impeachments of Oxford and Bolingbroke (*supra*, p. 283, n. 4), that of Ormond had been voted on the 21st of that month.

[3] Swift's curate, Tom Warburton, who had accompanied Chetwode to Woodbroke. It was evidently his duty at Laracor which Raymond was to take.

There is a collegian found guilty of speaking some words; and I hear they design in mercy to whip or pillory him.[1] I went yesterday to the Courts on purpose to show I was not run away.[2] I had warning given me to beware of a fellow that stood by while some of us were talking. It seems there is a trade going of carrying stories to the government and many honest folks turn the penny by it. I cannot yet leave this place but will as soon as possible. Tom this minute brought me up word that the Baron's man was here, and that his master[3] is in town. I hope to see him, and give him half a breast of mutton before he goes back. He is now with a lawyer. I believe old Lombard Street is putting out money.

The Report of the Secret Committee is published.[4] It is a large volume. I only just saw it at Manly's. It is but a part, and probably there will be as much more. I do not believe or see one word is offered to prove their old slander of bringing in the Pretender. The treason lies wholly in making the peace. Charles Ford[5] is with Lord Bolingbroke in Dauphiné within a league of Lyons, where his Lordship is retired, till he sees what the Secret Committee will do. That is now determined and his Lordship will certainly be attainted by Act of Parliament. The impeachments are not yet carried up to the Lords. I suppose they intend to make one work of it.

Addressed—To Knightley Chetwode, Esq., at Woodbrooke, near Portarlington, Queen's County.

[1] At that time several members of Dublin University were expelled or admonished for disloyalty (Stubbs, *op. cit.*, p. 156). On 27 June three had been expelled; one, a master of arts, for making a copy of a pamphlet called "Nero Secundus," and two, both bachelors of arts, for disrespectful language about the King.

[2] After recording the seizure of the letters to Swift, Boyer adds (*op. cit.*, ix, 455): "of which the famous libeller Swift having notice and that search was made after him, he thought fit to abscond."

[3] *I.e.*, Chief Baron Rochfort.

[4] Its appearance is thus announced in the "London Gazette": "Just Published, A Report from the Committee of Secrecy, appointed by Order of the House of Commons to examine several Books and Papers laid before the House relating to the late Negotiations of Peace and Commerce, etc. Reported on the 9th of June 1715, by the Right Honourable Robert Walpole, Esq.; Chairman of the said Committee. Together with an Appendix, containing Memorials, Letters, and other Papers referred to in the said Report. Publish'd by Order of the House of Commons. Printed for Jacob Tonson, Timothy Goodwin, Bernard Lintott, and William Taylor." [5] *Supra*, p. 254.

CCCXLIV. [*Elwin.*]

SWIFT TO ALEXANDER POPE

Dublin, *June* 28, 1715.

My Lord Bishop of Clogher gave me your kind letter full of reproaches for my not writing.[1] I am naturally no very exact correspondent, and when I leave a country without a probability of returning, I think as seldom as I can of what I loved or esteemed in it, to avoid the *desiderium* which of all things makes life most uneasy. But you must give me leave to add one thing, that you talk at your ease, being wholly unconcerned in public events: for if your friends the Whigs continue, you may hope for some favour;[2] if the Tories return, you are at least sure of quiet. You know how well I loved both Lord Oxford and Bolingbroke, and how dear the Duke of Ormond is to me. Do you imagine I can be easy while their enemies are endeavouring to take off their heads. *I nunc, et versus tecum meditare canoros.* Do you imagine I can be easy, when I think of the probable consequences of these proceedings, perhaps upon the very peace of the nation, but certainly of the minds of so many hundred thousand good subjects? Upon the whole, you may truly attribute my silence to the eclipse, but it was that eclipse which happened on the first of August.[3]

[1] *Supra*, p. 282.

[2] Pope had, however, been warned that his friendship with Swift was not likely to benefit him with the Whigs. Writing to him soon after the death of Queen Anne, his friend Jervas, the painter, tells him of a conversation with Addison and says: "he was afraid Dr. Swift might have carried you too far among the enemy, during the heat of the animosity; but now all is safe, and you are escaped, even in his opinion." To this Pope had replied: "For all that passed betwixt Dr. Swift and me, you know the whole, without reserve, of our correspondence. The engagements I had to him were such as the actual services he had done me, in relation to the subscription for Homer, obliged me to. I must have leave to be grateful to him, and to anyone who serves me, let me be never so obnoxious to any party; nor did the Tory party ever put me to the hardship of asking this leave, which is the greatest obligation I owe to it, and I expect no greater from the Whig party than the same liberty" (Elwin and Courthope, *op. cit.*, viii, 8, 9).

[3] This metaphorical allusion to the death of Queen Anne had its point in the fact that a total eclipse of the sun had taken place a short

I borrowed your Homer [1] from the Bishop—mine is not yet landed—and read it out in two evenings. If it pleases others as well as me, you have got your end in profit and reputation: yet I am angry at some bad rhymes and triplets, and pray in your next do not let me have so many unjustifiable rhymes to *war* and *gods*. I tell you all the faults I know, only in one or two places you are a little obscure: but I expected you to be so in one or two and twenty. I have heard no soul talk of it here, for indeed it is not come over; nor do we very much abound in judges —at least I have not the honour to be acquainted with them. Your notes are perfectly good, and so are your preface and essay.[2] You were pretty bold in mentioning Lord Bolingbroke in that preface.[3] I saw the Key to the Lock but yesterday: I think you have changed it a good deal, to adapt it to the present times.

time before. It caused great excitement, and was responsible in popular opinion for many calamities. Even Archbishop King seems to have lost his head, and attributed to its effects the death of Chief Baron Rochfort's successor, which took place a fortnight after it. "The cold and dew," he writes, "was complained of by everyone during the eclipse, and many got cold; my Lord Chief Baron was on horseback on his return from his circuit, and took then a shivering which was the beginning of a fever of which he died" (Mason, *op. cit.*, p. lvii).

[1] "The First Volume of Mr. Pope's Translation of Homer is now ready," announces the "London Gazette" a fortnight before, "to be delivered to the Subscribers upon producing their Receipts or paying the Subscription-money to Bernard Lintott between the Temple Gates. Where all Mr. Pope's Pieces which he has lately published may be had." There subsequently appeared a more elaborate advertisement: "This Day is publish'd, The first four Books of the Iliad of Homer translated by Mr. Pope, who has added a Critical Preface, an Essay on the Life, Writings and Learning of Homer, and large Notes to each Book, a new Map of Greece, and a Geographical Table of the Towns &c. in Homer's Catalogue of Greece, with the Authorities for their Situation as placed in the Map. Printed in Folio, for Bernard Lintott between the Temple Gates, who has obtained a Grant from his Majesty King George for the sole printing and publishing thereof. Price stitch'd 12ˢ or 14ˢ bound. N.B. A Small Number are printed on large Paper at a Guinea stitcht, or 25ˢ bound."

[2] The essay was written by Parnell and did not satisfy Pope himself.

[3] The reference to Bolingbroke was a guarded one: "Such a genius as my Lord Bolingbroke, not more distinguished in the great scenes of business than in all the useful and entertaining parts of learning, has not refused to be the critic of these sheets and the patron of their writer."

God be thanked I have yet no parliamentary business, and if they have none with me, I shall never seek their acquaintance. I have not been very fond of them for some years past, not when I thought them tolerably good; and therefore if I can get leave to be absent, I shall be much inclined to be on that side when there is a Parliament on this: but truly I must be a little easy in my mind before I can think of Scriblerus.[1]

You are to understand that I live in the corner of a vast unfurnished house. My family consists of a steward, a groom, a helper in the stable, a footman, and an old maid, who are all at board wages, and when I do not dine abroad, or make an entertainment, which last is very rare, I eat a mutton-pie, and drink half a pint of wine. My amusements are defending my small dominions against the Archbishop, and endeavouring to reduce my rebellious choir.[2] *Perditur haec inter misero lux.* I desire you will present my humble service to Mr. Addison, Mr. Congreve, and Mr. Rowe,[3] and Gay. I am, and will be always,

Extremely yours, etc.

CCCXLV. [*Copy.*[4]]

KNIGHTLEY CHETWODE TO SWIFT

Woodbrooke, *July* 2, 1715.

I CONSULTED Mr. Whalley's almanac[5] for the day of the month and casting my eye lower I find that he says on the

---

[1] *Supra*, p. 254.   [2] *Supra*, p. 271.

[3] Nicholas Rowe was amongst the Whig wits whom Swift had tried to serve in the days of his power (" Prose Works," ii, 406).

[4] In the Forster Collection. *Supra*, p. 241, n. 1.

[5]
> " Whalley bred up to end and awl,
> To work in garret or in stall,
> Who had more skill in cutting leather,
> Than in foretelling wind or weather,
> Forsook the trade of mending shoes,
> To deal in politics and news
> Commenc'd astrologer and quack,
> To raise the Devil in a crack."

He seems to have been an Irish duplicate of Partridge, and on his death Swift's epitaph on Partridge was applied to him (see Gilbert's " Hist. of Dublin," i, 188).

19th begin the dog days, but of no influence with us; he is a dog for saying so, for the dog days began sooner, and a great deal influence us as I think.[1] Now comes Laughlin to tell me the Dean of St. Patrick's and the Baron are coming into the court, and so I leave off writing.

Two hours after I writ the above lines I go on with my letter. The Baron leaves me with a parson, his brother-in-law,[2] who has got Philipstown living on Lightburne's death. Baron tells me you entertained him well, that some business of the Church keeps you in town, that you remember the Dame and Squire, and made him believe you intended us the greatest and most agreeable kindness to come down; for God sake persist in that good resolution, make me happy and leave the town.

Sub is here and *sub sigillo* is the worst improver of land alive; if it were not ungenerous since he came up in kindness and at my request, I would send you his journal, for I can tell with exactness what he will do every minute of the twenty-four hours of every day. But let that pass, to answer your queries. The Dean's field flourishes, the quicks are cleared and grow well; it is a fine thing to have a good lawn, they talk of mowing it, I assure you. Your river walk is thirty feet wide, has in all its windings and meanders, as we suppose, about five thousand foot in length. Madam with her long green legs, gamboled twice to see it, got several falls, laughed at her own ill-footing squalled with a tolerable grace, rose and so proceeded. For the regard you express for my health, I am infinitely obliged to you. Your recipes guide me. I drink wine more, small beer less, eat no salads, walk so much that Sub pronounces me distracted, complains of his forehead sweating, to be like somebody, when alas!

> Before, behind, behind, before,
> He puffs and blows and sweats all o'er;

declaims against men of fortune making themselves slaves, mentions Percival,[3] and at last recollects it is two o'clock.

[1] This letter is an answer to Swift's letter of 28 June (*supra*, p. 284).
[2] Rochfort's wife was the daughter of an ancestor of Lord Castlemaine. She had two brothers in holy orders, Matthew Handcock, Archdeacon of Kilmore, and Stephen Handcock, Dean of Clonmacnoise.
[3] *Supra*, p. 240, n. 2.

The Baron brought me a bond for two hundred pounds
lent by me to Ruler Benjamin,[1] not a word of the quondam
ten pounds he refused to lend me. He brought me [also]
a written newsletter from London, with an account of
your brother of Gloucester having prated in Convocation
against tumults more than against preferment ecclesiastical;
for God sake is the account true, I cannot believe it.[2]

To be a little serious: I hate your account of one man,
who saw another man, who saw a letter, which said you
would be sent for. I do not a great deal like matters. I
should, indeed, think less unless I could think better or
serve the world more. I wish my spirits were but barely
disturbed. I am sometimes half-mad. The treason of
making a peace seems as absurd to me as the articles
against the peers which we have in the prints. I wish this
provoking courage may end well; I never liked it. What
the disposition of people in England is at present I do

---

[1] A younger brother of Knightley Chetwode's father, the Rev. John
Chetwode (*supra*, p. 261, n. 6). He was a solicitor, and acted in that
capacity for the Revenue Commissioners in Ireland.

[2] The reference is to the elder brother of the Rev. John Chetwode,
the Very Rev. Knightley Chetwode, Dean of Gloucester. He was a
well-known ecclesiastic, whose gifts won for him the friendship of
Dryden and the accomplished Roscommon, and the favour of suc-
cessive sovereigns and their courts, and has left a reputation as a man
of letters (" D. N. B.," x, 210). But his career bears some similarity
to that of the Vicar of Bray. By James II he was nominated to the
episcopal bench, under William III he became chief chaplain of
Marlborough's command, by Anne he was promoted to his dignity,
and under George I he was on the fair road once more to a bishopric
when death intervened. His speech in Convocation, aimed as it was
at the High Church party, was calculated to propitiate the Whigs, and
was warmly applauded by Boyer, who records (*op. cit.*, ix, 425) that
" the learned and ingenious Dr. Chetwode, Dean of Gloucester, made
a very seasonable and loyal speech in the Lower House [of Convoca-
tion], upon the subject matter of the late tumults and riots," and gives
a summary of the speech which was afterwards printed in pamphlet
form. In addition to Swift's letters (*supra*, p. 241, n. 1) the dampness of
the Irish climate is said to have been responsible for the destruction of
many autograph letters addressed by the Duke of Marlborough to the
Dean while acting as his chaplain. He was also well known to the
Duke of Ormond. In a letter written in 1703 from Flanders to Ormond, who was then in Ireland, he describes the military operations
under Marlborough in that year, and tells Ormond that he cannot be
more valued in Ireland than he is abroad, and that " his mind pre-
sages " he will have some day a great command in Flanders. (Brit.
Mus. Addit. MS., 22,130, f. 6.)

not so well know as I should do were there fewer dogs and rascals in the offices for letters. I shall long to see the Report; I hear many ill-reports, but I long to see the worst of all reports. I wish our friends in the neighbourhood of Lyons continuation of life, welfare, honour, and to surmount the present difficulties. I hope and earnestly trust that in this great scene all our friends will show and approve themselves great men. I stay here till the week after next, bar accidents. I am always desirous to know how I could contribute to your service or satisfaction for I am, *toujours*,

Votre, etc.

CCCXLVI. [*Copy.*[1]]

SWIFT TO KNIGHTLEY CHETWODE

Dublin, *July* 7, 1715.

I HAD your letter[2] the other day by Mr. Foxcroft who was so kind to call on me this morning, but would not stay and dine with me though I offered him mutton and a bottle of wine. I might have been cheated of my ginger-bread for anything you said in your letter, for I find you scorn to take notice of Dame's kind present; but I am humbler and signify to her that if she does not receive by Mr. Foxcroft a large tin pot well crammed with the Duke of Ormond's snuff, holding almost an ounce, she is wronged. I wish Laughlin had not been mistaken when he saw me coming into your court. I had much rather come into it than into the Court of England. I used formerly to write letters by bits and starts as you did when Laughlin thought I was coming; and so now I have been interrupted these three hours by company, and have now just eaten a piece of beef-steak spoiled in the dressing, and drunk a cup of sour ale, and return to finish my letter. Walls sat by me while I was at my dinner, and saw me finish it in five minutes, and has left me to go home to a much better. I find by your journal of Sub's life for one day, that he was more careful of finding manure for your land in the

---

[1] In the Forster Collection. *Supra*, p. 241, n. 1.
[2] *Supra*, p. 288.

nasty Scotch meaning than in showing satisfaction or skill in what you are doing. Sure you stretch your walk when you talk of five thousand foot, but your ambition is to have it longer than Mr. Rochfort's canal, and with a little expense it will be made a more beautiful thing. Are you certain it was Madam's green legs you saw by the river-side, because I have seen in England a large kind of green grasshopper, not quite so tall but altogether as slender, that frequent low marshy grounds.

The Baron told me he was employed here by you in an affair of usury, of which I give you joy, but did not tell me the particulars. I believe the affair of your English uncle is true, I have had it from many hands. How is that worse than the Bishop of London's[1] letter to his clergy and their answer, both owning that the tumults were in order to bring in popery and arbitrary power, a reproach which the rabble did not deserve, and has done us infinite hurt. I have not seen the articles; I read no news and hear little. There is no mercy for the poor collegian, and indeed as he is said to have behaved himself, there could none be expected. The Report is printed here but I have not read it. I think of going for England, if I can get leave, when Lord Sunderland comes over,[2] but not before unless I am sent for with a vengeance. I am not much grieved at your being out of the peace; I heard something of it the day I left you, but nothing certain. Major Champagne has hard usage, and I am truly concerned for him and his lady.[3] I am told here that some of our army is to be transported for England.

I had a letter this day from thence, from the person who sent me one from a lady, with great satisfaction that hers to me was not seized.[4] That letter talks doubtfully of the Duke of Ormond; that the Parliament resolves to carry matters to the highest extremes, and are preparing to impeach the Duke of Shrewsbury which the King would not suffer at first, but at length has complied with;[5] that

---

[1] *I.e.*, the ex-Privy Seal and Utrecht plenipotentiary (*supra*, p. 141, n. 4).

[2] As has been mentioned, the Earl of Sunderland (*supra*, p. 275, n. 5) had been appointed Lord Lieutenant in the previous autumn but he never came to Ireland.

[3] *Supra*, p. 248, n. 1.   [4] *Supra*, p. 283.

[5] This rumour was without any foundation.

Prior is kept closer than Gregg,[1] to force him to accuse Lord Oxford though he declares he knows nothing, and that it is thought he will be hanged if he will not be an evidence;[2] and that Lord Oxford confounds them with his intrepidity etc.

I think neither of your places[3] is remote enough for me to be at, and I have some project of going further, and am looking out for a horse. I believe you will be going for England by the time I shall be ready to leave this. Nasty foolish affairs of the deanery keep me thus long here. My humble service to Dame; pray God bless her and her fireside. The Baron gave me hopes of doing something about Kilberry.[4] Did he tell you how I pulled Tom's locks the wrong way for holding a plate under his armpit and what cursed bacon we had with our beans? Adieu.

Addressed—To Knightley Chetwode Esq.

CCCXLVII. [*Original.*[5]]

SWIFT TO THE EARL OF OXFORD

July 19, 1715.

MY LORD,

IT may look like an idle or officious thing in me to give your Lordship any interruption under your present circumstances,[6] yet I could never forgive myself if, after having been treated for several years with the greatest kindness and distinction, by a person of your Lordship's virtue and wisdom, I should omit making you at this time the humblest offers of my poor service and attendance. It is the first time I ever solicited you in my own behalf, and, if I am refused, I think it will be the first request you ever refused me. I do not conceive myself obliged to regulate

---

[1] Harley's clerk, who revealed state secrets to the French Court (*supra*, vol. i, p. 69).

[2] On his return from France Prior had been examined before the Secret Committee, and the result had dispelled any doubts as to his fidelity (*supra*, p. 278, n. 4).

[3] *I.e.*, Woodbrooke or Martry.　　　　[4] *Supra*, p. 266.

[5] In the possession of the Duke of Portland. *Supra*, p. 160, n. 2.

[6] Oxford was then in the Tower, to which he had been committed on 9 July by the House of Lords.

my opinions by the proceedings of a House of Lords or Commons; and therefore, however they may acquit themselves in your Lordship's case, I shall take the liberty of thinking and calling you, the ablest and faithfulest minister, and truest lover of your country that this age hath produced. And I have already taken care that you shall be so represented to posterity, in spite of all the rage and malice of your enemies.[1] And this I know will not be wholly indifferent to your Lordship, who, next to a good conscience, did always esteem reputation your best possession. Your heroic and Christian behaviour under this prosecution astonisheth every one but me, who know you so well, and know how little it is in the power of human actions or events to discompose you. I have seen your Lordship labouring under greater difficulties and exposed to greater dangers, and overcoming both, by the providence of God, and your own wisdom and courage. Your life has been already attempted by private malice; as it is now by public resentment. Nothing else remained. You were destined to both trials, and the same power which delivered you out of the paws of the lion and the bear will, I trust, deliver you out of the hands of the uncircumcised.

I can write no more. You suffer for a good cause, for having preserved your country, and for having been the great instrument under God, of his present Majesty's peaceable accession to the throne. This I know, and this your enemies know; and this I will take care that all the world shall know, and future ages be convinced of. God Almighty protect you, and continue to you that fortitude and magnanimity He hath endowed you with. Farewell.

J. S.

CCCXLVIII. [*Copy*.[2]]

Swift to Knightley Chetwode

August 2, 1715.

CONSIDERING how exact a correspondent you are, and how bad a one I am myself, I had clearly forgot whether

---

[1] The reference is to " An Enquiry into the Behaviour of the Queen's Last Ministry," which is dated June 1715 (" Prose Works," v, 425).
[2] In the Forster Collection. *Supra*, p. 241, n. 1.

you had answered my last letter, and therefore intended to have writ to you to-day whether I had heard from you or no, because Mr. Warburton told me you were upon your return to Martry. Though it be unworthy of a philosopher to admire at anything, and directly forbidden by Horace, yet I am every day admiring at a thousand things. I am struck at the Duke of Ormond's flight.[1] A great person here in power read us some letters last night importing that he was gone to the Pretender, and that upon his first arrival at Calais he talked of the King only as Elector etc. But this is laughed at, and is indeed wholly unlike him, and I find his friends here are utterly ignorant where he is, and some think him still in England.

I was interrupted last post, but I just made a shift to write a few words to the Baron. The story of an invasion is all blown off; and the Whigs seem to think there will be no such thing. They assure us of the greatest unanimity in England to serve the King, and yet they continue to call the Tories all Jacobites. They say they cannot imagine why any Tory should be angry, since there never was the least occasion given; and particularly they cry up their mercy shown to Bingley.[2] There is no news of any more people gone off, though Lord Shrewsbury was named. The suspending the Habeas Corpus Act has frightened our friends in England. I am heartily concerned for poor Joe,[3] and should be more so if he were not swallowed up by his betters.

Give my service to Dame Pliant, and desire her to let me know what quantity of cherries she has for brandy; you may steep them in just enough to keep them alive, and I will send you some very good if I can and you will tell me how much. But here I want Joe. I hope Dame found the boys well, and that she gave them good counsel upon the subject of gooseberries and codlings, for I hear the eldest has been a little out of order.

I am glad to hear you and the Doctor are grown so well together, and was not Mrs. Raymond the civilest thing in

---

[1] The Duke of Ormond is said to have gone to France on 28 July.

[2] Lord Bingley was not by any means a strong party man, and this allusion is the more surprising in view of Ford's reference to him (*supra*, p. 216).

[3] Possibly Beaumont showed then some sign of mental derangement (*supra*, p. 276).

the world? I find you intend to take some very sudden resolution, and truly I was like to be as sudden, for I was upon the balance two hours whether I should not take out a license of absence immediately upon a letter I received;[1] but at last I thought I was too late by a week for the design; and so I am dropped again into my old insipidness, and the weather has been so bad, that together with my want of a horse, and my steward urging one every day about my tithes, I have not been a mile out of town these five weeks, except once on foot.

I hear Major Champagne was left half pay, and consequently that he will now have whole; so that he may yet eat bread.[2] God preserve you and Dame and the fire-side, believe me, ever,

Entirely yours etc.

Addressed—To Knightley Chetwode Esq., at Martry, near Navan, County of Meath.

CCCXLIX. [*Original.*[3]]

JOHN ARBUTHNOT TO SWIFT

August 6, 1715.

I RECEIVED your very Heraclitean letter. I am kinder than you. I desire to hear your complaints, and will always share them, when I cannot remove them. I should have the same concern for things as you, were I not convinced that a comet will make much more strange revolutions upon the face of our globe, than all the petty changes that can be occasioned by Governments and Ministries. And you will allow it to be a matter of importance to think of methods to save oneself and family in such a terrible shock, when this whole earth will turn upon new poles, and revolve in a new orbit. I consider myself as a poor passenger, and that the earth is not to be forsaken, nor the rocks removed for me. But you are certainly some first minister of a great

---

[1] Ormond was doubtless in both cases the cause of disquiet. Chetwode wished to join him in his desperate course, Swift to dissuade him from it.

[2] *Supra*, p. 292.   [3] In the British Museum. See Preface.

monarch, who, for some misbehaviour, are condemned, in this revolution of things, to govern a Chapter, and a choir of singing-men. I am sure I should think myself happy, if I had only such a province as the latter. Certainly your Chapter is too peaceable, and not like other Chapters; else they would give you more occupation.

You see I begin with philosophy. As to business, I this moment saw the Dragon.[1] He had your letters, and showed them to me some time ago, and seems to be mighty fond of the project; only he is to be at Wimpole, and not in Herefordshire, and it is but a step farther. He is to write this night, if you believe him, to that very purpose; nay, I am to have the letter to enclose, and I intend to keep mine open till eleven. It is strange that you should imagine the Dragon had cast his *exuviae* in his den, or that confinement is a cure for inactivity; so far from it, all these habits are ten times stronger upon him than ever. Lewis will furnish you with a collection of new stories that are as far beyond the old ones as you can imagine. Therefore I say again, come, and you will be far from finding such dismal scenes as you describe. Your own letter will furnish you with topics to conquer your melancholy. For in such a muta-bility, what is it that must not in time cast up? Even the return of that brother[2] you mention. And as philosophical as I am, I should be very sad if I did not think that very probable and feasible. As to your friends, though the world is changed to them, they are not changed to you; and you will be caressed as much as ever, and by some that bore you no good will formerly. Do you think there is no pleasure in hearing the Hanover club declaim upon the clemency and gentleness of the late reign, and a thousand stranger things? As for the constitution, it is in no more danger than a strong man that has got a little surfeit by drunkenness. All will be well, and people recover their sober senses every day.

Several of your friends dine with me to-day, Lady Masham, John Drummond,[3] the Judge, etc.; when you will be remembered. I wish I could return your compliments

---

[1] *I.e.*, Oxford (*supra*, p. 150, n. 4), who seems to have received more than one letter from Swift.

[2] *I.e.*, Bolingbroke.

[3] Swift had made the acquaintance of Drummond, Oxford's financial agent at the Hague, during his last visit to London.

as to my wife and bairns. Sure you are a very ill husband, for you had the complete thousand when you was in England, and sixpence of another thousand given by the Dragon.[1] I remember that full well. Lewis is gone his progress. I shall be at Bath in a fortnight. Come that way. Adieu.

I really think the person I recommended will do well; he will be quite another thing before Michaelmas, with Roseingrave's [2] teaching; and he has a good voice.

CCCL. [*Copy.*[3]]

KNIGHTLEY CHETWODE TO SWIFT

Woodbrooke, *August* 13, 1715.

THOUGH this leaves me perplexed beyond expression, and that I do not know you can extricate me, yet I would not omit to write to you, for sometimes imparting lessens affliction. My hurrying to this country, as I did, was to have an interview with an old lady,[4] whom I was directed to see, and by whose directions I was to form all my present measures. Either I am faulty in deferring it so long, or she is sooner called away than I expected. Be it whether it will, her being gone leaves me a great deal in the dark, pretty irresolute, and under all possible confusion. But if I resolve anything, it is to pursue my first resolution. I wish I were certain you knew her, or had seen her ere she embarked, but you are pleased to be sometimes so politic and dark that I never had reason from you to believe you of her acquaintance.

I hope to see you soon, so soon that I was in suspense if I should not have been the porter of this letter.[5] Your

---

[1] The reference is to the grant which Swift was promised (*supra*, p. 210, n. 2).

[2] The organist of St. Patrick's (*supra*, p. 59, n. 2).

[3] In the Forster Collection. *Supra*, p. 241, n. 1.

[4] In a note appended to the copy of this letter Forster's friend, Mr. Edward Wilmot-Chetwode, says that he believes "old lady" was the pass-word for the Duke of Ormond, but nothing is known of Ormond's visiting Ireland at that time.

[5] It now becomes an answer to Swift's letter of the 2nd (*supra*, p 294).

former resolution which you laid aside for being a week
too late, would have been better, in my opinion, pursued,
since three weeks would be allowed. You take me, I dare
say, without further *éclaircissement*. I have seen about sixteen of the clergy since I left you. I find them chagrined and
disobliged a good deal with some late steps made by your
friend, whom you call Proverb;[1] how justly or unjustly I
do not pretend to enter into. I writ to Dame about the
cherries. I cannot inform you of the fit quantity you say
you want, for that you cannot eat your cake and have your
cake; if he[2] be swallowed up by as many of his betters as
step aside, I cannot tell you what to say to it. I sent for the
Baron to come to me; he has promised, but I have not yet
seen him. I had a letter this morning from quondam Lady
Jenny to come to her. I could not go. She tells me *Monsieur
le Major* was to [take] post at Holyhead for London the
day I dined with you, his post not at that time given away
notwithstanding reports. I will see her to-morrow, and you
before Tuesday's post; I will not add more now, and wish
I have not said too much, but of this I am certain that I am
with the utmost affection and truth, ever,

Entirely yours.

CCCLI. [*Original.*[3]]

THE REV. ROBERT FREIND TO SWIFT

Westminster, *September* 20, 1715.

MR. DEAN,[4]
  I AM much obliged to Lady Kerry for giving you an
occasion of writing, and shall always be pleased to receive
any commands from you. Mr. Fitzmaurice is very promising, and a favourite of mine already.[5] I had never seen nor

---

[1] Possibly Provost Pratt is the person to whom the allusion is made,
and the action taken by the authorities about the disloyalty in the
College, the cause of dissatisfaction.

[2] *I.e.*, Joe Beaumont.

[3] In the British Museum. See Preface.

[4] To the writer of this letter, the eminent epigrammatist and Head
Master of Westminster School, there has been already allusion (*supra*,
p. 58).

[5] Swift's "great favourite," Lady Kerry (*supra*, vol. i, p. 188, n. 2),
had evidently asked him to commend her younger son, who was

heard from anyone that was concerned for him, till I had the favour of yours; but as I had taken particular notice of him on his own account, I shall now do it much more upon yours. This will be brought to you by your kinsman, Mr. Rolt.[1] I am glad I can tell you, that he has behaved himself very well here. He is not of the brightest sort, but is very sober and industrious, and will work out his way, and, I believe, deserve any encouragement you are pleased to give him. Things are in an odd posture with us at present, and the state of banishment you are in, may be endured without much regret; however, I shall hope in a little time to see you here, when more of your friends are in town.

The Bishop[2] and my brother[3] are much yours, and very desirous of a happy meeting with you. Before this can be with you, you will be able to guess how soon that may happen; and may it be as soon as is wished by, Sir,

Your most obedient and faithful humble servant,

R. FREIND.

CCCLII. [*Copy.*[4]]

SWIFT TO MRS. CHETWODE

October 7, 1715.

MADAM,

I FIND you are resolved to feed me wherever I am. I am extremely obliged to your care and kindness, but know not how to return it otherwise than by my love and esteem for you. I had one letter from Mr. Chetwode from Chester,[5] but it came late, and he talked of staying there only a week. If I knew where to write to him I would. I said a good deal to him before he went, and I believe he will keep

created Earl of Shelburne, to Freind's special care while in his school. Swift had already concerned himself about the entrance of her elder son into Christ Church, Oxford ("Prose Works," ii, 433).

[1] Possibly a son of Swift's cousin (*supra*, p. 172).

[2] *I.e.*, Atterbury.

[3] John Freind, who had been one of Swift's predecessors on the staff of the "Examiner" (*supra*, vol. i, p. 229, n. 1).

[4] In the Forster Collection. *Supra*, p. 241, n. 1.

[5] Chetwode had evidently determined to throw in his lot with the Duke of Ormond.

out of harm's way in these troublesome times. God knows what will become of us all. I intend when the Parliament meets here,[1] to retire somewhere into the country. Pray God bless and protect you, and your little fire-side. Believe me to be ever, with true esteem, Madam,

Your most obedient, humble Servant,
J. SWIFT.

Addressed—To Mrs. Chetwode.

CCCLIII. [*Original.*[2]]

THE DUCHESS OF ORMOND TO SWIFT

October 17, 1715.

SIR,

I WAS extremely pleased to find you had not forgot your friends, when it is so hard for them to write to you, and by their concern for you, put you in mind of them. But I find no misfortunes can lessen your friendship, which is so great as to blind you of the side of their faults, and make you believe you see virtues in them, it were happy for them they enjoyed in any degree; for, I am sure, some of those you named are much wanted at this time. I was, as you heard, very well pleased, that my friend[3] was safe as to his person, but very uneasy at seeing his reputation so treated. As to his fortune, it is yet in dispute. However, as long as he is well, I am satisfied. It is with difficulty I do hear, but now and then a straggling body brings me an account of him; for there has been no encouragement to write by the post, all letters miscarrying that either he or I have wrote that way, that we have given it over now, and trust to accident for news of each other. I hope I shall hear from you oftener than I have done for some months past; for no friend you have has more respect for you, than

Your most humble servant

Your niece Betty[4] is your humble servant.

---

[1] The first Irish Parliament of George I met on 12 November.
[2] In the British Museum. See Preface.
[3] *I.e.*, Ormond.   [4] *Supra*, p. 141.

CCCLIV. [*Copy.*[1]]

SWIFT TO KNIGHTLEY CHETWODE

December 17, 1715.

I HAVE had three letters from you, one from Chester,[2] another round a printed paper, and the third of the 6th instant. The first I could not answer for it came late, and you said you were to leave Chester in a week, neither did I know how to direct to you till your second came, and that was so soon followed by the third that now I answer both together. I have been miserably ill of a cruel cold, beyond the common pains, and so as to threaten me with ill consequences upon my health, else you should have heard from me three weeks sooner. I have been ten days, and am still at Mr. Grattan's four miles from the town,[3] to recover myself, and am now in a fair way.

I like the verses well. Some of them are very well though against my friends, but I am positive the town is out in their guess of the author. I wonder how you came to see the Dragon, for I am told none of his nearest relations have that liberty, nor any but his solicitors.[4] Had I been directed to go over some months ago, I might have done it, because I would gladly have been serviceable, but now I cannot, and agree with you and my other friends that I am safer here. I am curious to know how he carries himself, whether he is still easy and intrepid; whether he thinks he shall lose his head, or whether it is generally thought so.

I find you have ferreted me out in my little private acquaintance, but that must be *entre nous.* The best of it is you cannot trace them all. My service to them, and say I [would] give a great deal to be among you. I do not understand the rebus. I would apply it to myself, but then what means " narrow in flight "? I am sorry at heart for poor Ben.[5] He has in his life been so splenetic that it was past a jest. He should ride, and live in the country and

---

[1] In the Forster Collection. *Supra*, p. 241, n. 1.
[2] *Supra*, p. 300.   [3] *Supra*, p. 263.
[4] Apparently restrictions had been lately placed upon the number of Oxford's visitors (*supra*, p. 297).
[5] *I.e.*, Swift's publisher, Ben Tooke (*supra*, p. 173).

leave off his trade, for he is rich enough. As much as I hate news, I hear it in spite of me, not being able to govern the tongues of your favourite and some others. We are here in horrible fears, and make the rebels ten times more powerful and the discontents greater than I hope they really are; nay it is said the Pretender is landed or landing with Lord knows how many thousands.[1] I always knew my friend Mr. Attorney[2] would be as great as he could in all changes. When Cole of the Oaks comes to town assure him of my humble service, and that when storms are over I will pass some time with his leave among his plantations. Dame Pliant and I have had some commerce, but I have not been able to go there, by foolish impediments of business here. She has been in pain about not hearing from you. I lately heard your boys were well. The Baron called to see me here in the country yesterday, and said you had lately writ to him.

There is one period in your letter very full of kind expressions, all to introduce an ugly suspicion of somebody that told you I know not what. I had no acquaintance with you at all till I came last to this kingdom, and it is odd if I should then give myself the liberty of speaking to your disadvantage. Since that time you have used me so well, that it would be more than odd if I gave myself that liberty. But I tell you one thing, that when you are mentioned by myself or anybody else, I presently add some expressions, that he must be a rude beast indeed who would lessen you before me, so far am I from doing it myself, and I should avoid it more to you than another, because you are a man anxious to be informed, and have more of punctilio and suspicion than I could wish. I would say thus much to few men. Because generally I expect to be trusted, and scorn to defend myself; and the Dragon thought it the best compliment to him he ever heard, when I said I did not value what I said to him, not what I said of him. So much upon this scurvy subject.

You may direct to S. H. at Mrs. Holt's over against the Church in Bride's Street. The Parliament here[3] are as mad as you could desire them; all of different parties are used

---

[1] Five days later James landed in Scotland, but only attended by six persons.

[2] *I.e.*, ex-Lord Chancellor Harcourt.   [3] *Supra*, p. 301, n. 1.

like Jacobites and dogs. All conversation with different principles is dangerous and troublesome. Honest people get into corners, and are as merry as they can. We are as loyal as our enemies, but they will not allow us to be so. If what they said were true, they would be quickly undone. Pray keep yourself out of harm's way. It is the best part a private man can take unless his fortune be desperate, or unless he has at least a fair hazard for mending the public. My humble service to a much prouder man than myself; I mean your uncle.[1] Dr. P[ratt][2] showed me a letter from you about three weeks ago. He is well, I suppose, for I am a private country gentleman, and design to be so some days longer. Believe me to be ever, with great truth and esteem,

Yours, etc.

I direct to the Pall Mall Coffee-house, because you mention changing lodgings.

Addressed—To Knightley Chetwode, Esq., at the Pall Mall Coffee-house, in Pall Mall, London.

CCCLV. [*Original.*[3]]

THE DUCHESS OF ORMOND TO SWIFT

Jan. 23, 1715-16.

SIR,

YOUR letter[4] was a great while upon the road, before I had the good luck to have it, and [I] think I was happy that it ever arrived here; for it is the second letter I have received out of Ireland in above seven months. Either those few friends I have there are afraid of taking notice of me, or my enemies will not let me have the comfort of thinking I have any left, and therefore stop my letters. I give you a thousand thanks for so kindly remembering an absent friend. As you always think right, I do not wonder you are of the opinion our friend[5] has not all his good

[1] *Supra*, p. 290, n. 2.   [2] The Provost.
[3] In the British Museum. See Preface.
[4] Probably a reply to her letter of 17 October (*supra*, p. 301).
[5] *I.e.*, Oxford.

offices very well returned. But who live in this world, must arm themselves with patience, and a resolution able to bear ingratitude, reproach, poverty, and afflictions of all kinds, or submit to the discipline of Bedlam.

I have not heard from my master[1] these many months. I hope he is well, because the good-nature of the world would take care I should hear, if he were otherwise. The lady you name in your letter lives at her house in Berkshire.[2] I cannot entertain you with so much as the tittle-tattles of the town, having not seen it these four months, nor scarce anything but frost and snow, which makes me converse most with robin-red-breasts, that do me the favour to come in at the windows to see me. Your niece[3] is your humble servant, but not well, having a rash. I believe by this time you wish you had not provoked me to write, since you are troubled with so long a scrawl from me, who am with great truth, Sir,

Your most sincere friend and humble servant.

CCCLVI. [*Original.*[4]]

SWIFT TO ARCHDEACON WALLS

Trim, *February* 26, 1715-16.

I LAY at Forbes's[5] Friday night.[6] He had no horse to lend me, one was lame and the other sick, so I was forced to bring your scrub with me. You have reason to complain of Bolingbroke's shyness; your horse was like to cast Will half a dozen times.[7] I was very weary with my journey yesterday, but thank God am well to-day, and as bad as the weather is, I read prayers and preached at Laracor; for poor Warburton—who could believe it—is laid up with the gout. The roads were abominably bad from

---

[1] *I.e.*, Ormond.
[2] The reference is to Lady Bolingbroke, to whom Swift wrote soon afterwards (*infra*, p. 313).
[3] *I.e.*, Lady Betty.
[4] In the possession of Mr. John Murray. See Preface.
[5] *Supra*, p. 282.
[6] Swift had evidently left Dublin on Friday the 24th.
[7] As appears lower down Swift had exchanged Bolingbroke (*supra*, p. 280) for a horse of Walls.

Dunboyne[1] hither. My mare is brisker after the journey than before. I design to ride every day. I hope Bolingbroke carried you well this day to Castleknock.[2] I saw the gardens at Laracor and the grove too—tell Mrs. Johnson that—and they all look sadly desolate. My landlord and landlady[3] give their service to you and Gossip Doll and the ladies: I am very much theirs, and hope our Doll is better. Shift as you can without your nag till I return; he shall fare as well as the rest. My duty to my Lord Bishops of Clogher and Dromore.[4]

Yours.

Addressed—For the Reverend Mr. Archdeacon Walls, Queen Street, Dublin.

CCCLVII. [*Nichols.*]

SWIFT TO BISHOP ATTERBURY

Dublin, *March* 24, 1715-16.

MY LORD,

As much of your Lordship's thoughts and time are employed at present,[5] you must give me leave to interrupt them, and which is worse, for a trifle; though, by the accidents of time and party, of some consequence and great vexation to me. I am here at the head of three and twenty dignitaries and prebendaries, whereof the major part, differing from me in principles, have taken a fancy to oppose me upon all occasions in the Chapter-house;[6] and a ringleader

---

[1] The parish of which Forbes was rector.

[2] Castleknock parish, of which Walls was then the incumbent (*supra*, p. 67, n. 8), lies about five miles to the north-west of Dublin, embracing a part of the Phœnix Park.

[3] *I.e.*, Dr. and Mrs. Raymond.

[4] Bishops Stearne and Ashe were then in Dublin for the meeting of the Irish Parliament.

[5] Swift refers to the part taken by his friend (*supra*, p. 57) in resisting the latitudinarian influence of the Hanoverian administration on the Church. In the abilities of Atterbury, that "most brilliant tribune, orator, and pamphleteer of the High Church party" as Mr. Lecky (*op. cit.*, i, 251) calls him, Swift and those who agreed with him placed their chief reliance.

[6] In a contest between Swift and his Chapter a year before as to

among them has presumed to debate my power of proposing, or my negative, though it is what the deans of this
Cathedral have possessed for time immemorial, and what
has never been once disputed.[1] Our constitution was taken
from that of Sarum; and the knowledge of what is practised there in the like case would be of great use to me. I
have written this post to Dr. Younger, to desire he would
inform me in this matter;[2] but having only a slender acquaintance with him, I would beg your Lordship to second
my request, that the Dean would please to let me know the
practice of his cathedral, and his power in this point. I
would likewise desire your Lordship to let me know how it
is at Westminster, and the two other cathedrals, with whose
customs you may be acquainted.[3]

Pray, my Lord, pardon this idle request from one that
loves and esteems you, as you know I do. I once thought
it would never be my misfortune to entertain you at so
scurvy a rate, at least not at so great a distance, or with so
much constraint:

> Sis felix, nostrumque leves—I do not like *quicunque* [4]—laborem:
> Et quo sub coelo tandem, quibus orbis in oris
> Jactemur, doceas.

The greatest felicity I now have is, that I am utterly

the appointment of a proctor to the economy, an offer on Swift's part
to serve himself in that capacity was rejected in a chapter of fourteen
by a majority of two (Mason, *op. cit.*, p. 293).

[1] Writing five years later to the then Dean of Ossory on this subject,
Swift says that the chapter did not directly oppose his right of veto,
but only argued "the ill consequences which might follow if it had no
exceptions." The debates had evidently not any practical result, as
Swift adds: "it is an infallible maxim that not one thing here is done
without the Dean's consent; if he proposeth, it is then left to the
majority, because the proposal is his consent." The main responsibility
for raising the question Swift throws, in his letter to the Dean of
Ossory, on Theophilus Bolton, whose appointment as Chancellor of
St. Patrick's has been noticed (*supra*, p. 257, n. 2).

[2] Dr. John Younger was Dean of Salisbury and also a Prebendary
of St. Paul's. From Swift's letter to the Dean of Ossory, it appears
that Younger replied to Swift and gave him the same advice as Atterbury did in the letter printed below.

[3] It would appear that Swift refers to Carlisle and Christ Church,
Oxford, of which Atterbury had been successively Dean before his
appointment to the bishopric of Rochester and deanery of Westminster.

[4] The adaptation from the *quaecunque* of Virgil necessary to meet
existing circumstances.

ignorant of the most public events that happen in the world: *multa gemens ignominiam plagasque*, etc. I am with the greatest respect and truth, my Lord,

Your lordship's most dutiful and most humble servant,

JON. SWIFT.

CCCLVIII. [*Original.*[1]]

BISHOP ATTERBURY TO SWIFT

Bromley, *April* 6, 1716.

GOOD MR. DEAN,

MY gout kept me so long a prisoner at Westminster this winter, that I have fixed at Bromley[2] this spring much sooner than ever I yet did; for which reason my meeting with Dr. Younger will be more difficult than it would be, had I been still at the deanery.[3] The best, or rather the worst, is that I believe he can say nothing to you upon the matter about which you write, which will please you. His deanery is of the old foundation, and in all such foundations the deans have no extraordinary power or privilege, and are nothing more than residentiaries, with a peculiar corps belonging to them as deans; the first of the chapter, but such whose presence is not necessary toward the dispatch of any one capitular act, the senior residentiary supplying their absence, in every case, with full authority. Thus, I say, the case generally is in the old deaneries, unless where the local statutes may have expressly reserved some peculiar power or privilege to the deans of those churches. But none of them, I dare say, have a negative, either by canon law, custom, or local statute. Thus much to show you, that a nice search into the peculiar rights of the dean of Sarum will be needless, if not mischievous to you.

The three deaneries which I have had, are all of the new foundation, by Henry the Eighth or Queen Elizabeth. In the charters of all there is a clause, empowering the dean

[1] In the British Museum. See Preface.
[2] The palace of the Bishop of Rochester.
[3] *Supra*, p. 307.

to make, punish, and unmake all the officers. In the statutes of one of them, Carlisle, the dean's consent, in all the *graviores causae*, is made expressly necessary, and in the other two nothing from the foundation of those churches ever passed the seal without the dean's *sigilletur* first written on the lease, patent, presentation, etc., which is a manifest and uncontested proof of his negative. As to the power of proposing, that I apprehend not to be exclusive to the other members of chapters. It is a point chiefly of decency and convenience; the dean being the principal person, and supposed best to be acquainted with the affairs of the church, and in what order they are fittest to be transacted. But if anyone else of the body will propose anything, and the rest of the chapter will debate it, I see not how the dean can hinder them, unless it be by leaving the chapter; and that itself will be of no moment in churches where his absence does not break up and dissolve the chapter; as it does, where his consent to anything there treated of is expressly required before it can pass into an act. Where, indeed, he is allowed such a negative, he is generally allowed to make all proposals; because it would be to no purpose for anyone to make a proposition which he can quash by a dissent: but this is not, I say, a matter of right, but prudence.

Upon the whole, the best advice I can give you is, whatever your powers are by statute or usage, not to insist on them too strictly in either of the cases mentioned by you, unless you are very sure of the favour and countenance of your visitor. The lawyers, you will find, whenever such points come before them for a decision, are very apt to disregard statute and customs in such cases; and to say that their books make the act of the majority of the corporation the legal act of the body, without considering whether the dean be among the minority or not. And therefore your utmost dexterity and address will be necessary, in order to prevent such a trial of your right at common law; which, it is ten to one, especially as things now stand, will go against you. If the refractory part of your chapter are stout, and men of any sense, or supported underhand, the last of these is highly probable, you had better make use of expedients to decline the difficulty, than bring it at present to a decision. These are the best lights, and this the best advice, I can give you, after a long experience of the natural consequences of such struggles,[1] and a careful search into the foundation of the powers and privileges claimed and disputed on the one side and the other. I wish I could say anything more to your satisfaction, but I cannot; and I think, in all such cases, the best instance I can give you of my friendship is not to deceive you.

There is a statute in the latter end of King Henry the Eighth's reign[2] worthy of your perusal. The title of it relates to the leases of hospitals, etc. and the tenor of it did, in my apprehension, seem always to imply, that without the dean, master, etc. nothing could be legally done by the corporation. But the lawyers will not allow this to be good doctrine, and say that statute, notwithstanding the constant phrase of it, determines nothing of this kind, and, at the most, implies it only as to such deaneries, etc., where the dean, master, etc., has the right of a negative, by statute or usage; and few lawyers there are, who will allow even thus much. I cannot explain myself farther on that head; but, when you peruse the statute, you will see what I mean; though, after all, it does not, I believe, include Ireland. However, I look upon it as a declaration of the common law here in England.

I am sorry you have any occasion to write to me on these heads, and much sorrier that I am able to give you any tolerable account of them. God forgive those who have furnished me with this knowledge, by involving me designedly into those squabbles. I thank God, I have forgiven them. I will enter into nothing but the inquiries of

---

[1] Atterbury had indeed such experience of capitular conflict as falls to the lot of few ecclesiastics. The most extraordinary revelations as to the scenes under his rule as Dean, as well at Carlisle and Westminster as at Christ Church, are to be found in the correspondence between Stratford and Lord Harley (*supra*, p. 190, n. 3), and Smalridge, who succeeded him both at Carlisle and Christ Church, might well say that his business was to put out the fires which Atterbury had kindled. Even allowing for the fact that Stratford was, as Mrs. Lomas says ("Portland Manuscripts," vii, vi), "a good hater," and was prejudiced against the "Ruffian," it cannot be doubted that Atterbury was naturally imperious and quarrelsome, and his advice to Swift was probably largely prompted by the exigences of the moment. If Stratford is to be believed, Atterbury did not himself always follow the advice which he had given Swift during the remainder of his time at Westminster.

[2] 33 Hen. VIII, cap. 37.

your letter, and therefore add not a word more, either in English or Latin, but that I am, with great esteem, good Mr. Dean,

Your very affectionate humble servant,

FR. ROFFEN.

CCCLIX. [*Nichols.*]

SWIFT TO BISHOP ATTERBURY

April 18, 1716.

MY LORD,

I AM extremely obliged to your Lordship for the trouble you have given yourself in answering at length a very insignificant letter.[1] I shall entirely follow your Lordship's advice to the best of my skill. Your conjectures from whence my difficulties take their rise are perfectly true. It is all party. But the right is certainly on my side, if there be anything in constant immemorial custom. Besides, though the first scheme of this Cathedral was brought from Sarum, yet by several subsequent grants, from Popes, Kings, Archbishops, and Acts of Parliament, the dean has great prerogatives. He visits the chapter as ordinary, and the Archbishop only visits by the dean. The dean can suspend and sequester any member, and punishes all crimes except heresy, and one or two more reserved for the Archbishop. No lease can be let without him. He holds a court-leet in his district, and is exempt from the Lord Mayor, etc. No chapter can be called but by him, and he dissolves them at pleasure. He disposes absolutely of the petty canons and vicars-choral places. All the dignitaries, etc. swear canonical obedience to him. These circumstances put together, I presume, may alter the case in your Lordship's judgement. However, I shall, as your Lordship directs me, do my utmost to divert this controversy as much as I can. I must add one thing, that no dignitary can preside without a power from the dean, who, in his absence, makes a sub-dean, and limits him as he pleases. And so much for deaneries, which I hope I shall never trouble your Lordship with again.

[1] *Supra*, p. 308.

I send this enclosed, and without superscription, to be sent or delivered to you by a famous friend of mine, and devoted servant of your Lordship's. I congratulate with England for joining with us here in the fellowship of slavery.[1] It is not so terrible a thing as you imagine: we have long lived under it, and whenever you are disposed to know how you ought to behave yourself in your new condition, you need go no farther than me for a director. But, because we are resolved to go beyond you, we have transmitted a bill to England, to be returned here, giving the government and six of the Council power for three years to imprison whom they please for three months, without any trial or examination; and I expect to be among the first of those upon whom this law will be executed. We have also outdone you in the business of Ben Hoadley,[2] and have recommended to a bishopric one whom you would not allow a curate in the smallest of your parishes.[3] Does your Lordship know that, as much as I have been used to lies in England, I am under a thousand uneasinesses about some reports relating to a person that you and I love very well? I have writ to a lady upon that subject, and am impatient for an answer.[4] I am gathering up a thousand pounds, and intend to finish my life upon the interest of it in Wales.

God Almighty preserve your Lordship *miseris succurrere rebus*, whether you understand or relish Latin or no. But it is a great deal your fault if you suffer us all to be undone; for God never gave such talents without expecting

---

[1] *I.e.,* Whig rule.

[2] Hoadley was appointed to the bishopric of Bangor in December, 1715.

[3] The allusion is said to have been to Dr. Charles Carr, who was then chaplain to the Irish House of Commons, and who was promoted to the episcopal bench a few months later as Bishop of Killaloe. Judging by a sermon preached by Carr before the House of Commons on the anniversary of the martyrdom of Charles I in that year, there seems to have been justification for Swift's depreciatory remark, as well as evidence that denunciation of their enemies was more to the taste of the House than enunciation of Christian principles. It may be added that Carr was a son-in-law of Swift's friend, Joshua Dawson (*supra*, p. 204), who had lost his place on the advent of the Whigs.

[4] After acting for ten months as Secretary of State to the Pretender, Bolingbroke had been dismissed a few weeks before amidst charges of disrespect and even of treachery. The reply of the lady, otherwise Lady Bolingbroke, follows this letter.

they should be used to preserve a nation. There is a
doctor[1] in your neighbourhood, to whom I am a very
humble servant. I am, with great respect,
Your Lordship's most dutiful, etc.
JON. SWIFT.

Some persons go this summer for England, and if Dr.
Younger be talked with, I hope you will so order it that it
may not be to my disadvantage.[2]

CCCLX. [*Deane Swift.*]

VISCOUNTESS BOLINGBROKE TO SWIFT
London, *May* 5, 1716.

MR. DEAN,[3]
YOUR letter came in very good time to me,[4] when I was
full of vexation and trouble, which all vanishes, finding
that you were so good to remember me under my afflictions,
which have been not greater than you can think, but much
greater than I can express. I am now in town: business
called me hither, and when that is finished I shall retire
with more comfort than I came. Do not forsake an old
friend, nor believe reports which are scandalous and false.
You are pleased to inquire after my health; I can give you
no good account of it at present, but that country, whither
I shall go next week, will, I hope, set me up. As to my
temper, if it is possible, I am more insipid and dull than
ever, except in some places, and there I am a little fury,
especially if they dare mention my dear Lord without
respect, which sometimes happens; for good manners and
relationship are laid aside in this town—it is not hard for
you to guess whom I mean.[5] I have not yet seen her

---

[1] Dr. Robert Freind (*supra*, p. 299).

[2] *I.e.*, that they may not be supplied with precedents to use against
him.

[3] Bolingbroke's wife, Frances Winchcombe, the descendant of the
valiant Jack of Newbury, near which her Bucklebury estate (*supra*,
p. 211) lay, was one of Swift's special favourites, as is more than once
emphasized in the Journal to Stella.

[4] *Supra*, p. 312.

[5] The reference, in Mr. Sichel's opinion (*op. cit.*, i, 161) is to Bolingbroke's father, the "man of pleasure" whom Swift thought it so odd

Grace,[1] but design it in a day or two: we have kept a constant correspondence ever since our misfortunes, and her Grace is pleased to call me sister. There is nobody in the world has a truer respect and value for her than myself. I send this to my friend John,[2] and beg you, when you do me the favour of an answer, to send it to him, who will take care to convey it to me in the country; for your letter lay a long while before it came to my hands. I beg you to look with a friendly eye upon all my faults and blots in this letter, and that you will believe me, what I really am,

Your most faithful humble servant,

F. B.

CCCLXI. [*Original.*[3]]

SWIFT TO ARCHDEACON WALLS

Trim, *May* 6, 1716.

I AM at the Doctor's[4] house, where with great difficulty I have got half a sheet of paper to write to you. I was so hurt in my thigh with riding that being on horseback made my sore inflame, and I can now neither ride nor walk, but am mending, and hope to be on horseback in two or three days. Pray take some opportunity of seeing Tom Staunton and what he has done with Mr. Pratt about my papers.[5] Desire Mrs. Brent[6] to get the cellar window, where the hogsheads are, closer stopped, and the other if it wants. Gillespy[7] talked of his intending to be here in great haste; I hope he has given you some money in all this time. Tell Robin Grattan[8] I had his letter, and thank him for his

should be father of a secretary of state (" Prose Works," ii, 52). Two months later he was raised by the Whigs to the peerage as Viscount St. John.

[1] *I.e.*, the Duchess of Ormond.   [2] *I.e.*, John Barber.
[3] In the possession of Mr. John Murray. See Preface.
[4] *I.e.*, Raymond's. Swift had evidently been away from Dublin for some days.
[5] From a subsequent reference it is evident that the business related to a loan of money, possibly belonging to the Cathedral (see Mason, *op. cit.*, p. 296). Owing to his official position, the Provost's brother (*supra*, vol. i, p. 188, n. 2) was specially qualified to advise in such a matter.
[6] *Supra*, p. 256.   [7] *Supra*, p. 271.   [8] *Supra*, p. 262.

manuscript, which has been printed in every newspaper. My humble service to Gossip Doll, and the ladies. Are our two Bishops come to town? Will Clogher take Tuam, as the news says?[1] I am going to dinner. Adieu.

I have done dinner, and have nothing further to say to you. Dr. Raymond gives his service to you and the ladies. So does Warburton and Mr. Preston.

Addressed—To the Reverend Mr. Archdeacon Walls at his house over against the Blue-Coat Hospital in Queen Street, Dublin.

CCCLXII. [*Original.*[2]]

SWIFT TO ARCHDEACON WALLS

Martry,[3] *May* 15, 1716.

IF anything happen, to make you easy, *aliquisque malo fuit usus in illo.* If the sinecure be as you say, and that you are sure of it, and your friends advise you, and that after mature thinking it will make you perfectly easy, I believe I shall be brought to comply that Chamberlain should have St. Luke's and Dopping St. Nicholas's.[4] If that could be com-

---

[1] Archbishop Vesey (*supra*, p. 238, n. 2) had died on 28 March. Neither of "our two Bishops," *i.e.*, Ashe and Stearne, benefited by his death.

[2] In the possession of Mr. John Murray. See Preface.

[3] Swift had evidently sufficiently recovered (*supra*, p. 314) to admit of his proceeding from Trim to Martry on a visit to Mrs. Chetwode (*supra*, p. 300).

[4] Walls had been successful in securing the prospect of preferment for himself in the moves on Bolton's promotion to the Chancellorship (*supra*, p. 279, n. 5), and had been promised a rectory in the south of Ireland about to become vacant by Carr's elevation to the episcopal bench (*supra*, p. 312, n. 3), if Swift would appoint Chamberlain to the vacant cure of St. Nicholas. This Swift was unwilling still to do, but proposed to transfer Anthony Dopping, who was a brother of Swift's friend, Sam Dopping (*supra*, vol. i, p. 191), and who became, like their father, a bishop, from St. Luke's parish, which he had been given by Stearne, to that of St. Nicholas, and to give the former to Chamberlain. It is curious to find that Archbishop King, owing to the change of government, had been on Bolton's promotion as strong in pressing the claims of the Crown to the presentation as he had formerly

passed it would be a real pleasure to me, because I might have an opportunity of obliging a brother of Sam Dopping, whom I love and esteem above most men,[1] and therefore I beg you will push it, but you may trust me I shall not be backward in straining a point to do you good.

Pray be so kind to press Mr. Staunton to finish that affair with Mr. Pratt, and if he does not like the security I empower him to act as he would in his own case, or the case of a client, and I shall be extremely thankful and obliged to him.[2] Mr. Bindon[3] promised to preach a turn for me; I believe mine is Sunday next or the following. Some of the farmers at Laracor pretended they could not pay me till Gillespy came down, and a hint has been given me that the reason was he had some dealings with them for corn, which if it be true will breed a perplexity in my affairs that I shall not endure. Pray tell him what I say, and know the bottom of it, and give him a little advice.

I go to-morrow to Rochfort's if it be fair; when you write pray direct to me there to Mr. Rochfort's at Gaulstown in Westmeath; if there be a more particular direction Robin Grattan will tell you, to whom send the enclosed to Abbey Street.[4] This weather hath kept me from riding. The farmers here say the rain is come too late for the winter corn. You must be so kind to send the maid three shillings a week to live on. My humble duty to the two Bishops, and service to Gossip Doll and the ladies. I would fain have Sam Holt[5] paid his twenty-five pounds he lent me to buy wine.

Addressed—To Mr. Archdeacon Walls.

been in asserting the right of the Chapter (King to Addison, 18 December, 1714).

[1] Sam Dopping had proved himself a stout Tory and was one of Chancellor Phipps's great allies. In the "Long History of a Short Session" the Chief Secretary is censured for not nominating him as Speaker when Levinge was rejected, instead of consenting to the election of Brodrick.

[2] *Supra*, p. 314.

[3] Thomas Bindon, a Fellow of Trinity College, Dublin, who became afterwards Dean of Limerick.

[4] A street in the northern part of Dublin, so called from its being originally the approach to the Abbey of St. Mary's, one of the most important conventual establishments in Ireland.

[5] Sam Holt was a clergyman, and afterwards enjoyed a plurality of Church preferment, including one of the prebends in Swift's cathedral.

CCCLXIII. [*Original.*[1]]

SWIFT TO ARCHDEACON WALLS

Gaulstown, *June* 6, 1716.

I HAD yours this day sent me by express from Trim. I suppose there is no great haste about the instrument from me.[2] The government may lodge a warrant for a fiat for you in Chamberlain's hands, and then all will be safe. But I would have you inquire a little more carefully into the value and nature of the sinecure; for it would vex me to the heart to give that man a living without any substantial benefit to you. I hear it is near Cork;[3] it will be easy for you to get an answer from thence, and there can be no possible inconvenience if the warrant for the fiat be in Chamberlain's keeping. I do here promise, and will give it under my hand, that if the sinecure be what can be thought sufficient I will nominate him. And I have not been yet taxed with breaking my word. You may have sufficient information in ten days or a fortnight. I speak purely for your interest, and when you are satisfied in the value of the thing by good hands, and that the warrant for the fiat is drawn, I will come to town myself or [give] sufficient power. Worrall has my seal.

This is a plain path for the matter to go in, [and any-] body can tell you that there is no need of any [kind of] hurry. If the fiat itself was drawn there [would be a] consequence in it; but I would have no step [taken without] better information, and let Carr[4] tell you what he [knows]. My service to Gossip Doll and the ladies.

Addressed—To Archdeacon Walls.

---

[1] In the possession of Mr. John Murray. See Preface.
[2] *Supra*, p. 315.
[3] The "sinecure" was the rectory of Castlehaven, well known for its important harbour, in the county of Cork.
[4] As the former holder of the sinecure (*supra*, p. 315, n. 4).

CCCLXIV. [*Original.*[1]]

SWIFT TO ARCHDEACON WALLS

Gaulstown, *June* 14, 1716.

I AM not of opinion that your affair requires so much haste as you speak of.[2] If Mr. Chamberlain has the warrant by him in your name, it may keep this month without any manner of consequence, or a great deal longer, which I know very well, and my Lord Chief Baron now confirms to me. I have several reasons to keep me from returning till Tuesday sennight,[3] when I intend, God willing, to be in town. You may count upon it that it lies very much at my heart to make you easy. I writ by Paddy to the Bishop of Dromore, to have his judgement in one point; after which I will absolutely determine, and it is of no consequence at all when the Duke[4] or Archbishop go for England. My service to Gossip Doll.

Addressed—To Mr. Archdeacon Walls.

CCCLXV. [*Nichols.*]

SWIFT TO ARCHBISHOP KING

Gaulstown, *June* 17, 1716.

MY LORD,[5]
I HAVE an account by this post that your Grace intends in two or three days to go for England. I heartily wish you

---

[1] In the possession of Mr. John Murray. See Preface.
[2] *Supra*, p. 317.   [3] The 26th.
[4] The Duke of Grafton, then one of the Lords Justices of Ireland. To that position he had been appointed in the previous autumn, together with the Earl of Galway, and had come to Ireland shortly before the meeting of the Irish Parliament (*supra*, p. 301, n. 1).
[5] Since the appointment of Lindsay to the primacy the relations between Archbishop King and Swift had evidently been far from cordial, and after Swift's return to Ireland their conflicting interests had created much friction between them. The fault seems to have been largely on the Archbishop's side. In regard to civil affairs his distrust of Swift has been already seen with respect to the seizure of Swift's letters (*supra*, p. 276, n. 7), and in regard to Church affairs it

a good voyage, and a speedy return, with a perfect recovery of your health, and success in all your undertakings for the service of the Church. I lately applied myself to some persons who I thought had credit with your Grace, that they would prevail on you to consent that Mr. Dopping should have St. Nicholas, and that Mr. Chamberlain, upon surrendering a sinecure, fallen by the late promotion, to Mr. Walls, might succeed to St. Luke's;[1] and having heard your Grace was not disinclined to this scheme, I thought you had authority enough to make it go down with Mr. Chamberlain, who would be a gainer by the exchange, and, having already a plentiful fortune, would have as good an opportunity of showing his abilities in one parish as in the other.

I should add my humble entreaties to your Grace to consent to this proposal, if I had not so many reasons to apprehend that it would succeed just so much the worse for my solicitation. I confess, every friend I have discovered long before myself that I had wholly lost your Grace's favour, and this to a degree that all whom I was disposed to serve were sure to thrive the worse for my friendship to them; particularly, I have been assured that Mr. Walls would not have failed of the prebend of Malahidert, if he had not been thought too much attached to me;[2] for it is alleged, that, according to your Grace's own scheme of uniting the prebends to the vicarages, it would almost have fallen to him of course, and I remember the poor gentleman had always a remote hope of that prebend whenever Dr. Moore should quit it.   Mr. Walls came lately

was no less marked.   From a letter addressed by the Archbishop to Lord Sunderland (29 October, 1714) it appears that Bolton's appointment as Chancellor of St. Patrick's was in a great measure due to the Archbishop's wish to have a watch-dog in the Chapter: "Besides, I believe, your Excellency knows Dr. Swift, the Dean of my Cathedral, and what I am to expect from him, and except I have such a person as Dr. Bolton in a station in the Chapter I am afraid my affairs there will not go very well." It is therefore probable, as Mason says (*op. cit.*, p. 292), that the disputes in the Chapter were fomented by the Archbishop, and Swift's expostulation in this letter cannot be considered other than a temperate and deserved rebuke.

[1] *Supra*, p. 315.
[2] Moore, the occupant of the prebend which Walls coveted so much (*supra*, p. 132), had died on 1 June. The duties of Mulhuddart were evidently discharged by Walls as vicar of the adjoining parish of Castleknock.

down to me to Trim upon that disappointment, and I was
so free as to ask him, whether he thought my friendship
had done him hurt; but he was either so meek, or so fearful of offending, that he would by no means impute his
misfortune to anything beside his want of merit, and some
misrepresentations; which latter I must confess to have
found with grief, to have more than once influenced you
against some, who by their conduct to your Grace have
deserved a quite different treatment. With respect to myself, I can assure your Grace, that those who are most in
your confidence make it no manner of secret, that several
clergymen have lost your Grace's favour by their civilities
to me.

I do not say anything of this by way of complaint, which
I look upon to be an office too mean for any man of spirit
and integrity, but merely to know whether it be possible
for me to be upon any better terms with your Grace, without which I shall be able to do very little good in the small
station I am placed. The friendship I had with the late
Ministry, and the trust they were pleased to repose in me,
were chiefly applied to do all the service to the Church that
I was able. I had no ill designs, nor ever knew any in
them. I was the continual advocate for all men of merit
without regard of party; for which it is known enough that
I was sufficiently censured by some warm men, and in a
more particular manner for vindicating your Grace in an
affair where I thought you were misrepresented, and you
seemed desirous to be set right.[1] And upon the whole, this
I can faithfully assure your Grace, that I was looked upon
as a trimmer, and one that was providing against a change,
for no other reason but defending your Grace's principles
in Church and State, which I think might pass for some
kind of merit in one who never either had or expected any
mark of your favour. And I cannot but think it hard, that
I must upon all occasions be made uneasy in my station,
have dormant prebends revived on purpose to oppose me,[2]
and this openly acknowledged by those who say they act
under your Grace's direction. That instead of being able

---

[1] In regard to the report that the Archbishop had compared Harley
to Piso (*supra*, vol. i, p. 255).

[2] The reference is to the prebend of Timothan, to which no appointment had been made from the reign of Queen Elizabeth until then.

to do a good office to a deserving friend, as all my predecessors have been, it is thought a matter of accusation for
anyone to cultivate my acquaintance. This I must think
to be hard treatment, and though I regard not the consequences as far as they are intended to affect myself, yet
your Grace may live to lament those which from thence
may happen to the Church.

When I was first made dean, your Grace was pleased, in
a very condescending manner, to write to me that you
desired my friendship.[1] I was then in the service of the
Ministry, and the peace was made; and if I had any share
in their ill designs I was then guilty, but I do not know
that I have ever done anything since to forfeit your good
opinion. I confess I lost many friends by the Queen's
death, but I will never imagine your Grace to be of the
number. I have given your Grace too long a trouble. I
humbly beg your blessing, and shall remain ever, with the
greatest truth and respect, my Lord,

Your Grace's most dutiful and most humble servant,

JON. SWIFT.

CCCLXVI. [*Original.*[2]]

SWIFT TO ARCHDEACON WALLS

Gaulstown, *June* 18, 1716.

I SAT up till four this morning writing dispatches by
Mr. Rochfort who left us about two hours ago, and is not
very certain that he may not go for England to-morrow
about an appeal in some trial there. With him went a
large packet directed to you, containing letters to the
Archbishop, Bishop of Dromore, Dr. Travers[3] and Mrs.
Johnson, but not a word to yourself, because I had no
mind to say anything to you, and am now in no condition
to write, being quite disordered with scribbling over a dozen
letters at a heat and want of sleep, which I shall endeavour
to make up after I have answered some parts of your
letter.

I should be very glad to serve Mr. Dopping on his

---

[1] *Supra*, p. 27.
[2] In the possession of Mr. John Murray. See Preface.
[3] *Supra*, p. 273, n. 3.

brother's account,[1] and the man himself hath been always personally obliging to me, and I believe him an honest man that loves his own interest, but would not do an ill or a base thing to compass it, and being a man acceptable to that party I was glad of the opportunity; but you must needs suppose that if it were *res integra* I would certainly give it to yourself to hold with Castleknock, or if that were not possible that I have several people whom I love very well and know much better than I do Mr. Dopping, and who want it much more. Then in my conscience, I think Mr. Chamberlain doth not deserve such a living nor is equal to such a cure, being a man of very low parts and understanding, with a very high conceit of himself and party-mad into the bargain.[2]

I have let the Archbishop know my mind very freely in a long letter.[3] I have drawn up all his ill-treatment of me and shown him the injustice and ingratitude of it; how he is governed by favourites who misrepresent things and persons to him, and that if the Queen had lived he and his favourites would have used me better. I have reproached him with the dormant prebend, and other steps on purpose to oppose me; that his favourites openly profess that no man that is well with me should have any encouragement; that several persons assured me nothing else could have hindered you from Malahidert, wherein he broke his own scheme on purpose because you were my friend; that I tasked you with it, but your great meekness or fear of offending, made you impute your disappointment only to your want of merit, or misrepresentation of your enemies. I minded him how many friends I had lost, or at least gained enemies by supporting and defending his character in the late reign; that my intimacy and confidence with the late Ministry could be no just reason for his using me ill; because he had writ to me upon my being made dean to desire my friendship, and then the peace was made, and all the mischief done, if I had a hand in any. I said it was impossible for me to do any good in my station while I was upon this foot with him—with twenty other things I now

[1] *Supra*, p. 316.
[2] On the other hand the Archbishop says Chamberlain was a good man and an excellent preacher, and was not fairly used by the Tory government (King to Addison, 18 December, 1714).
[3] *Supra*, p. 318.

forget, as that he might make Chamberlain comply if he pleased, etc.

It is impossible for Dougatt to keep his honesty in the way and company he is.[1] The Bishop of Dromore did not move this matter of Dopping to me, but I wholly to him, and I blame him for dropping it, and that he hath not zeal enough to make the Archbishop cram it down Chamberlain's throat. How would it be inconvenient to the Archbishop to remove Chamberlain from his present cure of St. Nicholas? He may have a thousand Whig curates in Dublin. I told the Archbishop that Chamberlain was rich, and only wanted an opportunity to show his parts, which he might do as well at St. Luke's. I own he would get little by it, but he hath a further dependence on the Archbishop, and obligations to him, and therefore if his Grace pleased, the matter might easily be compassed. If Mr. Bolton apprehends I do him a kindness, and will give me any ironical thanks on that score, I shall either bear them or return them as well as I am able.

I know not what schemes you could form for Mr. Dopping unless St. Nicholas were not attended with a lawsuit. In that case I could wish Dopping had St. Nicholas and the sinecure, Chamberlain had Castleknock, and you Dopping's country living and St. Luke's; but as things are now this is all but vision. I have sent my last determination in the packet directed to you this morning. I have but two intentions, the first to do you a service, and the other to take some care of my own credit, and the good opinion of my friends. It is not hatred to Chamberlain or love to Mr. Dopping that makes me refractory. I could soon get over both of those. I believe you are uneasy enough, and so am I upon your account as well as my own. I am certain Chamberlain has made good use of what he has picked from you by your fears and uneasiness. He thinks I have personal malice to him, but he does himself too much honour. I do not so much as depise him. My ends were to make as good a bargain for you as I could, and to have some regard to my own credit.

I have said all I can think on. It is now between eight

---

[1] Robert Dougatt, who was Archdeacon of Dublin and a nephew of Archbishop King, is said to have been a chief opponent of Swift in the Chapter.

and nine, and I doubt I shall not pay myself in sleep. I leave the rest to your black Privy Councillor—be not frightened, I mean only Mrs. Johnson. My humble service to Gossip Doll and the ladies. I just now had a letter from the Bishop of Dromore; it was kept by going to Mullingar instead of Kinnegad.[1] My duty to him, what I writ this morning to him in the packet directed to you must serve for an answer. Pray send the enclosed to Dr. Coghill.[2]

Addressed—To Mr. Archdeacon Walls.

CCCLXVII. [*Copy.*[3]]

ARCHBISHOP KING TO SWIFT

June 20, 1716.

REVEREND SIR,

I AM favoured with yours of [the] 17th inst., by which I am heartily sorry to find that there are some very industrious to sow dissension between you and me, and do not wonder at it, because the same was much laboured in your predecessor's time as he himself can tell you, but he was aware of the snare and avoided it. I entreat you to do the like, and not give any credit to these false misrepresentations that self-interested persons make. Assure yourself they are neither your friends, nor mine, nor the Church's. Pray therefore give no ear to such whisperers as separate chief friends.

As to the business of Dr. Walls, Mr. Chamberlain, and Mr. Dopping, I am conscious to myself that in order to give you satisfaction, I have gone as far as either prudence or justice will allow me, and I am afraid a little farther. I never used my authority with any clergyman to oblige him to go farther than was consistent with his inclinations and interest, nor do I believe it is advisable I should.

I should be glad of an opportunity to convince you of

---

[1] Mullingar is the assize town of Westmeath, and Kinnegad a village on the main road from Dublin to it.

[2] Dr. Marmaduke Coghill, the Judge of the Prerogative Court.

[3] It is preserved, together with copies of other letters from Archbishop King, in Armagh Library in a volume lettered " MSS. Hibernica, vol. i." For a transcript of the copy, and permission to make use of it here, I am indebted to Dr. Morgan (*supra*, vol. i, p. 60).

the reality of my earnest desire and intention to live in all
good understanding with you, as being sensible it is necessary for our common quiet and good, and therefore again
entreat you to lay aside all surmises, and believe that I am
sincerely, Reverend Sir,

Yours etc.,

W. D[UBLIN].

I intend for the Bath, God willing, Tuesday [1] or Wednesday next. If you have any service of me in England you
may command me.

Dean Swift.

CCCLXVIII. [*Elwin.*]

ALEXANDER POPE TO SWIFT

June 20, 1716.

I CANNOT suffer a friend [2] to cross the Irish seas, without
bearing a testimony from me of the constant esteem and
affection I am both obliged and inclined to have for you. It is
better he should tell you than I, how often you are in our
thoughts and in our cups, and how I learn to sleep less and
drink more, whenever you are named among us. I look
upon a friend in Ireland as upon a friend in the other world,
whom, Popishly speaking, I believe constantly well-dis-
posed towards me, and ready to do me all the good he can,
in that state of separation, though I hear nothing from him,
and make addresses to him but very rarely. A Protestant
divine cannot take it amiss that I treat him in the same
manner with my patron saint.

I can tell you no news, but what you will not sufficiently
wonder at, that I suffer many things as an author militant,
whereof in your days of probation you have been a sharer,
or you had not arrived at that triumphant state you now
deservedly enjoy in the Church. As for me, I have not the

---

[1] The 26th.

[2] The bearer of this letter was Charles Ford, who had probably
separated from Bolingbroke (*supra*, p. 285) before the latter entered
into the service of the Pretender. He was accompanied to Ireland by
Jervas (*supra*, p. 98), who bore a letter from Pope to Parnell. It was
written on 29 June, and Elwin thinks (*op. cit.*, vii, 461) this letter to
Swift bore originally that date.

least hopes of the cardinalate, though I suffer for my religion in almost every weekly paper. I have begun to take a pique at the Psalms of David, if the wicked may be credited, who have printed a scandalous one in my name.[1] This report I dare not discourage too much, in a prospect I have at present of a post under the Marquis de Langallerie,[2] wherein if I can but do some signal service against the Pope, I may be considerably advanced by the Turks, the only religious people I dare confide in. If it should happen hereafter that I should write for the holy law of Mahomet, I hope it may make no breach between you and me. Every one must live, and I beg you will not be the man to manage the controversy against me. The church of Rome I judge from many modern symptoms, as well as ancient prophecies, to be in a declining condition; that of England will in a short time be scarce able to maintain her own family; so churches sink as generally as banks in Europe, and for the same reason—that religion and trade, which at first were open and free, have been reduced into the management of companies, and the roguery of directors.

I do not know why I tell you all this, but that I always loved to talk to you; but this is not a time for any man to talk to the purpose. Truth is a kind of contraband commodity which I would not venture to export, and therefore the only thing tending that dangerous way which I shall say, is, that I am, and always will be, with the utmost sincerity,

Yours, etc.

CCCLXIX. [*Original.*[3]]

VISCOUNTESS BOLINGBROKE TO SWIFT

London, *August* 4, 1716.

DEAR SIR,

I WISH your last[4] had found me in the country, but, to my misfortune, I am still kept in town, soliciting my unfortunate

---

[1] "An impious and indecent parody of the first Psalm," of which there is no doubt Pope was the author (Elwin, *op. cit.*, vii, 13).
[2] Langallerie was a French officer who had undertaken to lead the Turks against Italy (*ibid.*).
[3] In the British Museum. See Preface.
[4] Probably Swift's reply to her letter of 5 May (*supra*, p. 313).

business.[1] I have found great favour from his Majesty. But form is a tedious thing to wait upon. Since it is my fate, I must bear it with patience, and perfect it if I can; for there is nothing like following business oneself. I am unwilling to stir without the seals, which I hope to have soon. I have been very ill; this place never agreeing with me, and less now than ever, it being prodigious hot weather.

I know not what to say as to one part of yours, only this, that you will forgive the fears of a woman, if she says she is glad it is as it is, though it has almost ruined her.[2] I hope, one time or other, his Majesty will find my Lord has been misrepresented, and, by that means, he may be restored to his country once more with honour; or else, however harsh it may sound out of my mouth, I had rather wear black. These are my real sentiments. I never thought myself, nor my health, of any consequence, till lately; and since you tell me it is so to the unworthy, as you please to term it, I shall take care of it; for the worthy, which I once thought so, they are good for nothing, but to neglect distressed friends. Those few friends I meet with now, are worth a thousand relations, that I found long ago. We have the happiness of odd, half-witted relations, and silly, obstinate, opiniatre friends, that are a severe plague to me.

I never could have the pleasure of talking one moment to the Duchess of Ormond. She had always company, and some that I wish she had not. She is now out of town, and we do not correspond at present. I wish her all happiness, and in better hands as to her business. You have a much better opinion of me than I deserve; but I will study all I can to merit your favour, which you are kind to assure me of. I wish it were possible for us two to meet, that I might assure you, in person, that I am

Yours most faithfully.

Yours came safe: I hope this will to you. There is a lady

---

[1] Lady Bolingbroke was no doubt seeking indemnity for her estate from her husband's attainder. Of a great fortune which she had brought him, the larger part had been either spent or given to him when leaving England ("Portland Manuscripts," vii, *passim*).

[2] The loyalty of Lady Bolingbroke to her husband was marvellous. At that time it is believed he was living with the Marquise de Villette who became his second wife (Sichel, *op. cit.*, ii, 67).

who never forgets you, and a particular friend to me, and has been a great comfort to me in my trouble, I mean my tenant; she is now in the country, to my grief.

CCCLXX. [*Elwin.*]

Swift to Alexander Pope

August 30, 1716.

I HAD the favour of yours by Mr. Ford,[1] of whom, before any other question relating to your health, or fortune, or success as a poet, I inquired your principles in the common form, " Is he a Whig or a Tory?" I am sorry to find they are not so well tallied to the present juncture as I could wish. I always thought the terms of *facto* and *jure* had been introduced by the poets, and that possession of any sort in kings was held an unexceptionable title in the courts of Parnassus. If you do not grow a perfect good subject in all its present latitudes, I shall conclude you are become rich, and able to live without dedications to men in power, whereby one great inconvenience will follow, that you and the world and posterity will be utterly ignorant of their virtues. For, either your brethren have miserably deceived us these hundred years past, or power confers virtue as naturally as five of your Popish sacraments do grace.

You sleep less, and drink more. But your master Horace was *vini somnique benignus*; and, as I take it, both are proper for your trade. As to wine, there are a thousand poetical texts to confirm the one; and as to the other, I know it was anciently the custom to sleep in temples for those who would consult the oracles, " who dictates to me slumbering," etc.[2] You are an ill Catholic, or a worse geographer, for I can assure you, Ireland is not paradise, and I appeal even to any Spanish divine, whether addresses were ever made to a friend in hell, or purgatory? And who are

---

[1] *Supra*, p. 325. This reply was evidently sent to Pope by Ford, who was then setting out on a journey to Rome (*infra*, p. 335).

[2] " Paradise Lost," book ix, verse 23. In a footnote to this passage Nichols ("Works," xvi, 142) refers to a copy of " Paradise Lost " in which Swift had inserted marginal notes, " explanatory rather than critical," for the use of Stella and Miss Dingley.

all those enemies you hint at? I can only think of Curll, Gildon, Squire Burnet, Blackmore,[1] and a few others, whose fame I have forgot. Fools, in my opinion, are as necessary for a good writer, as pen, ink, and paper. And besides, I would fain know whether every draper does not show you three or four damned pieces of stuff to set off his good one? However, I will grant that one thorough bookselling rogue is better qualified to vex an author, than all his contemporary scribblers in critic or satire, not only by stolen copies of what was incorrect or unfit for the public, but by downright laying other men's dulness at your door. I had a long design upon the ears of that Curll, when I was in credit; but the rogue would never allow me a fair stroke at them, although my penknife was ready drawn and sharp. I can hardly believe the relation of his being poisoned,[2] although the historian pretends to have been an eye-witness; but I beg pardon, sack might do it, although ratsbane would not. I never saw the thing you mention as falsely imputed to you;[3] but I think the frolics of merry hours, even when we are guilty, should not be left to the mercy of our best friends, until Curll and his resemblers are hanged.

With submission to the better judgement of you and your friends, I take your project of an employment under Langallerie to be idle and unnecessary. Have a little patience, and you will find more merit and encouragement at home, by the same methods. You are ungrateful to your country; quit but your own religion, and ridicule ours, and that will allow you a free choice for any other, or for none at all, and

---

[1] Against those whom he mentions by name, Swift bore a grudge on his own account as well as on Pope's. Edmund Curll had exposed Swift to the chaff of Oxford "and the rest" by the trash which he had scraped up and published with Swift's "name at large" (*supra*, vol. i, p. 298, n. 2, and "Prose Works," ii, 176); Sir Richard Blackmore had pronounced the author of the "Tale of a Tub" to be "an impious buffoon" (Elwin and Courthope, *op. cit.*, viii, 22), and no doubt it was not without a sense of personal injury that Swift had called Bishop Burnet's son "a violent party jackanapes," and depreciated Charles Gildon's abilities when attacking the opinions of which Gildon was the exponent ("Prose Works," *passim*).

[2] The reference is to the tract entitled: "A full and true Account of a horrid and barbarous Revenge by Poison on the body of Mr. Edmund Curll, Bookseller, with a faithful copy of his Last Will and Testament published by an Eyewitness," which was written by Pope.

[3] *Supra*, p. 326, n. 1.

pay you well into the bargain. Therefore pray do not run and disgrace us among the Turks, by telling them you were forced to leave your native home because we would oblige you to be a Christian; whereas we will make it appear to all the world, that we only compelled you to be a Whig.

There is a young ingenious Quaker in this town who writes verses to his mistress, not very correct, but in a strain purely what a poetical Quaker should do, commending her look and habit, etc.[1] It gave me a hint that a set of Quaker pastorals might succeed, if our friend Gay could fancy it, and I think it a fruitful subject; pray hear what he says. I believe farther, the pastoral ridicule is not exhausted, and that a porter, footman, or chairman's pastoral might do well. Or what think you of a Newgate pastoral, among the whores and thieves there?[2]

Lastly, to conclude, I love you never the worse for seldom writing to you.[3] I am in an obscure scene, where you know neither thing nor person. I can only answer yours, which I promise to do after a sort, whenever you think proper to employ me. But I can assure you the scene and the times have depressed me wonderfully, for I will impute no defect to those two paltry years which have slipped by since I had the happiness to see you. I am with the truest esteem,

Yours, etc.

CCCLXXI. [*Original.*[4]]

THE DUCHESS OF ORMOND TO SWIFT

September 14, 1716.

SIR,

I HAD the ill-fortune to miss of that letter you upbraided me with.[5] I had deserved any reproaches you could make

---

[1] The Quaker is said to have been a linen draper named George Rooke. He was possibly related to Swift (*supra*, vol. i, p. 367).

[2] This suggestion is said to have given rise to the "Beggars' Opera" (Elwin and Courthope, *op. cit.*, vii, 17).

[3] Evidently the letter, which has been lost (*supra*, p. 286), and the one to which this is a reply (*supra*, p. 325) were the only letters which Pope had written to Swift since the latter came to Ireland.

[4] In the British Museum. See Preface.

[5] Probably a reply to her letter of 23 January (*supra*, p. 304).

me, if it had come to my hands, and I not made due acknowledgments for your inquiries after me. I will make you wish you had not been so angry with me; for I will scrawl out myself, what you would rather Betty or my maid had, for they would have made shorter work of it; but I will answer every part of yours, that you obliged me with by Mr. Ford.[1]

First, as to the lady you mention,[2] the reason I had not seen her in a great while was, my being in the country. To tell you the truth, I believe her husband has been a better courtier, than either she, or any of her sex could be; because men have it in their power to serve, and I believe hers has effectually done what lay in him.[3]

You kindly ask how my affairs go. There is yet no end of them, and God only knows when there will be. For when everything was thought done, a sudden blast had blown all hopes away, and then they give me fresh expectations. In the mean time I am forced to live upon the borrow; my goods all taken away, that I shall not have so much as a bed to lie upon, but what I must buy, and no money of my own to do that with; so that you may imagine me in a cheerful way. I pray God support me.

The gentleman[4] you inquired after is very well now. The illness you heard he had, he has been subject to a good while. What you desire, I wish were in the power of either his brother[5] or me; but all will go from both of us of every kind. Only they say, that the clothes upon my back I may perhaps call my own, and that is all. I was obliged to leave the country. I was so ill there, that if I had not come to the physicians, I cannot tell what might have happened. My daughter is your most humble servant, and is pretty well in health.

Am not I one of my word, and troubled you twice as long as you would have wished? But you will find by this,

---

[1] *Supra*, p. 328.   [2] *I.e.*, Lady Bolingbroke (*supra*, p. 326).
[3] The Duchess implies that by treachery to the Pretender, Boling-broke had earned the favour shown by George I to his wife in regard to her estate.
[4] *I.e.*, Ormond.
[5] *I.e.*, the Earl of Arran. Swift mentions him several times in writing to Stella, and says that he had very good sense, but was negligent of his own interests (" Prose Works," *passim*).

that a woman's pen should no more be set at work than her tongue, for she never knows when to let either of them rest. But my paper puts me in mind, that I have but just room to tell you, I wish much to see you here, if it could be with your satisfaction; and that I am, with great sincerity, Sir,

Your faithful humble servant.

CCCLXXII. [*Original.*[1]]

SWIFT TO ARCHDEACON WALLS

Trim, *October* 4, 1716.[2]

IT was very foolish in Joe[3] to alarm you as if I were in danger, as the Doctor[4] tells me, though he would not show your letter, nor do I know a word in it. I was ill but three days, and have been well since yesterday morning. I hope Gossip Doll is so. The Doctor tells me she is brought to bed, but not the sex; he therefore supposes it a girl. The weather mends, and I have yet thoughts of going to Mr. Rochfort's,[5] if it continues fair. Pray spur up Gillespy to get some arrear money. The Doctor said he expected you here last night. I should have thought you mad. Do you not believe that if I had any sickness of consequence I should have got a coach to come to town, or sent there for a doctor? I assure you I have been very careful of myself,

---

[1] In the possession of Mr. John Murray. See Preface.

[2] According to the theory of the Dean of St. Patrick's (*supra*, vol. i, p. xxiv, n. 2), it was during the preceding month that Swift went through the alleged form of marriage with Stella, if the tradition be true that the ceremony was performed in 1716 by Bishop Ashe at Clogher. The contents of this letter indicate, however, that Swift had been at Trim for some time before it was written, and that he had come thither from Dublin. It seems to me more probable that if Swift visited Clogher at all that year, it was during August, after the appointment of a Sub-Dean, as mentioned by Dean Bernard, on 28 July; but the references to Bishop Ashe in the Correspondence afford some ground for the conclusion that the only meetings between the Bishop and Swift were in Dublin.

[3] *I.e.*, Beaumont (*supra*, p. 276).   [4] *I.e.*, Raymond.

[5] *I.e.*, to Gaulstown (*supra*, p. 280).

and so have my friends been of me. I wish I had the deeds,[1]
or I shall lose all [this] year's opportunity of planting. My
service to the ladies. I hope they are well. Do you hear
anything of Jervas's going; for I hate to be in town while
he is there?[2]

Yours etc.

Addressed—To the Reverend Mr. Archdeacon Walls, at
his house over against the Blue-Coat Hospital in Queen
Street, Dublin.

CCCLXXIII. [*Original.*[3]]

VISCOUNT BOLINGBROKE TO SWIFT

October 23 [O.S. 12], 1716.

IT is a very great truth, that, among all the losses which I
have sustained, none affected me more sensibly than that of
your company and correspondence; and yet, even now, I
should not venture to write to you, did not you provoke
me to it.[4] A commerce of letters between two men who
are out of the world, and who do not care one farthing to
return into it again, must be of little moment to the State;
and yet I remember enough of that world to know, that
the most innocent things become criminal in some men, as
the most criminal pass applauded in others. Your letter
breathes the same spirit as your conversation, at all times
inspired, even when the occasions of practising the severest
rules of virtuous fortitude seemed most remote; if such

---

[1] By means of a grant from the Board of First Fruits, Swift had
arranged to purchase from Mr. Percival (*supra*, p. 289), twenty acres
of land as an addition to the existing glebe at Laracor. On June 22
the purchase had been approved by the Board subject to the opinion
of counsel on the title (Minutes in P.R.O. of Ireland).

[2] Whether Swift's dislike to be near Jervas (*supra*, p. 325, n. 2) was
due to that artist's ardent Whiggism or to the demands which he
made on his client's time does not appear. There is no doubt that
during his visits to Ireland Jervas began at least one portrait of Swift
(see Sir F. Falkiner's Essay, "Prose Works," xii, 12).

[3] In the British Museum. See Preface.

[4] Swift had evidently sent a letter to Bolingbroke by Ford (*supra*,
p. 328).

occasions could ever seem remote to men, who were under the direction of your able and honest friend Sir Roger.[1]

To write about myself is no agreeable task, but your commands are sufficient at once to determine and excuse me. Know, therefore, that my health is far better than it has been a great while; that the money which I brought over with me will hold out some time longer; and that I have secured a small fund, which will yield in any part of the world a revenue sufficient for one, *qui peut se retrancher même avec plaisir dans la médiocrité*. I use a French expression, because I have not one that pleases me ready in English. During several months after leaving that obscure retreat, into which I had thrown myself last year, I went through all the mortifying circumstances imaginable. At present I enjoy, as far as I consider myself, great complacency of mind; but this inward satisfaction is embittered, when I consider the condition of my friends. They are got into a dark hole, where they grope about after blind guides, stumble from mistake to mistake, jostle against one another and dash their heads against the wall, and all this to no purpose. For assure yourself that there is no returning to light; no going out, but by going back.

My style is mystic, but it is your trade to deal in mysteries, and therefore I had neither comment nor excuse. You will understand me; and I conjure you to be persuaded that if I could have half an hour's conversation with you, for which I would barter whole hours of life, you would stare, haul your wig, and bite paper more than ever you did in your life. Adieu, dear friend; may the kindest influence of Heaven be shed upon you. Whether we may ever meet again, that Heaven only knows; if we do, what millions of things shall we have to talk over. In the mean while, believe that nothing sits so near my heart as my country and my friends; and that among these you ever had, and ever shall have, a principal place.

If you write to me, direct " A Monsieur Charlot, chez Monsieur Cantillon, banquier, rue de l'Arbre Sec." Once more adieu.

[1] *I.e.*, Oxford.

CCCLXXIV. [*Original.*[1]]

CHARLES FORD TO SWIFT

Paris, *October* 28 [O.S. 17, 1716].

SIR,

IF I was to see you again, you would give twice as much as you offered six weeks ago,[2] not to have seen me. By the same rule, you might afford something not to hear from me; but the enclosed[3] came this morning to me, and I could not send it away, without adding a few lines in the cover. They are not to put you again into the spleen, but only to ask how you do, and how you employ yourself? Do the great designs go on at Laracor?[4] Or have the rains put a stop to your improvements, as well as to my journey? It will cost you but a penny,[5] and a few minutes to answer these questions; and in return you shall know anything you desire to know of me in my travels. I shall go on as soon as we have five or six days' sunshine to dry the roads, and make the finest country in the world supportable. I am laughed at here, when I talk of travelling, and yet of waiting for fair weather; but to me the journey is the greatest part of the pleasure. And whereas my companion is continually wishing himself at Rome, I wish Rome was a thousand leagues farther that I might have more way to pass in France and Italy. If you will do me the favour to write to me, direct to be left with Mr. Cantillon, banker in Paris.

Addressed—To the Rev. Dr. Swift, Dean of St. Patrick's, at his house in Dublin, Ireland.

---

[1] In the British Museum. See Preface.
[2] When Swift gave him the letter to take to Pope (*supra*, p. 328).
[3] The letter from Bolingbroke (*supra*, p. 333).
[4] *Supra*, p. 333, n. 1.
[5] Presumably the cost of the paper, as the postage would be paid by the recipient.

CCCLXXV. [*Sheridan.*]

Swift to Archbishop King

Dublin, *November* 13, 1716.

My Lord,[1]

The reason I never gave your Grace the trouble of a letter, was, because it could only be a trouble, without either entertainment or use; for I am so much out, even of this little world, that I know not the commonest occurrences in it; neither do I now write to your Grace upon any sort of business, for I have nothing to ask but your blessing and favourable thoughts; only I conceived it ought not to be said, that your Grace was several months absent in England, without one letter from the Dean to pay his respects. My schemes are all circumscribed by the Cathedral, and the liberties about it, where nothing of moment happened since your Grace left it, except the election of Mr. Chamberlain to St. Nicholas, which passed quietly while I was absent in the country. I am purchasing a glebe, by the help of the Trustees,[2] for the vicarage of Laracor, and I have vanity enough to desire it might be expressed by a clause in the deeds, as one consideration, that I had been instrumental in procuring the first fruits, which was accordingly inserted, but hints were given it would not pass.[3] Then the Bishops of Ossory and Killaloe had, as I am told, a sum of money for their labour in that affair, who, upon my arrival at London to negotiate it, were one of them gone to Bath, and the other to Ireland;[4] but it seems more reasonable to give Bishops money for doing nothing, than a private gentleman thanks for succeed-

---

[1] Until the close of this letter Swift ignores completely the subject of his correspondence with the Archbishop in June (*supra*, p. 318), and then he refers only indirectly to it. He had as his object in writing the letter a desire to serve his friend Provost Pratt, and so far as his humour would allow, he selected as subsidiary topics such as were likely to recommend him to the Archbishop in his capacity of a mediator.

[2] *I.e.*, of the First Fruits (*supra*, p. 333, n. 1).

[3] At a meeting of the Board of First Fruits on 12 October the deeds had been ordered to be engrossed, and to be perfected as a committee of the Board might appoint. There is no mention in the minutes of the question to which Swift refers.

[4] *Supra*, vol. i, p. 192.

ing where Bishops have failed. I am only sorry I was not a Bishop, that I might at least have got money.

The Tory clergy here seem ready for conversion, provoked by a parcel of obscure zealots in London, who, as we hear, are setting up a new Church of England by themselves.[1] By our intelligence, it seems to be a complication of as much folly, madness, hypocrisy, and mistake, as ever was offered to the world. If it be understood so on your side, I cannot but think there would be a great opportunity of regaining the body of the clergy to the interest of the Court, who, if they were persuaded by a few good words to throw off their fears, could never think of the Pretender without horror, under whom it is obvious that those refiners would have the greatest credit, and consequently everything be null since the time of the Revolution, and more havoc made in a few months, than the most desponding among the Tories can justly apprehend from the present management in as many years. These at least are, as I am told, the thoughts and reasonings of the High Church people among us, but whether a Court, in the midst of strength and security, will conceive it worth their while to cultivate the dispositions of people in the dust, is out of my reach.

The Bishop of Dromore has never been in town since he went to his diocese,[2] nor does he say anything of coming up. He is in good health.

I was told a week or two ago a confused story of the Anatomy Lecturer at the College turned out by the Provost,[3] and another put in his place.[4] I know not the

---

[1] The reference is to the efforts then being made by the later Nonjurors to maintain an independent Church, with a distinct episcopal succession. Three years before, Dr. George Hickes, the titular Bishop of Thetford, had, with the assistance of two of the Scotch Bishops, consecrated three successors to himself, and these three consecrated two more.

[2] The Irish Parliament was prorogued on 20 June. Probably the Bishop had then gone to his diocese (*supra*, p. 316).

[3] As we have seen, even before Queen Anne's death, Pratt's rule in Trinity College had given dissatisfaction (*supra*, p. 171). He spent evidently more time in London than in Dublin, and according to Stubbs (*op. cit.*, p. 327) he failed to sustain his proper authority in the College. By Archbishop King and his friends he was also censured for not taking sufficiently active steps in suppressing the Jacobite outbursts.

[4] A doctor who had delivered lectures in anatomy for some years was then superseded. He was reappointed in the following year.

particulars, but am assured he is blamed for it both by the Prince[1] and your Grace.[2] I take the Provost to be a very honest gentleman, perfectly good-natured, and the least inclined to speak ill of others of almost any person I have known. He has very good intentions; but the defect seems to be, that his views are short, various, and sudden, and I have reason to think, he hardly ever makes use of any other counsellor than himself. I talked to him of this matter since it was done, and I think his answers satisfied me; but I am an ill retainer of facts wherein I have no concern. My humble opinion is, that it would be much to his own ease, and of theirs who dislike him, if he were put into another station; and if you will not afford him a bishopric, that you will let him succeed some rich country dean. I dare be confident that the Provost had no other end in changing that Lecturer, than a design of improving anatomy as far as he could; for he would never have made such a step as choosing the Prince Chancellor,[3] but from a resolution of keeping as fair as he possibly could with the present powers, in regard both to his ease and his interest; and in hopes of changing a post, wherein, to say the truth, he has been used by judges and governors like any dog, and has suffered more by it in his health and honour, than I, with his patrimonial estate, would think it were worth.

Here has been one Whittingham,[4] in an ordination sermon, calling the clergy a thousand dumb dogs, and treating episcopacy as bad as Boyse;[5] yet no notice at all shall be taken of this, unless to his advantage upon the next vacant bishopric; and wagers are laid already, whether

[1] The Prince of Wales had been appointed Chancellor of the University in room of Ormond.

[2] As Archbishop of Dublin King was one of the visitors.

[3] See the "Parody on the Speech of Dr. Benjamin Pratt to the Prince of Wales" ("Poetical Works," ii, 189). I have much doubt, however, as to its being correctly ascribed to Swift.

[4] Charles Whittingham, who had been appointed to the prebend of Mulhuddart in room of Moore (*supra*, p. 319, n. 2) and who some years later succeeded Dougatt as Archdeacon of Dublin. In the succeeding sentences Swift intimates to the Archbishop that he is not deceived by the platitudes in his Grace's last letter, and that he knows that politics played a part in his Grace's bestowal of patronage.

[5] *Supra*, vol. i, p. 301.

he or one Monck[1] will be the man. But I forget myself; and therefore shall only add, that I am, with the greatest respect and truth, my Lord,

Your Grace's most dutiful and most humble servant, etc.

CCCLXXVI. [*Copy.*[2]]

ARCHBISHOP KING TO SWIFT

Suffolk Street, London, *November* 22, 1716.

SIR,

I READ yours of the 13th instant with great satisfaction. It is not only an advantage to me and you, that there should be a good correspondence between us, but also to the public; and I assure you I had much ado to persuade people here, that we kept any tolerable measures with one another, much less, that there was anything of a good intelligence, and therefore you judged right, that it ought not to be said, that in so many months I had not received any letter from you.

I do a little admire, that those that should be your fastest friends, should be so opposite to acknowledge the service you did in procuring the twentieth parts and first fruits. I know no reason for it, except the zeal I showed to do you justice in that particular from the beginning. But since I only did it, as obliged to bear testimony to the truth, in a matter which I certainly knew, and would have done the same for the worst enemy I had in the world, I see no reason why you should suffer because I, among others, was your witness. But be not concerned, ingratitude is warranted by modern and ancient custom, and it is more honour for a man to have it asked, why he had not a suitable return to his merits, than why he was overpaid. *Bene facere et male audire* is the lot of the best men. If calumny or ingratitude could have put me out of my way, God knows where I should have wandered by this time.

I am glad the business of St. Nicholas is over any way.

[1] Probably the Rev. Thomas Monck, a bachelor of divinity of Dublin University, who held then a living in the south of Ireland (Brody's "Records of Cork," ii, 295).

[2] In King's Correspondence. See Preface.

My inclination was Dr. Walls, that I might have joined the vicarage of Castleknock to the prebend of Malahidert,[1] which would have made a good provision for one man, served the cures better, and yielded more then to the incumbent, than it can do now when in different hands. But I could not compass it without using more power over my clergy, than I am willing to exert. But as I am thankful to you for your condescension in that affair, so I will expect that those, with whom you have complied, should show their sense of it by a mutual return of the like compliance, when there shall be occasion. Such reciprocal kind offices are the ground of mutual confidence and friendship, and the fuel that keeps them alive; and I think nothing can contribute more to our common ease, and the public good, than maintaining these between you and me, and with the clergy.

As to the zealots here, that you observe are setting up a new Church of England. It is true the word is new, but [the] thing has been all along, but kept close with the utmost fury, insomuch that Mr. Dodwell[2] did not know of it, and but very few of their own party, but when they supposed their game sure by the late rebellion, they took courage and spoke out. Dr. Hickes was made Suffragan Bishop of Thetford above twenty years ago, and there are others but not known.[3] They have published lately some of the Doctor's letters of which I have got a sight, and they go on such principles as these: That the Pretender is the only true and lawful king of these realms, and all that have occupied the throne since mere usurpers; that all persons owe allegiance to the Pretender under pain of damnation; that to own the King is a damnable sin and to pray for him like the sin of Balaam, if he had cursed Israel; that to be present at the prayers made for him is the like sin; that all the present Bishops and clergy that own the King are

[1] When urging, on Bolton's promotion, that the claim of the Crown to present to St. Nicholas should be pressed (*supra*, p. 315, n. 4), the Archbishop had suggested that Walls should be nominated, evidently hoping that in order to secure the appointment of his friend, Swift might be induced to surrender the right of himself and his Chapter. The Archbishop speaks of Walls as a grave and good man (King to Addison, 18 December, 1714).

[2] The well-known Nonjuror who had died in 1711.

[3] *Supra*, p. 337, n. 1. Hickes had died in 1715.

in a state of damnation, and that all the acts they perform
are of no use or benefit to the people, and all people that
join with them are in the case of those that joined with
Korah etc. against Moses etc.; that they must continue in
this case till they do penance, confess their guilt, and be admitted to their respective offices by new ordination, or laying
on of hands for confirmation, as the nonjuring church shall
think fit; that many of the English laws are unchristian, such
as that patronages are lay fees, that tithes may become lay
fees, that the King is supreme ordinary, that canons cannot
be made and oblige without the King's consent, *quare im-
pedits* and prohibitions and lastly appeals to the King in
Chancery are of the same nature; that the Revolution is
founded on the doctrine, resistance is lawful, and that
Bishops may be deprived by mere lay power, which are
heresies, and that those who were deprived suffered that on
account of their duty; that when a kingdom is conquered
by a greater power, the subjects are not to make the best
conditions with the conqueror they can, but rather suffer
all their throats to be cut, than own him; that it is better
to be present at the Popish prayers to saints, than at the
service where the King is prayed for.

I suppose that the present government do not owe many
good words to men of such principles, or that there would
be much good done by them. But as to the rest of the
clergy, that own the government and are under a maledic-
tion and excommunication, according to these men's
opinion, and their acts, sacraments and prayers void and
null, or at best of no use or benefit till they repent and
turn Jacobites, they may expect not only a few good words,
but also many good acts of favour and kindness. I verily
believe the bulk of these never designed to bring in the
Pretender, but these that were really in the design overreached them by persuading them that if they would keep
together and stand obstinately against the King and his
Ministry, they would be able to force him to come into
their measures; and by endeavouring this, they not only increased the number of the Jacobites, but brought matters to
such a pass, that the Jacobite plot had more than an even lay
for success. In order to [further] this, great care was taken
to prejudice the people, not only against the Ministry, but
likewise against the King's person and royal family; vile
libels, false, absurd and monstrous calumnies and slanders

were raised, handed about and fomented, and the danger of the Church rung from most pulpits, and at last an actual rebellion raised.

It is by these encouragements that these zealots ventured to show themselves [and] profess openly their principles, and Dr. Hickes's book that lay dormant was printed and dispersed about September 1715 amongst the party. It was by mere accident, that one of them came to be seized last summer, and an abstract of its principles published in the daily current, as I take it. It has put both the Universities here and the Bishops and clergy in a great ferment; all parties think themselves [compelled] to answer it, and several answers are already come abroad; they seem to have the same sense of it, that the clergy with you have according to your representation.

The Court seems mightily pleased with the effect of it, and have resolved to cultivate the opportunity of gaining the clergy by all good offices on their part, as being sensible that this [is] the best and surest method to fix the government on the affection of the people. The Prince manages himself with great civility to all people, and takes particular care that no reputed Tory shall have cause to complain of his reception. I have no fear but upon this ground: I have observed that an injured person can easily forgive, and I frequently have observed such forgiveness to be sincere, but it is much harder for the wrong-doer to be reconciled effectually; now it is manifest that the clergy have highly injured, affronted and abused the Court, but the Court has no ways injured them, and therefore though I am morally certain that the Court is ready and desirous to forgive them, yet I doubt whether the reconciliation will be so easy on the other hand. If these gentlemen should get their Pretender, it [will] fare with them as it did with the cavaliers on the restoration of King Charles the Second, but to be sure whatever favour they might have at first, the whole tide, as it soon did then, would turn into Popery.

As to the Provost's affair I heard a great deal of it, but was resolved not to take it from suspected or insufficient persons, and therefore writ to Dr. Coghill [1] for an account of it. I received one from him, and saw the Provost's account

---

[1] Dr. Coghill (*supra*, p. 324, n. 2) who was one of the members for the University.

to Mr. Molyneux,[1] and received a letter likewise from him.
I frame no judgement on the whole because I am not sure
but it may come before me in another way. Only I cannot but take notice of one passage. Mr. Molyneux has
been and is still the Provost's best friend; he writ him a
letter with the freedom of a friend, gave him his sense of
his proceedings and his reasons. The Provost, instead of
answering the objections and giving such grounds of his
acting as might justify himself, falls on some free and
friendly expressions in the letter, and scolds him most
heartily. This shows what you surmise, that he consults
only his own passions in what he does, and those are evil
counsellors, but Mr. Molyneux is wiser than to break with
[him] on this account. The scheme you mention for him is
the very thing I had projected, and as I believe had secured,
but how will it be after this, I cannot say, but to be sure I
will do my endeavour.

We have a strong report, that my Lord Bolingbroke will
return here, and be pardoned; certainly it must not be for
nothing. I hope he can tell no ill story of you.[2] I think you
have enough for once, and I add only my prayers for you
and am, Reverend Sir,

Your etc.
W. D[UBLIN].

Dean Swift.

CCCLXXVII. [*Original.*[3]]

SWIFT TO ARCHDEACON WALLS

Trim, *December* 6, 1716.

I NEVER was so weary in my life as this last journey, and
so were my horses. I struck in at Galtrim,[4] not being able
to go further. I find Warburton had writ to me not to come

---

[1] Samuel Molyneux (*supra*, vol. i, p. 375, n. 7), who was then secretary to the Prince of Wales.

[2] This remark seems to have been retaliation for Swift's reference
to Whittingham (*supra*, p. 338).

[3] In the possession of Mr. John Murray. See Preface.

[4] A parish adjacent to Trim.

here, because the small-pox was still in this town. But it
appears there is only one woman has it, so I shall continue
here. I wonder that rascal Gillespy does not come down.[1]
I beg you will inquire after him. What can the rascal
mean? I go this morning to inspect and settle the bounds
of the lands at Laracor.[2] Poor Joe is much out of the good
graces of everybody here.[3] I vindicate him sometimes, and
sometimes drop him. This is noble weather for you to walk
in. I hope the boy's picture is finished by this time.[4] My
service to friend Jervas; I heartily wish him a good
voyage. Pray send sweet-heart[5] some money to keep her
alive. Everybody here is well, and Mrs. Raymond and
[Mrs.] Chetwode most particularly give you their service,
and the former insists you should come down for a few
days and be merry with us this Christmas. Do if you can.
Remember, Sunday sennight is my turn at St. Patrick's.

Yours
J. S.

Addressed—To the Reverend Mr. Archdeacon Walls, at
his house over against the Blue-Coat Hospital in Queen
Street, Dublin.

CCCLXXVIII. [*Original.*[6]]

SWIFT TO ARCHDEACON WALLS

Trim, *December* 13, 1716.

I HAD yours yesterday. Gillespy[7] has been with me. I
have dispatched him, and allowed him his wages and board-
wages to this very day. I desire you will take notice of my

---

[1] *Supra*, p. 314.   [2] *Supra*, p. 336.   [3] *Supra*, p. 332.

[4] It appears from a later letter (*infra*, p. 351) that a portrait of
Walls's son had been painted by Jervas (*supra*, p. 333) as a present
for Gossip Doll.

[5] Delany describes ("Observations," p. 127) sweet-heart as a cook-
maid of a large size and robust constitution, with a face roughed with
the small-pox and furrowed by age.

[6] In the possession of Mr. John Murray. See Preface.

[7] *Supra*, n. 1.

kindness to him in as strong a manner as you can. I have given him a conditional note for twenty-two pounds odd money. I forgot to speak to him to deliver up his parchment bound folio of accounts, and all the rest of his papers relating to my livings. I here send you a list of the bonds[1] of Laracor for 1715 which he set, and which I ought to have had down with me, and which Mr. Gillespy says you have, though you have not set down the sums of any one of them in your great book. I cannot imagine how I came to forget bringing down these bonds of Laracor which Gillespy set for this year. I protest I do not remember any of them, but understand that he said that Doctor Raymond had taken care of all Laracor this year, whereas upon examining he said he had sent you all those which I here send you a list of, and that you have the bonds. I will therefore contrive to send somebody to you by whom they may be safely returned. I hope the messenger was with you early yesterday morning with the map of the glebe to be purchased.[2] I have given Gillespy a note upon you for one pound three shillings, which he paid by Doctor Raymond's order. I shall not have the countenance to give any more trouble to Mr. Staunton,[3] since we cannot prevail on him to take an acknowledgment.

As for going to Dromore,[4] the matter is so that I have not a horse strong enough to carry me there, as I found by coming down here, and I know not where to get one. Besides I cannot stir till I have settled this business of the glebe, and likewise till I have contrived some means to order my affairs now Gillespy hath left me. For I must have somebody to get in my arrears, and my present dues. Pray pay yourself what I owe you, and let me not be troubled with your lowsy debt; for I believe you are as great a beggar as I.

The tithes let by Gillespy at Laracor for this year 1716, of which he says you have the bonds, are as follows; some of the tenants may perhaps be changed, but you will know the denominations of the lands:

[1] For the farm of the tithe.
[2] From Percival (*supra*, p. 344).
[3] *Supra*, p. 316.
[4] As appears from subsequent letters, the St. Mary ladies and Gossip Doll spent that Christmas with Bishop Stearne at Dromore.

SET IN THE YEAR 1715.

		£ s d	£ s d
1. Part of Knockbeg.	Nicholas Dollan,[1]	£8 5 0	£6 0 0
2. Part of Summerstown.	Michael Heaps and Patrick Connell,		1 1 6
3. Part of Summerstown.	James Murphy,		1 1 6
4. Part of Summerstown.	Patrick and Maurice Murphy,		9 15 0
5. Part of Summerstown.	John Fay,	1 14 3	1 10 0
6. Clondoogan.[1]	Archibald Alexander,	16 16 0	16 4 0
7. Part of Summerstown.	Patrick Connell and Hugh Reilly,	2 12 0	2 10 0
9. Part of Summerhill.	George Bowsman,		0 15 0
14. Both Ginnets.	Mr. William Steers,	11 5 0	10 0 0
17. Part of Dangan.	Richard Babington,	0 14 0	0 13 6
20. Summerhill.	Mr. George Dennis,	11 0 0	10 0 0
23. Part of Summerhill.	John Fagan,		2 10 0
25. Laracor, Stokestown, Readstown.	Mr. John and Mark Tew,	16 0 0	20 0 0

£82 0 6[2]

These are bonds Gillespy says you have, and these are the sums they were let for in the year 1715, as I find in your book. Perhaps they may not be set now in the same manner. For instance, Summerstown which is now in five parcels you may have for this year in one; and tenants' names may be changed. However you will easily see whether they be the same tithes, and compare the sums.

The Doctor and Mrs. Raymond insists to have you Whigs down this Christmas upon condition that you and Mrs. Brent[3] will put two dozen bottles of wine into a large hamper and send it down before you, one dozen of gross lees, and the other dozen of the wine last drawn, but with a nick to distinguish; and I will likewise have a dozen of ten shilling wine for vulgar company; that must be marked too. Each bottle must be bundled in its own bit of hay.

Gillespy has a horse of mine in my stable, which he has so lamed as it will be never good for anything. Therefore I have given it to him, and will have it removed immediately from my stable, where it has ruined me in hay and oats. You will see Gillespy on Saturday as he says. I wish you would put the Provost[4] in mind of doing something for

---

[1] *Supra*, p. 54.

[2] The figures in the second column represent possibly the rate for the preceding year.

[3] *Supra*, p. 314.

[4] *Supra*, p. 337, n. 3.

himself in case the Bishop of Killala should die.[1] Service
to friend Jervas.[2]

Addressed—To the Reverend Mr. Archdeacon Walls at his
  house over against the Blue-Coat Hospital in Queen
  Street, Dublin.

CCCLXXIX. [*Original.*[3]]

SWIFT TO ARCHDEACON WALLS

Trim, *December* 16, 1716.

YOUR messenger came by noon when I was at Laracor,[4]
but I had your post letter before, and am disappointed at
not having the honour of Paddy's company. To-morrow we
all go to Mr. Percival's,[5] and if there be no difficulties
started, I will send Will on Tuesday, who shall be a witness.
Doctor Raymond desires you will keep the Trim charity
money till one of the churchwardens waits on you to
receive it, and gives you an acquittance. Whatever you
agreed to pay your messenger, let him have it, and I give
him a shilling into the bargain. You will know more I
hope on Tuesday night. I am sorry you disturbed yourself
so early this morning as four o'clock. I doubt you were
ready to sleep at your own sermon. All here give you their
service, and are angry you mention nothing of your coming
down. Pray put up those bonds you have of Laracor 1716,[6]
which Gillespy set, and return them to me by the messenger
I shall send; for now is my time of gathering money, if I
can. Adieu.

Addressed—To the Reverend Archdeacon Walls.

---

[1] Swift's old friend Lloyd (*supra*, p. 114) had died two days before.
[2] *Supra*, p. 344.
[3] In the possession of Mr. John Murray. See Preface.
[4] Swift was writing on a Sunday.
[5] To execute the lease of the land taken from Percival for the glebe
(*supra*, p. 345). On 5 December the Committee of the Board of
First Fruits had ordered the deeds to be sent down to be executed,
with a direction that the Vicar-General of the diocese of Meath and
two other credible witnesses should see and attest the due perfection
thereof.
[6] *Supra*, p. 345.

CCCLXXX. [*Sheridan.*]

SWIFT TO ARCHBISHOP KING

Trim, *December* 16, 1716.

MY LORD,[1]

I SHOULD be sorry to see my Lord Bolingbroke following the trade of an informer, because he is a person for whom I always had, and still continue, a very great love and esteem. For I think, as the rest of mankind do, that informers are a detestable race of people, although they may be sometimes necessary. Besides, I do not see whom his Lordship can inform against, except himself. He was three or four days at the Court of France, while he was Secretary, and it is barely possible, he might then have entered into some deep negotiation with the Pretender; although I would not believe him, if he should swear it, because he protested to me, that he never saw him but once, and that was at a great distance, in public, at an opera. As to any others of the Ministry at that time, I am confident he cannot accuse them, and that they will appear as innocent with relation to the Pretender as any who are now at the helm. And as to myself, if I were of any importance, I should be very easy under such an accusation; much easier, than I am to think your Grace imagines me in any danger, or that Lord Bolingbroke should have any ill story to tell of me. He knows, and loves, and thinks too well of me, to be capable of such an action.

But I am surprised to think your Grace could talk, or act, or correspond with me for some years past, while you must needs believe me a most false and vile man; declaring to you on all occasions my abhorrence of the Pretender, and yet privately engaged with a Ministry to bring him in, and therefore warning me to look to myself, and prepare my defence against a false brother, coming over to discover such secrets as would hang me. Had there been ever the least overture or intent of bringing in the Pretender, during my acquaintance with the Ministry, I think I must have been very stupid not to have picked out some discoveries

---

[1] This letter is an answer to the concluding paragraph of Archbishop King's letter of November 22 (*supra*, p. 343).

or suspicions. And although I am not sure I should have turned informer, yet I am certain I should have dropped some general cautions, and immediately have retired. When people say things were not ripe at the Queen's death; they say they know not what. Things were rotten; and had the Ministers any such thoughts, they should have begun three years before, and they who say otherwise, understand nothing of the state of the kingdom at that time.

But whether I am mistaken or not in other men, I beg your Grace to believe, that I am not mistaken in myself. I always professed to be against the Pretender, and am so still. And this is not to make my court, which I know is vain, for I own myself full of doubts, fears, and dissatisfactions, which I think on as seldom as I can, yet if I were of any value, the public may safely rely on my loyalty; because I look upon the coming of the Pretender as a greater evil than any we are likely to suffer under the worst Whig ministry that can be found. I have not spoke or thought so much of party these two years, nor could anything have tempted me to it, but the grief I have in standing so ill in your Grace's opinion. I beg your Grace's blessing, and am, etc.

CCCLXXXI. [*Original.*[1]]

SWIFT TO ARCHDEACON WALLS

Trim, *December* 17, 1716.

EVERYTHING is done as you ordered, and Will goes with this to-morrow morning early.[2] Mr. Percival keeps his own part of the deed, and I send you the other with the lease to give to Doctor Coghill.[3] I thought the Board[4] had no more to do with it, however they can now have it on Wednesday[5] to do what they please. I think all your particulars have been observed. Will is a witness and can swear what you please. Pray send by Will, and see him put

---

[1] In the possession of Mr. John Murray. See Preface.
[2] The lease had been executed that day as arranged (*supra*, p. 347).
[3] *Supra*, p. 342, n. 1.   [4] Of First Fruits.
[5] Swift was writing on Monday.

them up carefully, the bonds which Gillespy set for Laracor this year 1716, because I want the money.[1] Will is to wait your orders about his return. Some people here say there ought to be a memorial sent in order to have the deeds registered,[2] but since you only say a witness sworn is sufficient, and that Mr. Percival says so too, I have not done it.

Addressed—To the Reverend Mr. Archdeacon Walls.

CCCLXXXII. [*Original.*[3]]

SWIFT TO ARCHDEACON WALLS

Trim, *December* 19, 1716.

I HOPE Will got safe and timely to you yesterday.[4] I have since been thinking to propose it to you whether it might not be proper to order him to ride to the deanery,[5] and there give notice to some of the principal farmers, that is to say those who owe most, of whom you may give him a list both as to their names and habitations, that Gillespy hath left me, and that I require those who have their money ready would on the next market-day pay their money to you, who have their bonds and can give them receipts on the back of them. Will may likewise find out

---

[1] *Supra*, p. 347.

[2] The reference is to the system of registering deeds in Ireland which was established early in that century. As Swift found subsequently, a memorial reciting the contents of the deed is necessary, and one was lodged on 5 February following (" Registry of Deeds," bk. 18, p. 119). The deeds were witnessed by Anthony Raymond, Jonathan Preston, a notary public, and Swift's servant, William Geddes, who made the affidavit accompanying the memorial.

[3] In the possession of Mr. John Murray. See Preface.

[4] *Supra*, p. 349.

[5] By the deanery Swift means the possessions of the Dean of St. Patrick's in the southern part of the county of Dublin to which reference has already been made (*supra*, p. 56, n. 2). In the parish of Clondalkin, which adjoins that of Rathcoole, there are to be seen remains of a castle which provided a country residence for Swift's predecessors in Elizabethan times, who often dated their letters from their "poor house" of the Deansrath.

old Barnewall,[1] and say the same thing to him, and let old Barnewall inform the farmers. This will be useful that the farmers should know, and also help me get a little money, who have not a farthing to bless myself. Do not be frighted as if I intended to constitute you my receiver, but you know I am at a loss what to do. I wish also that Will had a list of those deanery men who owe me arrears, to give to Barnewall, who might tell those people that I shall proceed against them if they will not come and clear their old debts. The gentlemen of the deanery might be likewise desired to send their money by any servant who comes up to market, and you might draw up a paper of instructions pursuant to this for Will to give Barnewall. I suppose he knows, or can find out, where Barnewall lives; and you must let Will have what shillings he shall want to maintain himself, while he stays, for I could only give him eighteen pence. If you think what I say material you will please to do it, or alter it in whatever method you think fit. I wish with the bills of Laracor for this year 1716, you would send me in a paper, separate, the bills of arrears for Laracor, of which I find a list in your book from Parvisol; and see if I can pick up anything out of them.

Is Jervas gone? Has he finished Jacky's picture?[2] Will you come down this Christmas and send some wine before you?[3] Have you paid yourself your own debt out of the seventy pounds? When Jervas is gone, you must take Jacky's picture home. Do you know that one of the great packets you had for me was nothing but a scoundrel sermon of that rascal Smedley,[4] sent me either by himself

[1] Amongst the Anglo-Norman settlers in Ireland none occupied a more prominent place than the Barnewalls, who became ennobled under the titles of Trimlestown and Kingston. One of their principal seats, Drimnagh Castle, is adjacent to the Deansrath, but long before Swift's time it had passed out of their possession, and the family were only represented in the neighbourhood by persons in a humble walk in life.
[2] *Supra*, p. 344.   [3] *Supra*, p. 346.
[4] The defamatory manner in which Swift speaks of Smedley tends to confirm the truth of the report that Smedley's verses greeted Swift on coming to take possession of his cathedral (*supra*, p. 52). Their similarity in name and career is very remarkable. In each case the Christian name was Jonathan, in each case the first preferment was an obscure country living, in each case the final promotion was a deanery, and in each case politics, the one on the Tory side, the other on the Whig side, was the chief interest ("D. N. B.," lii, 397). The sermon was probably one preached on "the birthday of the

or some other dog, on purpose to put me to charge and vexation? Another large one was from the Archbishop,[1] and it is a civil letter and friendly, except in one article, for which I will be revenged by an answer.[2] He says it is confidently reported that Lord Bolingbroke is returning, that the consideration must be to discover secrets, and his Grace hopes that my Lord has no ill things to say of me; by which the Archbishop plainly lets me know that he believes all I have said of myself and the late Ministry with relation to the Pretender to be Court lies. My service in your next to our Dromore friends.[3] I hope they are well. I writ to Tew to measure out my ground and prepare for some other things relating to it.

Addressed—To the Reverend Mr. Archdeacon Walls, Queen Street.

CCCLXXXIII. [*Original.*[4]]

SWIFT TO ARCHBISHOP KING

Trim, *December* 22, 1716.

MY LORD,

I HAVE been here some days, to finish the purchase of a glebe for my country parish.[5] I prevailed on a gentleman to alienate twenty acres for two hundred pounds to be had from the Trustees of the First Fruits. He then sets me twenty-three acres more for nine hundred and ninety-nine years. Upon these last twenty-three acres, I am, by agreement, to lay out the said two hundred pounds in building, and to give the gentleman immediately fifty-five pounds out of my own pocket, and to pay him fourteen pounds per annum for ever, which is near the value of the whole forty acres; these last twenty-three acres, after I have built and

Prince of Wales" (the 6th of October) in that year, which was printed.
  [1] *Supra*, p. 339.
  [2] The answer to that portion of the letter had been written (*supra*, p. 348), but probably had not yet been sent.
  [3] *Supra*, p. 345, n. 4.
  [4] This is the sixth of the autographs preserved in the record room at Armagh (*supra*, vol. i, p. 60, n. 1).
  [5] *Supra*, p. 349.

LARACOR GLEBE

From a photograph by Mr. Thomas J. Westropp, M.A. Dubl.

improved, I design to leave my successors, who will then
have forty-three acres of good glebe, with house, gardens,
etc. for fourteen pounds per annum.[1] I reckon to lay out of
my own money above two hundred and fifty pounds, and
so to be an humble imitator of your Grace, *longo intervallo.*
This expedient was a project of Doctor Raymond, minister
of this town, to deal with a Jew,[2] who would not lessen his
rent-roll to save all the churches in Christendom. Doctor
Coghill,[3] and everybody else, approves the thing; since it
is a good bargain to the Church, a better to the gentleman,
and only a bad one to myself; and I hope your Grace will
have the same thoughts.

Since I came down here, I received the honour of a
large, and therefore an agreeable letter, from your Grace, of
November 22. I have reason to think myself hardly dealt
with by those of the side in power, who will not think I
deserve any place in your good thoughts; when they cannot but know that, while I was near the late Ministry, I
was a common advocate for those they called the Whigs,
to a degree, that a certain great Minister told me, I had
always a Whig in my sleeve; neither did I ever fail to
interpose in any case of merit or compassion, by which
means several persons in England, and some in this kingdom, kept their employments; for I cannot remember my
Lord Oxford ever refused me a request of that kind. And
for the rest, your Grace may very well remember, that I had
the honour of corresponding with you, during the whole
period, with some degree of confidence, because I know your
Grace had wished the same things, but differed only in
opinion about the hands that should effect them. It was on
account of this conduct, that certain warm creatures of this
kingdom, then in London, and not unknown to your Grace,
had the assurance to give me broad hints that I was providing against a change; and I observe those very men are
now the most careful of all others, to creep as far as they
can out of harm's way.

The system of the new zealots, which your Grace ex-
tracted, must be very suitable to my principles, who was

---

[1] The arrangement for the additional land was not carried through.
In 1836 the glebe of Laracor was returned as containing 21 a., 30 p.
plantation measure, or 34 a., 1 r., 11½ p. statute measure (Report on
Ecclesiastical Revenue and Patronage in Ireland).

[2] *I.e.*, Percival.   [3] *Supra*, p. 349.

always a Whig in politics. I have been told, that upon the death of the last nonjuring Bishop,[1] Dodwell and his followers thought the schism at an end. My notion was, that these people began to set up again upon despair of their cause by the rebellion being brought to an end, else their politics are, if possible, worse than their divinity. Upon the whole, it is clear, that the game is entirely in the hands of the King and his Ministers; and I am extremely glad of your Grace's opinion, that it will be played as it ought; or, if we must suffer for a name, however, I had rather be devoured by a lion than a rat.

That maxim of the injuring person never forgiving the person injured, is, I believe, true in particulars, but not of communities. I cannot but suppose that the clergy thought there were some hardships and grounds for fears, otherwise they must be very wicked, or very mad—to say more would be to enter into a dispute upon a party subject; a dog or a horse knows when he is kindly treated, and besides, a wise administration will endeavour to remove the vain, as well as the real fears of those they govern.

I saw the Provost yesterday in this neighbourhood, and had some little talk with him upon the occasion of the Bishop of Killala's death.[2] I believe he would accept of the deanery of Derry, if Doctor Bolton, the Dean,[3] should be promoted; but I said nothing of it to him. I believe he has written to Mr. Molyneux.[4] I find, since he cannot be trusted with a bishopric, that he desires to leave his station with as good a grace as he can, and that it may not be thought that what he shall get is only to get rid of him. I said in general, that such a circumstance, as things stood, was hardly worth the quiet of a man's whole life; and so we parted, only with telling him I intended to write to your Grace, in answer to a letter I had from you. I beg your Grace's blessing, and am, with great respect, my Lord,

Your Grace's most dutiful and most humble servant,

JONATH. SWIFT.

Addressed—To his Grace the Lord Archbishop of Dublin at his lodgings in Suffolk Street (at Mrs. Stoat's), near St. James's, London.

---

[1] *I.e.*, Ken.   [2] *Supra*, p. 347, n. 1.
[3] Swift's old rival (*supra*, vol. i, p. 33, n. 1).
[4] *Supra*, p. 343, n. 1.

CCCLXXXIV. [*Original.*[1]]

SWIFT TO ARCHDEACON WALLS

Trim, *December* 23, 1716.

I HAD all your dispatches by Will, and have thanks to give you upon a thousand particulars.[2] Pray ask Gillespy how it comes to pass that the several articles of Summerstown come this year to not above nine pounds six shillings, and in the year 1715 were near seventeen pounds.[3] Indeed I find he has set every article but scurvily. His method was to ask how it set last year, and then without further examining to ask the same rate, and so fall lower as they could agree. You are to know that when he came first to me he proposed to take a farm on the deanery from Whitshed, the Judge,[4] and did so as a thing of much advantage to me. You know I lost twenty-two pounds last year by it. Now he writes to Doctor Raymond and me to know whether I would yet hold it, which I am against, unless I could be sure of a tenant and without loss or care. It would certainly be of use to have a few acres there, but a rent of above forty pounds per annum is not to be thought on. However I desire you will speak to Mr. Gillespy to defer giving up the farms till Monday or Tuesday sennight, at which time a man will go from hence and meet Gillespy at Tallaght[5] or Dublin, but rather at the former, and view the land and talk with him first, and afterwards with you, and advise whether it be proper and safe to hold the land or no. Let Gillespy settle whether it can be Monday or Tuesday sennight, or whether at Tallaght or Dublin, that he can meet the man, and what hour of the day and place,

[1] In the possession of Mr. John Murray. See Preface.
[2] *Supra*, p. 350. [3] *Supra*, p. 346.
[4] Swift's future enemy, Chief Justice Whitshed, who had been appointed to the chief seat in the King's Bench in Ireland on the accession of George I. Whitshed's family appear to have been connected with the Clondalkin (*supra*, p. 350, n. 5) neighbourhood.
[5] Tallaght is a village not far from Clondalkin. It was the site in mediaeval times of a castle belonging to the Archbishops of Dublin, and Archbishop King's successor erected there a modern palace as a country residence for the holders of the see.

and the man shall be exact. Rather I say again at Tallaght, or if in Dublin at your house or the deanery, just as he and you shall settle.

Pray let Mrs. Brent buy a hamper to hold two dozen bottles, and send me by the first conveniency a dozen of gross lees, and a dozen of the last drawn wine, marking one dozen.[1] Come down and see us if you can. Let the wine be left at your house. The memorial is signed and shall be sent up.[2] I cannot leave this place till I have divided my ground, and done some other things; and when I leave it, I believe it will be for Rochfort's, for I cannot get to Dromore[3] without another horse, unless I walk it, which I will not promise to do. If you can govern your tongue, say nothing of the picture to Gossip Doll.[4] The letters are just going and I believe I have forgot to say twenty things; but I was so ill last night with a headache I could not write a line.

Addressed—To the Reverend Mr. Archdeacon Walls at his house over against the Blue-Coat Hospital, Queen Street, Dublin.

CCCLXXXV. [*Original.*[5]]

SWIFT TO ARCHDEACON WALLS

Trim, *December* 27, 1716.

I HAD yours this morning by your country messenger, which put me out of pain; for I apprehended mine of last Sunday miscarried.[6] I will contrive some way or other that a messenger shall see you and Mr. Gillespy either Saturday or Monday. It is plain there is some great mistake about the tithes of Summerstown, which Parvisol and another man have the accounts of as set for twenty pounds and Gillespy's bonds are but four, which amount to under

---

[1] *Supra*, p. 346.   [2] *Supra*, p. 350.
[3] *Supra*, p. 345.   [4] *Supra*, p. 344.
[5] In the possession of Mr. John Murray. See Preface.
[6] *Supra*, p. 355. Swift was writing on Thursday.

ten pounds. Pray let this matter be set right. It is thus
in his account:—

Part of Summerstown.	Michael Heaps and P. Connell	1	6	0
Part of Summerstown.	James Murphy	1	6	0
Part of Summerstown.	John Gray	1	14	6
Part of Summerstown.	John Greney	5	0	0
		£9	6	6

so that there wants ten pounds thirteen shillings and six
pence to make up the sum. Pray mention to Gillespy as a
piece of favour that he hath had the setting money for all
these bonds, which come to near four pounds. Mr. Gillespy,
as Will tells me, is every Saturday in Smithfield Market,
or Cornmarket; if you will send Paddy to enquire for him,
and fix him at your house on Monday evening, where Mr.
Proudfoot, one whom I shall partly employ, will attend
you. Pray let Paddy inquire diligently, and ten to one but
he will find him. Pray come down for two or three days,
and have the wine ready at your house, and I will send
for it.

Addressed—To the Reverend Mr. Archdeacon Walls, at his
house in Queen Street, over against the Blue-Coat Hospital, Dublin.

CCCLXXXVI. [*Original.*[1]]

SWIFT TO ARCHDEACON WALLS

Trim, *December* 30, 1716.

LAST post you sent me a letter from our friends at Dromore,
full of reproaches for my not writing to them or going
down there.[2] Pray in your next to Gossip Doll or the
Bishop, let them tell the two ladies that I will write to
them in a post or two; but for coming down it is impossible
for me unless I get a horse, which I am laying out for on all
sides in vain; neither can I stir till I have settled this
business of the land with Mr. Percival, who lies sick, and

---

[1] In the possession of Mr. John Murray. See Preface.
[2] *Supra*, p. 356.

is slowly recovering. We have, I know not how, let slip the opportunity of sending a messenger to meet you and Gillespy on Saturday.[1] We expect a letter from you this post, but I shall be at Laracor before it comes, and I will leave this for Doctor Raymond to finish. We have found out the secret of Summerstown;[2] for examining a farmer we found he had not given a bond, which yesterday we took from him for eleven pounds. It was very careless in Mr. Gillespy to omit this, and yet make no mention of it to us.

On second thoughts I stayed at home, and received yours, and Mr. Proudfoot[3] will be with you to-morrow night. Gillespy's excuse about Summerstown is a very sorry one, for he never said a word of it to you or me. You now have to adjust the matter about the farm,[4] or whether you would take it if you were as I. I cannot bear the thoughts of a heavy rent, without I am secure of some under-tenant to pay it. In that case it will be useful no doubt to have a bit of land to dry my tithes on occasion. You will direct and send away the enclosed.

Addressed—To the Reverend Mr. Archdeacon Walls, Dublin.

CCCLXXXVII. [*Original.*[5]]

SWIFT TO ARCHDEACON WALLS

Trim, *January* 3, 1716-17.

I HAD yours of the 1st which makes me remember to wish you a happy new year. One passage in your letter is odd; you say, if I write to the ladies it will be too late. Did not Proudfoot[6] give you a letter with one enclosed to Mrs. Dingley? And I hope you have sent it to save my credit. I approve all you say about the farm. I cannot think of meddling with paying rent. I wish you could send us our wine,[7] and come down and drink part of it. I am heartily sorry for poor little Dolly.

I will come to town as soon as I can settle the affair of

---

[1] The letter is dated on Sunday (*supra*, p. 355).
[2] *Supra*, p. 356.   [3] *Supra*, p. 357.   [4] *Supra*, p. 355.
[5] In the possession of Mr. John Murray. See Preface.
[6] *Supra*, n. 3.   [7] *Supra*, p. 356.

the lease with Mr. Percival, and have the lines of divisions etc., drawn upon the land, which meets with a hundred delays.[1] This would be a very good place for you to keep your Christmas in, for there are no cards nor diversions; only you cannot smoke or drink ale. If the Bishop of Down be in town, I would draw on him for sixty pounds, which he was to pay me at Christmas,[2] for which I have his bond in my cabinet and can direct you to it. If he be in town, I wish you would be so kind to tell him so, and see whether he be ready to pay the money, and I would return it to pay a debt in England.

The silly Tories here are just as you describe those in Dublin, very sanguine and feeding themselves with foolish imaginations.[3] Since you complain of spending your ream of paper, I wish you were Archbishop of Rheims to reimburse you. I wonder how Gillespy's northern modesty became him when you charged him about the Summerstown bond.[4] I despair about getting any odd acres from Gillespy or the Judge,[5] and I am sure the former will get rid of it as soon as he can.

Yours.

Addressed—To the Reverend Mr. Archdeacon Walls, at his house over against the Blue-Coat Hospital, in Queen Street, Dublin.

CCCLXXXVIII. [*Original.*[6]]

ERASMUS LEWIS TO SWIFT

London, January 12, 1716-17.

SIR,

ABOUT two months ago I sent you a very long epistle, and was in hopes you would either have made us a visit, or

---

[1] *Supra*, p. 352.
[2] The Bishop of Down at that time was Edward Smith, a former Dean of St. Patrick's. The transaction had relation to the Dean's lands at Kilberry (*infra*, p. 380).
[3] On the ministerial crisis caused by the removal of Lord Townshend from the position of chief minister.
[4] *Supra*, p. 358.   [5] *Supra*, p. 355.
[6] In the British Museum. See Preface.

have let us hear from you. Since you have done neither, we must flatter ourselves that you will be better the new year than the former.

Our friend Prior, not having had the vicissitude of human things before his eyes, is likely to end his days in as forlorn a state as any other poet has done before him, if his friends do not take more care of him than he has done of himself.[1] Therefore, to prevent the evil, which we see is coming on very fast, we have a project of printing his Solomon, and other poetical works, by subscription; one guinea to be paid in hand, and the other at the delivery of the book. He, Arbuthnot, Pope, and Gay, are now with me, and remember you. It is our joint request, that you will endeavour to procure some subscriptions: you will give your receipts for the money you receive, and when you return it hither you shall have others in lieu. There are no papers printed here, nor any advertisement to be published; for the whole matter is to be managed by friends in such a manner as shall be least shocking to the dignity of a plenipotentiary.

I am told the Archbishop of Dublin shows a letter of yours, reflecting on the high-flying clergy.[2] I fancy you have writ to him in an ironical style, and that he would have it otherwise understood. This will bring to your mind what I have formerly said to you on that figure. Pray condescend to explain this matter to me.

The removal of my Lord Townshend has given a little spirit; but that will soon flag, if the King, at his return, does not make farther changes.[3] What measures his Majesty will take is uncertain; but this we are very sure of, that the division of the Whigs is so great, that, morally speaking, nothing but another rebellion can unite them. Sunderland, Stanhope, and Cadogan are of one side; Townshend, Walpole, Orford, Devonshire, and the Chancellor,[4] on the other. The latter seem at present to be strongest; but when the former appear with a German reinforcement, they will un-

---

[1] Prior, after his return from France (*supra*, p. 293, n. 2), had been impeached, and appears to have been, like Oxford, confined in the Tower.

[2] *Supra*, p. 337.

[3] The King was in Hanover when he dismissed Lord Townshend (*supra*, p. 359, n. 3).

[4] Earl Cowper.

doubtedly turn the balance.[1] They are both making their court to the Tories, who, I hope, will be a body by themselves, and not serve as recruits to either of the other two. Lord Townshend's friends give out, that his disgrace is owing to refusing four things, viz. to keep up the army, repeal the limitations of the Succession Act, to send money to Germany for carrying on a war against Sweden, and to attaint Lord Oxford.[2] When Lord Sunderland comes over, he will probably cry whore again, and endeavour to saddle Lord Townshend in his turn; for these reproaches now are like that of Jacobitism in former reigns.

We are told, that Lord Bolingbroke has permission to stay in France, notwithstanding the late treaty, provided he retires from Paris.[3]

Addressed—To the Rev. Dr. Swift, Dean of St. Patrick's, Dublin, Ireland.

CCCLXXXIX. [*Copy.*[4]]

ARCHBISHOP KING TO SWIFT

Suffolk Street, London, *January* 12, 1716-17.

REVEREND SIR,
I HAVE yours of the 22nd of December last, but have been so much out of order by a most violent cough and cold, that I could not sooner acknowledge your kindness. I do not clearly apprehend your purchase of the glebe for the country benefice. It seems to me, that you have given two hundred pounds for twenty acres, and have laid out that two hundred pounds in building on another twenty acres, or are obliged to lay it out, and besides this it will cost you two hundred and fifty pounds, and after all you must pay fourteen pounds per annum for the last twenty

---

[1] The appointment of Stanhope as chief minister proved Lewis's surmise to be well founded.

[2] The rapacity of the Hanoverian ministers and favourites, and the King's jealousy of those who held any intercourse with his son were, in the opinion of Mr. Lecky (*op. cit.*, i, 319), the real cause of the changes in the Ministry.

[3] *Supra*, p. 312.   [4] In King's Correspondence. See Preface.

acres of land, and yet pay fourteen shillings per acre, though the other twenty acres are free to the Church. If I take the case right, the gentleman has indeed played the Jew: the Church is a gainer, but you have certainly had hard measure, but the gentlemen of Ireland are so deadly fond of land and love so extremely to live alone on the earth, that whoever would get a scrap for a clergyman must go into their own terms, though never so unreasonable. If some of your successors should be of the humour of some that I have known, they will let your house go out of repair, the rent run on ten or twelve years, and then the landlord will re-enter for want of distress. Pray take some care, if possible, to prevent such an accident.

As to the part of my letter that related to my Lord Bolingbroke,[1] you took it too seriously; for I assure you, when I wrote that letter, I neither believed that Lord Bolingbroke would return, or that he would tell any ill story of you. I was of opinion, and advised by several of my friends that were in a contrary party, to be quiet, give no disturbance, but to wait *reversum fortunae*—and if they had done so, they would soon have found that it was not in the nature of that gentleman to be constant in any one way; but many of them took all possible ways to fix her, and if she be long of coming about, let them remember it is their own fault. If I cannot be of the same opinion with my friends, I can easily bear their dissenting.

There is one thing I heard often whilst it was practised, but suspended my belief till I have had it confirmed by above half-a-dozen concerned in it, and it is that the Duke of Ormond, and several of the late Ministry used to closet gentlemen of interest and posts, and query was " will you come into the query measures? " If they desired to know what those measures were, no answer was given, but the question repeated, with a stern accent, and if they did not engage had no farther countenance but were turned out. I have a value for the Queen's memory, on which this seems to reflect, and wish somebody would explain the meaning of it to me; for the matter of fact is not to be doubted. I never believed you for the Pretender, but remember that when the surmises of that matter run high, you retired,

---

[1] This portion of the letter is a reply to Swift's letter of 16 December (*supra*, p. 348).

which agrees with what you say you ought to have done in that case.

The absence of his Majesty, and the unsettlement of the government of Ireland,[1] has kept me here longer than I designed, and I am afraid to very little purpose. If I had thought his Majesty would have stayed so long, I would have immediately gone to Ireland. I recommend you to God's good care and am, Reverend Sir,

Yours etc.,
W. D[UBLIN].

There is a foolish profane letter here in your name, but you may be easy under it. It is universally condemned, and thought to be writ by a Jacobite and Deist.

Dr. Swift.

CCCXC. [*Original.*[2]]]

SWIFT TO ARCHDEACON WALLS

Trim, *January* 13, 1716-17.

I AM glad your people are come home safe;[3] I suppose they have nothing in their mouth but Magheralin.[4] It was Doll's doings coming home so soon. How did the adventure of the picture pass?[5] I suppose you spoilt it by some circumstance or other; or was Gossip Doll not so pleased as you expected? My service to them all, and I hope to see them in a few days. Pray stop Mrs. Johnson's mouth with fourteen pounds, and if she or Mrs. Dingley want as much more, let them have it, if they will give you a receipt. You

---

[1] Lord Sunderland (*supra*, p. 278, n. 6), who had accompanied the King to Hanover (*supra*, p. 360, n. 3), was on the King's return appointed one of the Secretaries of State. Lord Townshend was appointed Lord Lieutenant in his room, but, like his predecessor, never came to Ireland.

[2] In the possession of Mr. John Murray. See Preface.

[3] *Supra*, p. 357.

[4] The see house of Dromore (*supra*, p. 103, n. 4) was situated in a parish of that name.

[5] *Supra*, p. 356.

are but a scurvy receiver with your ten pounds; talk to me
of hundreds. I have heard of Woodward, and wondered he
never applied before. I shall this year follow Dr. Raymond's
directions at a venture, whose strong side is employing able
fellows to set his tithes. I should be heartily glad of the
Provost's success.[1] We were positively told that the Bishop
of Derry is dead,[2] but you say nothing of it, any more than
of my aunt's death, which is certain. I wonder what sort of
will she hath made; we think she hath left all in her power
to the Forsters.[3] Dr. Raymond desires to know something
of the Bishop of Killala's will, if you can tell him anything
about it. He had some hopes that his daughter was not
forgot.[4] I suppose it will come to nothing. I read to the
Doctor what you say about the Bishop of Clogher, and he
must wait.

I saw a printed libel against myself, called a circular
letter.[5] It seems to be good-for-nothing, was it writ in
England or here? Mr. Percival still keeps his bed and I
wait to finish with him, after which I will come to town.[6] I
hope my visitation will pass to-morrow in form; or was it

---

[1] *Supra*, p. 354.

[2] Bishop Hartstonge (*supra*, p. 276, n. 7) was probably then ill. He
died on the 30th of that month.

[3] It is to the widow of his uncle William (*supra*, vol. i, p. 8) that
Swift alludes. With her Swift had kept up an acquaintance, and to
her Stella was known ("Prose Works," ii, 247, 343, 384), but there is
no mention of him in her will. It was made only two months before
his aunt's death, and possibly legacies in a former will, which she was
obliged to revoke "by reason of an expensive journey in England for
two years," may have included one to him. Some of the legatees
were near relations of Recorder Forster, the great exponent of Dublin
Whiggism, who had become, on the accession of George I, Chief
Justice of the Common Pleas (*supra*, p. 75, n. 1), and it seems not improbable that politics may have had something to do with Swift's
exclusion. For his aunt did not forget her step-daughter, her husband's
only surviving child, or even more remote relations, including Swift's
sister, and seems to have divided fairly enough between them and the
Forsters her property and personal possessions, including her black
japanned and pear-tree cabinets with the silver images, jars and china
belonging thereto, her diamonds and pearls, and her lace and em-
broidery. The Swift family portraits, now at Swiftsheath ("Prose
Works," xii, 57-63), were in her possession, and were left to her step-
daughter, as well as a painting of the Swift coat of arms to which
Swift refers in writing to Stella (*ibid.*, ii, 343).

[4] Bishop Lloyd (*supra*, p. 347, n. 1), made no mention of Raymond
or his family in his will.

[5] *Supra*, p. 363.   [6] *Supra*, p. 357.

last Monday? I have forgot. I was at Mr. Ludlow's[1] almost a week, and stayed three days longer than I intended by means of a broken shin, which is now well. I returned thence last Thursday.[2] We have the wine and find it marked; I imagine the mark is upon the new.[3] Your lemons they say are good, but I have seen none of them. I believe the pun of the northern shoemaker is your own, and that you are grown a profligate punner; for it is our custom to invent stories for the sake of a pun.

I know not whether to be glad or sorry that Jack Grattan[4] has, or has not, the gout. Did Gossip Doll play at ombre the first night of her return, or did she stay for the second? Poor Mrs. Dingley was likely to be robbed, and murdered seven times. And so I take my leave. Is Gillespy's horse gone from my stable;[5] and have I done with him for ever? I had a letter from Ned Synge[6] this post, enclosed in yours, in a most silly, starched, affected style. Somebody should go upon the leads of the deanery house and see whether all be right there.

Addressed—To the Reverend Mr. Archdeacon Walls over against the Blue-Coat Hospital, Queen Street, Dublin.

CCCXCI. [*Original.*[7]]

SWIFT TO ARCHDEACON WALLS

Trim, *January* 24, 1716-17.

I AM not assured whether I can be with you before the

---

[1] Peter Ludlow, a collateral descendant of the regicide, and grandfather of the first Earl Ludlow, was then residing at Ardsallagh, between Trim and Navan, to which he had succeeded through his wife, a member of Viscount Gormanston's family. He had sat for Dunleer in Queen Anne's last Parliament, and was returned some years later as one of the representatives for the county of Meath.

[2] The 8th.   [3] *Supra*, p. 356.   [4] *Supra*, p. 262, n. 3.

[5] *Supra*, p. 346.

[6] One of Swift's prebendaries, who became Bishop of Ferns. He was a son of Stearne's rival for the deanery of St. Patrick's (*supra*, vol. i, p. 53, n. 4), who had succeeded Vesey as Archbishop of Tuam (*supra*, p. 315, n. 1).

[7] In the possession of Mr. John Murray. See Preface.

beginning of next week. My friend Charleton[1] is still with us by our persuasions. We heard yesterday from Warburton, who appears to be very happy with his new wife, and finds her portion will be still greater than he expected, and that upon the death of an old uncle, one Finny, there will be hopes of some new addition. I am very sorry Mrs. Johnson had pre-intelligence of it. The jest was quite spoiled. We hear the town of Magherafelt is a very good one in a fine country.[2] I hope they will take care to air my room and bed. I intend to make two days' journey of it. I will provide somebody to preach here next Sunday, if I come home myself, so that Mr. Warburton need be in no pain. And now I think you must look out for a good curate, and he must preach well, or else it will not do after such a predecessor. I suppose I shall have offers enough, but I shall be hard to please. My service to the ladies and Gossip Doll. Adieu.

Postscript in another hand—The Doctor[3] writes to Mr. Warburton at your house and desires it may be sent to him as soon as possible, and he must buy a pair of black shirt sleeve buttons for the Doctor.

Addressed—To the Reverend Mr. Archdeacon Walls at his house over against the Blue-Coat Hospital, Queen Street, Dublin.

[1] Charleton was probably the Duchess of Ormond's chaplain (*supra*, p. 276, n. 7). He was the son of an Irish clergyman, and was born and educated in Ireland. His entrance in 1700 into Dublin University where he obtained a scholarship, is thus recorded : "Arthur Charleton, pensioner, son of Rev. Andrew Charleton, aged 15, born at Mallow, educated at Lisburn, college tutor John Wetherby." His relation Chiverton Charleton had died in 1716.

[2] Swift's curate had obtained a wife and a living at the same time. The rectory of Magherafelt, to which he was appointed, is in the diocese of Armagh, and possibly his promotion to it was due to Swift's influence with Primate Lindsay. He held the living until his death twenty years later (Leslie's "Armagh Clergy and Parishes," p. 364).

[3] *I.e.*, Raymond.

CCCXCII. [*Original.*[1]]

SWIFT TO ARCHDEACON WALLS

Trim, *January* 27, 1716-17.

I HAD both yours relating to poor Joe,[2] and care was taken to send his brother-in-law to town last night, which is all we could do. I have hardly time to say a word to you, because I am just come from Laracor, and all are at dinner here but I. You may expect me, I do not know what day; for Warburton coming down I shall have a mind to stay with him.[3] I wish you would step down here, and be merry three or four days, and we will all come back Monday sennight, and Dr. Raymond with us. My service to Gossip and the ladies. Pray inquire for a curate, and get me a large choice. I must have a good one, and soon, or I must return myself on Saturday sennight, for we are much out of parsons here.

Addressed—To the Reverend Mr. Archdeacon Walls at his house over against the Blue-Coat Hospital, in Queen Street, Dublin.

CCCXCIII. [*Original.*[4]]

SWIFT TO ARCHDEACON WALLS

Trim, *January* 28, 1716-17.

PARVISOL'S[5] son, the collegian, goes up to town, and a fellow follows him on foot to bring back his horse. Parvisol desires you would give that fellow the bills of Rathbeggan for 1716, and the arrears of the last or any other year for Rathbeggan, safely sealed and bound up; provided you think the fellow looks like one that will be careful of them;

---

[1] In the possession of Mr. John Murray. See Preface.
[2] As will appear from later letters, Beaumont's mind was then affected (*supra*, p. 276).
[3] *Supra*, p. 366.
[4] In the possession of Mr. John Murray. See Preface.
[5] *Supra*, p. 271, n. 2.

for Parvisol goes up to Dublin in two or three days, and as he goes he will receive what money he can get there and pay it to you. Joe is come home, and protests to me he is not mad,[1] and appeals to you; but we happen to be all against him. He talked to me a good while. A gentleman here showed us the finest large oranges with teats—the ladies know what I mean—that ever I saw, for twelve pence a dozen; I wish you would send us a dozen such by the fellow.

Addressed—To the Reverend Mr. Archdeacon Walls, Dublin.

CCCXCIV. [*Original.*[2]]

SWIFT TO ARCHDEACON WALLS

Trim, *January* 31, 1716-17.

I HAD your last. I am surprised to think curates should be so hard to get. Mr. Warburton's sudden going is very inconvenient to me.[3] I shall be able to get a preacher for Sunday sennight, but then I must come down if I cannot provide myself in the intermediate twelve days. Parvisol said there was a case on purpose for the papers;[4] however you were on the securer side, though the fellow said Mrs. Johnson would be engaged for him. Mr. Charleton stays here with me till Monday,[5] and then we all part, and the Doctor[6] designs to go with me; but I will make it two days. You must be taking your own methods about tobacco, instead of sending Mrs. Brent[7] to the old place, and so the Doctor will not take a whiff of it. I am glad you sent me the letters; one was from the Archbishop, the other from Mr. Lewis.[8] I am endeavouring to persuade Joe that he is mad.[9] I have given him twenty shillings to buy a periwig.

---

[1] *Supra*, p. 367, n. 2.
[2] In the possession of Mr. John Murray. See Preface.
[3] *Supra*, p. 366.   [4] *Supra*, p. 367.   [5] *Supra*, p. 366.
[6] *I.e.*, Raymond.   [7] *Supra*, p. 256, n. 6.
[8] *Supra*, pp. 359, 361.   [9] *Supra*, n. 1.

If you can get a coach to come six mile as far as Clonee [1] to fetch us for a crown or thereabouts, we will be there by one or two o'clock—the coach may be there as soon as it please. If you cannot, send us word by Saturday's post. My horses [are] the Doctor's. If you take a fancy to come, you may; and if the coach could come to Forbes's, [2] we would then dine with him. My service to Gossip and the ladies. All service here to you and them.

Postscript in another hand—The Dean is obliged to stay here a Monday so the coach must come a Tuesday. I tell you by order. Yours, A. RAYMOND.

Addressed—To the Reverend Mr. Archdeacon Walls.

CCCXCV. [*Original.*[3]]

SWIFT TO ARCHDEACON WALLS

Trim, *February* 3, 1716-17.

THERE might be some little difficulty in explaining our last letter, but I thought such wise persons as you and your co-inspectors might easily get over it. The matter is only that a coach and one pair of horses be sent to Clonee, [4] but six miles, on Tuesday next, to be there by twelve o'clock at noon, and not at midnight to avoid mistake; and therefore keep your four horses, and your "all the way to Trim" for your Magheralin folks; [5] they are above our reach.

The Doctor's [6] horses will go back from Clonee, and if you could get some hedge-interim-intermediate-temporary curate to trip down on Tuesday for a few weeks till I were better provided for, it would be very convenient both for the Doctor and me; but it must be such a one as we may cast

---

[1] A village on the main road from Dublin to Trim.
[2] Forbes's rectory (*supra*, p. 282, n. 5) was a little nearer Trim than Clonee.
[3] In the possession of Mr. John Murray. See Preface.
[4] *Supra*, n. 1.   [5] *Supra*, p. 363, n. 4.
[6] *I.e.*, Raymond's.

off without any consequence. Mr. Lightburne[1] writ to me a
very foolish letter to be my curate, but I do not intend it.
He will not answer my ends and I had rather serve him
another way. The Doctor will provide a place for whoever
comes down, and if any little parson desires only to take
the air for a fortnight till the Doctor returns here, it will be
a help.

You tell us nothing of your new Lords Justices, Conolly
and others.[2]

We have been considering the matter and broke open
the letter, and upon second thoughts we conceive it will be
more convenient not to stay till Wednesday, but to come
on Tuesday, as we at first intended; *vide* the beginning of
this letter. Mr. Warburton leaves us to-day, and Mr.
Charleton[3] and I are just walking to Laracor so that if I
have a letter from you I shall not answer it.

Postscript in another hand—I wish you may get one
to come down a Tuesday, though it be but for ten days or
a fortnight; for fear we may be called upon to do occasional
services etc. Yours, A. RAYMOND.

Addressed—To the Reverend Mr. Archdeacon Walls at his
    house over against the Blue-Coat Hospital in Queen
    Street, Dublin.

[1] Stafford Lightburne, who married Willoughby Swift's daughter
(*supra*, vol. i, p. 11, n. 1). To her Mrs. William Swift (*supra*, p. 364, n. 3)
left a mourning ring and her " black cloth gown and petticoat."
[2] On the appointment of Lord Townshend as Lord Lieutenant in
room of Lord Sunderland (*supra*, p. 363, n. 1), Archbishop King was
discarded as being too favourable to "the Irish interest," and the
Lord Chancellor, Alan Brodrick, who had been raised to the peerage
as Lord Midleton, and the Speaker, William Conolly, were appointed
as Lords Justices. In political influence Conolly, who was known as
"the great man of the North," had no rival, and his wealth has
become proverbial through Swift's use of it as an illustration in the
"Drapier's Letters" ("Prose Works," vi, 18), and through the great
mansion in the county of Kildare, "with a window for every day in
the year," of which he was the builder. He was, however, a self-made
man, by profession a solicitor, and his inclusion amongst the rulers
of Ireland gave no small offence to "the quality and old gentry."
[3] *Supra*, p. 368.

CCCXCVI. [*Sheridan.*]

SWIFT TO ARCHBISHOP KING

Dublin, *March* 2, 1716-17.

MY LORD,

YOUR Grace's letter[1] was a long time before it reached me; for I was several weeks in the country, dispatching the affair of the glebe, which, however, is not yet quite finished. Your Grace does rightly conceive the nature of my purchase, and that I am likely to be two hundred pounds poorer for it; only I shall endeavour to lose by degrees, which is all I have for it. I shall endeavour, as much as I can, to prevent the evil you foresee of my successors neglecting my improvements, and letting them all go to ruin. I shall take the best advice I can, and leave them to be fools, as well as knaves, if they do so; for I shall make so many plantations and hedges, that the land will let for double the value, and, after all, I must leave something to fortune.

As to what your Grace mentions of a practice in the late reign, of engaging people to come into the Queen's measures, I have a great deal to say on that subject, not worth troubling you with at present; farther than that I am confident those who pretend to say most of it, are conscious their accusation is wrong, but I never love myself so little as when I differ from your Grace, nor do I believe I ever shall do it, but where I am master of the fact, and your Grace has it only by report.

I have been speaking much to the Provost about the deanery of Derry,[2] or whatever other employment under a bishopric, may be designed him upon these promotions.[3] I find Dr. Coghill[4] has been upon the subject with him, but he is absolutely positive to take nothing less at present; and his argument is, that whatever shall be given him now, beneath the station his predecessors were called to, will be a mark of his lying under the displeasure of the Court, and that he is not to be trusted; whereas he looks

---

[1] *Supra*, p. 361.   [2] *Supra*, p. 354.
[3] Bishop Ashe had been translated a few days before from Clogher to Derry (*supra*, p. 364).
[4] *Supra*, p. 342.

upon himself to have acted with principles as loyal to the present government, as any the King employs. He does not seem to dislike either of the deaneries of Derry or Down,[1] but is persuaded it will reflect upon his reputation; and unless it could be contrived that he might have some mark of favour and approbation along with such a preferment, I believe your Grace may be assured he will not accept it. I only repeat what he says to me, and what I believe he will adhere to.

For my own part, who am not so refined, I gave my opinion that he should take what was given him; but his other friends differ from me, and for aught I know, they may be in the right, and if the Court thinks it of consequence that the present Provost should be removed, I am not sure but a way may be found out of saving his credit, which is all he seems to require; although I am confident, that if he were a bishop, the government might be very secure of him, since he seems wholly fallen out with the Tories, and the Tories with him, and I do not know any man, who, in common conversation, talks with more zeal for the present establishment, and against all opposers of it, than he. The only thing he desires at present in his discourse with me, is, that no proposal of a deanery should be at all made to him, but that he may go on as he is, until farther judgement shall be made of him by his future conduct. I thought it proper to say thus much to your Grace, because I did not know whether you and he perfectly understood each other.

I hear your Grace intends this spring for the Bath. I shall pray, for the good of the Church, that you may then establish your health. I am, with the greatest respect,

Your Grace's most dutiful and most humble servant,

JON. SWIFT.

Among other things, the Provost argued, that Dr. Forster[2] was promoted to a bishopric from being a Fellow,

---

[1] Then held respectively by Swift's former rivals, Bolton (*supra*, p. 354) and Lambert (*supra*, vol. i, p. 124, n. 3), who seem to have been first favourites for promotion to the episcopal bench.

[2] A brother of Chief Justice Forster, who had been appointed since the Hanoverian accession successively to the bishoprics of Killaloe and Raphoe. In the latter see, which he held until his death, he left a reputation of unexampled munificence; "What he was let gratitude tell."

and therefore he must conclude, that offering him a less preferment is a mark of displeasure, with which circumstance he is determined not to leave his present station.

CCCXCVII. [*Copy.*[1]]

ARCHBISHOP KING TO SWIFT

London, *March* 2, 1716-7,

REVEREND SIR,

I HAVE been informed that Mr. Duncan by a fall off his horse is like to make a vacancy in St. Bride's.[2] I know not how that may be, but I am told there will be three competitors for it, Dr. Howard,[3] Mr. Dopping,[4] and Dr. Drury.[5] As to the last I consider that he has the prebend of Tassagard,[6] and if he should be removed to St. Bride's, he would carry that prebend with him, which would leave the cures of Rathcoole and Kilteel[7] naked and without support, and therefore I hope you and the Chapter will not think it convenient to elect him. As to the other two, Dr. Howard and Mr. Dopping, they are brothers[8] and I will not interpose between them; either of them will be very grateful to me, if you and the Chapter be of the same opinion.

In yours of the 13th of November last, you gave me your opinion of the Provost very justly in my judgement, and intimated that you thought it would be much to his own ease, and theirs who dislike him, if he were put into another station, and if the government would not afford him a bishopric, that they would let him succeed some rich country dean. I have laboured that point, and brought it to bear as I hope, and I had this further reason to proceed

[1] In King's Correspondence. See Preface.
[2] The church of St. Bride, which has disappeared during recent years, lay a little to the north-east of St. Patrick's Cathedral, and the incumbency was in the gift of the Dean and Chapter. The Rev. James Duncan, to whom the Archbishop refers, had held the living for more than twenty years. He baptized Swift's biographer and cousin, Deane Swift (Carroll's "Clergy of St. Bride," p. 16).
[3] *Supra*, p. 268.   [4] *Supra*, p. 315.   [5] *Supra*, p. 94, n. 4.
[6] Or Saggart (*supra*, p. 56).
[7] A parish in the county of Kildare, not far from Rathcoole.
[8] Dopping married a sister of Howard.

in it, that he had signified to me that he was ready to come into my scheme. He now may, I believe, have an offer of Derry or Down,[1] but I hear he is fallen off, and scruples to take anything but a bishopric, to which, with my good will, I would never promote any man that had not gone through the degrees and served in proper stations in the Church.

I may trust you with it as a secret, that neither of these Deans had been removed at this time, if it were not to make room for him, and if he refuse the offer, he may assure himself, he will have cause to repent it. I think it is Tacitus who observed of governments, *si non vis ut bene tibi sit per eos facient ut male sit.* I hope you will give him better advice, and contribute to the execution of your own scheme, which as it will be a kindness to him and a benefit to the Society, for which I can expect nothing from the Government or Parliament whilst he is at the head of it, so it will be a great ease to, Reverend Sir,

Yours etc.,
W. D[UBLIN].

Dean Swift.

CCCXCVIII. [*Sheridan.*]

SWIFT TO ARCHBISHOP KING

[Dublin] March 9, 1716-17.

MY LORD,

I HAD yesterday the honour of a letter from your Grace,[2] wherein you first mention Mr. Duncan's accident, who, as it falls out, is quite recovered, and they say is since better of his asthma. I believe, whenever he dies, I shall be in some difficulties, although I am wholly indifferent who may succeed him, provided he may be a deserving person; unless I might say, that my inclinations are a little turned to oblige Mr. Dopping, on account of his brother,[3] for whom I have always had a very great esteem. It will be impossible for me to carry any point against that great majority of the Chapter, who are sure to oppose me whenever party interferes; and in those cases I shall be very

---

[1] *Supra,* p. 372.   [2] *Supra,* p. 373.   [3] *Supra,* p. 316.

ready to change my nomination, only choosing those I least dislike among such as they will consent to, wherein I hope I shall have your Grace's approbation.

About a week ago, I wrote to your Grace in relation to the Provost.[1] My Lord Bishop of Dromore, Dr. Coghill, and I were yesterday using our rhetoric to no purpose. The topic he perpetually adheres to is, that the Court offers him a deanery, because they look upon him as a man they cannot trust, which, he says, affects his reputation; that he professes to be as true to the present King, as any person in employment; that he has always shown himself so; that he was sacrificed by the Tories in the late reign, on account of the dispute in the College, and other matters; that he publicly argues and appears against the same party now, upon all occasions, and expects as little favour from them, if ever they should come into power, as any man now in employment. As to any hints dropped to him of any danger or uneasiness from Parliament or visitation, he declares himself perfectly safe and easy, and if it might not affect the Society, he should be glad of such inquiries, in order to vindicate himself; that he should like the deanery of Down full as well, and perhaps better, than the bishopric of Dromore,[2] provided the deanery was given him in such a manner, and with some mark of favour and approbation, that the world would not think he was driven into it as a man whom the King could not trust, and if any such method could be thought on, he would readily accept it; that he is very sensible he should be much happier in the other station, and much richer, and which weighs with him more, that it would be much for the present interest of the College to be under another head, but that the sense of his own loss of credit prevails with him above all considerations, and that he hopes in some time to convince the world, and the Court too, that he has been altogether misrepresented.

This is the sum of his reasoning, by all I could gather after several conversations with him, both alone and with some of his best friends, who all differ from him, as, he allows, most of his acquaintance do. I am no judge of what

---

[1] *Supra*, p. 371.

[2] Bishop Stearne had been translated to Clogher in the room of Bishop Ashe (*supra*, p. 371, n. 3).

consequence his removal may be to the service of the College, or of any favours to be shown it. But, I believe, it would be no difficult matter to find a temper in this affair; for instance, I speak purely my own thoughts, if the Prince[1] would graciously please to send a favourable message by his secretary, to offer him the deanery, in such a manner as might answer the Provost's difficulty. I cannot but think your Grace might bring such a thing about; but that I humbly leave to your Grace.

My Lord Bishop of Dromore received letters yesterday from your Grace, and the Bishop of Derry,[2] with an account of his succeeding to Clogher, of which I am sure all parties will be exceeding glad. I wish your Grace a good journey to the Bath, and a firm establishment of your health there. I am, with the greatest respect, my Lord,

Your Grace's most dutiful and most humble servant,

JON. SWIFT.

Not knowing but your Grace might be gone to the Bath, I have mentioned something of the Provost's affair, in a letter this post, to my Lord Bishop of Derry.

CCCXCIX. [*Copy.*[3]]

ARCHBISHOP KING TO SWIFT

London, *March* 12, 1716/7.

REVEREND SIR,

YOURS of the 2nd instant gave some trouble to me to find that after I had a prospect of bringing to perfection that scheme which all his friends came readily into and advised, and to which as I understand he himself consented, he should now go about to make objections to it, and to mar it. I ought to deal ingenuously with you, and tell you my mind honestly; I believe the Provost to be a good man, and to mean well, and that he may be of good use in the Church, but withal it does not appear to me that either

----

[1] The Prince of Wales, the Chancellor of the University (*supra*, p. 338, n. 1).

[2] *I.e.*, Ashe.   [3] In King's Correspondence. See Preface.

his heart or his talent lies in governing a College. If so, then why should he force his genius, and obstinately refuse what will certainly better suit that genius? As for his interpreting it a slight to take anything less than what was offered his predecessors, I answered that Dr. Huntington, after he became Provost, took a plain rectory and left the College, and though four bishoprics were then vacant none of them were offered him.[1]   But suppose the Court be jealous of him and therefore will not give a bishopric, will his refusing a deanery two or three hundred pounds better than the provostship contribute to remove that jealousy? Will it be either for his interest, or reputation, to be continually watched in a post, that exposed him more to the view and observation of his enemies than any other in the kingdom? You know he has many enemies, and that the gentlemen of the kingdom have great resentments against him, and will not easily be prevailed on to lay them aside. In what position then must he and the Society be, if he provoke the Court and government by refusing what they believe a favour? In the canon law *malitia plebis* is one reason of removing an incumbent, and for my own part I must own it to be a most uncomfortable thing for a man to be in a station where he is generally disliked, whether there be a reason for it or no. This is certainly the Provost's case, and what good can he expect to do in such circumstances?

If it be asked why do not they then make him a bishop? I answer for my own part, that I would never consent to make any head of a house a bishop without passing through other degrees. I think he is in a fair way to be one, when he has a deanery of a thousand pounds, but if he think to force himself into a bishopric by obstinately sticking to a post that is not thought proper for him, he may perhaps find himself mistaken, for which I should be very sorry. As to reputation, I will engage he will lose none by it; perhaps he doth not know what his circumstances as to that matter are at present. I believe you remember

---

[1] Dr. Huntington, who preceded Bishop Ashe as Provost (*supra*, vol. i, p. 362, n. 2), was appointed on his retirement from that office to an English benefice, and, although King was unaware of the fact, had refused to accept an Irish bishopric (Mant, *op. cit.*, ii, 104). Some years later he did so, however, but died within a few days of his consecration.

your former letter to me, but these things ought to be handled tenderly. I think it will be much for his reputation to do a thing, though cross to his humour, which will certainly be for his ease, and the generality believe for the good of the Society of which he has been so long head; he that humbles himself shall be exalted, and I am persuaded he will find his account in this conduct with all good men, and others are not valuable. If I did not think this of moment, I would not have troubled you with so long a letter, and I assure you it is with regard to the Provost, as well as to the Society, that I write this. I do not love to be trifled with, and if the Provost break his word with me after signifying himself satisfied with this scheme, it will lessen, to be sure, my opinion of him.

I have done what business I had to do in London, and nothing keeps me from the Bath but the very ill weather; if that mend, God willing, I shall go on Friday. In the mean time I am, Reverend Sir,

Yours etc.,
W. D[UBLIN].

Dean Swift.

CD. [*Copy.*[1]]

ARCHBISHOP KING TO SWIFT

London, March 21, 1716/7.

REVEREND SIR,

I RECEIVED yours of the 9th instant, and find by Mr. Duncan's recovery that we shall have time enough to adjust the affair of St. Bridget's. I think his life is entirely to be ascribed to Providence, for I am assured none else is, or would be, concerned to preserve it. I hope, if God grant me life, I shall be able to provide for one of the candidates before the vacancy happen, and that will take away all competition. I assure you, I am as well inclined to take care of Mr. Dopping as you can desire me to be.

As to the Provost, he is very much mistaken if he think it on account of party, that his friends desire to remove

---

[1] In King's Correspondence. See Preface.

him. No, it is with a view to make him easy and put him
in a post in the Church that I take to be more honourable than the provostship—which gives no place at all, is
more profitable, and may fit him for better preferment in
the Church, for which in my opinion the College government rather disqualifies a man; and let me assure you that
he has no other way to secure the favour of the Court, or
to give satisfaction to the kingdom, than by accepting a
better post when offered, and more suitable to his talent.
We have had a specimen of his conduct in governing the
College for about seven years, and I think it now full time
to try him in another post. Surely he cannot be so partial
as to think he has governed well, and I declare for my own
part, that without regard to any principle or party, I
should be for wishing him another post, and all that I am
acquainted with, whether friends or enemies to him, or
indifferent, are of the same opinion, and he ought to be
thankful to them that have so effectually recommended to
the Court, as to obtain this favourable remove for him;
it is intended and meant as a favour, and if he will not
take it as such, he will, if I be not mistaken, [have]
reason to repent it. It was a thing proposed to me by his
best friends, and he promised me under his hand to come
into it, and if he deceives me and them, I shall know what
to think of him. Mr. Molyneux [1] has writ to him in stronger
terms than you propose; what effect it will have I cannot
tell, but assure yourself the deanery of Down will not go
a begging.

The weather promises at last to be somewhat favourable, which will put me on my journey to the Bath, God
willing, to-morrow. I hope I shall hear from you, and that
you will tell something of what passes on your side to,
Reverend Sir,

Yours etc.,

W. D[UBLIN].

Dean Swift.

---

[1] *Supra*, p. 343, n. 1.

CDI. [*Original.*[1]]

SWIFT TO ARCHDEACON WALLS

Thursday night, *March* 28, 1717.[2]

PRAY, if Mrs. Brent[3] has sent my stockings, send them by the bearer; or if not, and if the bearer will call again, send to Mrs. Brent for them. I writ this day to the Bishop. The bearer gives you this to-morrow night, and returns on Saturday. I had a letter, which I suppose you sent me, from Mr. Deacon, the tenant of Kilberry, who tells me the Bishop of Down had ordered him to pay me last Michaelmas rent, which is the sixty pounds, for which you know I have his Lordship's bond.[4] Deacon desires further time till his garrons get flesh. I suppose the Bishop has paid his own rent, and puts the leavings upon me. I shall write to Deacon, and let him know I will not be so used. Tell the Bishop of Clogher[5] that Dilly Ashe[6] had a slovenly way of ******* as he lay in bed. I desire to know what sort of stone that was, make him guess, but I will tell you. It is *** *** ******: *lapis lazuli.* My service to Gossip and the ladies, and duty to the Bishop. I am,

Yours, etc.

Joe is as fain to know how le Mannian and Simmeri received you, and your excuses for him.[7]

Addressed—To the Reverend Mr. Archdeacon Walls at his house in Queen Street, Dublin.

[1] In the possession of Mr. John Murray. See Preface.
[2] Swift was again staying at Trim.
[3] *Supra*, p. 368.   [4] *Supra*, p. 359.
[5] *I.e.*, Stearne.
[6] Dilly Ashe (*supra*, vol. i, p. 376, n. 4) had died in the preceding May. He was buried in his church at Finglas on the 18th of that month.
[7] *Supra*, p. 367.

CDII. [*Original.*[1]]

SWIFT TO ARCHDEACON WALLS

Trim, *March* 30, 1717.

I SHALL not have a stocking to my foot, unless Mrs. Brent sends them to you to-morrow,[2] and you put them in the Bishop's bag on Tuesday.[3] I write early, because I go to Laracor. Make April fools of the ladies to-morrow. I have been three times with Joe upon my new estate, and three times I could not fix on the spot where the house is to be:[4] *tantae molis erat,* etc. Mr. Burne will be in town next term to receive my money, and give you ease.[5] I had yours last night. One of the enclosed was from Archbishop of Dublin,[6] all about the Provost and his taking the deanery. The Archbishop was to set out for the Bath a day after he writ. Pay sweet-heart her board-wages.[7] Pray desire Clem Barry[8] to negotiate by all means and methods for poor Prior's subscriptions: a guinea subscribed and another guinea on delivering the book.[9] Let him get others to take subscriptions as well as himself. I have had fresh entreaties from England about it just before I left you. Remember my turns at St. Patrick's. Let the Bishop[10] tell the Archbishop of Tuam[11] that he takes me down with him, and hinders me from appearing at the Archbishop of Dublin's visitation, which Tuam holds. Or rather I think he need not. It is a sort of condescension I am not obliged to, but it might be done occasionally or let alone. When the post comes in I will add a postscript.

Last night about ten we were called out to see an appearance in the sky like what was last summer, streams shoot-

---

[1] In the possession of Mr. John Murray. See Preface.

[2] *Supra,* p. 380.

[3] As appears subsequently, Bishop Stearne was going to Clogher for his enthronement (*supra,* p. 375, n. 2), and Swift was to accompany him. This letter is dated on Sunday.

[4] *Supra,* p. 352. The present glebe-house at Laracor, which was built in 1813, stands some distance from the site of Swift's "neat cabin." It is doubtful whether another residence for the clergymen was erected in Swift's time.

[5] *Supra,* p. 344.   [6] *Supra,* p. 376.   [7] *Supra,* p. 344, n. 5.

[8] *Supra,* p. 280.   [9] *Supra,* p. 360.   [10] *I.e.,* Stearne.

[11] *I.e.,* Synge (*supra,* p. 365, n. 6).

ing from the north, and the night very light, as at full-moon. But it differed from that of last year in this, that the rays which shot flew like lightning and flashed all over the sky, and darted, as we agreed, like the rays from a looking-glass when you turn it against the sun, as boys do out of a window, with sudden quivering motion. It was very amusing for about half an hour. The rays which flew about were distinguishable like a white thin cloud, and spent themselves soon. Some times they were in a circular motion. Doctor Raymond says it was like the quivering of the flame over burned brandy, when that flame is just going out. This appearance is for Sweden, as Mrs. Peggy says, as that of last year was for the Pretender. Was this appearance observed in Dublin?

I received the Bishop's letter just as I was going to Church. I find he does not think of going till Thursday. I expect next post to know from him what road he is to take. As to the gown, it was never intended for you; but, however, I believe it will not fit me. Pray pay Mr. Craven what charge he [has] been at; he says it is only two shillings and two pence; and the porter that brought the box. Young man, the gown and cassock will smooth of themselves. You must pay what they cost in London, and then you will save carriage and custom, for Craven passed them as old goods. I believe six pounds English will be the price. My humble service to Gossip Doll and the ladies. Doctor Raymond and she give all theirs, and Joe his respects.

Addressed—To the Reverend Mr. Archdeacon Walls at his house over against the Blue-Coat Hospital, in Queen Street, Dublin.

CDIII. [*Sheridan.*]

Swift to Archbishop King

Magheralin,[1] *May* 1, 1717.

MY LORD,

YOUR Grace's letter of March 23d was brought to me at Trim, where I went a month ago to finish my lease and

---

[1] *Supra*, p. 363, n. 4.

purchase for my country parish. In some days after, I met my Lord Bishop of Clogher at Drogheda, by appointment;[1] we went together to Clogher, where he was enthroned, and after three days came to this place, where his Lordship is settling everything against the coming of the new Bishop,[2] who is expected here next week. My great business at Clogher was to seduce his Lordship to lay out two thousand pounds in a new house, and for that end we rode about to find a situation. I know not whether I shall prevail; for he has a hankering after making additions to the old one, which I will never consent to, and would rather he should leave all to the generosity of a successor.[3] My notion is, that when a bishop, with good dispositions, happens to arise, it should be every man's business to cultivate them. It is no ill age that produces two such; and therefore, if I had credit with your Grace and his Lordship, it should be all employed in pushing you both upon works of public good, without the least mercy to your pains or your purses. An expert tradesman makes a few of his best customers answer, not only for those whom he gets little or nothing by, but for all who die in his debt.

I will suppose your Grace has heard of Mr. Duncan's death.[4] I am sure I have heard enough of it, by a great increase of disinterested correspondents ever since. It is well I am at free cost for board and lodging, else postage would have undone me. I have returned no answer to any; and shall be glad to proceed with your Grace's approbation, which is a less compliment, because I believe my Chapter are of opinion I can hardly proceed without it. I only desire two things; first, that those who call themselves my friends may have no reason to reproach me, and the second, that in the course of this matter, I may have something to dispose of to some one I wish well to.

Some weeks before Mr. Duncan's death, his brother-in-law, Mr. Lawson, minister of Galtrim,[5] went for England,

---

[1] *Supra*, p. 381.
[2] Dean Lambert (*supra*, p. 372, n. 1) had been appointed Stearne's successor in the see of Dromore.
[3] Stearne is said to have rebuilt the palace (Mant, *op. cit.*, ii, 586).
[4] *Supra*, p. 373, n. 2.
[5] The Rev. Wilfred Lawson had held the living of Galtrim, which, as has been mentioned, is near Trim (*supra*, p. 343, n. 4), for sixteen years.

by Mr. Duncan's consent, to apply for an adjoining living, called Kilmore,[1] in Mr. Duncan's possession, and now in the Crown by his death. I know not his success; but heartily wish, if it be intended for him, that the matter might take another turn: that Mr. Warren, who is landlord of Galtrim, might have that living, and Kilmore adjoining,[2] both not a hundred and fifty pounds, and Mr. Lawson to go down to Mr. Warren's living, in Clogher diocese, worth above two hundred pounds. But this is all at random, because I know not whether Kilmore may not be already disposed of, for I hear it is in your Grace's turn.

I heard lately from the Provost, who talked of being in the north in a month; but our Dublin account is, that they know not when the deanery is to be given him.[3] I do not find any great joy in either party on account of the person, who, it is supposed, will succeed him.[4] The wrong custom of making that post the next step to a bishopric, has been, as your Grace says, of ill consequence; and although, as you add, it gives them no rank, yet they think fit to take it, and make no scruple of preceding, on all occasions, the best private clergyman in the kingdom, which is a trifle of great consequence when a man's head is possessed with it.

I pray God preserve your Grace, for the good of the Church and the learned world, and for the happiness of those whom you are pleased to honour with your friendship, favour, or protection. I beg your Grace's blessing; and remain, with the greatest truth and respect, my Lord,

Your Grace's most dutiful and most humble servant,

JON. SWIFT.

[1] Duncan appears to have had a good estate in the county of Meath. His wife was a daughter of Sir Henry Echlin, the first of a line of baronets who have contributed a chapter to Sir Bernard Burke's "Vicissitudes of Families."

[2] Warren does not appear to have been given either Galtrim or Kilmore.

[3] Provost Pratt was presented to the deanery of Down on 17 June.

[4] Dr. Richard Baldwin, who succeeded Pratt in the provostship, was a school and college contemporary of Swift. He proved one of the most munificent benefactors the University of Dublin has known.

CDIV. [*Copy.*[1]]

ARCHBISHOP KING TO SWIFT

Bath, *May* 13, 1717.

REVEREND SIR,

I WAS favoured with yours of the 1st instant, which I perused with great pleasure, though I can claim but a little share in the good dispositions you are pleased to ascribe to me. As to Mr. Warren, if it be he that served the cure of St. Mary's,[2] I take him to be a good man, and shall be ready to serve him; as to Mr. Lawson I know him not, and to be sure, shall not be very forward to assist any man that leaves Ireland in order to solicit at Court here. As to the benefice you mention in the diocese of Clogher, it cannot be expected that I should concern myself in the disposal of it, without the Bishop's desiring it of me. I should be glad, and thank God, if all your friends and mine were common to us both, and will endeavour to make them so; in the mean time I promise you that no person shall fare the worse on the account of their reckoning themselves here your friend, but the better.

I am now in a fit of the gout and I hope that will excuse the shortness of this answer. I hope to see you in the beginning of the next month, and will endeavour so to settle a good understanding between you, your Chapter and me, that we may have but one common interest. I heartily recommend you to God's good care, and am, Reverend Sir,

Yours etc.,

W. D[UBLIN].

Dean Swift.

CDV. [*Original.*[3]]

SWIFT TO ARCHDEACON WALLS

Magheralin,[4] *May* 19, 1717.

TO-MORROW morning my Lord[5] and I set out towards

---

[1] In King's Correspondence. See Preface.
[2] The church in Dublin which gave the designation of the St. Mary ladies to Stella and her friend.
[3] In the possession of Mr. John Murray. See Preface.
[4] *Supra*, p. 363, n. 4.   [5] *I.e.*, Stearne.

Dublin. I leave my Lord at Ardee, or Drogheda,[1] and turn off to Trim for a few days to settle some things at Laracor, and then hope to see you in Dublin. I have had abundance of letters about St. Bride's,[2] and now Dr. Howard gravely writes to me that the Archbishop of Dublin has declared for him, and hopes I will consent. Nothing could put me more against him than the Archbishop's declaring, and I am now resolved to oppose it as long as I can.[3] Not but that next to a friend it is most to my interest that Howard should have it, because he hath something to give up which I may bestow [on] a friend; I mean the advowson of a town living which now will be worth something, and more in time; but there again I am at a loss who to give it to; for I had thoughts of a scheme with the Grattans,[4] and of Sam Holt,[5] and the Provost writes to me about Forbes,[6] and I know not what to think or say. But I will take time like my friend Lord Oxford.

I wonder at the Provost's formality about the deanery.[7] They say here that the government will not give it till he asks them, and he writes me word that they expect solicitation. If so, I think he acts right. I hope you have got money for me; and when I get to Trim, I shall know how Davy Burne has performed.[8] I writ to you about buying me some wine; I know not what you have done in it. I would have none unless it be extremely good, and that last vintage was a very good one in the opinion of the wise. I design to write to Deacon the Bishop of Down's tenant,[9] as soon as I can get to town and swinge him off if he does not pay me my money. It is pleasant to see my Lord mustering up his goods upon leaving this place, and missing sheets, tablecloths, napkins, candlesticks by the dozen, and bottles by the hundred, and all within half a year passed. He is now persuaded to take a house-keeper if he can get a good one.

---

[1] Both Ardee and Drogheda are on the main road from Dublin to the north of Ireland. Drogheda is situated on the borders of the counties of Meath and Louth, and Ardee, which is in the latter county and was then a parliamentary borough, is about eleven miles further to the north. A cross road thence, as well as one from Drogheda, would have brought Swift to Trim.

[2] *Supra*, p. 383.

[3] Howard (*supra*, p. 373) was, however, appointed to the incumbency of St. Bride.

[4] *Supra*, p. 262.   [5] *Supra*, p. 316.   [6] *Supra*, p. 282.

[7] *Supra*, p. 379.   [8] *Supra*, p. 381.   [9] *Supra*, p. 380.

CDVI. [*Original.*[1]]

SWIFT TO ARCHDEACON WALLS

Trim, May 23, 1717.

WHEN I left my Lord Bishop[2] at Drogheda, as he tells you, I rode ten miles to Navan, and there lay and came here yesterday. My Lord intended to lie at Drogheda, and there I designed to finish my letters to you and Mrs. Dingley, but stopping at the gate,[3] I was forced to seal them unfinished in a cabin. There has not been one thing done to my rooms at Laracor since I went; as I hear it was by the perverseness of that puppy Parvisol.[4] I am going there this morning about it. I hope my Lord Bishop got home safe, and desire my duty to him. We expected Mr. Warburton would have taken this town in his way home,[5] but we reckon he is gone a shorter road. I should have been very glad to see him. I have read Hoadly's sermon,[6] and the Bishop will tell you my thoughts of it. I wonder whether his will be the same, and what are yours, and whether the Whigs justify it.

If exchange be low, I must return a hundred pounds to England towards paying a debt there. I hope to get the money from the lands in Kildare. I wish Mr. Burne, who is in town, would write to Mr. Deacon near Athy about it[7]— there is sixty pounds due for half year last Michaelmas, and seventy-five pounds, by the advanced rent, due the 25th of March last—to let him know that I expect to receive both immediately, in all one hundred and thirty-five pounds. This sum with forty or fifty pounds, if I can get it, will I hope clear my grand English debt, returns and all; though I fear it hath increased by money paid to Mrs. Fenton[8] and others. However it will make it pretty light. Pray

[1] In the possession of Mr. John Murray. See Preface.
[2] *I.e.*, Stearne (*supra*, p. 385).
[3] The gate of St. Lawrence, through which this historic town is still entered.
[4] *Supra*, p. 367.   [5] To Magherafelt (*supra*, p. 366).
[6] His famous sermon, "On the Kingdom of Christ," which he had preached before the King in March, and which gave rise to the Bangorian Controversy.
[7] *Supra*, p. 386.   [8] Swift's sister (*supra*, vol. i, p. 30).

let me know whether Mr. Burne designs soon to leave Dublin. My humble service to my Gossip and the ladies. We expect Dr. Raymond here to-morrow.

Addressed—To the Reverend Mr. Archdeacon Walls at his house over against the Blue-Coat Hospital, in Queen Street, Dublin.

CDVII. [*Original.*[1]]

Erasmus Lewis to Swift

London, *June* 15, 1717.

LAST night I received yours of the 5th instant; and since you tell me I am your only correspondent, I think I ought to be the more punctual in my returns, and the more full in what relates to our friends here. You will see by the public prints that Monday next come sennight[2] is appointed for the trial of my Lord Oxford, and that no less than six-and-twenty doughty members are appointed to manage it.[3] The Lords have likewise settled the whole forms of the proceedings. My Lord has asked, that two lawyers more might be added to his counsel; yet is all this but a farce, for there is not a creature living who thinks he will ever be tried, for they publicly own, that they neither have, nor ever had, any evidence, and laugh at impeachments and attainders, and party gambols, and say, that all people deserve to be so punished, who presume to dispossess the Whigs of their indefeasible right to the administration. But since he is not to be tried, the next question is, in what manner he is to be brought off, so as to save the honour of his prosecutors. I think it will be by an Act of Grace. Others say, it will be by the Commons asking more time, and the Lords of their party agreeing to refuse it. But as we are wholly ignorant of their intentions, it is possible neither of these guesses may be right,

---

[1] In the British Museum. See Preface.   [2] The 24th.
[3] In May Oxford had lodged a petition that his case should be taken into consideration, and after a debate the Lords had decided that he should be brought to trial. The 13th of June was the date first named, but the trial was subsequently postponed to the 24th.

and that they may keep him yet another year in prison, which my Lord Marlborough seems passionately to desire.

We labour here under all the disadvantages in the world in every respect; for the tide of party runs still very strong everywhere, but in no place more than in Westminster Hall. Those on this side, whose honour and interest both require that all people, who pay obedience, should be protected, seem to want a capacity to govern, and the similitude of circumstances between the [King] and the Regent,[1] render the latter a firm ally, contrary to the natural interest of France. Thus we are secure from any foreign enemy.

I agree with you, that Snape's letter is really but a letter, and that it is much too short and too slight for such a subject.[2] However, his merit was great, in being the first to give the alarm to his brethren, and setting himself in the front of the battle against his adversaries. In those respects, his letter has had its full effect.

I desire you will be as quick as you can in the assistance you intend Prior;[3] for those who subscribed here are impatient to have their books; and we cannot keep it off much longer, without passing for common cheats. Dr. Arbuthnot and Mr. Charleton[4] and I, remember you often. Lady Masham always asks for you very affectionately. By the way, I am perfectly restored to grace there, and am invited to their house in the country. As soon as Lord Oxford's affair is over, I intend to go amongst my friends in the country, not to return hither till about Michaelmas. But if you will direct to me at my house in town, your letters will be conveyed to me, wherever I am. Mr. Rochfort seems to have a great many good qualities, and I am heartily glad he has met with success.[5] Adieu.

Addressed—To the Rev. Dr. Swift, Dean of St. Patrick's, in Dublin, Ireland.

[1] Philip, Duke of Orleans, who had governed France since the accession of his cousin, Louis XV, two years previously.

[2] Andrew Snape, then head master of Eton and afterwards Provost of King's College, Cambridge, was one of Hoadly's foremost opponents. His letter, which was a reply to Hoadly's sermon (*supra*, p. 387, n. 6), passed through seventeen editions in a few months.

[3] *Supra*, p. 381.

[4] The Duchess of Ormond's chaplain (*supra*, p. 370).

[5] The reference is apparently to "the Baron's" law business in England (*supra*, p. 321).

CDVIII. [*Original.*[1]]

ERASMUS LEWIS TO SWIFT

London, *June* 18, 1717.

HAVING acquainted you in my letter of last post,[2] that it was the universal opinion the Commons would not proceed to the trial of my Lord Oxford, I think myself obliged to tell you, that we begin now to be something doubtful; for the managers, who are twenty-seven in number, strenuously give out, that they shall be ready to proceed on Monday next. Therefore, if you have any thoughts of coming over, let not anything, which I have said in my last, have any weight with you to alter that resolution. I am wholly taken up with the men of the law, and therefore have nothing to say to you at present upon any public matters. I shall only just trouble you with one word relating to a private affair. My brother is chaplain to Sir Charles Hotham's regiment, which is now ordered to Ireland.[3] If you could find any young fellow, who would buy that commission, my brother thinks his patron, my Lord Carlisle,[4] will easily prevail with my Lord Duke of Bolton[5] for leave to dispose of it. I should be very glad you could find him a chapman.

Addressed—To the Rev. Dr. Swift, Dean of St. Patrick's, in Dublin, Ireland.

[1] In the British Museum. See Preface.
[2] *Supra,* p. 388.
[3] The regiment had seen much service during the rebellion; on being ordered to Ireland Sir Charles Hotham resigned the colonelcy, and the regiment was disbanded in the following year (Dalton's "George the 1st's Army," p. 172).
[4] Charles, third Earl of Carlisle, who after the accession of George I acted for some months as First Lord of the Treasury.
[5] The Duke of Bolton (*supra,* p. 212) had been appointed in April Lord Lieutenant of Ireland.

CDIX. [*Original.*[1]]

ERASMUS LEWIS TO SWIFT

London, *July* 2, 1717.

I HAVE the pleasure to inform you, that Lord Oxford's impeachment [2] was discharged last night, by the unanimous consent of all the Lords present, and, as nearly as I could count, their number was one hundred and six, the Duke of Marlborough, my Lord Cadogan,[3] Lord Coningsby,[4] and a few others of the most violent, having withdrawn themselves before the Lords came into Westminster Hall. The acclamations were as great as upon any occasion, and our friend, who seems more formed for adversity than prosperity, has at present many more friends than ever he had before, in any part of his life. I believe he will not have the fewer, from a message he received this morning from the King, by my Lord Chamberlain, to forbid him the Court.[5] You know the prosecution was at first the resentment of a party, but it became at last a ridiculous business, weakly carried on by the impotent rage of a woman, I mean of my Lady Marlborough, who is almost distracted that she could not obtain her revenge.

I am now going out of town, with an intention to roll about from place to place, till about Michaelmas next. If you write to me, direct to me hither, as usual, and your letter will be conveyed to me, wherever I am. Dr. Arbuthnot, Mr. Charleton,[6] and Mr. Currey, have dined with me to-day, and you have not been forgot. I was in hopes we should have seen you ere this. The Doctor says, you wait for the Act of Grace. If so, I hope to see you by next winter.

---

[1] In the British Museum. See Preface.   [2] *Supra*, p. 390.

[3] Cadogan had only been created a peer in the preceding year. He had distinguished himself under Marlborough, and naturally followed his old commander.

[4] Coningsby had been a member of the Secret Committee, and had moved Oxford's impeachment.

[5] The letter and Oxford's reply, both dated 2 July, are in the "Manuscripts of the Marquess of Bath," i, 249. Thomas Pelham, who had been created Duke of Newcastle (*supra*, p. 183, n. 2), held then the office of chamberlain, and emphasizes the fact that he acts under orders and has the most profound respect for Oxford.

[6] *Supra*, p. 389.

CDX. [*Sheridan.*]

SWIFT TO ROBERT COPE

Dublin, *July* 9, 1717.

SIR,[1]

I RECEIVED the favour of your letter before I came to town; for I stayed three weeks at Trim after I left you,[2] out of perfect hatred to this place, where at length business dragged me against my will. The Archdeacon, who delivers you this, will let you know I am but an ill solicitor for him.[3] The thing is indeed a little difficult and perplexed, yet a willing mind would make it easy, but that is wanted, and I cannot work it up. However, it shall not be my fault, if something be not made of it one time or other; but some people give their best friends reason to complain. I have at a venture put you down among poor Mr. Prior's benefactors,[4] and I wonder what exemption you pretend to as appears by your letter to Mr. Stewart. It seems you took the thousand pounds a year in a literal sense, and even at that rate I hope you would not be excused. I hope your sheep-shearing in the county of Louth hath established your health; and that Dr. Tisdall,[5] your brother of the spleen, comes sometimes, and makes you laugh at a pun or a blunder. I made a good many advances to your friend Bolton[6] since I came to town, and talked of you; but all

---

[1] The writer of this letter, an ancestor of the Copes of Loughgall Manor in the county of Armagh, had been introduced to Swift in London apparently by Charles Ford ("Prose Works," ii, 119). He had succeeded Mr. Justice Nutley in the representation of Lisburn (*supra*, p. 60, n. 7), and had sat for his own county in Queen Anne's last Irish parliament, but was too sound a Tory to secure election on the accession of George I. See Sheridan's " Life," p. 217.

[2] Swift would appear on his return from his expedition with Stearne to have paid Cope a visit at Loughgall.

[3] The Archdeacon was probably Theodore Morris, who held the living of Desercreat in the diocese of Armagh as well as the archdeaconry of Tuam (Leslie's "Armagh Clergy and Parishes," p. 219), and in whose company Swift had first met Cope.

[4] *Supra*, p. 389.

[5] Stella's old admirer, who, as has been mentioned (*supra*, vol. i, p. 47, n. 1), held a rectory in the county of Armagh as well as the vicarage of Belfast.

[6] *I.e.*, Theophilus Bolton (*supra*, p. 318, n. 5).

signified nothing; for he has taken every opportunity of opposing me, in the most unkind and unnecessary manner, and I have done with him. I could with great satisfaction pass a month or two among you, if things would permit. The Archdeacon carries you all the news, and I need say nothing. We grow mightily sanguine, but my temper has not fire enough in it. They assure me that Lord Bolingbroke will be included in the Act of Grace; which, if it be true, is a mystery to me.

You must learn to winter in town, or you will turn a monk, and Mrs. Cope a nun; I am extremely her humble servant. I have ventured to subscribe a guinea for Mr. Brownlow,[1] because I would think it a shame not to have his name in the list. Pray tell him so. I doubt whether Mrs. Cope will be pleased with the taste of snuff I sent her. Present my humble service to your mother and brother; and believe me to be, with great truth and esteem, Sir,

Your most obedient humble servant,
JON. SWIFT.

CDXI. [*Manuscripts of the Marquess of Bath.*[2]]

SWIFT TO THE EARL OF OXFORD

Dublin, *July* 9, 1717.

SINCE I am sure no event can have any power upon your mind, I cannot help believing that during this glorious scene of your life—I do not mean your discharge,[3] but your two years' imprisonment—you have sometimes found a minute to remember an inconsiderable man who ever loved you above all things. I write to you from an imagination I have always had, that as soon as you were freed from your jailers, you would retire for some months to Herefordshire, and that I should be a companion in your retirement. Therefore if you have any such thoughts, I beg you will command me to attend, for I have many

---

[1] An ancestor of the Earl of Lurgan who represented the county of Armagh at that time. Cope married, as his first wife, one of the family.

[2] Hist. MSS. Com., i, 249.   [3] *Supra*, p. 391.

things to say to you, and to inquire of you, as you may easily imagine. You will forgive me if I talk ignorantly; for perhaps you intend to live in town, or pass the summer with my Lord Harley, or perhaps, as some refiners say, you are again to be a Minister. In any of these cases, all I have said I desire may go for nothing, and I will wait your leisure. However, pray let me know as soon as you can by a line from yourself. I will trouble you no more at present.

CDXII. [*Scott.*]

SWIFT TO JOSEPH ADDISON

Dublin, *July* 9, 1717.

SIR,

I SHOULD be much concerned if I did not think you were a little angry with me for not congratulating you upon being Secretary.[1] But I choose my time, as I would to visit you, when all your company is gone. I am confident you have given ease of mind to many thousand people, who will never believe any ill can be intended to the constitution in Church or State, while you are in so high a trust, and I should have been of the same opinion though I had not the happiness to know you.

I am extremely obliged for your kind remembrance some months ago, by the Bishop of Derry,[2] and for your generous intentions, if you had come to Ireland, to have made party give way to friendship by continuing your acquaintance.

I examine my heart, and can find no other reason why I write to you now, beside that great love and esteem I have always had for you. I have nothing to ask you either for any friend or for myself. When I conversed among

[1] After the arrival of George I, on the termination of the regency (*supra*, p. 212), Addison had been appointed secretary to the Lord Lieutenant of Ireland, but though the contrary has been stated, like his chief, Lord Sunderland, he never went to that country. Three months before the date of Swift's letter he had been promoted to the position of a Secretary of State.

[2] *I.e.*, Ashe, of whom Addison had still "a thousand good things to say" (*supra*, vol. i, p. 158).

Ministers, I boasted of your acquaintance, but I feel no vanity from being known to a Secretary of State. I am only a little concerned to see you stand single; for it is a prodigious singularity in any Court to owe one's rise entirely to merit. I will venture to tell you a secret, that three or four more such choices, would gain more hearts in three weeks, than all the methods hitherto practised have been able to do in as many years.

It is now time for me to recollect that I am writing to a Secretary of State, who has little time allowed him for trifles; I therefore take my leave, with assurances of my being ever, with the truest respect, Sir,

> Your most obedient and most humble servant,
> JONATH. SWIFT.

CDXIII. [*Original.*[1]]

SWIFT TO THE EARL OF OXFORD

Dublin, *July* 16, 1717.

MY LORD,

I WROTE to you some days ago,[2] and enclosed the letter in a cover directed to your brother in Lincoln's Inn Fields; I need not repeat what I there said, but beg your Lordship will answer my letter as soon as you have an hour of leisure, and do not let civility force you to say anything against your mind, for if it doth not consist with your conveniency, the matter is at an end. But I imagine, if you have any thoughts of retiring for some time to Herefordshire, I ought to see you and ask you some questions, and receive your instructions, concerning some things I have often spoke to you about, that might employ my leisure in the present situation of affairs, which we then easily foresaw, etc. I will now give you no further trouble but remain, etc.

Addressed—To the Right Honourable the Earl of Oxford, at his house at St. James's, London.

[1] In the possession of the Duke of Portland (*supra*, p. 160, n. 2)
[2] *Supra*, p. 393.

CDXIV. [*Nichols.*]

SWIFT TO BISHOP ATTERBURY

Dublin, *July* 18, 1717.

MY LORD,

SOME persons of distinction, lately come from England, and not unknown to your Lordship, have made me extremely pleased and proud, by telling me that your Lordship was so generous as to defend me against an idle story that passed in relation to a letter of mine to the Archbishop of Dublin.[1] I have corresponded for many years with his Grace, though we generally differed in politics, and therefore our letters had often a good mixture of controversy. I confess likewise that I have been his Grace's advocate, where he had not many others. About nine months ago I writ a letter to him in London, for in my little station it is convenient there should be some commerce between us; and in a short time after I had notice from several friends, that a passage in my letter was shown to several persons, and a consequence drawn from thence, that I was wholly gone over to other principles more in fashion, and wherein I might better find my account. I neglected this report, as thinking it might soon die; but found it gathered strength, and spread to Oxford and this kingdom, and some gentlemen, who lately arrived here, assured me they had met it a hundred times, with all the circumstances of disadvantage that are usually tacked to such stories by the great candour of mankind. It should seem as if I were somebody of importance, and if so, I should think the wishes not only of my friends, but of my party, might dispose them rather to believe me innocent, than condemn me unheard. Upon the first intelligence I had of this affair, I made a shift to recollect the only passage in that letter which could be any way liable to misinterpretation.

I told the Archbishop, we had an account of a set of people in London, who were erecting a new church, upon the maxim that everything was void, since the Revolution, in the Church as well as the State, that all priests must be re-ordained, Bishops again consecrated, and in like manner of the rest, that I knew not what there was in it of truth,

---

[1] *Supra*, pp. 337, 360.

that it was impossible such a scheme should ever pass, and that I believed if the Court, upon this occasion, would show some good-will to the Church, discourage those who ill treated the clergy, etc., it would be the most popular thing they could think of. I keep no copies of letters; but this, I am confident, was the substance of what I wrote, and that every other line in the letter which mentioned public affairs, would have atoned for this, if it had been a crime, as I think it was not in that juncture, whatever may be my opinion at present; for, I confess, my thoughts change every week, like those of a man in an incurable consumption, who daily finds himself more and more decay.

The trouble I now give your Lordship is an ill return to your goodness in defending me; but it is the usual reward of goodness, and therefore you must be content. In the mean time, I am in a hopeful situation, torn to pieces by pamphleteers and libellers on that side the water, and by the whole body of the ruling party on this; against which all the obscurity I live in will not defend me. Since I came first to this kingdom, it has been the constant advice of all my Church friends, that I should be more cautious. To oppose me in everything relating to my station, is made a merit in my Chapter, and I shall probably live to make some Bishops as poor, as Luther made many rich.

I profess to your Lordship, that what I have been writing is only with regard to the good opinion of your Lordship, and of a very few others with whom you will think it of any consequence to an honest man that he should be set right. I am sorry that those who call themselves churchmen should be industrious to have it thought that their number is lessened, even by so inconsiderable a one as myself. But I am sufficiently recompensed, that your Lordship knows me best, to whom I am so ambitious to be best known. God be thanked, I have but a few to satisfy. The bulk of my censurers are strangers, or ill judges, or worse than either, and if they will not obey your orders to correct their sentiments of me, they will meet their punishment in your Lordship's disapprobation, which I would not incur for all their good words put together, and printed in twelve volumes folio. I am, with great respect, my Lord,

Your Lordship's most dutiful and most humble servant,
JON. SWIFT.

CDXV. [*Original.*[1]]

MATTHEW PRIOR TO SWIFT

Duke Street, Westminster,
July 30, 1717.

DEAR SIR,

I HAVE the favour of four letters from you, of the 9th, 13th, 16th, and 20th instant. They all came safe to me, however variously directed, but the last to me, at my house in Duke Street, is the rightest. I find myself equally comforted by your philosophy, and assisted by your friendship. You will easily imagine, that I have a hundred things to say to you, which for as many reasons I omit, and only touch upon that business, to which, in the pride of your heart, you give the epithet " sorry." I return you the names of those who were kind enough to subscribe,[2] that you may see if they are rightly spelt, as likewise the just titles put to them, as likewise if it has happened that any has subscribed for more than one volume. You will please to look over the catalogue, and return it to me at your leisure. You see that our calculation comes even; the gentleman's name that desired it being omitted. I am sensible that this has given you too much trouble, but it is too late now to make an apology. Let Mr. Lewis, who is now with me, do it for me, at what time, and in what manner, he pleases.

I take it for granted, that whatever I write, as whatever is writ to me, will be broke open, so you will expect nothing from me, but what you may have as particularly from the Postboy. We are all pretty well in health. I have my old whoreson cough, and I think I may call it mine for life. The Earl[3] is *semper idem.* Lord Harley is in the country. Our brotherhood[4] is extremely dispersed; but so as that we have been three or four times able to get as many of the Society together, and drink to our absent friends. I have been made to believe, that we may see your reverend person this summer in England; if so, I shall be glad to meet you at any place, but when you come to London, do

---

[1] In the British Museum. See Preface.
[2] *Supra*, p. 389.
[3] *I.e.*, Oxford.
[4] *I.e.*, the Brothers' Club.

not go to the Cocoa-tree, as you sent your letter, but come immediately to Duke Street, where you shall find a bed, a book, and a candle; so pray think of sojourning nowhere else.

Pray give my service to all friends in general. I think, as you have ordered the matter, you have made the greater part of Ireland list themselves of that number. I do not know how you can recompense them, but by coming over to help me to correct the book which I promise them. You will pardon my having used another hand, since it is so much better than my own; and believe me ever, with the greatest truth, dear Sir,

Yours,

M. PRIOR.

CDXVI. [*Original.*[1]]

THE EARL OF OXFORD TO SWIFT

August 6, 1717.

TWO years retreat has made me taste the conversation of my dearest friend with a greater relish, than even at the time of my being charmed with it in our frequent journeys to Windsor. Three of your letters have come safe to my hands. The first about two years since;[2] that my son keeps as a family monument. The other two[3] arrived since the 1st of July. My heart is often with you, but I delayed writing in expectation of giving a perfect answer about my going to Brampton; but the truth is, the warmth of rejoicing in those parts is so far from abating, that I am persuaded by my friends to go into Cambridgeshire, where you are too just not to believe you will be welcome before anyone in the world. The longing your friends have to see you must be submitted to the judgement yourself makes of all circumstances. At present this seems to be a cooler climate than your island is like to be, when they[4] assemble, etc. Our impatience to see you should not draw you into uneasiness. We long to embrace you, if you find it may be of no inconvenience to yourself.

---

[1] In the British Museum. See Preface.
[2] *Supra*, p. 293.   [3] *Supra*, pp. 393, 395.
[4] *I.e.*, the Irish Parliament which met on 27 August.

CDXVII. [*Original.*[1]]

SWIFT TO ARCHDEACON WALLS

Ardsallagh, *August* 19, 1717.

SIR,

I AM now with Mr. Ludlow,[2] and Mr. Gillespy is come hither to me. I have told him that there are several tenants in the deanery, who affirm they have paid him certain sums of money which he hath not accounted for. He can call nothing more to account than one or two odd sums all under twenty shillings, and ten loads of hay to be subtracted from one Murphy's bill, at four shillings and sixpence per load. He says he is ready to answer for everything, and desires I would advance the May rent for the farm from Judge Whitshed, which he was to pay; because I owe Mr. Gillespy near the said sum.[3] I know not well what to say in this matter. I would not use him hardly, and yet would be safe myself. Mr. Proudfoot can soon tell what people pretend to have paid Mr. Gillespy. He declares he received not one farthing of last year's tithes, so that the odd sums above mentioned are for the year before, which was 1715. And then if the tenants say they paid Mr. Gillespy one penny for 1716, he insists they wrong him; pray settle this matter as well as you can with Mr. Gillespy, which may be done by sending to Proudfoot. I know you have now no accounts by you of mine—however Mr. Gillespy insisting that he never received one single penny for 1716, I believe it may be made easy. I am,

Your most obedient servant,

J. SWIFT.

Mr. Proudfoot may tell Lord Chief Justice Whitshed that I have some accounts still with Mr. Gillespy, and that care shall be taken to pay his Lordship's rent, so that they need not be uneasy. If Mr. Proudfoot has not got me any hay, Mr. Gillespy says he has good, and will sell it at market rate, and I would rather he should have my money than another

---

[1] In the possession of Mr. John Murray. See Preface.
[2] *Supra*, p. 365.   [3] *Supra*, p. 358

as far as thirty loads. Desire Mr. Proudfoot to be easy with Mr. Gillespy about the tithes of four acres of wheat he has upon the farm of Newhall.

Addressed—To the Reverend Mr. Archdeacon Walls.

CDXVIII. [*Original.*[1]]

MATTHEW PRIOR TO SWIFT

Heythrop in Oxfordshire, *August* 24, 1717.

YOURS, my good friend, of the 6th[2] finds me in Oxfordshire with the Duke of Shrewsbury,[3] which would sooner have been acknowledged, had I stayed in London. Before I left that pious city, I made due inquiry into the methods and regularity of your correspondence with the Earl. He has received your letters; he will answer them, but not to-day, *sicut olim*. Nothing can change him. I can get no positive answer from him, nor can any man else; so trouble yourself no more on that head than he does. He is still in London; and possibly has answered you, while I am a little arraigning his neglect; but in all cases *liberavi animam meam*.

I wish you were in England, that you might a little look over the strange stuff, that I am to give our friends for their money. I shall be angry with you, if you are near and not with me; but when I see you, that weighty question may easily be decided. In the mean time, I am taking your good counsel, and will be in the country as much as I can. You have found two mistakes in the list, but have not corrected them. I presume we shall have it of the best edition, when you send the list back again, of which, I say, no haste is required. Give my service and thanks to all friends; reserve only to yourself the assurance of my being, beyond expression, my friend,

Yours, etc.

---

[1] In the British Museum. See Preface.
[2] A reply no doubt to Prior's letter of 30 July (*supra*, p. 398).
[3] Heythrop was a residence of the Duke of Shrewsbury, and was occupied by the Earls of Shrewsbury until the beginning of the nineteenth century.

SUPPLEMENTAL LETTERS

CDXVIIIA. [*Scott.*]

MISS ESTHER VANHOMRIGH TO SWIFT

Dublin, 1714.[1]

WELL! now I plainly see how great a regard you have for me. You bid me be easy, and you would see me as often as you could; you had better have said as often as you could get the better of your inclinations so much, or as often as you remembered there was such a person in the world. If you continue to treat me as you do, you will not be made uneasy by me long. It is impossible to describe what I have suffered since I saw you last; I am sure I could have borne the rack much better than those killing, killing words of yours. Sometimes I have resolved to die without seeing you more, but those resolves, to your misfortune, did not last long; for there is something in human nature that prompts one so to find relief in this world, I must give way to it, and beg you would see me, and speak kindly to me, for I am sure you would not condemn anyone to suffer what I have done, could you but know it. The reason I write to you is, because I cannot tell it you, should I see you; for when I begin to complain, then you are angry, and there is something in your look so awful, that it strikes me dumb. Oh! that you may but have so much regard for me left, that this complaint may touch your soul with pity. I say as little as ever I can. Did you but know what I thought, I am sure it would move you. Forgive me, and believe me, I cannot help telling you this, and live.[2]

---

[1] If this date is correct, the letter must have been written in the last three months of the year according to old style. It cannot have been sent before Vanessa's letter in December (*supra*, p. 259).

[2] To this letter Forster appends the comment, " flinging herself at him " (Forster Collection).

CDXVIIIB. [*Scott.*]

SWIFT TO MISS ESTHER VANHOMRIGH

Four o'clock.

I DINED with the Provost,[1] and told him I was coming here, because I must be at prayers at six. He said you had been with him, and would not be at home this day, and went to Celbridge to-morrow. I said I could, however, go try. I fancy you told him so, that he might not come to-night; if he comes, you must piece it up as you can, else he will think it was on purpose to meet me, and I hate anything that looks like a secret.

I cannot possibly call after prayers; I therefore came here in the afternoon while people were in church, hoping certainly to find you. I am truly affected for poor Moll, who is a girl of infinite value, and I am sure you will take all possible care of her, and I hope to live to see the sincerest friendship in the world long between you. I pray God of Heaven protect you both, and am, *entièrement*.

CDXVIIIC. [*Original.*[2]]

SWIFT TO ARCHDEACON WALLS

Thursday morning, Eight o'clock.[3]

THIS letter is to go to the Bishop of Clogher[4] on Saturday, and should have gone last night, if I had not thought you might be such a fool as to copy it to-day, and send it to the Bishop of Dromore[5] on Saturday likewise. If you will come this morning and do it here, we will dine together and get the Provost or Worrall. I send you the print also, which

---

[1] The fact that Pratt was appointed Dean of Down in June 1717 (*supra*, p. 384, n. 3) enables the date of this letter to be approximately fixed as between 1715 and 1717. In a subsequent letter Swift refers to him as Dr. Pratt. It is probable that Pratt had made Vanessa's acquaintance in London.

[2] In the possession of Mr. John Murray. See Preface.

[3] The original letter is endorsed 1716.

[4] *I.e.*, Ashe.   [5] *I.e.*, Stearne.

may go with your copy to Dromore; and because you will not understand some things in the letter, that are known well enough in London, I will explain them to you, and so send the notes with it to Dromore. If there be a greater fool than I, who took pains to write it, it must be he that copies it out. Adieu.

Addressed—To the Reverend Mr. Archdeacon Walls.

CDXVIIID. [*Original.*[1]]

SWIFT TO ISAIAH PARVISOL

Tuesday morning.[2]

MR. PARVISOL,

As you go into town,[3] pray call upon Archdeacon Walls, and desire him to send immediately to Mrs. Brent, that she would cover the hogsheads of wine with straw and litter, to prevent their being hurt by the frost, not only the three hogsheads in my cellar, but those two which are in the Bishop's cellar. I hope the paper will be sent to us by the Mite, so as to be sent by us by nine to-morrow morning; therefore you need not stay, but desire Mr. Walls to be at home at nine or ten o'clock to-morrow morning; for we design to send the map to him to be sent to Dr. Coghill or his clerk.

Yours,
J. SWIFT.

Leave [this] line for the Archdeacon if he be not [at home].

Addressed—For Mr. Parvisol.

[1] In the possession of Mr. John Murray. See Preface.
[2] This letter was evidently written at Trim while the negotiations for the purchase of the glebe lands were pending (*supra*, p. 345).
[3] *I.e.*, Dublin.

CDXVIIIE. [*Original.*[1]]

SWIFT TO ARCHDEACON WALLS

Saturday morning, Eight o'clock.[2]

YOUR acquaintance may possibly be a very honest man, and a good preacher, but he seems to have the least wit, manners or discretion in his jesting, of any pretender to it I ever knew; I mean except he were drunk when he writ the enclosed, as in charity to his understanding I would willingly believe. All I can further pick out of his note is that he does not intend to preach for me to-morrow, therefore I must beg you to provide somebody, for I have got so terrible a cold that I shall not be able, I fear, so much as to read at the altar. Adieu. I dine with you to-day, you know.

Pray show the enclosed to Mrs. Johnson, to see whether she be of my opinion.

CDXVIIIF. [*Copy.*[3]]

SWIFT TO KNIGHTLEY CHETWODE

Friday.

I LOOK[ED] over the enclosed some time ago, and again just now; it contains many good things, and wants many alterations. I have made one or two, and pointed at others, but an author can only set his own things right.

Endorsed—This was my advice to a young lady.[4]

[1] In the possession of Mr. John Murray. See Preface.
[2] Endorsed, 1716.
[3] In the Forster Collection (*supra*, p. 241, n. 1).
[4] Some verses with a few words altered by Swift are said to have been enclosed.

APPENDIX I

A LIE AND OTHER TRIFLES

A Lie

"THIS evening Lady Masham, Dr. Arbuthnot and I were con-
triving a lie for to-morrow," writes Swift on the eve of All
Fools' Day in 1713,[1] "that Mr. Noble, who was hanged last
Saturday, was recovered by his friends, and then seized again by
the Sheriff, and is now in a messenger's hands at the Black Swan
in Holborn.[2] We are all to send to our friends to know whether
they have heard anything of it, and so we hope it will spread."

A copy of the missive by which they sought to delude their
friends was found by Forster amongst the Narford manuscripts
(*supra*, vol. i, p. 153, n. 1), and is as follows: "Do you know that
Mr. Noble was but half-hanged, and was brought to life by his
friends, and was since seized again, and is now in a messenger's
hands at the Black Swan in Holborn—this was talked all over
the Court last night."[3] It is not surprising to find that their
friends declined to be deluded, and that Swift had to confess to
Stella the failure of "the lie."

The Story of the Baker

Is the story of the baker-man bran new? I shall sift it to-day.
Yeasterday I heard no such thing. Pray keep aloaf from such tittle-
tattle. I suppose it was told you by my Lord Crum-arty. O-vain
man to believe it. If Miles had told it me, I would have said to
him rot-you-low-rum.[4]

---

[1] "Prose Works," ii, 449.
[2] Richard Noble, who committed a murder in connection with an intrigue,
and was hanged on 29 March, 1713, has found a place in the "D. N. B."
(xl, 183).
[3] Forster Collection. The original was sold at Sotheby's Rooms on
15 December, 1906.
[4] *Ibid.*

Some Trifles

IF Bishop of Cloyne [1] coses, what vomit? Crow-coz.

Enemy burn London, Queen bid her not, what plaster? Spair-my-city.

If I say to you, House,[2] what medicine for clap? Call you mel (calomel); all bum Grecum; ox a meal of's quells; Asaph et Ida (asafoetida).

A medicine a farthing: a bolus (obolus).

Ratify—rot a fee—ratify.

Die of drinking sack, what plaster? Dia palma.

Gang-green: Newcastle's woodman.

Iliac (ill I act) passion.

Mary Snow: Molly-nix (Molyneux).

A man has a sore throat, why will he be a favourite? He has the Queen's eye (quinsy) upon him.

You sued her I feck (sudorific), went to law with her in troth, made lick on through pye (lycanthropy).[3]

APPENDIX II

LADY ORKNEY'S CHARACTER OF OXFORD

THE character of the man whom the Queen delighteth to honour:

Ambitious to serve his country, and yet knows its faults.

He never will tear up his own bowels from despair, but will ever act and show he expects a blessing from a superior power for every wise action.

He appears to be dilatory not from want of the satisfaction to serve all, but to search out those with the fewest faults.

Proud only by disregarding his own greatness.

Forgives, and unmindful if his enemy repents.

He is civil to all, without an ill-judged respect.

Careful of the public money, watchful to have that managed with faithfulness.

Concerned for its honour, proved by weighing how to pay the debts rather by advancing its interest . . .

Dutifully admires his Sovereign, and if things go amiss, he would rather have it thought his mistake or anybody's than hers.

---

[1] Charles Crow (*supra*, vol. i, p. 49). [2] *I.e.*, landlord.
[3] Forster Collection.

He adores God, he submits his doubts, endeavours to be perfect without presuming to hope for perfection.

He hates being commended, but must know he deserves it, reflecting his superiority cannot last without humility, ever suspecting he may err.

Lives without fear and will die with true honour.

This character, which is dated 1 January, 1712-13, is in Swift's handwriting and endorsed by him, "The Countess of ——'s Character of Lord Treasurer." To it Swift appends the following comment:

The lady who drew the above character of Lord Treasurer Oxford, is a person of as much good natural sense and judgement as I have ever known, and hath received all the improvements that Court and conversations of princes and other great persons could give her. Her advice hath many years been asked and followed in the most important affairs of state. Accordingly you see in this draft of hers an endeavour at something that is very judicious and uncommon; but her great misfortune was, that in her education she fell short even of that little share of reading which belongs to her sex, so that she has neither orthography, grammar, nor choice of proper words, which last never fails her in conversation, and in subjects she is conversant with. Besides there is a stiffness and affectation of something beyond her reach in what she writes. I think ladies thus qualified should never hold a pen but upon occasions of perfect necessity, or that when they do, they should employ some other hand to correct and put into English what they have to say.[1]

APPENDIX III

THE MONTAGU HOUSE LETTERS

THE three Swift letters in the possession of the Duke of Buccleuch, which were first published nearly seventy years ago in the "New Monthly Magazine" (vol. lxiv, p. 116), have caused much perplexity to Swift students. They are written from Northamptonshire, and at the time the first two were dated, there is ample

---

[1] "Manuscripts of the Marquis of Bath" (Hist. MSS. Com.), i, 225. To the document is attached a copy of Swift's character of Oxford in the "History of the Four Last Years of the Queen" ("Prose Works," x, 93).

proof, not only from his letters but also from his account-book, that Swift was in Ireland. In addition, the Dean of St. Patrick's (Introduction, *supra*, vol. i, p. xxii) from internal evidence has disproved their authenticity. The letters are addressed to John, second Duke of Montagu, who was then abroad, and as will be seen, relate mainly to business connected with his seat and estate at Boughton, near Kettering, and to questions affecting the interests of the Whig party to which the Duke belonged. In my opinion the letters were written by a clergyman named Charles Lamotte, who was for many years Rector of the parish of Warkton in which Boughton is situated.[1] As two essays, of which he was the author, denote some degree of classical scholarship,[2] it is not improbable that he may have acted in the capacity of tutor to the Duke, and from the fact that he held afterwards a position in the royal household,[3] which he doubtless owed to the Duke's influence, it may be concluded that he stood high in the Duke's favour. Besides, the titles of his essays indicate as well as scholarship, originality of thought. It seems, therefore, not a far-fetched idea, more especially since the Duke's claim to recollection is not least as a practical joker,[4] that as a retort to the appellation of "Reverend Doctor" which Lamotte confers on him, the Duke had distinguished his friend by the name of the great political writer of that age.

"JONATHAN SWIFT" TO THE DUKE OF MONTAGU

July the 31st your stile 1713.
[O.S. *July* 20.]

MY LORD,

I HAVE received the honour of your Grace's last orders, and have accordingly here sent you a draft of the wall to be done, which is I think very exact, and I have explained it as clearly as

---

[1] As I learn through the kindness of the Rev. H. G. Woods, late Rector of Warkton, Lamotte's name does not appear in the register until 1716, but there is handwriting similar to his from about 1714.

[2] An Essay upon Poetry and Painting, with relation to the sacred and profane history. With an Appendix concerning obscenity in writing and painting. Lond. 1730.

An Essay upon the state and condition of Physicians among the Antients occasioned by a late dissertation of . . . Dr. Middleton; asserting that physick was servile . . . among the old Romans and only practis'd by slaves. Lond. 1728.

[3] His burial is thus recorded in the register at Warkton: "Charles Lamotte, D.D., Chaplain to Frederick Prince of Wales, and Rector of Warkton twenty-seven years, was buried January 14, 1741/2." See also "Gentleman's Magazine" for 1742, pp. 51, 163.

[4] See "New Monthly Magazine," vol. lxiv, p. 116, and "D. N. B.," xxxviii, 253.

I can, but as it is somewhat late in the year, I am afraid, if your Grace resolves upon it, it must be put off till the spring; however it will certainly be of a great advantage, as well as beauty to the garden, that lies perfectly naked on one side. I desire your Grace next time you write to let me know whether you design our small beer shall be disposed of among the poor, for it begins already to be spoiled. The price of enclosing your garden, as is proposed, will amount to forty pound or thereabouts, but the season is so far spent, that to have it done well and to last, it will be proper, as I am informed by workmen, to put it off till the spring.

The weather has been so excessive bad that your surveyor has not been able to make any great progress in the drafts; he is about that of Boughton. I hear there is but one thousand pounds between you and Sir Caesar,[1] for God's sake, Doctor, do not lose so fair an opportunity. I saw the other day Lord Hinchingbroke,[2] who has grown a strenuous Tory, and besides that he is sure of being chosen for the town of Huntingdon, stands fair, as he told me, to fling out Sir Matthew Dudley,[3] but the last I do not believe, for his father has but little interest in the county. What does your doctorship think of the address of both houses against the Pretender? That confusion may light on all such as have any such designs is the hearty wish of, Reverend Doctor,

Your most obedient humble servant,

JONATHAN SWIFT.

Addressed—These for His Grace the Duke of Montagu.

"JONATHAN SWIFT" TO THE DUKE OF MONTAGU

August 12*th* your style [1713].
[O.S. *August* 1.]

MY LORD,

I RECEIVED the honour of your Grace's last letter, dated the 15th July. To the two queries you put to me, I return this answer: Mr. Morgan of Kingsthorpe is a friend, and was, as I am informed, put out of the commission of justice for being so. As for the other, I was at Hemington according to your order, and found no mansion-house there, and was informed it had been pulled down about thirty years before.

Last week one of your houses at Barnwell was struck with

---

[1] Sir Caesar Child, Baronet, Sheriff of Northamptonshire. See "New Monthly Magazine," lxiv, 117.

[2] Edward Richard Montagu, Viscount Hinchingbroke, son of Edward, third Earl of Sandwich, who was returned for Huntingdon that autumn (see *ibid.*).

[3] Frequently mentioned in the Journal to Stella.

thunder, and burnt with lightning. There was nobody in it, but a poor lame man, who called for help, and who, besides a little bruize, received no manner of harm from the fire. Some thieves broke into old Cole's house, and almost frightened him out of his wits; but they were discovered, and fled. I do not know who they are, but I am sure they came to a wrong man for money.

I have been threatened to be called to an account, because I did not keep the thanksgiving day for the peace in the church; but I do not hear any more of it. I find by Mr. Antony, that your Grace had sent a warrant to Mr. Bridges,[1] so you need not send one now, or if you have already done it, I will not have it served. There is Lady St. John[2] at Woodford, whose family always used to have the favour of venison from your Grace. I humbly conceive it would not be amiss, if your Grace gave a warrant to them; they are very well intentioned, and by the accession of my Lord Bolingbroke's[3] estate have an interest both in Northamptonshire and Bedfordshire. I begged a warrant also between Mr. Cole and Mr. Barton of Geddington[4] in one of my last letters. I have sent to Mr. Antony the plan of Boughton, done by our country engineer, and he is now going about the rest. I have examined it, and find it very exact; if your Grace has a mind to see it where you are, you may send to Mr. Antony who has it.

I do not know whether your Grace has any thoughts of buying Newton, but my Lord Bathurst, one of the worthy twelve lords, is about it, and very near buying it; who by his party, by his character, and by some words that he said when he was here, will, I doubt, prove a very ill neighbour, and in that case you are hardly master of Boughton. I humbly beg then, if it be not too late, that you would do your utmost to purchase a conveniency, and to keep off an enemy from your borders: that is the humble request of

Yours etc.,
Jonathan Swift.

Addressed—To the Duke of Montagu.

[1] John Bridges, to whom Northamptonshire owes its first county history ("New Monthly Magazine," lxiv, 118).
[2] The widow of Sir Andrew St. John (*ibid.*).
[3] Paulet, third Earl of Bolingbroke, who had died in 1711 (*ibid.*).
[4] The Rev. John Barton was Vicar of Geddington for forty years.

"JONATHAN SWIFT" TO THE DUKE OF MONTAGU

October 1*st* your style 1713.
[O.S. *September* 20.]

REVEREND DOCTOR,

I RECEIVED yours, and humbly conceive it will be better to put off the building of the garden wall till you come there yourself and see it. When I mentioned forty or fifty pounds which that work would cost, I did not understand brick and lime, which I believe you have almost enough of, but only the workmanship.

The election for Huntingdonshire went as well as heart could wish: I went on purpose to appear for Sir Matthew only as a faggot, for I had no vote, but that he might seem a little orthodox, for he had but very few of the clergy. It was a pretty great struggle; even Jeff Barton who always was so staunch before, and to whom I had told your intentions, wavered on this occasion, and made interest for my Lord Hinchinbroke, who lost it nevertheless by a great majority. It has also gone mighty well in Rutland, where two right Lords [1] are chosen.

I shall dispose of the beer according to your permission; for it will be so long before you come, it will not be fit at all for you to drink. I thank you for your advice about the scythe, which I shall not forget to follow. I have disposed of the warrant according to your permission.

My Lord Halifax has lately been here with Mrs. Montagu and Methuen; he liked your new plantation in the wilderness mighty well; I hope you will like it when you see it yourself, and that you will order the rest of the quarters to be done in that wood.

I am afraid Newton is gone; and that perfectly by the negligence of the managers of that affair. I am, most Reverend Doctor, with all possible respect,

Your most obedient servant,
JONATHAN SWIFT.

Addressed—These for his Grace the Duke of Montagu.

[1] Daniel, Lord Finch, and Bennet, Lord Sherard ("New Monthly Magazine," lxiv, 121).

APPENDIX IV

A LIST OF LETTERS

1 JANUARY 1712-13 to 1 NOVEMBER 1713[1]

TO	FROM
Jan. 3. MD. 57.	Jan. 23. MD. 37.
8. Abp. of Dublin.	Feb. 18 (about). MD. 38.
23 (about). MD. 58.	Apr. 24. MD. 39.
Feb. 14. MD. 59.	May 8. Bp. of Dromore.
28. MD. 60.	Dr. Coghill.
Mar. 2. MD. 61.	Idem.
Apr. 7. MD. 62.	Dr. Raymond.
28. MD. 63.	Mr. Walls.
May 16. MD. 64.	Bp. of Kildare.
Sept. 1. MD. 1.	Mr. Wesley.
17. MD. 2.	Mr. Diaper.
MD. 3.	
Oct. 22. MD. 4.	
Abp. of Dublin.	
Bp. of Clogher.	
Mr. Walls.	

APPENDIX V

BISHOP KENNETT'S PICTURE OF SWIFT

[Windsor Castle, *October* 1713.[2]]

DR. SWIFT came into the coffee-house, and had a bow from everybody but me. When I came to the ante-chamber to wait before prayers, Dr. Swift was the principal man of talk and business, and

---

[1] Taken from Swift's account-book (Forster Collection, No. 509).

[2] It is evident from the allusions that the scene which the Bishop depicts, must have taken place at that time, when, as the Correspondence has shown, the Court was at Windsor. The picture was first printed by Nichols ("Works," xv, 287) with the heading, "Extract from the manuscript diary of Bishop Kennett in the library of the Marquis of Lansdowne," and a further brief extract from the same source which that editor gives, and which shows the Bishop's intense antagonism to the government of that day, is dated 3 November, 1713.

acted as a Master of Requests. He was soliciting the Earl of Arran to speak to his brother the Duke of Ormond, to get a chaplain's place established in the garrison of Hull for Mr. Fiddes, a clergyman in that neighbourhood, who had lately been in gaol, and published sermons to pay fees. He was promising Mr. Thorold to undertake with my Lord Treasurer, that, according to his petition, he should obtain a salary of two hundred pounds per annum, as minister of the English church at Rotterdam. He stopped F[rancis] Gwyn, Esq.,[1] going in with the red bag to the Queen, and told him aloud he had something to say to him from my Lord Treasurer. He talked with the son of Dr. Davenant to be sent abroad, and took out his pocket-book and wrote down several things, as memoranda, to do for him. He turned to the fire, and took out his gold watch, and telling him the time of the day, complained it was very late. A gentleman said, he was too fast. "How can I help it," says the Doctor, "if the courtiers give me a watch that won't go right?" Then he instructed a young nobleman, that the best poet in England was Mr. Pope (a Papist), who had begun a translation of Homer into English verse, for which he must have them all subscribe. "For," says he, "the author shall not begin to print till I have a thousand guineas for him." Lord Treasurer, after leaving the Queen, came through the room, beckoning Dr. Swift to follow him; both went off just before prayers.

APPENDIX VI

A DISCOVERER'S LETTER

L. M. to the Earl of Oxford

March 18, 1713-14.

MAY IT PLEASE YOUR LORDSHIP,[2]

PURSUANT to her Majesty's proclamation of the 15th of this instant March, for discovering the author of a false, malicious, and factious libel, entitled, "The Public Spirit of the Whigs;" wherein her Majesty is graciously pleased to promise a reward of three hundred pounds, to be paid by your Lordship, which said dis-

---

[1] There is an interesting account of Gwyn, who then held the office of Secretary at War, in the "D. N. B.," xxiii, 403.

[2] This letter is preserved in the collection in the British Museum (see Preface) and was evidently given to Swift by Oxford. Sir Walter Scott takes the view ("Life," p. 189) that the offer of discovery was a genuine one, but the supposition that it was a hoax seems at least as probable.

covery I can make. But your Lordship, or some persons under your Lordship, have got such an ill name in paying such rewards: instance two poor men, viz. John Greenwood and John Bouch, who took and brought to justice six persons, vulgarly called Mohocks; which the said two poor men never received so much as they were out of pocket beside time and expenses, the former never received but twenty pounds, and the latter thirty; and they had no partners concerned with them, as appears by the Attorney General's reports to your Lordship; which if I should be so served, to cause any persons to be punished, and be no better rewarded, will be no encouragement for me to do it; for these two poor men being so plain a precedent for me to go by.

Your Lordship's most humble and most obedient servant,

L. M.

APPENDIX VII

OXFORD AND THE SCRIBLERUS CLUB

An Invitation to Oxford [1]

Chiefly written by the Dean

LET not the Whigs our Tory club rebuke,
Give us our Earl, the devil take their Duke.
Quaedam quae attinent ad Scriblerum,
Want your assistance now to clear 'em.
     One day it will be no disgrace,
     In Scribler to have had a place;
Come then, my Lord, and take your part in
The important history of Martin.

Another

Written by the Dean

     A pox on all senders
     For any pretenders,
Who tell us these troublesome stories
     In their dull humdrum key,
     Of *arma virumque,*
Hanoniae qui primus ab oris.

[1] First printed by Hawkesworth.

A pox too on Hanmer,
Who prates like his gran-mere,
And all his old friends would rebuke [1]
In spite of the carle,
Give us but our Earl,
The devil may take their Duke.
Then come and take part in
The memoirs of Martin;
Lay down your white staff and grey habit:
For trust us, friend Mortimer,
Should you live years forty more,
Haec olim meminisse juvabit.

AN ANSWER

Written by Gay

Backstairs, St. James's Palace,
Past eight, *April* 14, 1714.

In a summons so large, which all clergy contains,
I must turn Dismal's [2] convert, or part with my brains,
Should I scruple to quit the Back-stairs for your blind ones,
Or refuse your true junto for one of——

ANOTHER

Written by Oxford

April 14, 1714.

I honour the men, sir,
Who are ready to answer,
When I ask them to stand by the Queen;
In spite of orators,
And blood-thirsty praters,
Whose hatred I highly esteem.
Let our faith's defender
Keep out every pretender,
And long enjoy her own;
Thus you four, five, [3]
May merrily live,
Till faction is dead as a stone.

---

[1] Sir Thomas Hanmer had a few days before, when the House was in committee and the Speaker's chair unoccupied, supported a motion that the Hanoverian succession was in danger under the Tory Ministry.

[2] *I.e.*, the Earl of Nottingham.

[3] Owing to his indolence (*supra*, p. 163) Parnell appears to have been regarded in the light of an extra member of the club.

II   E E

APPENDIX VIII

THE VISIT OF THE SCRIBLERUS ENVOYS TO LETCOMBE

A NEWSLETTER [1]

From Letcombe, near Wantage,
Sunday, *July* 4, 1714.

THIS day the envoys [2] deputed to Dean S[wift] on the part of his late confederates, arrived here during the time of Divine Service. They were received at the back-door, and having paid the usual compliments on their part, and received the usual chidings on that of the Dean, were introduced to his landlady, and entertained with a pint of the Lord Bolingbroke's Florence. The health of that great Minister was drank in this pint, together with the Lord Treasurer's, whose wine we also wished for; after which were commemorated Dr. Arbuthnot, and Mr. Lewis, in a sort of cider, plentiful in those parts, and not altogether unknown in the taverns of London. There was likewise a sideboard of coffee, which the Dean roasted with his own hands in an engine for the purpose, his landlady attending all the while that office was performing. He talked of politics over coffee, with the air and style of an old statesman, who had known something formerly, but was shamefully ignorant of the last three weeks. When we mentioned the welfare of England he laughed at us, and said Muscovy would become a flourishing empire very shortly. He seems to have wrong notions of the British Court, but gave us a hint as if he had a correspondence with the King of Sweden. As for the methods of passing his time, I must tell you one which constantly employs an hour about noon. He has in his windows an orbicular glass, which by contraction of the solar beams into a proper focus, doth burn, singe, or speckle white or printed paper, in curious little holes or various figures. We chanced to find some experiments of this nature upon the votes of the House of Commons. The name of Thomas Hanmer, Speaker, was much singed, and that of John Barber entirely burnt out. There was a large gap at the edge of the Bill of Schism, and several specks

---

[1] Elwin and Courthope's "Works of Pope," vii, 468.
[2] *I.e.*, Pope and Parnell (*supra*, p. 185).

upon the proclamation for the Pretender. I doubt not but these marks of his are mystical, and that the figures he makes this way are a significant cypher to those who have the skill to explain them.

APPENDIX IX

BOLINGBROKE AND THE HISTORIOGRAPHER'S OFFICE

VISCOUNT BOLINGBROKE TO THE DUKE OF SHREWSBURY [1]

Windsor Castle, *January* 5, 1713-4.

MY LORD,

MY brother, the Dean of St. Patrick's, is, you know, an historian, and has brought forth from folios down to duodecimos. We have often talked him up to an undertaking, which it is some degree of shame to our nation was never yet performed as it ought to be, and which I believe he is fitter for than any man in the Queen's dominions, I mean the writing a complete history of our own country. Rymer's [2] death creates an opportunity of making this his duty, if your Grace will be so good as to bestow the place of Historiographer upon him.

I submit this to your Grace's good pleasure, assuring you that in the proposition which I presume to make, I have the public much more in mind than Jonathan. I am, etc.,

B.

APPENDIX X

A MISSING LETTER FROM THE CHETWODE CORRESPONDENCE

"IN first describing this Correspondence to me, before I had myself seen it," says Forster, [3] "Mr. Wilmot-Chetwode [4] wrote: 'It betrays enough of human nature to retrieve the old Dean from many a fiend-like imputation; whilst it also proves that his

---

[1] "Letters and Correspondence of Viscount Bolingbroke," ii, 581.
[2] That well-known author and archaeologist had died on 4 December, 1713. Forster Collection.   [4] *Supra*, p. 241, n. 1.

sad malady in his head was of sufficiently long growth, before it
bowed him down at last, to excuse many an eccentricity, and to
appeal to the generosity, rather than the severity, of right minded
critics.' He refers them to Thackeray's criticism, and adds: 'I
think that all he says against Swift's heart might be answered by
the grateful mewing of a cat, which forms a pretty little episode
in one of his letters to my kinsman, as well as I can remember to
the following effect'—the letters at this time were at Woodbrooke,
Mr. Chetwode writing from Torquay:—

He (Dean Swift) returned on horseback, as was his wont,
from the county of Meath to his house in Dorset Street,[1] which
during his absence was left in the single guardianship of an
old woman: his cook, his housekeeper, his everything. It
was a winter's day, and dark evening, when he reached the
door—cold, wet, hungry after his long ride. The old woman
looked blue as she opened the door, and still more blue
when he asked her for some dinner. On repeating the
question, she muttered something about having no fire. He
became a little angry at first, until she slowly admitted the
entire truth, which was that the cat had kittened that day
in the kitchen grate, and that either puss must be disturbed,
or the Dean must lose his dinner. Hunger strove hard
against compassion, but poor pussy pleaded not in vain; and
so the Dean went to bed without his dinner.

Unfortunately, upon Mr. Chetwode, at my urgent solicitation,
sending over for the letters to Woodbrooke, this particular letter
was missing; and in announcing the arrival of the rest he writes:
'I must add a postscript to say that I would not for a hundred
pounds have lost one of Swift's letters which I fear is gone. It
contained a story about a cat, which, I think, I retailed to you
when first I wrote an answer to your first. It did honour to the
much maligned Dean's heart—but alas! I fear it is gone.
Whether some enemy of his memory, or some dishonest col-
lector, made away with it—or whether my love of the little story
induced me to keep this letter to show, and separate from the
rest—I know not; but I cannot find it now. By the honour of
my ancestor's blood, however, I declare that the story was in
Dean Swift's own handwriting to Knightley Chetwode.'"

---

[1] Dorset Street, which in Swift's time was known as Drumcondra Lane, is
a continuation of Capel Street, where Swift is said to have lodged before
his promotion to the deanery.

APPENDIX XI

CORRESPONDENCE RELATING TO THE INTERCEPTED LETTERS

ARCHBISHOP KING AND THE EARL OF KILDARE TO MR. SECRETARY STANHOPE [1]

Dublin Castle, *May* 19, 1715.

SIR,

WE presume you have received our last of the 10th instant. This morning one Mr. Jeffreys, a gentleman who is agent to the Bishop of Derry, arrived here from England. An officer belonging to the Custom House searching his trunks and pockets as usual to see if he brought over any prohibited goods, found about him two packets directed to Dr. Swift, which considering the present circumstances of affairs, he thought proper to carry to the Commissioners, who immediately brought them to us. One of them contained nothing but the enclosed pamphlet entitled, The Conduct, etc., which we judged convenient to transmit to you, not knowing whether or no it may be yet published in England. The other packet, together with several libels, such as English Advice to the Freeholders; [2] a Defence of the King against what is commonly called his Speech; Sir William Wyndham's Case, and the Ballad on the late Lord Wharton, had in it the two enclosed letters which we thought proper to convey to you by a packet-boat sent on purpose; conceiving it might be of no small importance to his Majesty's service could the last instructions to the Lord Bolingbroke mentioned in one of these letters be intercepted.

We are further to inform you that Mr. Jeffreys being examined upon oath, declares that he received the above mentioned packets from Mr. Charleton, chaplain to the Duchess of Ormond, by whom he was desired to deliver them carefully into the Dean of St. Patrick's own hands.

Upon searching Mr. Jeffreys's portmanteau we found several other letters directed to persons here, of a seditious nature, but

---

[1] State Papers relating to Ireland in P.R.O.

[2] For the discovery of the author of this pamphlet, which it has been suggested was written by Bishop Atterbury, a reward of £1,000 was offered by the Government.

which we do not think material enough to trouble you with a particular account of. We are, Sir,

Your most humble Servants,
WILL. DUBLIN.
KILDARE.

To Mr. Stanhope.

Endorsed—From the Lords Justices.

EUSTACE BUDGELL TO THE EARL OF SUNDERLAND [1]

Dublin, *May* 19, 1715.

YESTERDAY morning [2] Mr. Jeffreys, agent to the Bishop of Derry, arrived here from London. A custom-house officer searching his trunks found two packets directed to Dr. Swift; one of them only contained a book entitled, The Conduct of the Duke of Ormonde; the other, together with several libels such as English Advice, Sir W. Wyndham's Case, the Ballad on the late Lord Wharton, etc., had in it two letters which the Lords Justices thought proper to send the same night to Mr. Stanhope, and of which I send copies.

ARCHBISHOP KING TO BISHOP ASHE [3]

Dublin, *May* 23, 1715.

. . . Two days ago one Mr. Jeffreys being searched as he landed at Ringsend, several letters and packets were seized on him and brought to the Custom House, and by the Commissioners sent to the [Lords] Justices. Two were directed to the Dean of St. Patrick's, in which were several treasonable or seditious pamphlets, such as the English Advice to the Freeholders, etc., a Defence of the King against a Speech, etc., the Impartiality of the Parliament in Sir William Wyndham's Case, etc., with several letters neither directed nor subscribed, but plainly meant for the Dean. They contained very bad matter. Mr. Jeffreys swears they were given to him by Mr. Charleton, chaplain to the Duchess of Ormond, and that he received the packets sealed from Mr. Charleton and knew not what was in them.

---

[1] Hist. MSS. Com., Rept. 8, App., pt. i, p. 58. It was in this letter that the copies from which the intercepted letters (*supra*, pp. 276-8) have been printed were enclosed. Budgell was then the permanent secretary in Dublin Castle, the office previously held by Joshua Dawson.

[2] This letter, although dated the 19th, was not despatched until the 20th.

[3] In King's Correspondence.

These and several other letters represent Jeffreys as an ingenious man, that they durst not write their minds, but he knew *arcana imperii*—I use their words—and could inform them of everything, that these were iniquitous times, and that there was no place for honest men—that the Pretender's men increase daily by the ill-usage of such men. They complain that the Dean did not write to them, and look on that as a forbidding them to write to him, which they greatly regret. I am of opinion they will have very little thanks from him for their unseasonable kindness. Amongst other pamphlets there is one entitled the Conduct of the Duke of Ormond. I had not time to read it, nor was I desirous to do it, since it had no name to it. It is wrote in his Grace's favour, and hath many orders sent him about the cessation. If I understand them right, they may magnify his obedience, but I did not see how they justified his conduct.

This Jeffreys seemed to me to be an agent sent over to manage for the party here. He was bound over to the good behaviour, and we sent some of the letters to the Secretary there. . . .

ARCHBISHOP KING TO EDWARD SOUTHWELL [1]

Dublin, *May* 23, 1715.

. . . MR. JEFFREYS declared that he had them [the letters] all sealed up from Mr. Arthur Charleton, chaplain to my Lady Duchess of Ormond, which cleared him, though the letters intimated that he knew *arcana imperii*, and could inform them of such things as were not safe for them to write, and some suspected from the letters that he came over as an agent for a party, but I believe nothing of it; [2] yet this suspicion bound him to his good behaviour, but being the lawyer's business I have nothing to say to it. There were two letters of the Bishop of Derry that were not very prudent I confess, but there being nothing directly against his Majesty we ordered them to be restored. . . .

CHRISTOPHER DELAFAYE TO ARCHBISHOP KING [3]

Bath, *May* 25, 1715.

MY LORD, [4]

I RECEIVED yesterday a letter from Mr. Manley giving an account of the seizing of a parcel of treasonable papers with one

---

[1] In King's Correspondence.
[2] It will be observed that in the preceding letter the Archbishop expresses an absolutely contrary opinion. Perhaps the explanation is to be found in the fact that Ashe was a Whig and Southwell was a Tory.
[3] Hist. MSS. Com., Rept. 2, App. xix, p. 234.
[4] The writer was one of the Earl of Sunderland's secretaries.

Jeffreys directed to Dr. Swift. I acquainted my Lord Lieutenant with it, who was very well pleased with this fresh instance of your Grace's zeal and diligence in the King's service, which cannot fail of being highly acceptable to his Majesty. His Excellency commanded me to give you his thanks for it; and he hopes that if there appears enough against the Doctor to justify it he is kept in confinement, and Mr. Haughton also,[1] but how far that may be justifiable your Grace is best able to judge; I presume they are at least held to very good and sufficient bail. If anything can add to your Grace's character, this application to the public service will undoubtedly heighten it in the esteem of all good men, which, like all other things that may happen to your advantage, will give a peculiar satisfaction to, my Lord,

Your Grace's most dutiful and most obedient humble servant,
CH. DELAFAYE.

My Lord Lieutenant's health is improving.

ARCHBISHOP KING TO CHRISTOPHER DELAFAYE[2]

Dublin, *June* 4, 1715.

... THE letters directed to Dean Swift we sent to England with an examination where they were found. They could affect none here because not delivered to them, and they seemed to acquit the Dean by complaining of his not writing, which they interpreted as a forbidding them to write. Mr. Jeffreys told us on oath from whom he had them, and that he knew not what was in the packet. The utmost could be done to him was to bind him over on suspicion as the lawyers told us. ...

---

[1] A few days before Jeffreys landed, letters addressed to Haughton, who was Controller of the Ordnance, and a kinsman of Francis Annesley, had been intercepted.

[2] In King's Correspondence.

CHISWICK PRESS: PRINTED BY CHARLES WHITTINGHAM AND CO.
TOOKS COURT, CHANCERY LANE, LONDON.